SOUTHERN BIOGRAPHY SERIES
Bertram Wyatt-Brown, Editor

WILLIAM HENRY DRAYTON

South Carolina Revolutionary Patriot

Keith Krawczynski

Louisiana State University Press

Baton Rouge

Copyright © 2001 by Louisiana State University Press
Manufactured in the United States of America
First printing
10 09 08 07 06 05 04 03 02 01
5 4 3 2 1

Designer: Barbara Neely Bourgoyne
Typeface: Janson Text and Trajan
Typesetter: Coghill Composition Co., Inc.
Printer and binder: Thomson-Shore, Inc.

Library of Congress Cataloging-in-Publication Data:

Krawczynski, Keith.
   William Henry Drayton : South Carolina revolutionary patriot / Keith Krawczynski.
      p.   cm. — (Southern biography series)
   Includes bibliographical references and index.
   ISBN 0-8071-2661-6 (alk. paper)
      1. Drayton, William Henry, 1742–1779.   2. Revolutionaries—United States—Biography.   3.
Legislators—South Carolina—Biography.   4. South Carolina—History—Revolution, 1775–1783.
5. United States—History—Revolution, 1775–1783—Biography.   I. Title.   II. Series.

E302.6.D7 K73   2001
975.7'03'092—dc21
[B]   00-069434

CONTENTS

ILLUSTRATIONS

PREFACE

Five months before the thirteen American colonies formally declared their independence from Great Britain, William Henry Drayton, president of the South Carolina provincial congress, became the first prominent Carolinian to openly call for a break from the mother country. Speaking before that body on February 8, 1775, Drayton declared that the British "hand of tyranny" threatened to "spoil America of whatever she held most valuable." The colonists' numerous "humble petitions" had failed to gain them redress from the king, who remained "deaf to the cries of his American subjects." Forced into an "unlooked-for defensive civil war," Drayton concluded, Americans must quickly decide between either "independence or slavery."[1]

Such excitable revolutionary rhetoric is ironic considering that William Henry Drayton actually began the struggle with Great Britain as a member of His Majesty's government in South Carolina, serving in the royal council and the judiciary. During the early 1770s, however, he grew frustrated over the increasing incidence of local offices he ambitiously sought going instead to "placemen" from Great Britain and disgruntled with Whitehall's increasing infringement on Americans' liberties. When Parliament passed the Coercive Acts in 1774, Drayton, who could no longer utter even "one word in favor of administration," quickly joined the American rebellion.[2] With

1. *JPC*, 179–80.
2. William Henry Drayton, *A Letter from Freeman of South Carolina to the Deputies of North America Assembled in the High Court of Congress at Philadelphia* (Charleston: Peter Timothy, 1774), 5.

youthful energy, enormous self-confidence, relentless ambition, and the zeal-otry of a recent convert, Drayton served the Revolutionary cause in a variety of roles: the most effective Whig polemicist in the lower South, a member of all the state's important Revolutionary governing bodies, commander of a frigate of war, president of the provincial congress, chief justice, privy coun-cilor, assemblyman, coauthor of the state's 1778 constitution, and delegate to the Continental Congress. Through such allegiance, energy, and influence, Drayton did more to resist British rule than any other South Carolinian. A biography of William Henry Drayton is therefore crucial in gaining a satis-factory understanding of South Carolina's rebellion.

Despite Drayton's conspicuous service, historians have largely ignored his contribution to the Revolutionary movement in South Carolina. His un-timely death in 1779 at the age of thirty-seven is largely to blame for this neglect. As a member of the second gallery of revolutionary leaders, Drayton has also been greatly overshadowed by the more distinguished patriots of his generation. His reputation is so buried by these more prominent Revolution-aries that one historian has sadly professed that Drayton "will probably never be rescued from the dust bin of history." The only full-length biography, *William Henry Drayton and the American Revolution* by William Dabney and Marion Dargan, does little to rescue him from "undeserved obscurity."[3] Written originally as a dissertation in the late 1920s, the biography's brevity, loose organization, pedestrian style, hazy generalizations, and failure to make maximum use of Drayton's many political writings result in an inadequate treatment of his youth, his conversion to the American cause, his revolution-ary activities, and his political philosophy.

More recent articles and monographs on Drayton also fail to adequately detail his fascinating life and to explain his puzzling conversion to the Whig persuasion. J. Russell Snapp tackles the latter issue in two separate works, ar-guing that the Crown's appointment of outsiders to local offices Drayton as-pired to transformed him from an "aristocratic opponent of the resistance movement to a fiery revolutionary." To be sure, Drayton was upset over these royal rebuffs. However they were not enough to draw him into the revolu-tionary movement; had they been, he would have left the royal fold in the

3. Solomon Lutnick, "William Henry Drayton's Memoirs," in *The Colonial Legacy: Early Na-tionalist Historians*, ed. Lawrence H. Leder (New York: Harper & Row, 1973), 200; H. Trevor Colbourn, *The Lamp of Experience: Whig History and the Intellectual Origins of the American Revolu-tion* (Chapel Hill: University of North Carolina Press, 1965), 157 n. 72.

early 1770s when these slights against him occurred. That Drayton did not join the American cause until after Parliament passed the Coercive Acts against the colonies in 1774 suggests that other less personal and more political factors played an equally important role in his conversion. Other motivating influences for his transformation are offered by Dorothy Gail Griffin, whose examination of the early Drayton family includes a brief summary of Drayton's pre-Revolutionary political career and intimates that his relationship with his father and local revolutionaries also pushed him toward the patriot party.[4]

Even when taken together, these works provide a less-than-satisfactory explanation of Drayton's early life, his conversion to the American cause, and his involvement in it. The present work attempts to provide a fuller, more detailed examination of Drayton's youth, education, family relations, character, political philosophy, and revolutionary activities in South Carolina and abroad. It also strives to revise earlier explanations for his joining the American rebellion, his efforts and successes at suppressing loyalism in the South Carolina backcountry, and his ideas on the creation of a federal government.

In addition to rescuing Drayton from the ash heap of history, this biography is intended to add to our understanding of the causes and characteristics of the Revolution in South Carolina. Of all the mainland colonists, South Carolinians were, according to Robert Weir, the "most improbable of rebels." Lowcountry planters and merchants were firmly bound to the imperial system of trade, exporting staples to England while importing its much valued manufactured and luxury goods. Inhabitants of the backcountry, many of whom were recent immigrants from Great Britain, also strongly identified with the king. White South Carolinians, moreover, were reluctant to show any kind of division among themselves for fear of encouraging a slave rebellion. "Under the circumstances," Weir claims, "it almost seems, no sane man would have wished or dared to revolt."[5] When South Carolinians did dare to break away from the British commonwealth, they refused to follow the example of their neighbors in radically altering their political and social practices.

4. J. Russell Snapp, *John Stuart and the Struggle for Empire on the Southern Frontier* (Baton Rouge: Louisiana State University Press, 1996), 165 n. 38; Dorothy Gail Griffin, "The Eighteenth Century Draytons of Drayton Hall" (Ph.D. diss., Emory University, 1985), 255–81. The other work on Drayton by Snapp is "William Henry Drayton: The Making of a Conservative Revolutionary," *JSH* 57 (November 1991): 637–58.

5. Robert M. Weir, *"A Most Important Epocha": The Coming of the Revolution in South Carolina* (Columbia: University of South Carolina Press, 1970), 3.

To attain a better understanding of the forces behind the uniqueness of South Carolina's rebellion, one must study the individuals who composed it, particularly the leaders. An examination of the powerful and complex forces that compelled Drayton, after having been a member of the royal government early in the struggle between the colonists and Great Britain, to turn so angrily against the mother country may shed some light on why other South Carolinians, particularly the elite, also rebelled. As a member of the ruling oligarchy, moreover, Drayton's energetic attempts to preserve the provincial hierarchy and keep the reigns of government firmly in the hands of the local aristocracy may also help to explain why South Carolina's revolution was politically conservative compared to those of the other states. Drayton's life also provides a rare and important opportunity to illustrate the complexity of his state's rebellion by situating it in broader ethnic, social, political, and geographical contexts, since he had dealings with Native Americans, African Americans, frontiersmen, the urban masses, and Revolutionary leaders in Georgia, North Carolina and Virginia. Finally, Drayton's service in the Continental Congress helps place the Revolution in a national setting.

Like all biographers, I have been influenced by the availability of records related to my subject. Unfortunately, the information surrounding Drayton offers only enough to tantalize us; these documents, additionally, deal almost exclusively with his political activities. Only a few personal letters to or from family members and colleagues have survived; there is also no existing will, inventory, or financial records. Even with such data an author could never completely uncover Drayton's ideas and motivations. Early in the twentieth century Mark Twain illustrated the biographer's dilemma:

> What a wee little part of a person's life are his acts and words! His real life is led in his head, and is known to none but himself. . . . His acts and words are merely the visible, thin crust of his world . . . a mere skin enveloping it. The mass of him is hidden. These are his life, and they are not written, and cannot be written. Biographies are but the clothes and buttons of the man—the biography of the man himself cannot be written.[6]

Considered in this light, a dearth of private correspondence and personal records does not seem an impassable obstacle for writing a life of Drayton. But with little information on his personal life, any biography of Drayton, to continue Twain's analogy, will be missing a few articles of clothing. I can only hope that my efforts have not left Drayton indecently exposed.

6. Samuel L. Clemens, *Mark Twain's Autobiography* (New York: Harper & Bros., 1924), 1: xviii.

ACKNOWLEDGMENTS

This work has benefitted from the assistance of many people. Robert M. Weir proved most helpful; the eyebrow-raising questions he posed in his graduate seminars on Colonial and Revolutionary America forced me to look at early American history in ways I never would have otherwise. His demanding and exacting standards in research, methodology, and interpretation taught me much about proper historical scholarship. Concerning the present work in particular, Rob Weir pointed me toward many sources I would have otherwise missed, caught an embarrassing number of blunders, forced me to rethink or strengthen some of my assertions, curbed my often prolix writing, and always pushed me to do better. I hate to think how this book might have turned out without his careful guidance. The manuscript has also benefitted enormously from careful readings by Clyde Wilson, William Rivers, and most especially my copy editor, Sara Anderson.

Many other people and institutions also helped in various ways. Those deserving special recognition include Tracy Hayes, research assistant at Drayton Hall; John Jones, archivist of Balliol College; Susan Corrigall, assistant registrar at the National Register of Archives in Edinburgh, Scotland; James H. Hutson, historian in the Manuscript Division of the Library of Congress; Peggy Clark, associate editor of the Papers of Henry Laurens; and the staff members at the Scottish Records Office, Edinburgh; the Clements Library, University of Michigan; the Historical Society of Pennsylvania, Philadelphia; the South Caroliniana Library, University of South Carolina; the South Car-

olina Department of Archives and History, Columbia; and the South Carolina Historical Society, Charleston.

Although they may not realize it, my four siblings—Doug, Ken, Tim, and
Thea Jo—helped push me to complete the work sooner than I would have
otherwise by constantly asking me: "For God's sake, Keith, when are you
going to finish it?" I thank them for encouraging me in ways only siblings
can.

However, my parents, Ken and Frances Krawczynski, made the greatest
contribution by not only providing much financial and moral support but,
more importantly, encouraging me to set lofty goals and instilling within me
the qualities necessary to achieve them. Of course, no material offering can
ever repay such an enormous debt. Knowing my parents, though, I am certain that the love and appreciation with which I dedicate this book to them
will be payment enough.

ABBREVIATIONS

BPROCO   British Public Records Office, Colonial Office, Series 5

BPROSC   British Public Records Office Relating to South Carolina, South Carolina Department of Archives and History, Columbia, South Carolina

CL   Clements Library, University of Michigan, Ann Arbor

DHAR   Robert W. Gibbes, ed. *Documentary History of the American Revolution: Consisting of Letters and Papers Relating to the Contest of Liberty, Chiefly in South Carolina.* 3 vols. New York: D. Appleton, 1853–1857. Reprint. Spartanburg, S.C.: Reprint Co., 1972.

GHQ   *Georgia Historical Quarterly*

HLP   Philip M. Hamer, George C. Rogers, and David Chesnutt, eds. *The Papers of Henry Laurens.* 16 vols. Columbia: University of South Carolina, 1961–2000.

JCC   Worthington C. Ford, ed. *Journals of the Continental Congress, 1774–1789.* 34 vols. Washington, D.C.: Government Printing Office, 1904–1937.

JPC   W. Edwin Hemphill and Wylma Wates, eds. *Extracts from the Journals of the Provincial Congresses of South Carolina, 1775–1776.* Columbia: University of South Carolina Press, 1960.

JSH   *Journal of Southern History*

LDC	Paul H. Smith, ed. *Letters of Delegates to Congress, 1774–1789.* 24 vols. to date. Washington, D.C.: Library of Congress, 1976-.
NYHS	New York Historical Society
NYPL	New York Public Library
SC&AGG	*South Carolina & American General Gazette*
SCDAH	South Carolina Department of Archives and History
SCG	*South Carolina Gazette*
SCG&CJ	*South Carolina Gazette & Country Journal*
SCHM	*South Carolina Historical Magazine*
SCHS	South Carolina Historical Society, Charleston
SCL	South Caroliniana Library, University of South Carolina, Columbia
W&MQ	*William and Mary Quarterly*

WILLIAM HENRY DRAYTON

PRIVILEGED YOUTH

From his birth in September 1742, circumstances destined William Henry Drayton for leadership among South Carolina's ruling oligarchy. His father, John, a wealthy planter and member of the royal council, and his grandfather and uncle—both of whom served as lieutenant governors of the province—expected William Henry to eventually take his rightful place alongside them. He certainly received all the prerequisites necessary for the tasks of government: a college education, a sizable inheritance, and political connections. Despite these advantages, however, young Drayton's initial attempt at realizing his preordained position fell far short of his family's high expectations. The reasons for his early failure seem to lie in his childhood experiences.

Drayton spent the first decade of his life at his father's palatial 660-acre plantation, located twelve miles up the Ashley River from Charleston. At the plantation's center was Drayton Hall, a two-story Georgian-style "Palace and Garden" constructed in the early 1740s. In planning and building the estate, John Drayton strove to re-create the atmosphere of English country life. His success in this endeavor was unrivaled by any other Carolinian. In fact, very few colonial mansions matched the splendor and show of Drayton Hall. At over 7,680 square feet, it was more than twice the size of any other plantation house in the province, and one of the largest in the thirteen American colonies. Stationed on a high basement, the richly variegated brickwork of the mansion embraced several bedrooms, two drawing rooms, a parlor, ballroom, dining room, and library—all finished with cypress paneling and elegant molding and richly outfitted with mahogany furniture and gilt-framed mirrors.

The grounds surrounding the manor were just as impressive, containing a lake, a deer park, and octagonal and semicircular gardens framed with boxed hedges and filled with roses, lilacs, magnolias, poinsettias, and gardenias. Commanding the entire estate was a legion of large, rugged, majestic oaks. A retinue of black servants, who continually ministered to the needs of the white inhabitants, made the manor as accommodating as it was elegant. Besides functioning as a home, center of business, and place for formal gatherings, Drayton Hall symbolized John Drayton's power and place in South Carolina's social order. It also served as a microcosm of William Henry Drayton's environment during his formative years.[1]

The grandness and opulence encompassing Drayton's youth did not emerge overnight, but developed slowly over sixty years following the arrival of the first Drayton to the shores of the nascent colony in 1678. Three years earlier, thirty-year-old Thomas Drayton Jr. had left his home in Warwickshire, England, for Barbados on the *Willing Wind*. Nothing is known of his status or wealth in England. Like most of the approximately 400,000 Britons in the seventeenth century who risked their lives in dangerous and terribly unpleasant voyages to the New World, he was probably searching for opportunities not available at home. A decrease in plague mortality in Britain during the preceding century caused a rapid increase in the population, which, in turn, placed severe pressure on the limited availability of land. Meanwhile, prices rose some 250 percent while the workingman's real wages dropped nearly in half, resulting in widespread poverty. Nearly eight out of ten inhabitants in some Warwickshire villages were so poor they could not afford to pay taxes. Because Thomas Drayton was able to pay for his passages to Barbados and Carolina, it is unlikely that he belonged to this pathetically impoverished group. Nevertheless, even the gentry found it increasingly difficult to provide a younger son with sufficient land or capital to establish him on a farm or in a trade.[2]

1. *SCG*, 22 December 1758; Henry A. M. Smith, "The Ashley River: Its Seats and Settlements," *SCHM* 20 (April 1919): 92–3; Griffin, "The Eighteenth Century Draytons," 104–18, 126–7, 207–17; Lynne Lewis, *Drayton Hall: Preliminary Archaeological Investigation at a Low Country Plantation* (Charlottesville: University Press of Virginia, 1978), 12, 101–11; Jane Brown Gillette, "American Classic," *Historic Preservation* 43 (March–April 1991): 23–7, 71–2.

2. J. M. Martin, "The Rise in Population in Eighteenth-Century Warwickshire," *Dugdale Society Occasional Papers* 23 (1976): 9–10; Marie Rowlands, "Society and Industry in the West

To many young Englishmen, the boundless opportunities of the New World offered a welcoming remedy for their desperate dilemma. Thomas Drayton may have been enticed to leave Warwickshire by a flood of propaganda encouraging "industrious and ingenious" persons to come to Carolina so they may "obtain the greater advantages" of the "Felicities of this Country,"—an abundance of rich fertile soil, a mild climate, and a virgin wilderness gorged with deer, turkeys, and other wild game. As a further inducement, the eight Lords Proprietors organizing the colony made an offer irresistible to many land-hungry Englishmen by granting 150 acres to each free male, with an additional 150 acres for every male over age sixteen he brought with him, as well as 100 acres for females and boys fifteen or under. In May 1678 Thomas Drayton took advantage of this generous offer by applying for a land warrant of 200 acres on New Town Creek. However, Drayton did not establish permanent residence in Carolina until sometime after April 25 of the following year, when he sailed from Barbados on the ship *Mary*. He and Elizabeth Carpenter, whom he either brought with him or met and married in the colonies, began a family with the birth of a son, Thomas, around 1680.[3]

When Drayton arrived in Carolina the colony had not yet reached its tenth anniversary. In 1680 malaria forced the colonists to remove from Albemarle Point on the Ashley River to a healthier site open to the Atlantic breezes at the junction of the Ashley and Cooper Rivers. Here the settlement began showing signs of growth and prosperity. Population doubled to approximately 2,200 within two years of the removal, and the rugged pioneers, described by a contemporary as a "Hotch potch" of "bankrupts, pirates, decayed Libertines, Sectaries and Enthusiasts of all sorts," no longer suffered

---

Midlands at the End of the Seventeenth Century," *Midland History* 4 (spring 1977): 56–8; D. C. Coleman, *The Economy of England, 1450–1750* (London: Oxford University Press, 1977), 13, 18–9; L. A. Clarkson, *The Pre-Industrial Economy in England, 1500–1750* (London: B. T. Batsford, 1971), 232–5.

3. Alexander S. Salley Jr., ed., *Narratives of Early Carolina, 1650–1708* (New York: Charles Scribner's Sons, 1911), 66–70, 290, 308; Robert K. Ackerman, *South Carolina Colonial Land Policies* (Columbia: University of South Carolina Press, 1977), 24; South Carolina Royal Grants, 39: 331, SCDAH; John C. Hotten, ed., *The Original Lists of Persons of Quality . . . Who Went from Great Britain to the American Plantations, 1660–1700* (New York: Empire State Books, 1874), 363; John Drayton, "History and Genealogy of the Drayton Family," SCHS; Peter Campbell, *Some Early Barbadian History* (St. Michael, Barbados: Caribbean Graphics & Letchworth, 1993), 157–60.

from "continual want," but had such "plenty of provisions" that "it was to be admired rather than beleeved."[4]

Unfortunately, there are no surviving documents revealing Thomas Drayton's economic and social circumstances during these early, difficult years of colony building. Like most other Carolinians at the time, he probably focused his efforts on producing a diversity of agricultural provisions for the English plantations in the Caribbean—trading salt meat, lumber, and naval stores in exchange for slaves, sugar, and cash. Because records show that he did not enlarge his original grant, it appears that Thomas Drayton's agricultural pursuits were limited to subsistence farming and the production of the aforementioned export items. He died in 1700, leaving behind a wife and son.[5]

Drayton's only surviving child, Thomas Drayton III, greatly improved upon the financial standing of his trailblazing father by taking advantage of the province's increasingly sophisticated and developed economy. In the late seventeenth century, the introduction of rice, which thrived in the swampy land of the lowcountry, quickly transformed Carolina's economy and, concomitantly, its society. By the early 1700s the delicate and shallow-rooted plant became the dominant commodity in the province's production of staples, with exports to Europe increasing from 394,000 pounds in 1700 to nearly 20 million pounds by 1730. The enormous profits resulting from this trade brought Carolinians vast opportunities for economic and social advancement.[6]

Thomas Drayton III and his wife Anne were one couple who greatly profited from the lucrative rice trade. By the time of his death in 1724,

4. Frank J. Klingberg, ed., *Carolina Chronicle: The Papers of Commissary Gideon Johnston, 1707–1716* (Berkeley: University of California Press, 1946), 22; Maurice Mathews, "A Contemporary View of Carolina in 1680" *SCHM* 55 (July 1954): 153.

5. David L. Coon, "The Development of Market Agriculture in South Carolina, 1670–1785" (Ph.D. diss., University of Illinois, 1972), 95–108; Converse D. Clowse, *Economic Beginnings in Colonial South Carolina, 1670–1730* (Columbia: University of South Carolina Press, 1971), 60–9; Miscellaneous Records of Charleston County, South Carolina, 52: 43–4, Charleston County Library.

6. Henry C. Dethloff, "The Colonial Rice Trade," *Agricultural History* 56 (January 1982): 234; Aaron M. Shatzman, "Servants into Planters, The Origin of American Image: Land Acquisition and Status Mobility in Seventeenth Century South Carolina" (Ph.D. diss., Stanford University, 1981), 215, 260, 302–3; Richard Waterhouse, "Economic Growth and Changing Patterns of Wealth Distribution in Colonial Lowcountry South Carolina," *SCHM* 89 (October 1988): 203, 211–2.

Thomas Drayton owned 1,380 head of cattle, 112 horses, 3,027 acres, and 91 slaves to labor on his five rice plantations. Anne, an inveterate businesswoman in her own right, continued expanding and improving the estate through astute management until her death in 1742. The couple also benefitted by constructing their plantations alongside the Ashley River. Not only was the Ashley blessed with fertile soil along its banks, but its accessibility by water to Charleston made it easier and less expensive to transport produce to market. This land acquisition began a long-standing relationship between the Draytons and the Ashley River.[7]

The most prominent Drayton associated with the Ashley River during the eighteenth century was John Drayton, although he probably seemed the least likely member of all to achieve such a distinction. As the youngest of Thomas and Anne's three sons (born in early 1716), John Drayton received only 350 acres of his father's sizable estate, the lion's share going to his eldest brother Thomas as prescribed by the custom of primogeniture. Yet he was able to overcome the disadvantage of this relatively paltry inheritance and ascend to membership in South Carolina's patrician society through mercenary marriages, the advantages of political office, and the colony's unrivaled economic prosperity.

John Drayton acquired the greater portion of his wealth and political connection through three very advantageous marriages. His first wife, Sarah Cattell, was the daughter of Charleston merchant and Ashley River planter William Cattell, one of the wealthiest men in the colony at the time of his death in 1752.[8] Sarah quickly bore John two sons: Stephen Fox, born nine months after their marriage in February 1737; and William, who arrived in December 1738. Sadly, both boys left the young couple's world just as quickly as they entered it when they died on the same day one year apart—Stephen Fox

7. South Carolina Royal Grants, 38: 398, 399, 440, 462, 463, 532, SCDAH; Charleston County Wills, 1722–1724: 99–101, SCDAH; Elizabeth Lucas to Thomas Lucas, 22 May 1742, in Elise Pinckney, ed., *The Letterbook of Eliza Lucas Pinckney, 1739–1762* (Chapel Hill: University of North Carolina Press, 1972), 39; Smith, "The Ashley River," 3.

8. The marriage between John and Sarah may have been strongly encouraged by Thomas Drayton and William Cattell, who were neighbors and close friends. The elder Drayton, in fact, trusted Cattell to be the executor of his estate. See will of Thomas Drayton in Charleston County Wills, 1722–1724: 101, SCDAH. The estimate of William Cattell's wealth is found in the *SCG* of 24 August 1752. In addition to his lucrative mercantile business, William Cattell owned four plantations worked by 120 slaves. See Charleston Inventories, 1751–1753: 491–500, SCDAH.

on September 9, 1739, and William the following year. Still despondent over the death of his second son, Drayton experienced another heartrending loss three months later when Sarah died on Christmas Eve, on what would have been her son William's second birthday. Stephen Fox, William, and Sarah Drayton were most likely the victims of a smallpox epidemic that ravaged the lowcountry in 1739 and 1740.[9] In the brief span of just fifteen months, twenty-three-year-old John Drayton lost his entire family.

Possibly as a way to fill the emptiness of these tragic losses, John Drayton waited less than a year before marrying his second wife, twenty-two-year-old Charlotta Bull, on November 14, 1741, during a "festal day" at the lieutenant governor's house. This marriage to the daughter of that official, William Bull, wedded John Drayton to the most powerful family in the province. The Bulls had been among the first settlers of the colony when Stephen Bull arrived from Warwickshire in 1670. The elder Bull made a fortune in the Indian trade and became a member of the Grand Council (the governing body of the province while it was owned by the Lords Proprietors), serving as a specialist in Indian affairs. His son and grandson—both named William—greatly augmented the family's political authority by monopolizing the office of lieutenant governor from 1737 to the Revolution. As an ally of this powerful family, John Drayton now commanded enormous influence among the Carolina aristocracy.[10]

Together, John and Charlotta had two children: William Henry, born in September 1742, and Charles, who arrived two days before Christmas the following year. Sadly, Charlotta died less than a week after giving birth to her second child, robbing her of the joy of nurturing and raising her two sons and preventing William Henry and Charles from experiencing a mother's love and care.[11] Although in the eighteenth century early death was considered an

9. Mabel L. Webber, "Register of St. Andrews Parish, Berkeley County, South Carolina 1719–1774," *SCHM* 13 (October 1912): 219, 223, and 14: (January 1913): 20; Dana P. Arneman, "The Medical History of Colonial South Carolina" (Ph.D. diss., University of South Carolina, 1996), 213–4, 366; John Duffy, "Eighteenth-Century Carolina Health Conditions," *JSH* 18 (August 1952): 289–94.

10. "The Bull Family of South Carolina" *SCHM* 1 (January 1900): 77–8; Pinckney, *Letterbook*, 25; Kinloch Bull Jr., *The Oligarchs in Colonial and Revolutionary Charleston: Lt. Governor William Bull II and His Family* (Columbia: University of South Carolina Press, 1991), 9. Eleven years earlier, John's brother Thomas had married Charlotta's older sister Elizabeth, thus beginning the Drayton-Bull alliance.

11. According to Dr. Dana P. Arneman, South Carolina had one of the lowest maternal mortality records among British North American colonies, with only seven deaths per thousand births. The two leading causes of death from childbirth in South Carolina were postpartum

act of Providence and accepted as a matter of course, John Drayton was devastated by the loss of two wives in just three years. He waited nearly a decade before remarrying.

Without a wife to care for and occupy his time and energy, Drayton concentrated his efforts on government service. He served as a local justice of the peace and church warden before winning a seat in the Commons House in 1745. Eight years later the governor and the council appointed him to serve as an assistant justice for the province. When not toiling as a public servant, Drayton devoted much attention toward increasing his property holdings, purchasing a town home in Charleston and more than three thousand acres by 1747.[12]

With John Drayton busy making his way in the world, William Henry (or "Billy," as he was called as a youth) grew up with little parental guidance or nurturing. The elder Drayton invested only money in his sons; instead, he devoted nearly all his time, attention, and energy into his manor, land, and slaves. Southern patriarchs like John Drayton simply did not want to be bothered with children and "scorned to spend time with their little ones." Instead, they abandoned them to governesses, personal slaves, tutors, and relatives. Not surprisingly, Drayton later reaped much disappointment and frustration in the careless and carefree actions of his undisciplined and unfocused children.[13]

As if this negligence were not enough to alienate himself from his children, John Drayton's demeanor toward his sons was apparently both indifferent and harsh. According to family history, the Drayton patriarch was a "Tyrant in his Family" and his sons "could never by their utmost attentions, retain his affection and confidence. The least thing which crossed his will or even his expectations as relating to them, set him against them anew." On the rare occasion that Drayton was in the company of his sons, he demanded deference, respect, and dispassionate affection. Once in 1761, William Henry greatly displeased his father by showing "too much warmth" in one of his letters home while attending school in England. Indeed, the elder Drayton's interest in his boys was piqued "only when they forced themselves on his con-

hemorrhaging and puerperal fever, an infection of the birth passage. See Arnemen, "Medical History of Colonial South Carolina," 302, 313–4, 328.

12. Thomas Cooper and David J. McCord, eds., *Statutes at Large of South Carolina* (Columbia, S.C.: A. S. Johnston, 1838–1841), 3: 504; 7: 492; 9: 126; "Historical Notes," *SCHM* 20 (January 1919): 73; Charleston Deeds, vol. 50, section 2CO: 234, 260, and section 2DO: 309, SCDAH; Charleston Memorials, 7: 483, SCDAH.

13. Michael Zuckerman, "Penmanship Exercises for Saucy Sons: Some Thoughts on the Southern Colonial Family," *SCHM* 84 (July 1983): 156, 159; Griffin, "The Eighteenth Century Draytons," 314.

sciousness, either by their conduct or by their expenses, and then this concern only manifested itself negatively." Apparently William Henry and his brothers impinged on their father's consciousness on numerous occasions. John Drayton frequently complained of his sons' disrespectful and "very wild and ungovernable" behavior, which he said caused him years of suffering, unhappiness and disappointment.[14]

In part, the boys' recalcitrant conduct was the result of child-rearing practices common among southern colonial gentry, who, preferring the "tacit morality of indiscipline to the official one of obedience," rarely inflicted bodily punishment on their children. To them, willfulness, autonomy, and self-assertion were the most important characteristics to cultivate in their offspring. Consequently, impudence, licentiousness, and incapacity for self-control were endemic among southern sons. John Drayton, in a belated, desperate, and punitive attempt to improve his children's conduct, threatened disinheritance in 1761 if they, after reaching the age of twelve, behaved "undutyfully" toward him. William Henry Drayton would learn years later that this was no idle caveat.[15]

While his sons were still too young to cause him maddening frustration, John Drayton married Margaret Glen, a thirty-nine-year-old spinster and sister of the province's ambitious governor, James Glen. Politics, not love, appears to have brought this couple together. Glen, who had arrived in South Carolina as governor in 1743, had lost considerable political support in both the colony and England in the intervening years and was in jeopardy of losing his post. To bolster his flagging power base, he attached himself to the powerful William Bull by providing his family members with important offices; the alliance was consolidated with the marriage of Glen's sister Margaret to John Drayton, the lieutenant governor's former son-in-law. In return for rescuing his sister from spinsterhood, John Drayton received from Glen finan-

14. John Drayton, *The Carolinian Florist of Governor John Drayton of South Carolina* (Charleston, 1798; reprint, Columbia: South Caroliniana Library of the University of South Carolina, 1943), xxv; Eliza L. Pinckney to Billy [William Henry] Drayton, 16 April 1761, in Pinckney, *Letterbook*, 169; Griffin, "The Eighteenth Century Draytons," 244; John Drayton to James Glen, 5 April 1768, 24 December 1769, 13 August 1772, and 6 February 1773, all in James Glen Papers, SCL; Philip J. Greven, *The Protestant Temperament: Patterns of Child-Rearing, the Religious Experience, and the Self in Early America* (New York: Knopf, 1977), 276–7; Daniel Blake Smith, *Inside the Great House: Planter Family Life in Eighteenth-Century Chesapeake Society* (Ithaca, N.Y.: Cornell University Press, 1980), 32, 34, 181–2.

15. Zuckerman, "Penmanship Exercises," 164; Greven, *Protestant Temperament*, 276–7; Glen-Drayton Marriage Contract (Abstract), 15 June 1761, Glen Papers (legal size folder), SCL.

cial offerings, social prestige, and political aggrandizement. His middle-aged bride, generously described by an obsequious local press as a "lady of celebrated Beauty and merit," was more importantly "endowed with every Qualification that can render the Nuptial State a Happiness." If colonial society defined happiness by wealth and political and social connections, this February 1752 marriage certainly brought John Drayton immense bliss. He received £5,000 sterling from Glen and quick appointment by the governor to serve as an assistant judge of the Court of General Sessions, despite having no legal training. Glen also made several earnest recommendations on behalf of his new brother-in-law for a position on the royal council. The Board of Trade refused all of the governor's endorsements, however. Not until May of 1761, after Glen was replaced, did the board feel that Drayton's age, political experience, and affluence rendered him "well qualified for the important trust of assisting His Majesty's Governor with his advice."[16]

As a council member, John Drayton was in an ideal position to increase his property holdings. Councilmen and the governor were the sole grantors of land in the colony, and when land was distributed, they were there to see that a substantial share went to themselves and friends. Indeed, between 1762 and 1765, Drayton received royal grants for 4,724 acres in South Carolina and 2,000 in Georgia. He continued his frenzied pursuit of wealth and property through the remainder of his life, eventually becoming one of the richest men in the province. In addition to his grand and gorgeous plantation home, Drayton owned a residence in Charleston, approximately 16,000 acres of land (consisting of numerous cow pens and thirty plantations, twenty-five rice and five indigo), and over nine hundred slaves. He also purchased two schooners to transport his rice, indigo, and cattle down the Ashley River to market in Charleston.[17]

Drayton did not accumulate his vast wealth just from advantageous marriages and the benefits of political office. Timing, too, played an important role in his success. Between 1730 and 1770 lowcountry planters, by cultivat-

16. *SCG*, 2 March 1752; Glen-Drayton Indenture Tripartite, 27 February 1752, Glen Papers, SCL; BPROSC 25: 4, 93; 26: 115; 29: 14; 36: 195–6.

17. M. Eugene Sirmans, *Colonial South Carolina: A Political History, 1663–1763* (Chapel Hill: University of North Carolina Press, 1966), 252; Leonard W. Labaree, *Conservatism in Early American History* (Ithaca, N.Y.: Cornell University Press, 1948), 29–30; South Carolina Royal Grants, 10: 229, 241; 11: 10, 49; 12: 82, 448, SCDAH; Griffin, "The Eighteenth Century Draytons," 117; R. Nicholas Olsberg, "Ship Registers in the South Carolina Archives," *SCHM* 74 (October 1973): 217–8.

ing the extremely profitable rice and indigo plants—the latter introduced into
the economy in the early 1740s—gloried in the highest per capita income in
America.[18] This wealth, power, and cultural affluence established the planters
(and the merchants who marketed the crops) as the dominant social class. In
less than forty years, this aggressive planting caste came to dominate the life
of the colony, setting the tone and pace of South Carolina society.

After nearly two decades of struggling, John Drayton finally attained
membership in this elite circle. Yet one cannot relegate his economic and political acquisitiveness entirely to self-interest. By attaining political influence,
property, and wealth, Drayton was planning for his family's future by providing an economic base for his sons to continue the leadership role he began.
The prerequisite for such a station was personal independence, which an individual acquired by the ownership of sufficient property to provide leisure
to participate in government affairs. But wealth and property alone were insufficient to protect such independence. Education, too, was important in
safeguarding the material base of freedom. Through schooling one learned
the skills necessary to accumulate and preserve a fortune. Also essential were
genteel manners, taste, refinement, eloquence, and carriage—traits that
played an important role in establishing social position.[19]

John Drayton perhaps understood the importance of these qualities better
than anyone in the colony. For all his vast wealth and political position, the
elder Drayton commanded little esteem from his peers. A coarse, irascible,
and avaricious personality contributed to his low regard. Even more damaging to his social standing, though, was an "indifferent education" and a "confined mind." The poor grammar and frequent misspellings in Drayton's correspondence suggest that he received only a superficial education. His third
wife, Margaret, worked to improve her husband's writing, understanding as
a cultivated and educated English aristocrat that learning was the true mark
of gentility. Only through years of hard study and training could one acquire
the broad knowledge and social graces her husband's position in the community demanded. Men like Drayton who had wealth but lacked refinement, eloquence, comportment, and knowledge of books were looked down upon by

18. The next highest regional or subregional figure was £660.4 sterling for Anne Arundel
County, Maryland. Peter A. Coclanis, "The Rise and Fall of the South Carolina Low Country:
An Essay in Economic Interpretation," *Southern Studies* 24 (summer 1985): 151–2.

19. Frederick P. Bowes, *The Culture of Early Charleston* (Chapel Hill: University of North
Carolina Press, 1942), 10, 115, 121–3; Robert M. Weir, *Colonial South Carolina: A History* (Millwood, N.Y.: KTO Press, 1983), 252–3.

the better educated and socially refined elites. According to family tradition, John Drayton lived "without public esteem" and died "without public commiseration."[20]

Not wanting his sons to suffer the same disadvantages and derision, John Drayton did "his Utmost" to provide them with a superior education. To this end, he paid particular attention to William Henry, for it was the eldest son who would inherit Drayton Hall and eventually take his place as a leading member of the South Carolina ruling elite. Although nothing is known about William Henry Drayton's early education in South Carolina, he most likely received private instruction from a tutor either at Drayton Hall or at his uncle Thomas's nearby Magnolia plantation with his cousins. By early 1753 John Drayton felt Billy was ready for more formal schooling. Since South Carolina lacked a college, advanced education necessitated a journey to a northern colony or Europe. John Drayton ultimately decided to send William Henry and Charles "home" to England to receive the instruction considered essential for young men of the upper class. Many Carolina gentry were distrustful of the Calvinist influence of Princeton and Yale, as well as the skepticism reputed of William and Mary. They also selected British schools over other European institutions of higher learning out of snobbery, their love for all things English, and a belief that a stay in England was an important part of a young gentleman's education.[21]

On April 5, 1753, John Drayton placed nine-year-old William Henry and his younger brother Charles on board the *Edinburgh* for England.[22] They sailed under the protection of Charles Pinckney and his wife Eliza Lucas, who were to serve as their guardians while abroad. John Drayton made a fine choice in selecting the Pinckneys to guide the development of William Henry's education and character. Pinckney had already been a successful planter, lawyer, and influential member of the Commons House and the royal council when the Board of Trade appointed him to serve as interim chief justice in September 1752. Just six months later, however, the board replaced Pinckney with an English placeman, Peter Leigh, who had recently been forced to resign as

20. Bowes, *Culture of Early Charleston*, 10, 53; Griffin, "The Eighteenth Century Draytons," 174; John Drayton's "schoolbook," Drayton Family Papers, SCHS; John Drayton, *Carolinian Florist*, xxv.

21. Judith R. Joyner, *Beginnings: Education in Colonial South Carolina* (Columbia, S.C.: Wentworth, 1985), 53.

22. *SCG*, 11 April 1753.

high bailiff of Westminster for improper conduct. Pinckney's quick displacement by a foreigner tainted with scandal galled the proud Carolinian and served as a warning to him and other colonists that the British administration would not reward American-born citizens with top provincial offices for their party service. Incensed by this slight, Pinckney took the opportunity, when the council offered him the position as the colony's agent in London, to leave South Carolina and oversee the education of his sons in England. His anger and frustration with British placemen undoubtedly rubbed off on young William Henry Drayton and helped ferment a feeling within the boy that Americans were a distinct group of Englishmen treated differently by royal authorities.

Charles's wife, Eliza Lucas, was an even more remarkable person. While still in her early twenties, she had been largely responsible for developing the colony's second great staple crop—indigo. In addition to her botanical interests, Eliza Pinckney played music and even read law to help some of her poorer neighbors draw up their wills. The diary she kept shows her to be a devoted mother and wife, qualities she certainly showed toward her new, young charges. She had been friends with Charlotta Drayton, the young boys' late mother, and was committed to their upbringing while in England. Even after her return to South Carolina in 1758, Eliza continued to correspond with Billy, providing moral encouragement and guidance during his remaining years away from home.[23]

The Pinckneys' two young sons, Charles Cotesworth and Thomas, were also a favorable influence. They were both excellent scholars and received the highest praise for their conduct and character from masters and tutors. Their achievements and distinction later in life reflect their determination to succeed. Charles Cotesworth fought as a brigadier general in the Revolution, attended the Constitutional Convention of 1787, served as a diplomat to France under Washington, and ran as the Federalist candidate for the presidency in 1804 and 1808. His younger brother Thomas fought as a major general in the War of 1812 and served as governor of South Carolina and minister to Spain, where he arranged a treaty bearing his name in 1795, which secured to the United States the free navigation of the Mississippi. Alto-

23. David L. Coon, "Eliza Lucas Pinckney and the Reintroduction of Indigo Culture in South Carolina," *JSH* 42 (February 1976): 61–71; Sam S. Baskett, "Eliza Lucas Pinckney: Portrait of an Eighteenth Century American," *SCHM* 72 (October 1971) 207–19; G. Terry Sharrar, "Indigo in Carolina, 1671–1796," *SCHM* 72 (April 1971): 94–103.

gether, it was an outstanding group to stimulate a maturing and malleable boy.

In England, the Pinckneys first settled in an expensive villa in Ripley, near London. Soon thereafter Charles Pinckney hired a private instructor for his sons and the Drayton boys to bring their education up to standard before placing them into the prestigious Camberwell Academy. After several years there, the boys attended another private school, this one in Kensington Borough, run by a Mr. Longmore. Here they learned basic grammar, arithmetic, and Latin, in preparation for university.[24]

Schoolwork did not consume all of young Drayton's youthful energy, though. He devoted much of his spare time sightseeing throughout England; with more than two dozen Carolinians residing in the country for one reason or another, he had a large circle of friends and relatives with whom to fraternize. In the summer of 1753, the Pinckney family and the Drayton brothers made a seven-hundred-mile trip during which they visited the popular tourist attractions of Stonehenge, Old Sarum, and Salisbury Cathedral. In between sights, they stopped to rest and visit with fellow Carolinians residing in Bath and Wiltshire. The following winter, Charleston lawyer and planter Rawlins Lowndes took the Drayton brothers on a two-week Christmas holiday trip in a "Post Chays" to the Crowfields, South Carolina planter William Middleton's country estate in Suffolk, then to Norwich and London before returning to Ripley.[25]

The Draytons' tutelage under the Pinckneys ended in 1758 when a downturn in the economy resulting from the French and Indian War forced Charles and Eliza to return to South Carolina to supervise their plantations more closely. They left their children and the Drayton boys under the care

24. Pinckney, *Letterbook*, 111–2, 156–8; Marvin R. Zahniser, *Charles Cotesworth Pinckney: Founding Father* (Chapel Hill: University of North Carolina Press, 1967), 10–1.

25. Harriott H. Ravenel, *Eliza Lucas Pinckney* (New York: Charles Scribner's Sons, 1898), 156–7; "Fragment of a Diary of Charles Lowndes," William Lowndes Papers, SCDAH. This diary, which was actually kept by Rawlins Lowndes, is mistakenly attributed to his brother Charles. See Carl J. Vipperman, *The Rise of Rawlins Lowndes, 1721–1800* (Columbia: University of South Carolina Press, 1978), 79 n. 1.

Some of the Carolinians (and their families) residing in England at the time of Drayton's visit include: Ralph Izard, John and Hugh Rutledge, Arthur and William Middleton, William Drayton (cousin), Thomas Drayton (uncle), Rawlins Lowndes, Thomas Corbett, Thomas Lynch, George Bellinger, Paul Trapier, Thomas Heyward, William Moultrie, John Grimke, John Watsones, Jermyn Wright, Edmund Atkin, Samuel Brailsford, and James Abercromby. See Vipperman, *Rise of Rawlins Lowndes*, 80.

of a Mrs. Evance and George Marley, Charles Pinckney's business manager in England.[26]

Before leaving England, the Pinckneys placed William Henry and Charles into the old and prestigious Westminster School in London. It seems that John Drayton, who knew little or nothing about the reputation of schools in Britain, trusted the Pinckneys, both of whom were educated in England, to enroll his boys in a proper English school. They selected Westminster because "of all the Publick schools Westminster I think is to be preferred," Eliza explained, even though "the morals of Youth are little taken care of." This neglect of moral guidance, coupled with the corruption and dangers in nearby London, made Westminster "not the best place for every Boy," according to Henry Laurens, wealthy planter, Charleston merchant, and future political nemesis of William Henry Drayton. Still, Westminster was the favored choice among the English nobility, at least, for its heavy emphasis on academic excellence, manners, and deportment.[27]

The curriculum at Westminster was demanding—at least according to Charles Cotesworth Pinckney. In a slightly embellished account of his years spent attending the school, he describes a very structured and rigorous course of instruction. Students advanced through seven grades according to their ability to translate from Latin and Greek the works of Marital, Ovid, Horace, Virgil, Homer, Xenophon, and Sallust. The curriculum at Westminster was highly classical, too. The only subjects avowedly taught, according to Pinckney, were Latin, Greek, and the basic tenets of the Christian religion. In fact, a student could not go through Westminster, he claimed, "without being a fair Latin and Greek scholar and being able to assign a reason for the faith that is in [him]."

Students also followed a demanding work schedule, attending classes from six in the morning to twelve noon, then again from two to five in the afternoon. They sometimes had a half-holiday on Thursday, if it were "begged by some nobleman or gentleman who had been educated at the school." Weekends often brought no relief from studies, either, with Bible lessons on Sun-

26. Ravenel, *Eliza Lucas Pinckney*, 164–80.

27. G. F. Barker and Alan H. Stenning, comps., *The Record of Old Westminster: A Biographical List of All Who Are Known to Have Been Educated at Westminster School* (London: Chiswick, 1928), 1: v, 285; John Drayton, *Carolinian Florist*, xxv; Eliza L. Pinckney to Charles Pinckney, 7 February 1761, in Pinckney, *Letterbook*, 158; Henry Laurens to Alexander Garden, 20 August 1772, *HLP*, 8: 434; John D. Carleton, *Westminster School: A History* (London: Rupert Hart-Davis, 1965), 30–3.

day and homework to complete by Monday morning. Those who failed to turn in their exercises or perform them to the instructor's satisfaction were "liable to corporal punishment by a Master," who registered any shortcoming in a book.[28]

In 1760 William Henry was made liable to discipline from another "master" when John Drayton placed him and his brother Charles under the guardianship of their step-uncle James Glen, who had recently lost his position as governor of South Carolina. Before leaving for London in June of that year, Glen made an arrangement with his brother-in-law in which he promised to oversee the welfare and education of Drayton's sons in return for Drayton's managing his business affairs in South Carolina. A conscientious man who tried to please, Glen took his kinship responsibilities quite seriously and quickly grew fond of his "Dearest nephews." However, because William Henry and Charles were away at school and rooming together, Glen's parental role was limited to offering guidance and money (too much of the latter, according to John Drayton), thus leaving the two boys largely to their own devices.[29]

Not long after making this agreement, John Drayton considered having Billy sent back home. He wrote Glen asking his opinion on whether his eldest son required additional schooling. Unconcerned with his son's knowledge of the law, classics, history, or mathematics, the elder Drayton only desired that the youngster's "awkwardness" be replaced with a "Genteel behavior and carage." If this "can be accomplished without [him] going to College," the frugal-minded Drayton added, "he need not go . . . but let him not, at all events come out before he attains an easy Air, carage & Good behavior in company." However, Glen had already anticipated his brother-in-law's concerns and entered both Drayton boys into Balliol College on October 10, 1761—one day before their father wrote of his preferences concerning their future.[30]

28. St. Julien Ravenel, *Charleston: The Place and the People* (New York: Macmillan, 1906), 149–51.

29. Mary F. Carter, "James Glen, Governor of South Carolina: A Study in British Administrative Policies" (Ph.D. diss., University of California at Los Angeles, 1951), 2, 146, 178; W. Stitt Robinson, *James Glen: From Scottish Provost to Royal Governor of South Carolina* (Westport, Conn.: Greenwood Press, 1996), 34–5, 125–8, 137; James Glen to John Drayton, May 1775, Glen Papers, SCL.

30. John Drayton to James Glen, 11 October 1761, Glen Papers, SCL; Joseph Foster, *Alumni Oxonienses: The Members of the University of Oxford, 1715–1886* (Nendeln, Liechtenstein: Kraus Reprint, 1968), 1: 387; Griffin, "The Eighteenth Century Draytons," 194.

Why Glen entered the Drayton brothers into Oxford without John Drayton's approval is not

Undergraduates at Balliol College in the mid–eighteenth century entered a strictly hierarchical society, presided over by the head of the college and teachers and stratified by various grades of students: noblemen, gentlemen-commoners, commoners, and servitors. Every undergraduate was distinguished by the gown and cap he wore at all times, the fees he paid, the privileges he enjoyed, the table he sat at in the dining hall, and the place he occupied in chapel. The Drayton brothers were ranked among the second class of students—gentlemen-commoners—which entitled them to certain privileges not given to lower-ranking pupils: use of the library, admittance into the buttery and cellar, and permission to sit with instructors during dinner.[31]

Balliol College offered a varied, although unstimulating, course of instruction. For the bachelor of arts degree, candidates had to study logic, Latin, rhetoric, morals, politics, and religion, and examine the works of three classical authors of their choice. Part of a student's education also involved learning to dress and behave like a gentleman—attributes that were most important to John Drayton. At dinner and formal occasions, students were required to wear swallow-tailed coats, knee breeches, silk stockings, pumps, and a wig. Classes in drawing, fencing, dancing, and music (William Henry Drayton studied the violin) completed the elegant portion of a young gentleman's education.[32]

The amount of time devoted to studies obviously varied from student to student. Generally, undergraduates were expected to spend from 9:30 A.M. to

known. Perhaps the two boys' character and manners needed additional polishing. More than likely, Glen, a university graduate himself (University of Leyden), probably felt a few years in college were necessary for the proper upbringing of a young gentleman. Regardless, his decision reflects a close relationship, trust, and understanding between himself and John Drayton.

Glen's selection of Balliol over the many other English colleges is also a mystery. The school was not a popular place of learning among the South Carolina scions. Only one other Carolinian, in fact, had entered Balliol before the Draytons during the previous half century. However, geographical location, reputation, connections of its headmaster and tutors, and personal recommendations may have played a role in Glen's decision. See John Jones, *Balliol College: A History, 1263–1939* (Oxford, U.K.: Oxford University Press, 1988); V. H. H. Green, "The University and Social Life," in Lucy S. Sutherland and L. G. Mitchell, eds., *The History of the University of Oxford: The Eighteenth Century* (Oxford, U.K.: Clarendon Press, 1986), 315–6.

31. I. G. Doolittle, "College Administration," in Sutherland and Mitchell, *History of the University of Oxford*, 260–2; V. H. H. Green, *A History of Oxford University* (London: B. T. Batsford, 1974), 316–7.

32. John Drayton to James Glen, 10 September 1773, Glen Papers, SCL; Green, "The University and Social Life," 334; E. Manigault and Gabriel Manigault, "The Manigault Family of South Carolina from 1685–1886," *Transactions of the Huguenot Society* 4 (April 1897): 65–6.

1:00 P.M. on college work, and the rest of the day on their own avocations. However, for gentlemen-commoners like Drayton, who were not subject to any real control by the college, the exercises for the degree of bachelor of arts were "near-meaningless formalities." Tutors and students met so rarely, according to one Oxford graduate, they often "lived in the same college as strangers to each other." Thus freed from the demands of university exercises and examinations, Drayton could read what he liked, study when he felt inclined, or pass the time in recreation.[33]

If it was the latter activity Drayton sought, London held countless diversions to lure him away from his studies. The most popular pastime among undergraduates was frequenting the many coffeehouses in the English capital. Here students could sit by a warm fire while drinking, eating, gossiping, writing letters, and playing billiards, cards, and backgammon—all in the "Midst of Tobacco Smoak & an eternal buz of busy Gentry." Drayton certainly frequented the Carolina Coffee House, the unofficial headquarters for Carolinians in London. Here he could pick up and send mail and visit fellow Carolinians, some of whom brought news from home. Other popular attractions in London included the tombs in Westminster Abbey, the Tower of London, and the annual fair. Those interested in the unusual and morbid could view the lunatics at Bedlam hospital or the public executions held within the capital. For the more athletically inclined there was bowling, cricket, boat trips up the Thames, ice skating and horseback riding. Both Drayton brothers owned horses, which they undoubtedly rode in the parks and surrounding countryside. Affluent and daring students often played assorted games of chance, a pastime that was practically a national obsession in England at the time.[34]

Evidence suggests that William Henry Drayton may have participated in these popular but financially risky diversions. It would certainly help to explain why he amassed debts while in England that "greatly embarrassed his

33. Lucy Sutherland, *The University of Oxford in the Eighteenth Century: A Reconsideration* (Oxford, U.K.: Oxford University Press, 1972), 22–3; Doolittle, "College Administration," 267; Sutherland, "The Curriculum," 475–7; Green, *A History of Oxford University*, 87; Jan Morris, ed., *The Oxford Book of Oxford* (Oxford, U.K.: Oxford University Press, 1978), 153.

34. Mabel L. Webber, ed., "Peter Manigault's Letters," *SCHM* 33 (January 1932): 55; G. E. Mingay, *Georgian London* (London: B. T. Batsford, 1975), 65–7, 70–9; Richard B. Schwartz, *Daily Life in Johnson's London* (Madison: University of Wisconsin Press, 1983), 55–74; William L. Sachse, *The Colonial American in Britain* (Madison: University of Wisconsin Press, 1956), 17–8.

[financial] affairs"; it would also partially explain his reckless gambling habits later in life. Exacerbating Drayton's pecuniary problems while in school was his "proud and stingy" father, who provided each of his two sons with only £145 a year while at Balliol, an amount considerably less than the £175–200 spent annually by the average gentleman-commoner at Oxford in the mid–eighteenth century. The elder Drayton simply could not allow his sons to spend his hard-earned money "with care and pleasure," he explained to James Glen, while he worked "many hot summer days . . . out in the field boiling my head." Yet William Henry continued to spend beyond his means, believing his father would cover his expenditures. When the expected funds failed to arrive, he borrowed from his ever-generous step-uncle, James Glen, promising not to spend the money in an "improper manner," but to "make the most advantageous use of it that lies in my power."[35]

However, Drayton could not afford to spend all his money and energy on extracurricular endeavors. As the future patriarch of Drayton Hall, he had to live up to his father's high expectations. John Drayton certainly instilled the importance of education and genteel manners in his eldest son from an early age. Wanting to please his father and prepare himself for his eventual place among the Carolina ruling oligarchy, William Henry Drayton devoted a substantial portion of his time and effort toward his studies. His later political writings, which are heavily peppered with quotes from classical authors, references to historical events, and analyses of complex legal and constitutional tracts, reflect the learning of a conscientious student. This thirst for knowledge is also demonstrated in an unrequired anatomy course Drayton took with his brother Charles, who was studying medicine.[36]

In early 1763 John Drayton decided his eldest son had acquired enough formal schooling and called him back home. There were several reasons for the elder Drayton's abrupt decision. Because William Henry Drayton was fi-

35. "Expense Account of John Drayton's Sons While in Britain," John Drayton to James Glen, 30 April 1762, 5 April 1768, 24 December 1769, 6 February 1773, 10 September 1773, all in Glen Papers, SCL; John Drayton, *Carolinian Florist*, xxvi; William Henry Drayton to James Glen, 11 March 1762, Dalhousie Muniments, Papers Relating to the Drayton Family, Scottish Records Office, Edinburgh. Information on the average annual financial expenditures of eighteenth-century Oxford students can be found in Green, *A History of Oxford University*, 118–9; Green, "The University and Social Life," 328–9; Morris, *Oxford Book of Oxford*, 157–8.

36. William Henry Drayton to James Glen, 11 March 1762, Dalhousie Muniments, Papers Relating to the Drayton Family, Scottish Records Office, Edinburgh.

nancially set for life through inheritances, John Drayton did not feel it was crucial for him to receive a degree, just as long as he did not return home "as awkward a Lad as Tom Middleton's son." Moreover, the senior Drayton was in the process of expanding his planting operations. Cutting expenses in England would enable him to purchase more land, more slaves, and an additional schooner to transport his produce to Charleston. Finally, he wanted his prodigal son home before he acquired further financial obligations he could not meet. Twenty-one-year-old Billy had no alternative but to return home to a disappointed father.[37]

Drayton did not sail directly to South Carolina on his way home; instead, he went to a northern port city, most likely New York, and from there traveled overland to Charleston. This detour was more than likely the suggestion of James Glen. He had made a similar trip a few years before and probably thought it beneficial for a young, up-and-coming gentleman to become familiar with the life and customs of the northern colonies. Glen even advanced Drayton £300 in May 1763 for the return trip, certainly more money than was needed for a transatlantic voyage.[38]

Returning to Drayton Hall in mid-1763 with a college education, patrician manners, and a large inheritance awaiting him, young William Henry Drayton was anxious to make his mark and take his place among the South Carolina gentry.

37. John Drayton, *Memoirs of the American Revolution As Relating to the State of South Carolina* (Charleston: A. E. Miller, 1821; reprint, New York: Arno Press, 1969), 1: xiii; John Drayton to James Glen, 11 October 1761, Glen Papers, SCL; Olsberg, "Ship Registers," 217–8. The alleged awkwardness of William Middleton (1744–1768) did not prevent him from winning a seat in the South Carolina assembly in 1765.

38. The *SCG*, which faithfully listed the arrival and departures of prominent citizens, makes no mention of Drayton's arrival between 1762 and 1764. Griffin, "The Eighteenth Century Draytons," 249; Glen-Drayton Account, 1761–1763, Glen Papers [legal size folder], SCL.

EARLY SUCCESSES AND FAILURES

Having not seen his eldest son since the boy was a child of nine, John Drayton probably did not recognize the fully grown twenty-one-year-old who greeted him in the summer of 1763. He had to have been pleased with William Henry's elegance, learning, and cosmopolitan bearing. But the elder Drayton was an unforgiving man, difficult to get along with, and his allegedly tyrannical behavior toward all his children, exacerbated by Billy's profligacy while in England, caused a large rift between the two, compelling the son to strike out on his own as soon as he was able.[1] The young Drayton soon established himself in the upper class, marrying a wealthy heiress, inheriting a sizable estate, and winning election to political office. Within a few years, however, he squandered everything he had so quickly attained. His chances of ever achieving his foreordained station among Carolina's ruling elite seemed bleak.

Drayton's first step in his methodical march toward high social and political position had been to establish himself in some profession. Because of his carelessness in England, his father did not yet trust Billy with his inheritance. Without a plantation to manage, Drayton turned his attention to the study of law and entered on a private course of reading with "great industry" until he became "well informed" in English, ancient and modern history, the "Laws of Nations," and the "rights of his own country." Like many young

---

1. Reputedly, John Drayton behaved like a "Tyrant" toward his sons, "so that they lived little with him after they grew up." See John Drayton, *Carolinian Florist*, xxv.

Americans of his generation, Drayton also read the works of the English Whigs and opposition theorists of the late seventeenth and early eighteenth centuries. Although not egalitarians nor revolutionaries, these men were proponents of enlightened conservatism, believing in the natural rights of everyone, checks and balances on government, separation of powers, freedom of thought and expression, and the right to oppose tyranny, while condemning standing armies, placemen, and party cliques and cabals. The Whigs insisted that Englishmen were entitled to be ruled by laws to which they had themselves consented. Drayton and other revolutionary-minded Americans later used this idea to deny the right of Parliament to determine cases in the colonies. Drayton also valued the study of history, where he found resemblances between historical accounts and contemporary criticisms of English society that he later applied to the context of American debate over imperial relations.[2]

While improving his mind, Drayton also pursued the one thing absolutely necessary for becoming a member of the ruling elite—economic independence. Without having received his inheritance, and with his legal studies still uncompleted, he decided to take a lesson from his father and marry wealth. Fortunately for him, Drayton happened to return to South Carolina at an opportune time to meet such women, for, according to the elder Drayton, there were "many a girl of fine fortune" then in the market. And with his English education, debonair deportment, enormous future inheritance, and influential connections—young William Henry Drayton was one of the most eligible bachelors in the colony. His profligate tendencies constituted no mark against him, either. Carolina parents readily accepted an "abandoned fellow" with a "polite disorder" as an appropriate match for their daughters. Instead, they measured a man by the number of slaves or amount of land in his possession, "without the least regard to temper, parts or education."[3]

Possessing all the qualities favored by women in potential husbands, Dray-

2. Drayton, *Memoirs*, 1: xiii–xiv; Caroline Robbins, *The Eighteenth-Century Commonwealthmen: Studies in the Transmission, Development and Circumstance of English Liberal Thought from the Restoration of Charles II until the War with the Thirteen Colonies* (Cambridge: Harvard University Press, 1959), 4–21, 382–6; H. Trevor Colbourn, *The Lamp of Experience: Whig History and the Intellectual Origins of the American Revolution* (Chapel Hill: University of North Carolina Press, 1965), 4–7; Bernard Bailyn, *The Ideological Origins of the American Revolution* (Cambridge: Harvard University Press, 1967), 22–42.

3. John Drayton to James Glen, 24 December 1769, Glen Papers, SCL; *SC&AGG*, 1 April 1768; *SCG*, 26 January 1738.

ton began confidently pursuing the available young ladies of wealth in the colony. He soon set his sights on sixteen-year-old Dorothy Golightly, a "very amiable young lady," according to the *South Carolina Gazette*, and an heiress of "great fortune and merit." One can only speculate on the circumstances surrounding the couple's first meeting. They may have been introduced by Eliza Pinckney, who had a reputation as a matchmaker and who was a close friend to the families of both. Believing that the two youngsters were compatible and would make a nice match, she possibly initiated the courtship at one of the many dances, balls, and barbecues where courting frequently began; with the venerable Eliza Pinckney involved in the arrangements, both sets of parents would have approved the match. John Drayton would certainly have been pleased that Dorothy brought to the marriage a £40,000 dowry.[4]

Following a short, formal courtship, William Henry and Dorothy married on March 28, 1764—one day before the bride's seventeenth birthday—in a ceremony performed at St. Andrews Church outside Charleston. As with most eighteenth-century couples, the Draytons' matrimonial history has not been preserved. One can only speculate regarding their relationship, based upon the few surviving records concerning their marriage and the general marital customs, laws, and behavior of the time.

Not much is known about Dorothy Golightly Drayton beyond her birth, marriage, children, and death. She was born at her father's Fairlawn plantation on the Ashley River on March 29, 1747. Like her new husband, she, too, lost a parent (her father) at an early age. Unlike William Henry, however, she received a superficial and ornamental education. In 1758 her mother boarded Dorothy and her younger sister Mary at a school managed by Miss Sarah

4. *SCG*, 31 March 1764. Dorothy was the daughter of Culcheth Golightly, a wealthy rice planter who died in 1749. In addition to owning three rice plantations in St. Batholomew Parish, Golightly held many local offices and served in the provincial assembly. In his will, Golightly designated that his property be equally divided between his two daughters, Dorothy and Mary, which eventually amounted to £40,000 each. See Charleston County Wills, 6: 244–6, 276–7, 534–46; 7: 340–1, SCDAH; and Florence G. Geiger, "St. Bartholomew Parish as Seen by Its Rectors, 1713–1761," *SCHM* 50 (October 1949): 188–9.

Charles Pinckney served as executor of Culcheth Golightly's will and guardian of his two young daughters. When Pinckney died in 1758, his wife Eliza stayed at Mary Golightly's Fairlawn plantation, receiving "great tenderness" and support from her. See Ravenel, *Eliza Lucas Pinckney*, 181; Pinckney, *Letterbook*, 169; Griffin, "The Eighteenth Century Draytons," 250–1. For evidence of Eliza Pinckney as matchmaker, see Thomas Corbett to Peter Manigault, 2 April 1755, Manigault Family Papers, SCL.

Simpson, who instructed a small group of girls on the "polite accomplish-ments" necessary to become a lady: reading, writing, arithmetic, needlework, drawing, dancing, and music. Because girls were not trained in any profession "except music and dancing," they reputedly made "very agreeable Compan-ions, but very expensive wives."[5]

Like all women in eighteenth-century America, domesticity was Dorothy Drayton's inevitable destiny. She was to find pride, satisfaction, and fulfill-ment in her life through her many roles as wife, housekeeper, and mother. As a wife, her main purpose was to please her husband by being an agreeable and obedient companion, a gracious hostess to his guests, and a capable and industrious manager of his house. It was this latter responsibility that placed enormous demands on her time and energy. As the mistress of a large planta-tion she was involved in the day-to-day and season-to-season domestic opera-tions of the plantation enterprise: creating adequate supplies of food and clothing for white and blacks; supervising activities of the house slaves and domestic producers; performing domestic tasks that could not be entrusted to slaves, such as cutting out garments to be sewn together by domestic pro-ducers; preparing special meals, preserving food and handling prized, scarce, or fragile objects; and, finally, nursing the sick (both white and black), provid-ing religious instruction, and teaching slaves domestic skills. Together, these activities made mistresses' days an endless stream of work.

Additionally, because William Henry Drayton was occasionally away from his plantation for months or even years at a time, Mrs. Drayton found herself in the position of surrogate master or "deputy husband," performing many traditionally male tasks in the day-to-day operation of the estate. These in-cluded making careful arrangements for the management of the property, from paying taxes to attending to concerns about the labor force. Whether or not Dorothy Drayton relished the independence and power bestowed upon her as plantation manager or reluctantly shouldered the responsibility is uncertain. What is known is that she took her managerial duties quite seri-ously, even representing her husband in court on several occasions to protect their property from seizure by creditors. However, Dorothy did not bear this burden alone. She relied on assistance from her husband through his corre-

5. Griffin, "The Eighteenth Century Draytons," 250; Julia Cherry Spruill, *Women's Life and Work in the Southern Colonies* (Chapel Hill: University of North Carolina Press, 1938; reprint, New York: W. W. Norton, 1972), 185, 197–8; Joyner, *Beginnings,* 54–7; Walter J. Fraser, *Patri-ots, Pistols and Petticoats: "Poor Sinful Charlestown" during the Revolution* (Columbia: University of South Carolina Press, 1976), 27.

spondence, Eliza Pinckney, an experienced and astute plantation manager in her own right, and her brother-in-law Benjamin Huger, a prosperous low-country rice planter.[6]

Bearing and raising children competed directly with Mrs. Drayton's household responsibilities for her limited resources and energy. Insurance for old age, the isolation of plantation life, and high infant mortality were all reasons for having many children. The Draytons, however, did not begin having children until more than three years after exchanging their wedding vows. The reason for the delay is unknown. Perhaps their first attempts ended in miscarriage. Yet once the births began, they came regularly until William Henry's temporary departure from South Carolina in 1770. The first child, a son they named John—possibly in an attempt to placate Drayton's father—was born on June 2, 1767. Like nearly all parents at the time, the couple suffered the loss of a child when a second son, born the following year, died in October 1769. Their sadness over this loss was partially supplanted by the arrival one month later of a third son, whom they named after his father. The child brought them added excitement and joy before he, too, died seventeen months later in May 1770. The Draytons had their fourth and last child in March 1774, a daughter they named Mary, after Dorothy's sister who had died three years earlier.[7]

Household chores and child care did not consume all of Dorothy Drayton's time and energy. The numerous slaves, overseers, and servants allowed her time to occasionally escape the boredom of the isolated plantation life and pursue sundry social gatherings and entertainments. Though she lived in a world dominated by men, Dorothy's closest friends were other females—particularly her mother and sister and Eliza Pinckney and her daughter Harriott—whom she turned to for support and companionship. Mrs. Drayton needed a great deal of support and friendship from others during her mar-

6. Marli F. Weiner, *Mistress and Slaves: Plantation Women in South Carolina, 1830–1880* (Urbana: University of Illinois Press, 1998), 24–48; Cara Anzilotti, "Autonomy and the Female Planter in Colonial South Carolina," *JSH* 63 (May 1997): 239–68; Elise Pinckney, ed., "Letters of Eliza Lucas Pinckney, 1768–1782," *SCHM* 76 (July 1975): 152–3; Spruill, *Women's Life and Work*, 64–77, 104–5; Mary Beth Norton, *Liberty's Daughters: The Revolutionary Experience of American Women, 1750–1800* (Boston: Little, Brown, 1980), 26–7, 34–8, 60; Smith, *Inside the Great House*, 77, 191–200.

7. Mabel L. Webber, "Register of St. Andrews Parish," *SCHM* 15 (April 1914): 98; Alexander S. Salley Jr. and D. Huger Smith, eds., *Register of St. Andrews Parish* (1927; reprint, Columbia: University of South Carolina Press, 1971), 332.

riage as her husband was often away absorbed in affairs of state. During such times she sometimes took social sojourns to see her closest friends and relatives, spending the day dining, drinking tea, attending balls, and traveling through the countryside. Of course, the "sickly" summer season (May to November) and the social winter season (January and February) occasioned extended visits to Charleston, where Dorothy temporarily escaped from her numerous duties as plantation mistress.

William Henry Drayton's role as planter, husband, and father was far different from that of his wife. In the patriarchal society of the eighteenth century, he governed his family and estate like a little kingdom. He was paternal lord over his wife, children, and slaves, responsible for their physical, moral, and spiritual welfare. His word was final in all matters both inside and outside the home: the education of their children, control over the servants, selection of a homesite, and even planning and furnishing the house. Although information is scant concerning Drayton's paternal abilities and concerns, his son John considered him "a fond and attentive father."[8]

Drayton gained more than a dutiful wife and adoring children in his marriage to Dorothy Golightly. The union with his teen-aged bride brought him £40,000 and a "very considerable real and personal Estate" consisting of lands, plantations, town lots, buildings, slaves, money, livestock, household furniture, and "other things of value." The bulk of this estate consisted of a Charleston townhouse and a 1,076-acre rice and indigo plantation (called the Horseshoe) on the Ashley River in Colleton County.[9]

Unfortunately, neither Drayton's Horseshoe country home nor information about it has survived. Indeed, the precise location of the residence is uncertain, for Drayton owned several plantations acquired between 1764 and 1769 and a house in Charleston obtained through marriage. Drayton and his family probably resided in the capital during much of the summer "sickly sea-

8. Spruill, *Women's Life and Work*, 43–4; John Drayton, *Carolinian Florist*, xxviii.

9. Marriage Settlement between William Henry Drayton and Dorothy Golightly, *Marriage Settlements*, 2: 185–92, SCDAH. The settlement allowed William Henry access to only half of Dorothy's £40,000. Parents of brides were only too aware of the profligate tendencies among aristocratic men and regularly set aside a portion of their daughter's inheritance in a trust to provide her with a measure of financial security during marriage and widowhood and protection from creditors from a husband's mismanagement, business misfortune, or extravagant living. This agreement would later prove to be a wise financial move for Dorothy Drayton. See Marylynn Salmon, "Women and Property in South Carolina: The Evidence from Marriage Settlements, 1730–1830," *W&MQ*, 3d. ser., 39 (October 1982): 657–61, 675.

son," the winter social season, and especially after 1771 when he became heavily involved in local politics. While not in Charleston, Drayton perhaps lived at his Horseshoe estate on the Ashley River. However, complications arising from the execution of Culcheth Golightly's estate prevented him and Dorothy from receiving official ownership of this plantation until September 1768, so they may have been forced to reside elsewhere during their first years of marriage. One possible residence was a 1,000-acre plantation in Prince William Parish on Lewis's Neck that Drayton inherited from his grandfather William Bull soon after his marriage. A less likely residence was the Ponds, a 3,400-acre rice plantation situated on the upper part of the Ashley River Swamp in Berkeley County, which he acquired in 1769.

No matter the location of his permanent country home, it was most likely modest in size. Certainly it did not rival the splendor or scale of his father's palatial Ashley River estate. No other Carolina plantation manor did, in fact, largely because most planters preferred investing their money in lucrative land and slaves rather than in a plantation manor. But despite its relatively modest size, Drayton's country home was elegantly furnished with expensive china and mahogany pieces that included dining, tea, and card tables and an infant cradle.[10]

All this wealth and property gave Drayton the financial security and independence to pursue political office. The reason for his interest in government service was offered by his son, who explained that his father's "ardent mind" would not allow him to "move in a common sphere." But there were deeper psychological reasons behind Drayton's entrance into the political arena. An important motivating factor was a desire to please his father and attain the position of authority demanded of him. Throughout his life William Henry Drayton reputedly sought "affection and confidence" from his father, who,

10. The legal battle over Drayton's Horseshoe estate is found in the Miscellaneous Records of Charleston County, 91-A: 251–61, Charleston County Library. Information on the Ponds plantation is located in Henry A. M. Smith, "The Upper Ashley and the Mutations of Families," *SCHM* 20 (July 1919): 174–5, while data on Drayton's household furnishings is found in Mabel L. Webber, "The Thomas Elfe Account Book, 1765–1775," *SCHM* 39 (April 1938): 84, (July 1938): 135, and 40 (July 1939): 81.

The plantation Drayton inherited from his grandfather Bull was originally his mother Charlotta's future inheritance from her father. When she died in 1744, William Bull willed the property to her two infant sons. John Drayton was furious over the loss of this property, which he thought rightfully belonged to him. When he revised his will years later, the greedy patriarch deducted the amount William Henry and Charles had received from their grandfather from what they would ultimately collect from his estate (Bull, *Oligarchs*, 42).

by providing his eldest son with a superior (and costly) education, expected that son to rise to his preordained station. A secondary yet still powerful influence was a desire on Drayton's part for public recognition. His uncle William Bull II recognized this trait, remarking that his nephew was "ever fond of appearing at the Tribunal of the Publick." In seeking fame, however, Drayton was merely emulating a general cultural feature among the South Carolina elite. Because there was no titled nobility in the colonies, political office was the only area for formal public recognition of social prominence. Election to public office signified that a man had arrived, that he had assumed the role appropriate to his station.[11]

Drayton entered government service in October 1765 amidst great political turmoil caused by Parliament's increasing involvement in governing the colonies. Prior to 1763, Britain had paid little attention to administering its North American possessions. But after expanding an already enormous debt and increasing an already vast territory as a result of the Seven Years' War with France, the Crown had to find ways to raise new revenue and better manage its expanding empire. The American colonies, used to the mother country's "salutary neglect," hotly protested its increased meddling, especially its attempts to increase taxes and reduce the local legislature's authority to govern. This policy reversal quickly sparked two conflicts in South Carolina—the Boone-Gadsden Affair and the Stamp Act controversy—which embroiled the province in nearly a half decade of political warfare between the Commons House of Assembly and local Crown officials. It was within this bitter partisan feuding that Drayton received his political training.

The Boone-Gadsden Affair, one of the colony's most pernicious and protracted contests prior to the Revolution, erupted in the spring of 1762 when newly appointed governor Thomas Boone tried to achieve a membership within the assembly that was more favorable to royal instruction. In trying to realize this end, Boone made the politically fatal mistake of attacking the lower house's right to control the election of its own members. In March 1762 the governor requested the Commons to revise the election law of 1721, complaining that it was too loose, too general, and nonbinding on the church wardens who administered the elections. The legislature replied that there

11. Drayton, *Memoirs*, 1: xiv; John Drayton, *Carolinian Florist*, xxv; William Bull to Lord Dartmouth, 22 February 1775, BPROSC 35: 23; Robert M. Weir, "The Stamp Act Crisis in South Carolina" (Ph.D. diss., Case Western Reserve, 1966), 33; Richard Waterhouse, "South Carolina's Colonial Elite: A Study in the Social Structure and Political Culture of a Southern Colony, 1670–1760" (Ph.D. diss., Johns Hopkins University, 1964), 277.

was no need to change the law because it had proved effective for more than four decades. The obstinate and tactless Boone refused to drop the matter, however. To prove his point, he refused to administer the oath of office to Christopher Gadsden, a Charleston merchant and strong proponent of American rights, because church wardens of St. Paul's Parish had failed to administer the required oaths before opening the polls. Boone's use of this trivial oversight to force the issue started a nearly two-and-one-half-year caustic contest between the Commons, the governor, and leading planters and merchants—all of whom addressed their grievances in the local press and to imperial authorities at Whitehall. In the end, the Crown sided with the South Carolina assembly and Boone left for London to explain his disruptive behavior to disgruntled Crown officers.[12]

This experience in political upheaval proved invaluable when South Carolinians contested Parliament's right to tax the colonies, which that body attempted to do with the passage in March 1765 of the Stamp Act, a broad internal tax that required Americans to purchase and use special stamped paper for newspapers, customs documents, various licenses, college diplomas, and legal forms for purchasing land, recovering debts, and making wills. At first, South Carolinians, not ready to oppose the act upon the "uncompromisable grounds of absolute principle," took a negative but cautious approach to the decree. However, with encouragement from the "laudable example" of the northern provinces in "endeavering to repell the manifest encroachments thereby made on their liberty," Charlestonians finally began "opening their Eyes" to the efficacy of violence in preventing this precedent from being set.[13]

South Carolinians then joined their northern brethren in the defiance by sending three delegates—Thomas Lynch, Christopher Gadsden, and John Rutledge—to the Stamp Act Congress held in New York in early October 1765. Meanwhile, the local press and pro-American leaders aroused popular opposition to the act by organizing a violent but ordered program of protest. When the "obnoxious" stamped paper arrived off Charleston on October 18, the rebels, loosely formed by Christopher Gadsden into an association called the Sons of Liberty, soon gathered near the docks with the intention of seiz-

12. Jack P. Greene, "The Gadsden Election Controversy and the Revolutionary Movement in South Carolina," *Mississippi Valley Historical Review* 46 (December 1959): 469–92.

13. Weir, *"A Most Important Epocha,"* 15; Richard Hutson to Joel Benedict, 30 October 1765, "Letters of the Honorable Richard Hutson," *Charleston City Year Book* (1895): 313.

ing and destroying the cargo if the ship's crew attempted to land it. When Lieutenant Governor Bull learned of this scheme he ordered the stamp paper placed under the protection of Fort Johnson. Undeterred, the rebels quickly initiated a program of intimidation. The next day they paraded an effigy of a stamp distributor through Charleston in a coffin and set it ablaze that night amidst boisterous applause from the city's inhabitants. They followed up this symbolic warning with a more overt one by rummaging through the stamp distributors' homes and threatening them with violence if they attempted to execute their duties. The paper remained at Fort Johnson.[14]

Twenty-three-year-old Drayton had jumped headlong into this political pandemonium earlier in October with his appointment as justice of the peace for St. James Parish and his election to the assembly. It is uncertain why he even accepted the first office, which was a lowly judicial post "of no profit and some trouble." Few people, in fact, ever accepted the position unless they were "much courted." Drayton's father and uncle possibly encouraged him toward this entry-level post as an appropriate introduction to political office. The many duties a justice of the peace had to perform—issuing warrants, examining and committing trespassers, enforcing the many slave codes, inspecting weights and measures, and settling minor contractual disputes—certainly prepared him for the tedium of public service. These many tasks evidently were not too onerous for Drayton, who remained a local justice for four years.[15]

Yet service as a justice of the peace did not satisfy Drayton's lofty political ambitions. While being courted for this relatively insignificant berth, he sought the much more prestigious office of assemblyman. The colonists' dispute over the Stamp Act caused a great deal of excitement and partisanship among local voters during the 1765 election. One Carolinian calling himself "A Native" pleaded with his readers to elect only those candidates "who will use their best endeavours to *preserve, support and defend the enjoyment of every*

14. *SCG*, 19 October 1765; Maurice A. Crouse, "Cautious Rebellion: South Carolina's Opposition to the Stamp Act," *SCHM* 73 (April 1972): 59–71; Weir, "The Stamp Act Crisis," 191–4; Drayton, *Memoirs*, 1: 36–41.

15. *SCG*, 12 October 1765; *SCG&CJ*, 7 December 1765; William Bull to Earl of Hillsborough, 30 November 1770, BPROSC 32: 381; Cooper and McCord, *Statutes at Large*, 2: 330; William Simpson, *The Practical Justice of the Peace and Parish-Officer, of His Majesty's Province of South Carolina* (Charles Town: Robert Wells, 1761; reprint, New York: Arno Press, 1972), 1–5, 49, 62, 127, 163, 253; Rayford B. Boles, "The South Carolina Judiciary, 1669–1769" (Ph.D. diss., University of Georgia, 1978), 43–4, 164–7.

constitutional LIBERTY, RIGHT and PRIVILEGE that has been handed down to us by our FOREFATHERS, and which we CLAIM as BRITISH Subjects." Voters in St. Andrews Parish evidently thought Drayton professed such ideals, for they elected him to represent them in the assembly. Equally important to his election, though, were his wealth, education, and family connections.[16]

Drayton's high aspirations did not surface in his indifferent execution of his office. He was frequently absent from his seat, compelling the speaker of the assembly to send special messengers to Drayton's residence in Charleston calling for his immediate attendance "on the services of the House." Fines imposed on him failed to curtail his delinquency. When Drayton did honor the assembly with his presence, legislative leaders assigned him to committees charged with improving the economic and cultural conditions in the province. Some of the specific issues these panels considered were the utility of a "pounding machine" for rice, methods to improve the lot of the poor and civilize the local Indians, and plans to construct a seminary, chapel, and canal.[17]

16. *SCG*, 28 September 1765. Drayton's stance on the Stamp Act is still a point of debate among historians. Previous biographers have argued that Drayton was "in the minority" over the Stamp Act resolution (William M. Dabney and Marion Dargan, *William Henry Drayton and the American Revolution*. [Albuquerque: University of New Mexico Press, 1962], 28). They base their argument on his years spent in Great Britain (which supposedly would attract him toward the Crown's position), the influence of his father and uncle, both of whom opposed the measure, and a statement made by General Charles Lee to Drayton asserting that "it was strong evidence of the mercy of the American patriots that they did not long ago hang up you and every Advocate for the Stamp act." Charles Lee to William Henry Drayton, 15 March 1779, "Charles Lee Papers," New York Historical Society *Collections*, vol. 4 (New York: NYHS, 1873), 318.

However, because there is no corroborative evidence of Drayton's support of the Stamp Act, it is more plausible that General Lee was misinformed, perhaps confusing the Carolinian's backing of the Townshend Acts in 1769—knowledge of which was printed in handbills throughout the colonies—with his stance on the Stamp Act. Consequently, except for the assumption that his father and uncle may have initially steered young Drayton toward supporting Crown measures, there is no evidence that he was ever a devoted defender of the royal prerogative. In any event, if Drayton did support the Stamp Act, it was a timid and reticent patronage, for had he made it public, he probably would have lost his bid for a seat in the assembly during this political controversy with the mother country.

17. Journals of the Commons House of Assembly, special microfilm edition labeled "South Carolina Public Records Office, Colonial Office," Series 5/491: 193; 5/489: 101, 152; 5/491: 193; 5/484: 41, 74, 77; 5/488: 99, 104, 107; 5/489: 98; 5/491: 3–5, 143, SCDAH. In all fairness to Drayton, absenteeism was not uncommon in the South Carolina assembly, which was probably the hardest-working legislature in British North America. The numerous inconveniences of sitting in extraordinarily long legislative sessions, often lasting eight months a year for as many

Unfortunately for Drayton, his aristocratic heritage and indifferent service in the assembly caused him to lose his seat the following election. As in 1765, the election of 1768 coincided with conflict between the colonists and Great Britain. The previous summer Parliament had passed the Revenue Act (or Townshend duties), an external tax on glass, paint, lead, paper, and tea imported into the colonies. Americans, stoked by their success in securing the repeal of the Stamp Act in March 1766, once again opposed this attempt to undermine colonial self-government. Patriot leaders instructed voters to choose unwavering defenders of American liberty, and Charleston artisans and shopkeepers urged greater recognition of the common people's views by replacing elitist assemblymen with more ordinary men. Accordingly, voters in St. Andrews Parish elected George Sheed Jr., a forty-three-year-old schoolmaster, to take Drayton's all too frequently vacant seat in the Commons.

Drayton's political defeat cannot be attributed solely to his aristocratic background, however, for voters reelected vocal, genteel loyalists like William Wragg and John Freer. Instead, Drayton's business failures and profligate habits (both of which are discussed later in the chapter) and indifferent service played an equally prominent role in his defeat. These failures and character flaws of his were evidently well known among South Carolinians. During the heated public debate over the nonimportation association, in which Drayton participated the following year, a group of Charleston mechanics acridly asserted that despite his liberal education, the "good fruits thereof have not hitherto been conspicuous either in his public or private life" and that "surely no parish in this province will ever think it prudent to trust their interests in such hands." In the end, this political defeat proved no real loss for Drayton. Governor Charles Montagu dissolved the assembly a few days after it convened for joining with legislatures in the northern colonies to repeal the Revenue Act. Still, Drayton must have been disappointed. As a member of the Commons he was recognized as a leading member of society; with his defeat, he lost some of that public respect.[18]

---

as six days a week and six hours a day, taxed even the most energetic and dedicated assemblyman (Sirmans, *Colonial South Carolina*, 241).

18. David R. Chesnutt, " 'Greedy Party Work': The South Carolina Election of 1768," in *Party and Political Opposition in Revolutionary America*, ed. Patricia Bonomi (New York: Sleepy Hollow Press, 1980), 75, 78, 84–5; Marc Egnal, *A Mighty Empire: The Origins of the American Revolution* (Ithaca, N.Y.: Cornell University Press, 1988), 237–8; David M. Knepper, "The Political Structure of Colonial South Carolina, 1743–1776" (Ph.D. diss., University of Virginia, 1971), 31–5; *SCG*, 5 October 1769.

*   *   *

Drayton's failure in politics also carried over to his financial affairs. In less than five years he managed to squander a significant portion of his fortune. This fiscal irresponsibility was partly due to his own mismanaging of his estates. Although he had received a good education in Latin, history, and classical authors, he apparently was never taught basic accounting or business management, and his financial woes accelerated following the 1768 assembly defeat. Thereafter, his youthful energies became leisurely and unfocused as he devoted an increasing portion of his time to the genteel social life of Charleston. In this environment of self-gratification, Drayton's passion for gambling, which he probably acquired in England, surfaced in a reckless flurry. In the absence of corrective influences, this undisciplined and dangerous lifestyle nearly devoured all his time, energy, and wealth.

However, some of Drayton's financial difficulties were a result of misfortune, overspending, and the expense of establishing himself as a planter. Although he inherited two plantations with slaves to work them, he continued to enlarge his property holdings. Between 1765 and 1769, he purchased three plantations and the accompanying slaves, thereby incurring not only these property costs but also the expenses of furnishing the plantations and households. In a one-year period in 1769–1770, for example, Drayton paid at least £450 sterling for assorted merchandise: nails, rum, milk pails, cheap cloth, silk cloth, Irish linen, hats, shoes, a chafing dish and a 255-pound anchor for an eighteen-ton schooner (the *Tryton*) he purchased in 1766 to transport his produce to the Charleston market. In addition to these enormous expenditures, Drayton suffered a financial setback in 1767 when he lost rice worth £3,000 currency in a riverboat accident.[19]

Drayton lost an even greater portion of his wealth through his gambling. Without politics to guide him, he directed his attention to the frenzied social scene of the lowcountry elite. Immensely rich and secure, and without a tradition of religious piety to inhibit them, planters and merchants devoted a great deal of time and money toward recreation. And Charleston, although only the fourth largest metropolis in North America in 1770 with approxi-

19. Colonial Plats, 8: 12; Colonial Memorials, 2: 499; 9: 123, SCDAH; Smith, "The Upper Ashley," 174–7. Unfortunately the deeds do not note the amount Drayton paid for his properties. The list of Drayton's mercantile purchases for 1769–1779 is located in South Carolina Court of Common Pleas, Judgment Rolls, Box 90A, no. 51A, SCDAH. On his purchase of the *Tryton*, see Olsberg, "Ship Registers," 274. The lost rice cargo is mentioned in Judgment Rolls, Box 72A, no. 387A.

mately 12,000 inhabitants, offered them more amusing diversions than any other city on the continent. Here the Carolina gentry immersed themselves in an uninterrupted chaotic whirl of merriment. Ladies fancied the more elegant amusements of the symphony, theater, and balls, while gentlemen preferred frequenting the more boisterous private clubs, meeting regularly in taverns to drink, gamble, argue politics, and discuss land, slaves, and rice. Some wives thought their husbands spent far too much time and money in such "parties of pleasure." One woman publicly complained: "There is not one Night in the Week in which they are not engaged with some Club or other at *the Tavern* where they *injure their Fortunes* by gaming in various Ways, and impair their Health by the intemperate Use of Spirituous Liquors and keeping late Hours, or rather spending whole Nights, sometimes, in these disgraceful and ruinous Practices."[20]

Drayton's profligate lifestyle in the late 1760s conforms well with this generalization regarding men's destructive social bonding. Yet his participation in these "ruinous practices" was partly a result of how he comported himself as a gentleman. Because aristocratic men already possessed wealth, office, and power, they expressed their aggressive drives, personal ambition, and masculinity through their play, particularly horse racing, hunting, and gambling. It was this latter activity, especially, that consumed South Carolina gentlemen. In fact, gaming was a social obligation at barbecues, taverns, jockey clubs, and racetracks. Not to participate in the games of chance implied cowardice and antisocial behavior. Such pressure made it difficult for a young man not accustomed to self-denial to resist the temptation.[21]

Far from resisting such temptations, Drayton jumped with abandon into the risky, high-stakes diversions of lowcountry gentlemen—possibly in an effort to regain acceptance and respect from his peers following his assembly defeat. He enjoyed games involving dice and cards, but his favorite form of

20. *SCG*, 5 October 1769. Information on Charleston's social life was culled from Thomas J. Wertenbaker, *The Golden Age of Colonial Culture* (New York: New York University Press, 1942), 127–49; M. Eugene Sirmans, "Charleston Two Hundred Years Ago," *Emory University Quarterly* 19 (fall 1963): 129–36; Carl Bridenbaugh, *Myths and Realities* (Baton Rouge: Louisiana State University Press, 1952), 56–117; Fraser, *Patriots, Pistols and Petticoats*, 1–27; Bowes, *Culture of Early Charleston*, 3–12.

21. Timothy H. Breen, "Horses and Gentlemen: The Cultural Significance of Gambling among the Gentry of Virginia," *W&MQ*, 3d ser., 34 (April 1977), 239–42, 247–8; Bertram Wyatt-Brown, *Honor and Violence in the Old South* (New York: Oxford University Press, 1986), 134–5.

entertainment was horse racing, a popular pastime among South Carolinians at least since the 1730s. Ironically, Drayton may have fallen in with the "thickest of the sport" quite by chance after winning two thoroughbreds valued at £1,825 in a game of dice from Edward Fenwicke, owner of the most famous stable in the colony. But whether his thoroughbred was purchased or won in a game of chance, possession of a racehorse was a social necessity among Carolina gentlemen, a conspicuous emblem of wealth and status from which a man could prove himself and become "known" to other members of the gentry as one of their own.[22]

Drayton's introduction to the sport of kings came in February 1768 when he entered his roan colt Partner against William Cattell's horse Havanna in the annual races held at New Market Course. Partner easily defeated the older horse, winning Drayton an expensive silver plate valued at approximately £1,000. Confident following this victory, he entered Partner in a race at Ferguson's Ferry in March; again, his colt came away with first prize, beating Thomas Ferguson's Scrub.[23]

Drayton's racing fortune changed drastically the following season at the New Market races when he lost over £1,000 after his horse Adolphus was beaten by "half a head." He was not the only one to lose considerable money on the race. Charleston newspapers reported "very great sums were laid on this match," and that the "friends of *Adolphus* were much hurt." Undaunted, Drayton entered Adolphus in the Charleston Subscription Plate at New Market against Thomas Nightingale's English-bred Shadow. Erroneously promoted as the first contest between a locally bred horse and an English thoroughbred, this "great match" was the first race to produce any unusual excitement in the province. The match did not live up to the fanfare, however. Adolphus, although running "a good and honest" race, was "easily defeated" by the English thoroughbred in the best of three four-mile heats. Drayton continued racing his horses until early 1771 when Adolphus came in "a distant last" in a race for the silver plate held at New Market. Following

22. Judgment Rolls, Box 90A, no. 27A, SCDAH. Useful works on horse racing include Randy J. Sparks, "Gentlemen's Sport: Horse Racing in Antebellum Charleston," *SCHM* 93 (January 1992), 16–8; John B. Irving, *The South Carolina Jockey Club* (Charleston: Russell & Jones, 1857; reprint, Spartanburg, S.C.: The Reprint Co., 1975), 35; Wyatt-Brown, *Honor and Violence*, 134; and Breen, "Horses and Gentlemen," 249.

23. *SCG&CJ*, 9 February 1768; *SCG*, 15 March 1768; Breen, "Horses and Gentlemen," 251.

this humiliating defeat, Drayton abstained from horse racing and focused his attention on resurrecting his political career.[24]

It is impossible to determine how much money Drayton lost gambling. However, if wagering £1,000 on the speed of a horse and £1,800 on the toss of dice is any indication of his extravagance, then it is understandable how easily and quickly he, in the words of his father, "ran through a great part of his fortune." When Drayton lost in these games of chance he never failed to pay his debts. Failure to do so would cost him his honor as a gentleman, a commodity much more valuable than the lost money. Moreover, race covenants were considered binding legal contracts, so that if a gentleman failed to fulfill the agreement, the other party had grounds to sue. Drayton took his gambling debts so seriously, in fact, that he voluntarily attached interest to it—an unheard-of act even among men so constrained by honor. Peter Manigault, a beneficiary of Drayton's gambling misfortunes, was so pleasantly surprised by this generous deed that he wrote to a friend that it was "the first Instance I Believe of the kind that ever happened. . . . It was his own Doing, for I sh'd never have thought of demanding Interest upon a debt of this Nature."[25]

One person certainly not pleased with Drayton's generosity in paying his debts was his wife. There is no record of Dorothy Drayton's exact feelings concerning Drayton's profligacy, but another woman calling herself "Margery Distaff" spoke for many wives married to such irresponsible husbands when she exclaimed in the local press that they "throw away *Hundreds*, nay *Thousands of Pounds*, in one Evening without the least Remorse, [though] their *helpless Infants* may suffer for the *future* by their *present* Imprudencies." This publicized rebuke probably had little effect in changing the hedonistic habits of lowcountry gentlemen; husbands at this time kept the reins of financial management firmly in their own hands, rarely informing their wives (most of whom were ignorant of financial affairs) about monetary transactions. Drayton, too, attempted to hide his financial losses from his wife by borrowing enormous sums of money. Between 1765 and 1769 he secured over £50,000

24. *SCG*, 12 January 1769 and 2 February 1769; *SCG&CJ*, 12 February 1769 and 12 February 1771; Irving, *South Carolina Jockey Club*, 36.
25. John Drayton to James Glen, 14 March 1770, Glen Papers, SCL; Peter Manigault to Ralph Izard, 4 October 1769, Peter Manigault Letterbook, 1763–1773, Manigault Family Papers, SCHS; Breen, "Horses and Gentleman," 253.

in currency from friends and relatives in South Carolina, Florida, England, and Scotland.[26]

Although Drayton faithfully paid his gambling debts, he was less faithful in repaying his loans. He was in financial distress throughout much of his early adulthood, with creditors constantly harassing him. On occasion Drayton tried to avoid paying some of his loans by taking advantage of an eighteenth-century social code that allowed southern elites to manipulate tradesmen and others of lesser social standing (within some bounds) without tarnishing their reputation and honor. For example, in 1772 Drayton attempted to escape paying an £800 loan from Susannah Hall, an elderly widow. He claimed before the Court of Common Pleas that Hall never gave him such a bond, yet court documents clearly show he received the loan in December 1768. Drayton also attempted to renege on his debts to several Charleston merchants, who accused him of "contriving and fraudulently intending craftily and subtilly to deceive and defraud" them from their rightful money.[27]

---

26. Drayton received nearly one-third this sum from James Glen (Papers Relating to the Drayton Family, GD45/16/2635, Scottish Records Office, Edinburgh; and Account of James Glen, 1767–1770, Glen Papers, SCL). Information on his other loans can be found in Judgment Rolls, Box 89B, no. 12A; Box 90A, nos. 27A, 30A, 51A, 53A, SCDAH. Webber, "Thomas Elfe Account Book," *SCHM* 35 (April 1934), 68; and Bond between William Henry Drayton, Stephen Bull and James Grant, James Grant Papers, Manuscripts Division, Library of Congress, Washington, D.C. The Distaff quote is from *SCG*, 5 October 1769. Norton, *Liberty's Daughters*, 5–7, and Spruill, *Women's Life and Work*, 78, provide insight into who controlled the family purse strings in colonial America.

27. Judgment Rolls, Box 92A, no. 44A; and Box 90A, no. 51A, SCDAH. Previous biographers use one particular instance of Drayton's refusal to pay a debt as a partial reason for his conversion to the revolutionary cause. In 1769 Drayton secured a £2,400 sterling loan from James Grant, governor of East Florida and friend and colleague of Drayton's cousin William Drayton, chief justice of East Florida and member of the royal council. Drayton continued to pay interest on the bond until February 1774 when a lack of hard currency in the province prevented him from answering Grant's "many calls for it" (William Henry Drayton to James Grant, 6 February 1774, James Grant Papers, Library of Congress). Because Drayton stopped payment on this loan at the outset of British-American hostilities, Dabney and Dargan (*William Henry Drayton*) believe it "cast doubt" upon Drayton's later assurances that his conversion to the revolutionary cause was "entirely one of principle" (47). However, as demonstrated above, Drayton had a habit of attempting to welsh on his nongambling debts. Consequently, it is specious to argue that his decision to cease repayment of the Grant loan was a factor in his decision to join the Whig party. In addition, he stopped this payment six months before he joined the American cause, which suggests that his reason for discontinuing payment—a lack of currency in the province—was the initial cause for the delay in repayment. When war did finally break out between America and Britain, Drayton probably saw the conflict as an easy way to dispense with an enor-

All this borrowing and debt dodging was not enough to rescue Drayton from his financial predicament; his debts continued to grow. Finally, he was forced to confront Dorothy and tell her he had squandered much of their fortune through both the gambling and the incompetent management of their estates. Although eighteenth-century customs dictated that wives were not to dispute their husbands nor to disclose their imperfections, Dorothy Drayton must surely have voiced her disappointment. No longer certain of her future financial security, she took her husband to court in late 1769, forcing him to relinquish the agreed-upon portion of her dowry (£20,000 sterling). Drayton complied by placing his 1,076-acre Horseshoe estate and his 1,000-acre plantation inherited from his grandfather William Bull directly into his wife's hands through a complicated legal arrangement between Eliza Pinckney, Dorothy's mother, Dorothy's sister Mary, and Mary's husband Benjamin Geurard.[28]

Drayton's wife was not the only person displeased with him. John Drayton, too, was "unhappy" and "miserable" over his eldest son's profligacy. Unlike Dorothy, though, the elder Drayton had been aware of his son's extravagance and "closely taxed" him several times about it. Upon these personal inquiries, Drayton denied that his gambling was causing him pecuniary problems. When he was finally forced to admit his financial distress to his father, the elder Drayton offered little assistance. John Drayton most likely believed that his paternal responsibility for Billy ended with his son's acquisition of enormous property and cash through marriage and inheritance. Moreover, he had considerable financial obligations of his own at this time—enlarging Drayton Hall and supporting three sons studying abroad and a sickly wife recuperating in England.[29]

Drayton's reckless extravagance was not the only thing that upset his

---

mous debt with the possibility of never facing court proceedings. Thus the instance was just another one of Drayton's "craftily and subtilly" contrived means of escaping a portion of his debts. To use this one example (out of many) of Drayton's attempts to dodge payment of his debts as a reason for joining the Revolution merely trivializes the serious factors contributing to his conversion.

28. Charleston Deeds, vol. O-3 (1769–1770), 119–30; vol. P-3 (1770), 134–7, SCDAH; Renunciation of Dower (1767–1774), part 1: 79 and part 2: 500, SCDAH; Miscellaneous Records of Charleston County, 91-B: 588, Charleston County Library; Spruill, *Women's Life and Work*, 164, 169; Weiner, *Mistress and Slaves*, 65, 71.

29. John Drayton to James Glen, 14 March 1770, Glen Papers, SCL; Griffin, "The Eighteenth Century Draytons," 258–60.

father. According to John Drayton, his eldest son also behaved "undutifully" and "extreamly amiss" to him in "sundry matters."[30] He did not elaborate on the nature of these insults, but there were significant differences in the two men's upbringing and character which may explain their growing estrangement. John Drayton had received only superficial schooling and lacked cultural refinement. William Henry, on the other hand, possessed a college education, genteel bearing, and worldly knowledge acquired through travels in England and the northern colonies—all the result of his father's benevolence and financial sacrifice. With these highly esteemed attributes, it is possible that William Henry, whose later writings reveal a supercilious character, may have developed a superior attitude toward his father, who lacked these valued traits. John Drayton, however, measured men by a different standard. Amassing a large fortune through years of difficult labor, he believed that frugality and hard work were qualities equally important as education and carriage. Because William Henry had acquired the bulk of his wealth and property through inheritance and quickly lost most of it through mismanagement and gambling, John Drayton perhaps considered his eldest son an indolent wastrel and withheld any respect until Billy had enlarged his inheritance through the sweat of his brow and shrewd business practices.

Such speculation aside, John Drayton was evidently tormented by his eldest son's disrespectful behavior. In a letter to Billy he declared that "you are the sad cause of my late ilness and all of those heavie and many complaints I have had for Some years past." The father therefore decided the son should "reap the fruit of his disobedience" by "cutting him short" of his inheritance. True to his word, John Drayton revised his will in April 1767, leaving his eldest son with significantly less than his other children. James Glen, upon learning of this disparate disbursement, came to William Henry's defense, encouraging his brother-in-law to reconsider his decision: "You talk of casting off a son as you say you have done Billy . . . but the forgiveness of a Father is unlimited, a thousand faults must be forgiven." Yet John Drayton was an irascible and unforgiving man. Just months before his death in May 1779, the elder Drayton made another will, bequeathing £3,000 sterling to each of his daughters and dividing the rest of his estate among his five sons, giving the largest share not to William Henry but to the youngest, John.[31]

30. John Drayton, "History of the Drayton Family of South Carolina," 56.
31. Ibid., 14, 56–8; John Drayton to James Glen, 11 June 1771 and James Glen to John Drayton, 24 August 1774, Glen Papers, SCL; Henry William DeSaussure, *Reports of Cases Argued and*

In defense of John Drayton, his decision to reduce William Henry's birthright was simply a wise fiscal move. He had accumulated enormous wealth through considerable effort, only to witness his eldest son go through a greater part of his own fortune in a few years, giving him a legitimate fear that the same fate would befall his inheritance. The elder Drayton obviously did not want to see the accumulated efforts of a lifetime turned over to sons whom he considered "all bad and extravagant to the last degree."[32] Nevertheless, William Henry, who expected to inherit Drayton Hall, must have felt betrayed by his father's punitive act, causing an already distant and strained relationship to decay further.

In 1765, at the age of twenty-three, Drayton possessed all the ingredients necessary for a promising future—an excellent education, genteel bearing, high political office, enormous wealth, and a lovely young wife. These advantageous attributes, however, were not enough to overcome serious character flaws. As a result of his mismanagement and irresponsible gambling, Drayton plummeted to the nadir of Carolina patrician society as quickly as he had soared to its zenith. By the fall of 1769 he had lost a great portion of his wealth, political influence, and respect from his peers. Drayton's home life also suffered. His wife lost all confidence in him as a provider, and his father withdrew most of his inheritance. The death of an infant son in October of that year only intensified his anguish. As much as Drayton's situation had deteriorated, however, it was about to decline even further.

Determined in the Court of Chancery of South Carolina (Philadelphia: R. H. Small, 1854), 2: 324, 329, 468, 493, 557.

32. John Drayton to Margaret Drayton, 30 July 1772, Charles Drayton Papers, Drayton Hall, Charleston.

OPPOSING NONIMPORTATION

As relations between Drayton and his father deteriorated, so did the bond between the American colonies and the mother country. Parliament's repeal of the Stamp Act was a fleeting victory for the Americans. Determined to tax the colonies and punish the recalcitrant citizens, the English lawmakers passed a series of measures that caused many colonists to view the Stamp Act as not an isolated decree but part of a sinister design by corrupt ministers to deprive them of their liberties and their right to self-government. Americans in nearly every colony responded by establishing extralegal "associations" encouraging a boycott of British goods to compel Parliament to repeal its most recent measures.

However, not all Americans believed that the distant Parliament posed a serious danger to their liberties. Some, like William Henry Drayton, saw these hastily organized local nonimportation associations, which used threats, social ostracism, and financial ruin to force individuals into their agreements, as the gravest threat to their way of life. Drayton was undaunted by such bullying and challenged the coercive methods in the local press. His acerbic attack ignited a fiery five-month public debate with leaders of the Charleston nonimportation movement. Although the dispute changed few minds, it nevertheless provided historians with a valuable record of the developing fears, motives, personalities, and political ideology of some of South Carolina's future revolutionary leaders. The record also helps explain why some people joined the American cause while others remained loyal to the Crown. And perhaps most graphically, it reveals the extreme methods American patriots were willing to employ to crush their opposition, as demonstrated by their success in ostracizing Drayton from Carolina society and forcing him to flee to England where he hoped his unpopular stance would find greater acceptance.

Parliament did not surrender its claim to tax the colonies with its March 1766 repeal of the Stamp Act. Indeed, on the same day it passed the face-saving Declaratory Act, affirming its supremacy over the colonies "in all cases whatsoever." To impress this authority on the Americans, Charles Townshend, chancellor of the Exchequer and acting prime minister, then engineered the passage of the Revenue Acts (or Townshend duties) levying duties on a new class of previously untaxed articles—glass, lead, paint, paper, and tea—imported into the colonies from England. To ensure collection of this new revenue, the act called for a reorganization of the American customs service under a special board of commissioners residing in Boston, with vice-admiralty courts placed in all the major ports in North America to hear disputed cases. As distasteful as this measure was to the Americans, they found even more unpalatable the provision directing revenues from these duties toward paying the salaries of governors and other royal officials in the colonies. This stipulation robbed the colonial legislatures of their most potent weapon—the power to withhold salaries from uncooperative royal officers. American assemblies now faced the frightening prospect of losing their controlling position in government to unelected royal officials.[1]

Most South Carolinians were hesitant to take a strong stand on the Townshend duties until notice arrived of the king's decision regarding the Americans' petitions for redress on this legislation. By late spring 1769 they had their answer when the Crown "rejected with contempt" all colonial appeals. South Carolinians now realized it would be "evidently necessary" to pursue "Schemes of Oeconomy, Industry and Manufactures" and enter into nonimportation agreements similar to those already implemented in New England and New York. Accordingly, lowcountry planters, encouraged by pleas in the local press to prevent British statesmen from "mak[ing] Asses of us," organized themselves into "Societies of Gentlemen" who agreed to boycott all

---

1. P. D. G. Thomas, "Charles Townshend and American Taxation in 1767," *English Historical Review* 83 (January 1968): 49–51; Robert J. Chaffin, "The Townshend Act of 1767," *W&MQ*, 3d ser., 27 (January 1970): 107–19.

British goods that could be manufactured in America and to dress themselves in homespun "as soon as it could be got."[2]

Support for a nonimportation agreement received an enormous lift in late June when Christopher Gadsden made an agitated appeal for a boycott of British goods in the *South Carolina Gazette*. Gadsden's previous successful fight with Governor Boone launched him into the public spotlight as a strong defender of colonial rights and helped transform him into "a very violent enthusiast in the [American] cause," according to Lieutenant Governor William Bull. The Charleston factor's defiant behavior developed partly from his readings of English Whig philosophers such as John Locke, who believed that people had a right to revolt when their rulers violated an unwritten social contract and denied their natural rights of life, liberty, and property. Gadsden's rebelliousness was intensified by his ambitious, egocentric, moody, pious, and quite humorless personality. During the Stamp Act crisis he had become the leading spokesman of the Sons of Liberty, a loosely organized group of men composed chiefly of artisans, merchants, and a few planters who sought to oppose Parliament's taxation attempts. Gadsden's leadership earned him an appointment to the Stamp Act Congress in Philadelphia, where he arrogantly claimed that "no man in America strove more (and more successfully) first to bring about a Congress in 1765, and then to support it afterwards, than myself." An "impetuous zealot," given almost to "paranoid suspicions," Gadsden by the late 1760s became convinced that Parliament was plotting to enslave the American colonies and viewed all British measures with a "jaundiced eye."[3]

Labeling himself "Pro Grege Et Rege" (For the People and the King), Gadsden warned his fellow citizens that Britain was preparing the "deepest scheme of Systematical Slavery upon Americans" through the adoption of "oppressive and unconstitutional" measures: raising revenues without the consent of those taxed and depriving Americans of "our best inheritance, a trial by Jury and the Law of the Land." He urged Carolinians not to "hesitate one moment longer" in uniting "with our brother sufferers in the other

2. Charles Montagu to Earl of Hillsborough, 30 June 1769, BPROSC 32: 81; *SCG*, 18 May 1769, 1 June 1769, and 15 June 1769.

3. E. Stanley Godbold Jr. and Robert H. Woody, *Christopher Gadsden and the American Revolution* (Knoxville: University of Tennessee Press, 1982), 18–20; Richard Walsh, "Christopher Gadsden: Radical or Conservative Revolutionary?" *SCHM* 63 (October 1962): 198; Robert M. Weir, ed., *The Letters of Freeman, Etc.: Essays on the Nonimportation Movement in South Carolina* (Columbia: University of South Carolina Press, 1977), xiv.

colonies" in a general boycott of British goods. To guide further discussion on the matter, Gadsden appended a tentative draft of a nonimportation agreement.[4]

Prodded by this public plea, leading planters, mechanics, and merchants met the next month to determine which items they could reasonably live without. By July 22 they had worked out an agreement. In a solemn ceremony held under what became known as the Liberty Tree, nearly 270 men pledged to abide by the following resolutions: to encourage American manufacturing and frugality; to maintain current price levels; to boycott all British imports except necessary items such as coarse cloth and blankets, tools, ammunition, books, pamphlets, salt, and coal; to refrain from doing business with anyone refusing to sign the agreement; and to treat with the "utmost contempt" any subscriber who did not strictly adhere to the "Association." As a symbol of the democratic tendencies of the movement, the committee drafting the final proclamation appointed thirteen planters, merchants, and artisans to form a "General Committee of Thirty-Nine" charged with doing whatever was necessary to enforce the agreement.[5]

In executing the rigid observance of the resolutions, the General Committee and its adherents, according to Lieutenant Governor Bull, used "threats of vengeance . . . impetuosity of behavior and reproachful language" to "deter the moderate, the timid and the dependent" from "stepping forth in a body to assert their own opinion & wishes." Drayton, who was neither timid nor dependent, was not intimidated by the bullying tactics of this extralegal organization. What particularly upset Drayton was the group's provision promising to treat nonsubscribers as enemies to the province. Incensed by this affront to his loyalty, Drayton immediately wrote a rebuttal attacking the committee for its arbitrary and punitive measures. However, he waited nearly

4. Christopher Gadsden, "To the Planters, Mechanics, and Freeholders of the Province of South Carolina . . . ," in Richard Walsh, ed., *The Writings of Christopher Gadsden* (Columbia: University of South Carolina Press, 1966), 77–88.

5. *SCG*, 3 August 1769. The name "Association" was adopted by several different groups of rebels during the course of the Revolution, but it always signified a group bound together in an economic boycott of British goods. Some Associations were continental in scope, while others, such as this one, were local, but their purpose was always the same. The terms *Association* and *Associators* are thus proper nouns referring to these groups or the individuals within them.

The Liberty Tree, a noble live oak in Isaac Mazyck's cow pasture on Charleston Neck, was so named following a meeting held beneath it by Gadsden and some of his followers celebrating the repeal of the Stamp Act.

a month before submitting his letter to the local press, hoping "some abler pen" would "take up the cause." But with no one else willing to risk the "heavy loss of property and of acquiring a heavy load of public odium" that might befall anyone questioning the Association's authority, Drayton finally submitted his acrid attack to Peter Timothy, who promptly published it in the August 3 issue of his gazette. This preemptive strike commenced a caustic, five-month public debate between Drayton and Christopher Gadsden. John Mackenzie, a thirty-one-year-old planter, Cambridge graduate and member of the General Committee, soon joined the fray on Gadsden's side, while William Wragg, a fifty-five-year-old planter, former council member, and staunch defender of royal authority, came to Drayton's aid to even things up.[6]

To understand why Drayton chose to risk further financial ruin and public censure by attacking the popular and powerful nonimportation association, one must examine his convictions, character, and circumstances. Of greatest importance to Drayton was preservation of the English constitution, which he held in esteem above all else. It is unlikely that he would risk so much if he did not truly believe in the cause for which he was fighting: the preservation of his rights as an Englishman against what he considered unconstitutional measures imposed by a capricious and extralegal organization. That he continued the dispute until economic and social ostracism compelled him to leave the province lends credence to this hypothesis.

Drayton also risked so much because he stood to lose even more if the democratic tendencies of the nonimportation movement (and in the province generally) were allowed to continue. His defeat for a second term in the Commons House by a lowly schoolteacher obviously upset him. This loss caused him to view the emergence of the lower classes into the political arena as a threat to his personal ambition as well as to the existing political and social establishment. His concern for maintaining control of statecraft in the hands of the wealthy and educated is reflected in a subsequent supercilious assault against artisans, in which he asserted that they were unqualified to serve in political office. Drayton attacked the Association's leaders with the same severity because he believed they encouraged the breakdown of the political tradition, thereby threatening to bring additional economic, social, and political instability at a time when he was already suffering considerably in

6. Bull to Hillsborough, 20 October 1770, BPROSC 32: 342; Weir, ed., *Letters of Freeman*, 7; Drayton, *A Letter from Freeman*, 5.

these areas of his life. Drayton also distrusted the motives of the movement's leaders, who he believed were using the crisis to further their own political ambitions.

Yet Drayton was guilty of the same charge. He was exploiting the controversy surrounding the Townshend duties to resurrect his public image and regain the respect and affection of his father, whose attention was now focused on the three younger sons. Drayton understood that in a society like eighteenth-century South Carolina where men measured each other's worth by their status and power, a gentleman was in some measure dependent upon his peers for his own self-image. By publicly exposing the unconstitutional elements of the nonimportation agreement through eloquent and erudite arguments, Drayton hoped to acquire a political significance he had failed to achieve with his notorious Commons House service by portraying himself as a staunch defender of individual rights. What he failed to realize, however, is that during the 1760s South Carolinians had begun developing greater appreciation for politicians who put public welfare above private rights.[7]

Drayton was obviously taking the chance that readers might misconstrue his protest as an attack against everything the General Committee championed. He tried to prevent such a misinterpretation by explaining that he supported the encouragement of home manufactures and a voluntary boycott of British goods. The only element of the Association he condemned was the use of coercive methods to gain adherence to its principles. Moreover, as the son of a council member and nephew of the lieutenant governor, Drayton may have expected his high connections to protect him from retribution and hostility. Drayton, with his carefree gambler's attitude, regarded the opportunity as a worthwhile risk.

The essence of the debate over nonimportation concerned the preservation of liberties. Both sides wanted to safeguard the rights of Englishmen; what they disagreed on was where the real danger to colonial liberty lay. Gadsden and Mackenzie believed it derived from corrupt English ministers attempting to wrongfully tax Americans who had no voice in Parliament. The boycott against British goods would not only force Parliament to repeal these taxes, Gadsden and Mackenzie argued, it would also increase colonial prosperity by encouraging other avenues of trade. If the embargo failed to pres-

7. Weir, ed., *Letters of Freeman*, xxxvi; Robert M. Weir and Robert M. Calhoon, "The Scandalous History of Sir Egerton Leigh," *W&MQ*, 3d ser., 26 (January 1969): 73.

sure the British legislature into repealing the Townshend duties, suggested Gadsden, then Americans should contemplate more drastic methods— perhaps even independence, if necessary.

Drayton and Wragg, on the other hand, believed the greatest threat came from within the colony, principally from the extralegal organization that, in cooperation with the assembly, instituted arbitrary and punitive policies designed to coerce others into supporting a cause they had a constitutional right to oppose. Drayton ignored the issue of the Townshend duties entirely, refusing to reveal whether he favored or opposed them. He did disclose, however, his vision of an empire whose unifying bond was the British constitution. The General Committee's resolutions, according to Drayton, violated the constitution by restricting an individual's inherent, natural, and constitutional right to think and act for himself; if such illegal measures were allowed to continue, they might eventually lead to the creation of a tyrannical confederacy. Preserving the British constitution was more important to Drayton than perceived cases of circumscribed colonial rights. He also maintained there was room for compromise and offered suggestions to end the controversy.

Signing himself FREE-MAN, Drayton opened his assault by protesting the final clause of the nonimportation agreement, which branded a nonsubscriber, in his words, "*an enemy to this province.*" This form of intimidation by men "*overcharged* with *intemperate zeal,*" argued Drayton, was "like the Popish method of gaining converts to their religion by fire and faggot" and introduced "infinitely *greater evils*" than the Revenue Acts themselves because its goal was to "*curb, subdue,* and *guide the will,* and *set bounds* to the *opinions of men!*"[8]

After completing his attack on the "*base, illegal decree,*" Drayton next directed his pen at its primary author and leading proponent, Christopher Gadsden. He denounced the merchant as a power-hungry megalomaniac possessed by a "most fervent zeal to *steer* the state" and accused him of exploiting the present crisis to portray himself as a patriot in hopes of acquiring an influential and lucrative post. If Gadsden were a patriot, charged Drayton, he more resembled Oliver Cromwell, the "*patriot of his day*" who fought against monarchical tyranny so that "he might introduce a *tyranny*

---

8. Weir, ed., *Letters of Freeman,* 7–8. Subsequent citations to this work will be given parenthetically in the text.

of a more *horrible species.*" In any event, Drayton concluded, Gadsden was either a "traitor or a *madman,*" and should be lodged in the Charleston insane asylum at public expense "to prevent any ill consequence from his disorder" (8).

"What a pity it is that mama of that pretty child . . . FREE-MAN had not now and then whipt it for lying," replied Gadsden, for nowhere was the "paw-paw word 'enemy'" to be found in any of the proposed nonimportation agreements (11). The Charleston factor took particular offense at Drayton's "ungenerous insinuations" that he was using the current crisis to establish himself in a position to receive a lofty government post. Such accusations, he replied, must come from a man "void of every trace of public spirit and generosity" (13). Gadsden went on to suggest that since Drayton's mind was unable to "undergo the fatigue and trouble of thinking and reasoning," the older and wiser William Wragg should continue the quarrel in his place (13–14).

Gadsden's motive for inviting Wragg to join the dispute was not to improve the level of debate. During the Boone-Gadsden controversy back in 1762, Wragg had initiated a brief public polemic with Gadsden by defending the actions of the governor in a letter to the press. Now Gadsden, whose hotheaded temperament made it difficult for him to forgive and forget, was trying to use the present argument to seek revenge against Wragg.

But Drayton, who was just as impetuous as Gadsden, was not about to let anyone replace him in the fight he had initiated. Lashing back at the merchant in the August 17 issue of the *South Carolina Gazette*, Drayton scoffed that the "silly nibbling thing" (Gadsden's letter) had failed to confute "any one period of my paper" (14). Drayton stood by his charge that the Association treated nonsubscribers as enemies of the province, explaining that "we cannot be too cautious of . . . people who make secret use of such a hostile word, and endeavor to conceal it from the public" (17). He reminded his readers of the nefarious conduct of Octavius, Anthony, and Lepidus, who, upon taking control of the Roman Empire following the death of Julius Caesar, proscribed senatorial opponents as public enemies and had them executed. As a compromise in the disagreement over the final clause of the resolutions, Drayton suggested that the General Committee follow the example set by the Virginia nonimporters, who omitted sanctions against individuals who refused to join. If this had been done originally, he argued, "no free man in the province could have had any objection to them." The proposal reveals the crux of Drayton's reasoning for opposing the clause: "Free men must have free wills in all cases where the laws of our country do not restrain them." No man could be genuinely free unless he had the "undoubted right to think and act" for himself. "I then must say," Drayton concluded, "fie upon that naughty person who hath promulgated a doctrine which violates the constitution of our country in such a manner as to have laid a restraint upon, and endeavoured to intimidate free-men into novel opinions and politics" (18).

John Mackenzie strongly objected to Drayton's attempts to "transfer his poison" among the people "to the utter ruin of his native land" and penned a rebuttal the following week in "A LETTER to the PEOPLE" (19). He argued that the people had a right to adopt such a scheme because Parliament, in its recent measures against the colonies, had violated the "inherent rights" of Americans derived from the Magna Charta, Bill of Rights and the Act of Settlement.[9] The long list of violations included laws preventing the colonies from making paper money; the creation of vice-admiralty courts that were "almost equally oppressive to the innocent as terrible to [the] guilty"; frequent dissolutions of the legislatures and attempts to limit their size; and a military force sent to terrify the people into "servile submission." Not even Niccolò Machiavelli, claimed Mackenzie, could have "invented a plan on a broader bottom for the total eradication of every trace of liberty!" (21).

When a government failed to protect its citizens from such draconian policy, continued Mackenzie in a second "LETTER to the PEOPLE" published on

9. Although essentially a feudal document, exacted by feudal barons from their lords, the Great Charter of 1215 did contain clauses with implications for national reforms. The most important such clauses were those preventing the king from selling, denying, or deferring justice to any man; preventing a free man from being arrested or imprisoned except by the lawful judgment of his peers or by the law of the land; and requiring the Court of Common Pleas to remain in a fixed place.

A product of the Glorious Revolution of 1688, the Bill of Rights established parliamentary supremacy over the Crown by making it illegal for the monarch to suspend or dispense with any laws, to collect taxes by prerogative, to maintain a standing army or levy taxes without Parliament's consent, to interfere in Parliamentary elections, or to tamper with juries or impose excessive fines or bail.

A charter of liberties passed by Parliament in 1701, the Act of Settlement stipulated that no person who held an office of profit under the king should sit in the House of Commons; that all resolutions taken in the Privy Council should be signed by the councilors; that judges should hold office for life unless judged guilty of misconduct by both houses of Parliament; and that in an impeachment no pardon should be allowed to be pled. Parliament, however, repealed the first two of these resolutions in 1705, thus setting the stage for the growth of the British cabinet.

September 14, citizens "have a right to fall upon such measures as they may think conducive to their own preservation" (22). Mackenzie warned his readers that if the colonists allowed Parliament to continue violating their rights, such violation would result in "certain death to your constitution" and "nothing less than the prostration of a whole continent . . . insulted, bullied, treated like emasculated eunuchs" (23). Therefore Americans must unite in boycotting British goods to force Parliament into reversing its oppressive policy. Those refusing to heed the Association would meet certain financial ruin, Mackenzie concluded threateningly, "dashed to pieces like a small craft against the reefs" (24).

William Wragg, described by a peer as a vigorous defender of the Crown's prerogative with a notoriously intractable "spirit of opposition," eagerly swallowed the bait old nemesis Gadsden had set out several weeks earlier and responded to Mackenzie's overt threats to nonsubscribers.[10] In a letter in the September 21 issue of the *South Carolina Gazette*, Wragg defended his right to oppose the Association's resolutions, arguing that the English constitution gave him an "indisputable right" to withhold his assent to propositions he disapproved of and believed were "altogether discretionary" (26). The General Committee's methods of enforcing its resolutions were tyrannical and punitive, according to Wragg. "Where is the reason, the justice, the charity," he asked, "in locking up my property, with endeavors to force a compliance or starve men?" (26). Unlike his young ally Drayton, Wragg defended the Revenue (Townshend) Act, claiming that its intent was not to raise revenue, but to regulate imperial commerce. However, he agreed with everyone that a plan of general economy would greatly benefit the province. To help facilitate that "laudable purpose," Wragg suggested reducing the interest rate from eight to six percent, a change he believed would "give great assistance to the laborious manufacturer, and relief to the industrious planter" (28).

Meanwhile, the Associators had held another mass meeting on September 1 under the Liberty Tree to consider what to do about those persistent few who still refused to sign their agreement. After much deliberation, they finally decided to give these delinquents one week to comply. When the deadline arrived, the General Committee printed and distributed handbills

---

10. Henry Middleton to William Middleton, 8 February 1770, Middleton Papers, ref. no. SA/1/4/59, Shrubland Hall, Coddenham, Suffolk, Ipswich, U.K. Quoted by kind permission of Lord de Saumarez, in whose family archives the papers reside.

throughout the city listing the thirty-one individuals, exclusive of Crown officials, who had still refused to sign. Among the names registered on the handbills were William Henry Drayton and his debating partner William Wragg.

The General Committee's activities placed Drayton's uncle, Lieutenant Governor Bull, in a difficult position. He certainly did not agree with the behavior of either the committee or the assembly. But his main objective as executive of the province was to maintain peace, and dissolving the Commons and dispersing the Associators would simply feed the popular discontent. In any event, Bull believed it was Parliament's responsibility—not that of a lone American governor—to enforce its will. The only positive thing he believed he could do to protect his nephew and other nonsubscribers from harassment by Associators was to inform its leaders that Britain soon planned to repeal part of the Townshend duties. This intelligence failed to pacify the Liberty Tree party, however, which continued to compel compliance to its resolutions until Parliament repealed the Revenue Acts as a whole.[11]

If the General Committee believed its handbills would terrify Drayton into complying with the Association, it greatly underestimated his resolve. The handbills, in fact, only pleased Drayton, who considered them "a public testimony of my resolution and integrity to persist in acting agreeably to the dictates of my reason" (30). Still, he felt obliged to "defend the constitution of my country" from the "*laying [of] illegal restraints upon the free wills of men who have an undoubted right to think and act for themselves*" (29–30). Drayton accused the "harlequin medley committee" with violating the "first principles of liberty" and acting in a "despotic and unjust manner" by assuming a power not recognized by law and using it to intimidate innocent people into surrendering the "liberty and right of thinking, judging, and acting for themselves" (31). Drayton claimed he had not broken any law by refusing to join the Association; consequently, there was no justifiable reason for printing his name on handbills and dispersing them throughout North America "with [a] design to prejudice my countrymen against me" (32). This "prejudice" against Drayton was so pervasive that it forced him to market his own crops in London at a financial loss. Thus the Association's coercive tactics not only violated his civil liberties, but also what he believed was his natural right to enjoy the fruits of his own labor.

11. Bull, *Oligarchs*, 148–51.

Not content with lambasting the General Committee, Drayton next vilified the mechanics and artisans of Charleston, who wielded substantial power in the nonimportation movement.[12] Believing that only the wealthy and educated possessed the qualifications necessary to govern, he disdainfully remarked that the ability to "cut up a beast in the market . . . to cobble an old shoe . . . or to build a necessary house," did not prepare a person for the "difficulties of government" (31). He added that only a fool would hire an illiterate person to prosecute a lawsuit or place a landsman at the helm of a ship caught in a storm near a rocky shore.

Mackenzie responded to Drayton's attack by first pointing out that the word "enemy," which Drayton made so much of, had been used only in earlier Association drafts and had been removed from the final subscription (35). Nor did the General Committee curb men's actions or opinions in any way. As for the handbills, explained Mackenzie, they were not intended to stigmatize nonsubscribers; if they had been, the committee would have published nonsubscribers' names in the more widely read newspapers. Furthermore, Drayton should not blame the committee for the means it used to accomplish its ends, because Britain's unlawful colonial policies have "rendered such measures necessary" (38). Finally, the Cambridge graduate took issue with Drayton for attacking the Charleston mechanics and "sorting mankind" much like a "botanist does the different species of plants." The common people are the "bones and sinews" of society, he replied obsequiously, and have as much right as anyone else to protect their liberties (39).

The Charleston mechanics and artisans were dissatisfied with Mackenzie's passionless and perfunctory defense of their right to participate in political affairs and penned their own acerbic reply to Drayton that was replete with personal attacks. "We are pleased Mr. William Henry Drayton, in his great condescension," has allowed us "a place amongst human beings," the mechanics began (111). They reminded him that not everyone is "so lucky as to

---

12. The mechanics of Charleston comprised a wide variety of skilled artisans and an endless number of less skilled plain craftsmen. These artisans functioned as an independent faction within the resistance movement in South Carolina and were not pawns of their social superiors. Instead, the mechanics worked within the colonial opposition to Great Britain and were "subject to cooperation, compromise, and political juggling," as were the planters, merchants, and professionals. Eva B. Poythress, "Revolution by Committee: An Administrative History of the Extralegal Committees in South Carolina, 1774–1776" (Ph.D. diss., University of North Carolina, 1975), 21; Richard Walsh, *Charleston's Sons of Liberty: A Study of the Artisans, 1763–1789* (Columbia: University of South Carolina Press, 1959).

have a fortune ready provided to his hand, either by his own or his wife's parents" (113). More seriously, they challenged his pompous conviction that wealth and education were qualities necessary for participation in government and insisted that one needed only enough common sense to distinguish between right and wrong in order to serve in political office (112). The group believed Drayton lacked common sense, though, a mental deficiency they surmised had led him to conjure up "many phantoms of danger" and, like Don Quixote, be misled by the "freakish caprices of his own vacant head" (113). This may explain his recent imprudent attack on the common people, they continued, whereby he disturbed the "peace and good order" of the province by "knock[ing] his head against ninety-nine out of every hundred of the people" (112). If all these shortcomings were not enough to convince everyone not to take Drayton seriously, the group reminded readers of his recent financial and political troubles. The young parvenu was so deficient of any abilities, either in head or hand, they claimed, that without his inherited fortune, he would be forced to earn only "a scanty pittance" by hiring himself as a packhorseman in the Indian trade or serving as an artisan's assistant (113). Like Gadsden, the mechanics believed that Drayton's unsound yet dangerous mind entitled him to a private room in the asylum where he would be barred from using pen, ink, and paper, "lest they aggravate his disorder" (114).

Drayton was obviously hurt by this stinging attack. In his next essay, he tried to placate the mechanics by reexplaining his views about their proper role in society. The wealthy planter remarked that he had always considered the industrious mechanic a useful and necessary member of society. But when a man steps out of his "proper sphere" to become a statesman, he continued, he "exposes himself to ridicule, and his family to distress, by neglecting his private business." Moreover, because the common man lacked the education and wealth necessary to make himself independent, Drayton argued, he would easily be "converted into cats paws," and "made to serve a turn" by unscrupulous special interest groups (49).

Drayton's self-centered reasoning undoubtedly failed to appease the lower classes. After intensifying the mechanics' hatred of him, he returned to the safer and more familiar arguments on English law. He began this essay in the October 12 issue of the *Gazette* asserting that members of the General Committee had formed an illegal confederacy designed to injure innocent individuals. Drayton based his claim upon an early-seventeenth-century court decision defining a confederacy as an alliance formed when there was a voluntary combination by bonds or promises; when the combination injured (physically or financially) an innocent person; when there was unjust revenge intended; and when the injury was unprovoked (135, n.13).[13] Because the General Committee was using physical and financial coercion to force people to join the Association, he argued, it "fall[s] clearly under the description of confederates," who are punishable by law (48). In concluding, Drayton warned his opponents that he would continue to defend the English constitution with utmost vigor no matter how much abuse the Associators directed against him. "I will not be intimidated from my duty," Drayton resolutely announced (49).

Neither was Mackenzie easily intimidated, especially not by a man he claimed "whose reading is principally confined to a few Latin poets" (50). He quickly dismissed Drayton's charge that the General Committee was a confederacy by simply claiming that his definition of one did not fit the Association's resolutions. Mackenzie next justified the committee's behavior using John Locke's idea of civil government, which argued that whenever a corrupt government violated the people's liberties, they possessed the right to break any constitution or contract in their endeavor to retrieve their natural rights. If any protested such extreme conduct, Mackenzie warned in concluding, the General Committee would silence them one way or another (53).

Drayton, feeling the pressure from such unveiled threats and the increasing public odium vented toward him, tried to clarify his unpopular position in a way the people would find more acceptable in "*Another* LETTER *from* FREEMAN," published on October 26. He explained that throughout his previous writings he had only censured the last resolution of the nonimportation agreement, which he believed was punitive and unconstitutional, and those few men enforcing it. The remaining elements of the agreement, particularly the plan of greater economy and the boycott of British goods, were beneficial to the province and received his full endorsement (54).

Having clarified his position, Drayton next turned Gadsden and Mackenzie's favorite philosopher against them. Using arguments made by Locke in *Two Treatises of Government*, Drayton declared that by establishing and enforcing new rules throughout the province, the General Committee had

---

13. Recently, historians have questioned Drayton's interpretation of the concept of confederacy. See Pauline Maier, *From Resistance to Revolution: Colonial Radicals and the Development of American Opposition to Britain, 1765–1776* (New York: Knopf, 1972), 131–2.

overturned the assembly and established a new legislature; since the last resolution of their Association was un-Christian, unjust, and unconstitutional, South Carolinians, urged Drayton, should follow the teachings of Locke and oust the General Committee from its self-imposed position of authority. "Oh my countrymen! suffer not an arbitrary power to get footing in this state," he pleaded. Remember, Rome was enslaved by "almost imperceptible degrees" (57).

Drayton removed himself from the debate for the next six weeks. The death of his namesake just days after he wrote "*Another* LETTER" caused him much heartache. While grieving over the loss of this infant son, Drayton was also busy salvaging his deteriorating financial and family situation, as discussed in the previous chapter. In the meantime, he left the cause he had commenced in the able hands of his elder partner William Wragg.

In the following two issues of the *Gazette*, Gadsden tried to overwhelm his opponents with a redundant and convoluted twelve-thousand-word harangue. For the first third of the essay, the Charleston factor repeated his well-worn sermon about "ministerial schemes" to enslave the colonists, America's futile attempts at peaceful redress, and their right, under Lockean theory, to resist oppressive rulers (61). Nearly hidden amid his tautological verbosity was a radical suggestion that Americans should seek independence if Parliament did not yield to the pressures of their boycott. Although Gadsden believed separation from Great Britain would be "the greatest misfortune that could befall" the colonists, it would not compare to the calamity of "losing their rights and liberties" (64).

Apparently, Drayton and Wragg's arguments were gaining some support among wealthy and influential planters, for Gadsden next tried to repair a potential breach in the Association's ranks by defending the General Committee's actions and attacking his opponents' suggestions for compromise. The patriot leader claimed that the Associators had done nothing unconstitutional in uniting to redress their grievances because they had a right to spend their money as they wished (65). The final resolution, which Drayton so lamented, only censured those who were "base enough to forfeit their honour, and openly violate or craftily evade" the agreement they had signed (67). It did not apply to nonsubscribers like Drayton and Wragg. Nor did the General Committee behave in a "violent or arbitrary" manner in enforcing the Association, Gadsden maintained (66). However, he conveniently failed to explain why the committee dispersed handbills across the country listing the names of those men unwilling to sign the agreement (67).

Gadsden next attacked Drayton and Wragg's proposals for compromise. In one short sentence, he quickly disposed of Drayton's recommendation to remove the last resolution of the boycott as a "thread-bare trick" designed to weaken the agreement by deterring "real friends of the people" from enforcing it (75–76). Similarly, he made short shrift of Wragg's bid to decrease interest from eight to six percent by asking "what service could that be towards getting the acts of Parliament . . . repealed" (77). As for Drayton's argument that the General Committee had usurped power from the elected assembly and established a confederacy, Gadsden curtly dismissed the whole of it, charging it "not to be of the least consequence" (69).

Gadsden realized that the success of the nonimportation movement rested with the support of influential and wealthy planters. He therefore used a combination of humiliation, humanitarianism, and horror to compel them to lead others in backing the boycott. Possibly referring to Drayton and Wragg, Gadsden charged that only a planter of "so miserably selfish a disposition" would withdraw his example and influence at such a crucial moment in this important crisis (83). The wealthy are "providentially constrained" to "make the public good" their aim, the merchant moralized, and assist those in less fortunate circumstances (82). If the wealthy lowcountry planters refused to perform their civic and religious duty by helping their less affluent brethren in this cause, he warned, then the numerous small backcountry farmers might refuse to help subdue their "very precarious property" (i.e., their slaves) in the event of a rebellion (84).

Gadsden's "incoherent discourse" and "barbarous jargon" made little impression on Wragg, who dismissed the merchant's trumpet calls about oppression and slavery brought on by wicked and cunning ministers as unwarranted because "the degeneracy of the times," he explained, was not any "greater than those which preceded" (87–89). Even if a designing and arbitrary ministry were truly enslaving Americans, ruling authority would not automatically revert back to the people as Locke asserted. Under such desperate circumstances, argued Wragg, the constitution has "pointed out the remedy: . . . impeach, prove, find guilty, condemn and decapitate" (88). Deviations from this process would only lead to anarchy or the rise of a tyrannical leader like Oliver Cromwell.

Wragg agreed with Drayton that one of the most serious departures from constitutional procedure was the creation of a confederacy in the guise of the General Committee. He viewed this illegal organization as possessing three serious flaws: it was formed to the "prejudice of third persons," it was "highly criminal in the eye of the law," and it was "contrary to the first principles of common honesty" (91). Since Drayton's legal arguments on this point had had little influence on their opponents, Wragg used an English maxim to demonstrate his assertion: "The agreement of individuals cannot annul the public law. Things done between strangers ought not to injure those not parties" (91; 142, n 21).

Do not forget, shot back Gadsden with a frequently quoted maxim of his own, that the "public welfare is the highest law" (102; 144, n 11). To protect the public welfare from unjustifiable opposition, Gadsden in the November 30 *Gazette* made the astonishing assertion that minorities have no right to oppose an organization of men supported by a majority of the people (96). He evidently failed to realize that the Crown could have made a similar argument to denounce the American revolt.

While Wragg and Gadsden were dueling with quill and ink, the Association was enjoying great success. According to Lieutenant Governor Bull, all but a few stalwarts complied with the General Committee's resolutions rather than "stem a torrent of popular opinion [and] resentment." Those that did dare oppose the Association, Peter Manigault wrote, were "treated with universal contempt." This unity caused Drayton serious financial injury. Unable to sell his produce and forced to borrow money to cover his losses, he petitioned the Commons on December 5, 1769, humbly asking for "protection and support" from those resolutions he maintained were illegally operating to "deprive him of the benefits of society" (106). Drayton explained that he was forced to seek redress from the assembly because a fair trial was impossible, considering that all judges sitting on the Court of Common Pleas were Association members. Any jury, too, would "in all probability consist of men under the same disqualification," he argued (104). But the legislators possessed an "overbearing spirit of democracy," according to Bull, and refused to even read Drayton's petition.[14]

Drayton fully expected the legislature to reject his petition because he knew that by approving his request, the lower house (where all bills originated) would be admitting that the Association was illegal and injurious to

14. Bull to Hillsborough, 7 September 1769 and 20 October 1770, BPROSC 32: 101, 344; Peter Manigault to Ralph Izard, n.d., Peter Manigault Letterbook, SCHS; Journals of the Commons House of Assembly, 38, part 2: 215, SCDAH.

innocent men and would set a precedent encouraging others to come clamoring forward with similar grievances. Indeed, Drayton did not even suggest measures the representatives might adopt for his relief. Knowing the assembly would deny his request, he instead made it his purpose to publicly expose that body as an unsympathetic group controlled by Association members. Accordingly, he sent his petition—appended with an explanation of the legislature's rejection of it—to Peter Timothy, who reluctantly printed it in the December 14 issue of his paper.

While the assembly was rejecting Drayton's petition for relief, it was lavishing money upon an English politician and publicist named John Wilkes, the newest hero among Americans opposing Parliament's colonial policies. Wilkes first gained popularity while a junior member of Parliament in the early 1760s, when he published editorials in his newspaper the *North Briton* excoriating the ministry for destroying rights gained during the Glorious Revolution of 1688. Young King George III ignored these attacks until April 23, 1763, when Wilkes lamented in his now famous *North Briton No. 45* that the Crown had "sunk even to prostitution." The royal ministry, determined to rid themselves of this rake, charged Wilkes with seditious libel, prompting him to seek refuge in France. After four years of profligate living and womanizing on the Continent, Wilkes's indebtedness forced him to return to England in hopes of securing reelection to Parliament. He succeeded in winning a seat in March 1768, but authorities soon arrested him on the original charges and sentenced him to two years in prison. While incarcerated, Wilkes continued writing inflammatory squibs against the ministry, further increasing his popularity among the masses as a martyr of liberty. Citizens from Middlesex even elected him to Parliament three additional times the following year; each time the Crown disavowed the election. Early in 1769 friends and sympathizers of Wilkes formed the Society of Gentlemen Supporters of the Bill of Rights in London to uphold his cause and pay his debts.

Wilkes was nearly as popular in America as he was in England. To Americans, the ministry's harassment of Wilkes and Parliament's attempt to tax the colonies became part of the same general assault upon liberty. What also made Wilkes a particular object of enthusiasm to Americans was their belief that he, by his influence within Parliament, could effect reforms calculated to check monarchical encroachment. When Parliament continually refused Wilkes his seat, the colonists believed that government malfeasance was at the root of the problem, leaving a lasting disillusionment among Americans with the British government.[15]

South Carolinians were perhaps the most ardent sympathizers of Wilkes and his cause. "Wilkes & Liberty is all the cry," Charleston merchant Miles Brewton wrote, and "he [has] become the Idol." On the evening of October 2, 1768, a number of workmen showed their support of the Englishman with a public procession down Broad Street, preceded by forty-five of their number bearing candles as a salute to his *North Briton No. 45.* Knowing the sympathy and support South Carolina and the other colonies had for Wilkes, the Society of Gentlemen Supporters of the Bill of Rights solicited the provincial legislatures for economic assistance to help them uphold his cause. The South Carolina Commons, "sympathyzing with those noble Spirits" who were standing against the "whole collected Fury of Ministerial Vengeance," directed treasurer Jacob Motte to pay a local committee £1,500 sterling to be sent to the English society "for the support of the just and constitutional Rights and Liberties of the People of Great Britain and America." Although other provinces sent various gifts, South Carolina was the only colonial government to respond officially to the request for funds from Wilkes supporters.[16]

Drayton, having just been denied assistance by the legislature, was furious over this ample donation to a foreign scoundrel. In a letter published in the December 28 *Gazette,* he sarcastically congratulated his fellow citizens upon the "sudden increase" of wealth in the province and snidely complimented "those of our patriots who were most active" in helping to defray the bills of a "private gentleman" in London (110). Switching quickly from sarcasm to outrage, Drayton next accused his opponents of falsely portraying themselves as American patriots. "'Tis not because a man is always bellowing, Liberty! Liberty! that he is to be exalted into the ranks of patriots!" he cried. If the Association classified their own behavior as patriotic, he continued, then "rage, fury and wanton persecutions" must be the true characteristics of a patriot (108). It was this malicious harassment by Associators against nonsubscribers that convinced Drayton that the greatest danger to American liber-

15. Pauline Maier, "John Wilkes and American Disillusionment with Britain," *W&MQ*, 3d ser., 20 (July 1963): 373–9, 385, 395; Jack P. Greene, "Bridge to Revolution: The Wilkes Fund Controversy in South Carolina, 1769–1775," *JSH* 29 (February 1963): 19–52.

16. Miles Brewton to Peter Manigault, 10 January 1769, Manigault Family Papers, SCL; *SCG&CJ*, 4 October 1768; Joseph Barnwell, ed., "Correspondence of Charles Garth," *SCHM* 31 (April 1930): 132; Journals of the Commons House of Assembly, 38, part 2: 215, SCDAH.

ties came not from a distant government, but from his own neighbors. If these breaches of the English constitution were not quickly plugged, he cautioned, society would deteriorate "'till things are thrown into utter confusion; the liberties of the people destroyed, and a galling tyranny erected upon their ruins" (109).

Drayton's alarmist rhetoric failed to raise the public's ire against the Association. Instead, most Charlestonians continued to support the actions of the General Committee, especially its leader Christopher Gadsden. Following the public debate with Drayton and Wragg, the merchant continued battling against perceived threats to colonial liberty into the next decade, becoming one of the province's most influential leaders for the American cause. Gadsden's colleague John Mackenzie also gained much public notoriety and respect for his efforts during the nonimportation crisis. Unfortunately, Mackenzie's untimely death from an unknown illness in May 1771 prevented him from reaping the benefits of his popularity. Meanwhile, the venerable William Wragg, unlike Drayton, was able to retain his respected standing among the Carolina elite following the controversy. He continued supporting royal authority in South Carolina until July 1777 when Whig leaders, who by that time controlled provincial affairs, banished him from the state. This eviction ultimately proved to be his demise. While sailing to Holland, a storm struck the ship and washed his young son overboard. Wragg drowned trying to rescue the boy.

Drayton, having alienated himself from the common people and most social and political leaders in the colony, suddenly became directly dependent on the British government for any favors and any opportunity to regain his position and respect in provincial society. He therefore decided to leave South Carolina for England, where he hoped his views would find a more favorable response and acquire for him at least one lucrative post back home that would help him pay off the numerous creditors who were about to take legal steps to seize his property. Apparently Drayton could not flee the province fast enough. On January 1 and 2, less than a week after making his last public protest, he managed to procure £30,000 currency for his passage and living expenses while in England. The following day Drayton left his wife and two young children and boarded the ship *London*. Ironically, the vessel was one that the General Committee had run out of the province for carrying a large quantity of "returned goods," merchandise the Associators would not allow to be sold.[17]

17. Judgment Rolls, Box 90A, nos. 51A, 52A, and 30A, SCDAH; *SCG*, 4 January 1770.

Drayton's opponents undoubtedly thought it fitting that he was sailing back to Britain among these returned goods. However, there is evidence that Drayton was not as strong a Crown supporter as his adversaries believed— and modern historians still contend. There is no evidence that he endorsed either the Stamp Act or Townshend duties. Granted, he did not publicly renounce them, either. Nevertheless, Drayton showed some sympathy for America's predicament by verbally supporting the advantageous aspects of the boycott of British goods. This attitude reveals that he may have already begun developing doubts about the legality of Parliament's claim to govern America "in all cases whatsoever." Thus Drayton appears not to have been the fanatical and uncompromising champion of royal authority that earlier biographers have classified him, a factor which helps to explain his later willingness to join the patriot cause.

Drayton's involvement in the nonimportation controversy also reveals much about his character. It shows that he was not above using a crisis to help rescue his waning reputation among the South Carolina elite. Yet he was also a man of strong principles who was not afraid to submit his opinions to a hostile public for approval or rejection. His behavior during the dispute is testimony to his dedication to these principles and willingness to make enormous sacrifices to defend them. By attacking the popular Association, Drayton demonstrated a healthy disregard of the possibilities of loss or failure— another personal characteristic enabling him to risk everything to join the American rebellion five years later.

Drayton gained valuable knowledge from the humiliating public defeat he suffered at the hands of the Associators. He would never again underestimate the power and importance of the common folk in any communal controversy. Indeed, he eventually came to realize that popular consensus could serve as a base from which to assist traditional elitist leadership. He also came to understand South Carolinians' concern for the public welfare over individual rights. Finally, the debate provided Drayton with the opportunity to hone his debating skills and further refine his political and legal doctrines.

During his transatlantic voyage to England, Drayton must have spent a great deal of time reflecting on the downturn his life had made during the preceding year. In that brief time he had lost a young son, much of his fortune, his seat in the assembly, and considerable respect from his peers and family. So many misfortunes in such a short period would have driven lesser men to either suicide or the frontier. But if this public quarrel reveals anything, it is that Drayton possessed fearlessness, self-confidence, and an intense desire for political power and public approval. Perhaps during his journey Drayton focused on these qualities and motives rather than his recent reversals, thus enabling him to survive this very difficult time in his young life.

QUARRELING WITH THE KING'S MEN

Drayton spent the following year in England, where he courted members of the English nobility for royal offices back in his home province. Through persistent self-promotion and flattering recommendations from his uncle, he received a seat on the South Carolina Council. Given this second chance, Drayton made significant lifestyle changes to ensure that his past failures would not reoccur. He stopped gambling recklessly and devoted a year toward repairing his broken finances before taking his place in the upper house alongside his father, where he diligently carried out his legislative duties. By making these beneficial modifications, Drayton managed to regain much of the lost respect from his peers.

At the same time, though, Drayton was also making new enemies of his fellow councilors, particularly the British placemen, by questioning their dedication and loyalty. His hostility toward these foreign officeholders stemmed in part from the Crown's appointment of Englishmen to two local offices that he felt justly belonged to him. Drayton's bitterness increased further when some of the placemen successfully thwarted his plan to wrest 144,000 acres of land from the Catawba Indians. When the Britons displayed behavior injurious to the colony's welfare, Drayton could no longer contain his emotions and publicly denounced them. They, in turn, censured him. This feud quickly lured Drayton into the culmination of an intense, long-standing power struggle involving the Commons House, the council, and the governor.

When Drayton arrived in England in February 1770, he wasted no time trying to gain the attention of royal officials. Continuing where he had left off in his FREEMAN letters, he penned a satirical note to several London newspapers in which he applauded the patriotism of the South Carolina Commons for "breaking loose from the Shackles of their Constitution, and the imperious Restrictions of a Royal Commission and Instructions" by issuing £1,500 to Wilkes without the proper warrant required from the governor. Cleverly blended in Drayton's attack against the assembly was a sycophantic expression of gratitude to King George III for generously offering a lucrative bounty to American silk growers and allowing South Carolina to appoint its own sheriffs. Unfortunately for Drayton, his editorial aroused responses in London similar to those the *Freeman* essays had elicited in Charleston. One London native even wrote to inform South Carolinians that Drayton was held "in equal Esteem with us, as he was with you when he quitted his Country."[1]

John Drayton did not have much regard for his eldest son, either, whom he feared would continue his profligate ways in Britain and be "quite Ruined" before returning home. Characterizing William Henry as "the most imprudent lad I ever heard of," the elder Drayton even felt constrained by "honor & honesty" to advise his brother-in-law James Glen against offering his improvident son any financial assistance. "Should he want any money of you I now put you on your Guard," Drayton warned, "he Probabelly may make some proposals to you of money matters which if he does I beg you to avoid them, or at least do not blame me hereafter." John Drayton also advised against a meeting between Drayton and his younger brother Charles, who was still studying medicine in Scotland, fearing that "Billy" would "lead him into Gaming." John Drayton was already upset with Charles for refusing his earlier "commands" to give up his medical training and return to South Carolina. "I am so unhappy and made so miserable in two of my Sons," he lamented to Glen, for "taking no council from me nor . . . pay[ing] no obedience." Despite the elder Drayton's requests, Glen could not prevent the two brothers from meeting. During the summer of 1770 William Henry Drayton made a trip to Edinburgh to visit Charles and his stepuncle. It is not known whether Drayton enticed his younger brother into games of chance as John Drayton feared, but if he did, Charles apparently did not find them especially appealing, for he never suffered from gambling-related financial difficulties.

1. *Publick Advertiser* (London), 20 March 1770; *Lloyd's Evening Post and British Chronicle* (London), 19–21 March 1770; *SC&AGG*, 23 May 1770; *SCG*, 17 May 1770.

What is certain is that the two brothers spent much time reminiscing about their school days and bringing one another up to date on their experiences since they had last been together seven years before.[2]

Drayton, however, had not traveled to Britain to reflect on the past but to ameliorate his seemingly dismal future. Having failed to gain recognition through his newspaper editorials, Drayton took a more direct approach and began courting Crown officials, recounting to them his efforts and sacrifices opposing the South Carolina Association. John Montagu (Fourth Earl of Sandwich) and Wills Hill (Lord Hillsborough) were particularly interested in Drayton's story. Hillsborough, as the no-nonsense secretary of state for the colonies, was certainly interested in assisting the efforts of such a valiant opponent of the troublesome American rebels. Montagu, who served as First Lord of the Admiralty among many other offices, also developed a kinship with Drayton upon hearing his recent misfortune. He, too, was suffering from an enormous amount of public opprobrium from his participation in the prosecution of the popular John Wilkes. Any opponent of Wilkes was a friend of his. Drayton hoped the Englishmen's strong influence and vast patronage would help secure him at least one royal office back in South Carolina.[3]

To call further attention to his outspoken loyalty, Drayton gathered, edited, and published *The Letters of Freeman*, a slight volume containing the newspaper debate over nonimportation. But this immodest attempt to gain public or political recognition failed, too. Neither the South Carolina newspapers nor the popular English literary magazines mentioned the publication of *The Letters of Freeman*. Had South Carolinians paid closer attention to Drayton's work, however, they would have learned that he was not going to quit his cause so easily. The emblem and motto he illustrated for the title page of *Freeman*—a quill pen and the ancient Roman freedmen's felt hat, accompanied by the phrase "indignante Hydrae"—demonstrated that Drayton still held to his interpretation of the English constitution and common law; that no matter how many times his opponents might slay him, he would always angrily return to fight again.

Drayton had greater success in gaining the attention of British authorities from the efforts of his uncle William Bull, who recommended his nephew

2. John Drayton to James Glen, 14 March 1770, and James Glen to John Drayton, 26 March 1771, Glen Papers, SCL. While in Scotland, Drayton was made a "Burgess and Gild-brother" of the Burgh of Linlithgow on August 21, 1770 (John Drayton, *Carolinian Florist*, xxvi).

3. Drayton, *Memoirs*, 1: xiv.

for positions in the South Carolina judiciary and the council. Both of these governmental branches had numerous vacancies which the lieutenant governor had to quickly fill. However, Bull had difficulty finding men willing to accept a seat on the bench because Charleston lawyers made much more in private practice than the £300 the office paid. Desperate, he nominated Drayton to serve as an assistant justice. The lieutenant governor defended the selection of his nephew by pointing out that although he was "young and not bred to the Law," his "liberal education" enabled him to "acquire some knowledge thereof with a little application." More importantly, Drayton was "attached to the King's person & Government and free from unconstitutional prejudices." These commendations, however, could not overcome Drayton's lack of legal training. The Board of Trade summarily denied Bull's nomination. At the same time, the British ministry did not want to risk offending Bull, who was a responsible and excellent servant. To keep him in good graces, as well as to reward Drayton for his apparent loyalty, the Board of Trade approved the lieutenant governor's nomination of his nephew to a seat on the South Carolina Council. But Drayton's appointment cannot simply be reduced to nepotism and gratitude. Problems within the council itself explain why Drayton, who did not possess the usual qualities necessary to serve as an adviser to the governor, received appointment to the upper house.[4]

Beginning in the first decade of the eighteenth century, the South Carolina assembly began an ad-hoc, piecemeal acquisition of power by questioning every dubious prerogative of the governor and the council. A succession of weak executives after 1730 offered little opposition to the assembly's ravenous pursuit. By midcentury the Commons had assumed ironclad control over all aspects of government: initiating laws, appointing revenue officers, establishing courts, supervising the Indian trade, selecting the colonial agent in London, auditing and reviewing all accounts of public officers, overseeing elections, and administering all governmental expenditures. The council, in addition to losing much of its powers, also lost a considerable amount of its prestige after 1757 when Governor William Henry Lyttleton arbitrarily suspended William Wragg from that body for opposing the governor's unwillingness to defend the council's right over partial control of the colonial agent. Wragg's dismissal led to a wave of resignations in the upper house, which

4. Bull to Hillsborough, 7 March 1770, and 5 December 1770, BPROSC 32: 205–8, 411–2.

quickly gained the reputation of being "a dependent body" whose members were "removable at pleasure." Consequently, most men of fortune found the council a "contemptible" body, according to Henry Middleton, and no amount of inducement could persuade them to serve on that advisory board. The Crown accelerated the council's deteriorating reputation by attempting to create an absolutely subservient upper legislative body, one that would give unwavering support of its measures and resist the assembly's determined efforts to gain complete control over local administration. With this objective in mind, the ministry selected men financially dependent on the Crown, most of whom were British bureaucrats of mediocre abilities. By the early 1770s only two native South Carolinians served on the council. So although Drayton lacked the wealth, political experience, and social standing ordinarily required to serve in the upper house, the Board of Trade felt his loyalty to and dependence on the Crown justified his appointment to the council on February 6, 1771.[5]

With no tangible prospects of further political appointments, Drayton boarded the packet boat *Sandwich* in early March 1771 for a seven-week voyage back to Charleston. Also encouraging him to return home at this time was Parliament's repeal of most of the Townshend duties, which prompted the General Committee to terminate the South Carolina Association in December 1770. With the committee no longer agitating the people, Drayton hoped his fellow South Carolinians would be in a more pacific mood when he arrived.[6]

But when Drayton returned to Charleston in late April 1771, he found the capital still in political discord. The assembly's conspicuous £1,500 sterling gift to John Wilkes in December 1769 had produced a furious reaction in London. Crown officials were not so much incensed that the house had disobeyed royal instructions forbidding it to spend public funds without the consent of the council and the governor—a practice that had become common by midcentury—but that it was aiding their leading critic. King George III responded by issuing an "Additional Instruction" for the South Carolina

5. Bull to Hillsborough, 9 January 1771, BPROSC 32: 373; Henry Middleton to William Middleton, 8 February 1770, Middleton Papers, ref. no. SA/1/4/59, Shrubland Hall, Ipswich; M. Eugene Sirmans, "The South Carolina Royal Council, 1720–1763," *W&MQ*, 3d ser., 18 (July 1961): 381–91; Jack P. Greene, "The Role of the Lower Houses of Assembly in Eighteenth-Century Politics," *JSH* 27 (November 1961): 451–74; Jack P. Greene, *The Quest for Power: The Lower Houses of Assembly in the Southern Royal Colonies, 1689–1776* (Chapel Hill: University of North Carolina Press, 1963), 440–2.

6. Charleston Deeds, W-3: 188–91; *SCG&CJ*, 27 April 1771.

executive and councilors, threatening them with removal from office if they failed to veto any revenue bill raising money for other than local services. The governor, the council, and the Commons soon clashed over the repayment of the funds borrowed from the treasury to pay for the contribution. Neither side was willing to compromise its authority, resulting in a political deadlock that virtually paralyzed the government for the remainder of royal rule. As a result, no annual tax bill was passed after 1769 and no legislation at all after 1771. In a sense, royal government ended in South Carolina four years before the other colonies.

The controversy centered around the question of which political body would gain ultimate control over the provincial government. British officialdom was determined to retain its superiority by forcing the Commons to repudiate the grant to Wilkes by preventing its repayment in future tax bills. The ministry maintained that the colonies and their legislatures were subordinate political units with constitutions completely derived from the Crown, through charters, commissions, and instructions. Therefore, Whitehall had the authority to repudiate any precedents the lower house might cite to justify the exercise of rights. The council, dominated by the king's yes-men, was determined to ensure the Crown's superiority on colonial matters by forcing the assembly to capitulate to the king's controversial instructions.

Arguing for home rule, the assemblymen insisted that they should have greater power than an appointed council and executive because they were the people's representatives. The Commons further based its opposition to the king's additional instructions on the principle of a dynamic constitution, similar to but separate from the one in Britain, in which the legislature played a forceful role in the continuing changes to the system of government. One of these alterations was the established tradition of allowing the lower house to exercise control over money bills. The assembly asserted its right, based upon precedent and established custom, to spend funds for whatever services it thought fit; and denied the Crown's ability to supersede over two decades of tradition and practice.[7]

However, Governor Charles Montagu was determined to persuade the lower house to comply with the king's instructions. Against the advice of William Bull and others, he unwisely ordered the temporary removal of the assembly to Beaufort, an inconvenient and difficult place to reach, in hopes

7. Weir, "*A Most Important Epocha*," 40–3; Bull, *Oligarchs*, 161–4; Godbold and Woody, *Christopher Gadsden*, 105.

that the legislators from Charleston, the principle promoters of opposition, might arrive late, and their absence might make it possible to push through a tax bill acceptable to the Crown. To Montagu's surprise, the assembly turned out in full force in Beaufort when the session opened in early October 1772. His machinations thwarted, the governor dissolved the house and sent its members back to Charleston. Montagu called for new elections twice more in hopes of gaining a legislature more to his liking. On both occasions voters returned most of the recalcitrant members; the governor replied each time by proroguing the Commons. Lord Charles's behavior in the "Beaufort removal" greatly upset the new secretary of state, the Earl of Dartmouth. Complaining of health problems, Montagu sailed for England in March 1773, leaving the reigns of government for the fifth time in the able hands of William Bull.[8]

While provincial leaders were locked in this intense power struggle, Drayton was busy mending his wrecked financial and personal affairs. When he returned to South Carolina in April 1771, he was no longer the irresponsible young man who had left the province in financial, political, and social disgrace fifteen months before. Because so little information survives concerning Drayton's brief time in England, it is impossible to fully understand how or why he modified his reckless behavior. Disgust with his financial and family problems, fear of losing his remaining wealth, and a desire to regain the lost respect from his peers were perhaps all factors driving him to correct his irresponsible lifestyle. His motivations aside, when Drayton returned home from England he stopped gambling and worked hard to stabilize his situation.

One sign of his new attitude was his waiting a year before taking his council seat so he could concentrate on getting his plantation activities and finances back in order. While his stay in England had advanced his political career, it had only exacerbated his financial difficulties. On at least four occasions magistrates requested Dorothy Drayton's appearance in court to either pay William Henry's debts or explain why she could not honor them at that time; with the help of her friend Eliza Pinckney and others she managed to successfully fend off the numerous creditors seeking to seize portions of her

8. Journals of the Commons House of Assembly, 36, pt. 2: 158, SCDAH; Charles Montagu to Earl of Hillsborough, 20 October 1772, BPROSC 33: 183; Greene, "Bridge to Revolution," 19–52; Robert M. Weir, "Beaufort: The Almost Capital," *Sandlapper* 9 (September 1976): 43–4; Alan D. Watson, "The Beaufort Removal and the Revolutionary Impulse in South Carolina," *SCHM* 84 (July 1983) 121–35.

husband's estate. Drayton's own early efforts in repairing his affairs were apparently unsuccessful, as illustrated by a bond for £10,000 he obtained from his cousin Edward Fenwicke in July 1772. Making it difficult for Drayton to get back on his financial feet were torrential rains that produced massive flooding throughout the lowcountry during the spring and summer of 1772, ruining much of the region's rice crop. Specific losses on Drayton's plantations are unknown, but Peter Manigault reported that the incessant rains had done "immense damage" throughout the area.[9] Drayton's efforts at mending his pecuniary problems ultimately proved successful, as records show that after 1773 he never again borrowed enormous sums of money, mortgaged portions of his property, or defended himself in court from creditors seeking attachments against his personal estate.

Less clear is the precise extent of Drayton's wealth. Soon after his arrival in South Carolina in mid-1763 he began accumulating sizeable property, enabling him to move into the province's ruling elite. By 1770 he owned three lowcountry plantations, totaling nearly 5,000 acres, on which he grew rice and indigo. After 1772 he used his powerful position as a member of the council to obtain 7,000 additional acres of land in various areas of the backcountry. He undoubtedly acquired this property for speculative purposes, but he was probably also reserving certain portions for family development. It is not known whether he used the land to cultivate and market indigo, tobacco, wheat, and hemp—all important upcountry commodities. Drayton acquired no additional land following the fall of royal rule in 1776, as the South Carolina government placed a temporary halt on all land sales during the Revolution.

Just as important as his landholding to Drayton's economic and social standing among the ruling class was his ownership of slaves. As one visitor to the region remarked, "if a man has not as many slaves as they, he is esteemed by them their inferior." Unfortunately, little is known about the number of Drayton's human chattel. The only available evidence is a 1770 document revealing that Drayton gave one hundred slaves as security to his mother-in-

9. Judgment Rolls, Box 90A, nos. 30A, 27A, 51A and 53A, SCDAH; William Henry Drayton to Henry Middleton, Lease of a Plantation, 1 July 1772, Charleston Deeds, B-4 (1772–1773), 167, SCDAH; William Henry Drayton and Henry Middleton to Edward Fenwicke, Bond, 1 August 1772, Signers of the Declaration of Independence/Henry Middleton, Simon Gratz Collection, Historical Society of Pennsylvania, Philadelphia; George W. Lane Jr., "The Middletons of Eighteenth Century South Carolina: A Colonial Dynasty, 1678–1787" (Ph.D. diss., Emory University, 1990), 419–20.

law to protect his Horseshoe estate from creditors. One may assume that this number would not include all of his slaves, as he would need some to work his several plantations. Thus Drayton owned perhaps several hundred slaves. However, it appears that the number of slaves in his possession dropped precipitously during the Revolution and following Drayton's death in 1779. According to executor Charles Drayton, his brother's estate counted a mere forty-nine slaves in 1784. One can only speculate on the reasons for the decline. Perhaps some of the bondsmen, like thousands of others, fled to or were stolen by the British upon their capture of the state in 1780. Others may have been sold to pay off debts owed by Drayton's estate upon his death.[10]

Even more obscure than the number of Drayton's slaves is evidence of how he treated and cared for them. In addition to operating largely as an absentee planter, even when home he employed overseers to manage the daily plantation operations, including the disciplining of recalcitrant or uncooperative bondsmen. Drayton's personal duties were mostly limited to that of an administrator: keeping accounts of productivity, transactions involving the sale of surplus products and acquisitions of goods, statistics on slaves, and balance sheets of profits and losses. Although Drayton therefore had little contact with his slaves, he nonetheless had to follow the provincial slave code adopted by the assembly in 1740, which prevented masters from "exercising too great rigour and cruelty" over their bondsmen and from working them on Sunday or more than fifteen hours a day during the week. The slave code also required owners to provide adequate food and clothing, the former usually consisting of corn, peas, and rice of unmarketable quality while the latter was commonly made of coarse, cheap English linen. However, many planters did allow their slaves to hunt, fish, and cultivate garden plots to supplement their meager diets. Quarters provided to slaves varied significantly, from hovels to brick cabins, while medical care was surprisingly good, as masters sought to protect their investments. How closely Drayton followed the slave codes and common slave-management customs is impossible to determine. However, the fact that he never advertised the sale or escape of his slaves may imply a relatively humane treatment of his black chattel.[11]

---

10. Robert Olwell, *Masters, Slaves, and Subjects: The Culture of Power in the South Carolina Lowcountry, 1740–1790* (Ithaca: Cornell University Press, 1998), 44; Charleston Deeds, P-3 (1770), 134, 140–3, SCDAH; Bull, *Oligarchs*, 372 n. 23.

11. Philip D. Morgan, "Work and Culture: The Task System and the World of the Lowcountry Blacks, 1700–1880," *W&MQ*, 3d ser., 39 (October 1982): 566–9; M. Eugene Sirmans, "The Legal Status of the Slave in South Carolina, 1670–1740," *JSH* 28 (November 1962):

Also requiring Drayton's attention at this time was his marriage, which, along with his finances, suffered during his year-long preferment-seeking trip to Britain. Dorothy was already upset with him for gambling away much of their fortune, the behavior that prompted his trip across the "Pond" in the first place. Drayton's absence only stoked her anger, as she was left alone to care for the couple's extensive property holdings as well as their two young sons. Dorothy's disgust must certainly have risen on each of the four occasions when she was forced into the embarrassing position of having to go to court to fend off creditors trying to seize portions of the estate. The death of seventeen-month-old William Henry Jr. in May 1770 only intensified Dorothy's misery and her resentment toward her husband, whose absence robbed her of the comfort she needed during this melancholy time. Given these circumstances, Drayton must have devoted some attention toward placating his wife in order to restore a relatively peaceful domestic environment. His success in this endeavor is uncertain, but the birth in 1774 of Mary perhaps attests to some reconciliation between the two.

While Drayton was attending to his plantations and marriage, his uncle William Bull was working on his behalf for the position of postmaster general for the Southern District of North America. This position suddenly became vacant on August 16, 1773, when Peter DeLancey was killed in a duel with Dr. John Haley in Charleston. So that "no interruption or delay might happen in the business of that office," Bull quickly selected his nephew to serve as pro tempore postmaster general. In a letter to Hillsborough, the lieutenant governor justified his decision by explaining that Drayton's "loyalty and attachment to His Majesty's Government" along with his "integrity and abilities" rendered him "equal to the duties of that office."[12]

To increase his chances of receiving the position, Drayton wrote Lords Sandwich and Hillsborough, requesting their assistance. Unfortunately for Drayton, his petition reached the noblemen after Lord Le Despencer, the Crown's postmaster general, had already selected English-born George Roupell, the deputy collector of customs and commissioner of fortifications for Charleston, to replace DeLancey. Drayton boasted years later that he was "not disgusted" by this snub, an assertion that may be partially true, since the post paid only £300 sterling annually and held little prestige. Still, the

471–2; Anzilotti, "Autonomy and the Female Planter," 254; Olwell, *Masters, Slaves, and Subjects,* 186, 193, 212; Weir, *Colonial South Carolina,* 187.

12. Bull to Hillsborough, 19 August 1771, BPROSC 33: 82.

assignment would have brought Drayton much-needed cash to help pay off his creditors and would have aligned him more closely with the royal government. The Crown's selection of an Englishman who already held three local government offices sharply reminded Drayton of the British ministry's low regard for provincials.[13]

On April 2, 1772, Drayton finally assumed the duties for the one office to which the Crown appointed him and took his seat alongside his father in the council chamber. Unlike his neglectful service as an assemblyman seven years before, Drayton worked diligently and conscientiously as a councilor. He viewed his new, powerful office as the means by which to rebuild his political and economic fortunes, and his service reflected the dedication of a man determined to turn his life around. Drayton's industry so impressed Governor Montagu that he informed Hillsborough that the young Carolinian was one of only two members who were "constant attendants" at council. The other councilors, on the other hand, attended meetings so infrequently that the governor often had difficulty securing even the three members necessary for a quorum. Frustrated, Montagu beseeched the secretary of state to remove several members, including John Drayton, for dereliction of duty. William Henry Drayton similarly had little respect for his irresponsible associates, whom he believed sometimes performed their duties in an indifferent and unparliamentary manner. Unwisely, Drayton reported his colleagues' transgressions to Montagu, conduct that endeared him to the governor but alienated him from the other councilors.[14]

This alienation undoubtedly contributed to Drayton's failure later in the year to swindle 144,000 acres from the Catawba Indians in a shrewd and calculating arrangement. Drayton had first conceived this scheme in November 1772 when King Trow, leader of the Catawba nation, and ten of his headmen went before the council to complain of white settlers encroaching on their lands. The Catawbas were particularly offended by four families who they claimed "did not behave well" and implored the upper house to have them removed from the reservation.[15]

Until the 1760s, the Catawbas had been a numerous and powerful nation

13. Drayton, *A Letter from Freeman*, 5 n.; *SCG&CJ*, 14 January 1772; Ruth L. Butter, *Doctor Franklin: Postmaster General* (New York: Doubleday, Doran, 1928), 115–24.

14. South Carolina Council Journals, no. 36, pt. 2: 67, 126, SCDAH; *SCG&CJ*, 14 April 1772; *SCG*, 16 April 1772; Montagu to Hillsborough, 2 August 1772, BPROSC 33: 169–71.

15. South Carolina Council Journals, no. 36, pt. 2: 225–6, SCDAH.

inhabiting a region ranging from the upper waters of the Pee Dee River in North Carolina south to the Santee River in South Carolina. During the first half of the eighteenth century, the friendly Catawbas provided a valuable service to South Carolinians by acting as a bulwark against the more powerful and hostile Cherokee, Creek, Westo, and Tuscarora Indians living farther west. During the 1750s and 1760s, however, a shift in the Indian trade, a decline of game, smallpox epidemics, raids from northern tribes, and participation in the French and Indian and Cherokee Wars greatly weakened the Catawbas' livelihood and ability to defend themselves. The smallpox epidemic of 1759–1760 alone wiped out two-thirds of their population, reducing them to less than five hundred in number. The Catawbas were physically and perhaps emotionally destroyed by the quick succession of calamities and never recovered from these terrible years. Alcoholism and apathy soon spread among the survivors. Had the South Carolina government not come to their aid with food and clothing, the Catawbas probably would have been completely wiped out within a few years.

Nearly reduced to extinction, the once strong and proud Catawba nation was now unable to prevent land-hungry whites from encroaching on their land. Under the direction of John Stuart, Superintendent of Indian Affairs for the Southern Colonies, a congress was held in Augusta, Georgia, in November 1763 to settle grievances from the French and Indian War. The Catawbas, complaining of white encroachment and a lack of hunting territory, asked for a reservation of thirty square miles. In the final Treaty of Augusta, British officials granted them a reservation half that size (144,000 acres) in a region around the Catawba River and Sugar Creek near the North and South Carolina boundary. However, this agreement carried little influence among frontiersmen, who immediately began settling on the reservation. Encroachment increased tremendously as immigration into the backcountry more than doubled in the following decade, leaving the South Carolina government at a loss as to how to stop the illegal intrusion.[16]

On the other hand, Drayton conceived his own plan for solving the Catawbas' encroachment problem while at the same time enabling him personally to make a small fortune. Several days after King Trow voiced his griev-

16. James H. Merrell, *The Indians' New World: Catawbas and Their Neighbors from European Contact through the Era of Removal* (Chapel Hill: University of North Carolina Press, 1989), 193–9; Charles M. Hudson, *The Catawba Nation* (Athens: University of Georgia Press, 1970), 46–51.

ances to the council, Drayton proposed that the government lease the Catawba lands to him for twenty-one years. In return for allowing him to rent small tracts on the reservation to colonists, Drayton promised to protect the approximately 350 remaining Catawbas from abusive whites and provide them with blankets, coats, guns, powder, shot, and paint. Moreover, the Catawbas would retain all rights over their cornfields and towns and the privilege of hunting throughout the entire tract. While Drayton's ability to protect the Indians was dubious, there is no doubt that he stood to reap enormous economic gains from the deal. The cost of providing the promised goods would only amount to about £80 sterling annually, a fraction of the amount he could make renting land to the thousands of colonists immigrating into the region every year.[17]

After hearing Drayton's offer, the other council members could not believe their good fortune. The South Carolina government had been trying to distance itself from the Catawbas for more than a decade, no longer needing their services after the defeat of the Cherokees in 1761, and no longer willing to continue feeding, clothing, or protecting them from white settlers. Delighted to relieve themselves of this custodial role, the council quickly approved Drayton's proposal, provided the Catawbas were agreeable and no treaty or instruction from the Crown forbade the lease.[18]

With the council's blessing, Drayton immediately left Charleston to sell his proposal to the Catawbas. Speaking condescendingly before King Trow and his headmen on January 8, Drayton promised to be "a father to them," to protect them from injury by whites, and to provide them with goods necessary for their survival in exchange for their allowing him to rent small parcels of their land to colonists. Before the headmen had time to ponder this astonishing offer, Drayton delivered a shocking message from the governor and the council advising the Indians to accept the Carolinian's proposal, describing it as the "best method" to protect their lands from "such injustice as you complain of."[19]

Drayton's remarkable offer caused vast dissension among Catawba leaders. Some of them were "tolerably well satisfied" with the proposal while others were "not so well content." Most apparently did not grasp the full implications of the proposal. John Wyly, the province's agent to the Cataw-

17. John Stuart to Earl of Dartmouth, 26 February 1773, BPROCO 5/74, pp. 119–20.
18. Merrell, *Indians' New World*, 202–4.
19. John Stuart to Lord Dartmouth, 26 February 1773, BPROCO 5/74, pp. 119–20; South Carolina Council Journals, no. 36, pt. 2: 248.

bas and a witness to much of the proceedings, thought the Indians failed to understand that Drayton planned to settle the "whole of their Land." In the end, King Trow and his headmen, stunned by the announcement that the South Carolina government was no longer willing to address their grievances, felt they had no other choice but to accept the offer. Before agreeing to it, however, the Catawba leader made certain Drayton understood that their land would still belong to them "as long as there was one Catawba Indian left." But with the number of Catawbas quickly dwindling and recent rumors that they were planning to abandon the reservation, Drayton was confident that this obstacle to absolute control of the tract would soon vanish. Indeed, Wyly understood Drayton's true intentions and was glad that he had missed the final talks as he "did not want to have anything to do" with such a disgraceful transaction.[20]

One person who certainly wanted a voice in the matter was John Stuart, whose vehement opposition to Drayton's land-lease scheme revealed a deeper struggle between the local gentry and Crown officials over the imperial government's role in frontier affairs. Born around the turn of the century in Scotland, Stuart emigrated to South Carolina in 1748. He soon became a successful planter and married Sarah Fenwicke, an heiress and member of one of the colony's most influential and respected families. While serving as an officer in the French and Indian War, he displayed some ability in the management of Indians, which gained him the appointment as Superintendent of Indian Affairs for the Southern Department. Stuart took his duties seriously and worked hard to gain full imperial status for his department, believing that a uniform, centralized administration was crucial in managing land transfers, trade, and diplomatic relations with the Indians. In the process, he managed to usurp much of the virtually unfettered control that governors had traditionally maintained over both land and Indian policy. Within a few years after taking office, Stuart was answerable only to the British secretary of state. In 1770 Lord Hillsborough strengthened the Scotsman's authority by appointing him "councillor extraordinary" to advise the governors and councils on Indian affairs. Possessing a vain and pompous personality, Stuart jealously guarded his considerable influence.[21]

20. John Wyly, "A Copy of the Talk Delivered by Mr. Drayton to the Catawba Indians, 8th January 1773," Joseph Kershaw Papers, SCL; Hudson, *Catawba Nation*, 48.

21. John Alden, *John Stuart and the Southern Colonial Frontier: A Study of Indian Relations, War, Trade, and the Land Problems in the Southern Wilderness, 1754–1775* (Ann Arbor: University of Michigan Press, 1944); Snapp, *John Stuart*, 149–53; Philip M. Hamer, "John Stuart's Indian Policy during the Early Months of the American Revolution," *Mississippi Valley Historical Review* 17 (December 1930): 351–2; Snapp, "William Henry Drayton," 643–4.

Drayton had first clashed with Stuart in October 1763 over the issue of the superintendent's rank as an ex-officio member of the council. Stuart, an ambitious Scotsman who yearned for higher status, argued that as the eldest member of the upper house, he should be first in rank. Moreover, he demanded that the governor and fellow councilors consult him on all matters related to frontier policy, not just Indian affairs. Drayton, although more than forty years Stuart's junior and having only a few months of experience in the council, was not intimidated by the presumptuous superintendent. Nor was he afraid of antagonizing an influential member of the imperial government. Drayton called Stuart's demands absurd, arguing that he was not even a regularly appointed councilor because he was not "vested with the powers of the ancient twelve." The secretary of state only appointed Stuart as an ex-officio member of the council to better execute the duties of his office, continued Drayton, not to "authorize him constantly to interfere in the domestic legislative affairs of any such Colony." The other councilors agreed with Drayton and blocked Stuart's demands.[22]

Drayton's attack on the powerful superintendent came back to hurt him two months later when he introduced the land-grabbing scheme to the council. Stuart attended this meeting, but the journals do not record any protest on his part, nor did he oppose the other councilors when they approved Drayton's plan a few days later. The opportunity to get even with this arrogant young upstart was too good to squander with a hastily conceived dissent. Stuart's earlier confrontation with Drayton taught him not to underestimate the young Carolinian's talent and passion for argument. In preparing his protest, Stuart diligently gathered all the information he could find that disputed his colleague's scheme and carefully drafted a convincing case against it. But in making his dissent, Stuart was not simply seeking revenge against Drayton, he was also defending the powers of his office from a plan he believed circumvented his authority over Indian affairs. One of his duties as superintendent was to protect the Indians from being swindled by avaricious and cunning colonists. With ten years of experience in managing relations between Indians and colonists, Stuart knew all too well that direct negotiations between private individuals and tribes were frequently fraught with deception. He believed Drayton's scheme was no different. As head of the province's Indian affairs, Stuart considered it his duty to declare his objection.[23]

22. Drayton, *Memoirs*, 1: 237; *SCG*, 15 October 1772.
23. Stuart to Dartmouth, 26 February 1773, BPROCO 5/74, pp. 119–20.

On January 20 Stuart presented his protest, in which he used the law, fear, and compassion to try to persuade the governor and the council to block Drayton's plan. Beginning with legal evidence, Stuart argued that the land transfer was unlawful because it violated the king's instructions and the Treaty of Augusta, both of which prohibited private land transfers from natives. He warned that breaking this treaty with the Catawbas would set a bad precedent and might incite other Indian tribes to retaliate. The Catawbas had "always been faithfully & Cordially attached to the British Interest," the superintendent added, and deserved fair treatment and protection. According to Stuart, the present land transfer was not favorable to the nation because Drayton had no concern for the Indians' welfare. He only wanted to use their land for his own personal interest and emolument. In concluding, Stuart notified the council that he had discussed the matter with Attorney General Egerton Leigh, who told him that, according to his legal expertise, the land transfer clearly violated the Treaty of Augusta as well as the king's instructions to the superintendent.[24]

Stuart's argument impressed the council. Following a short deliberation, the upper house reversed its previous decision and "unanimously rejected" Drayton's plan as "an improper and impolitic measure which might be attended with bad consequences." The threat of an Indian uprising pointed out by the superintendent was certainly one of the bad consequences the councilors had in mind when reevaluating their decision.[25]

Drayton was furious, and he blamed both Stuart for instigating resistance to his plan and Leigh (also a councilor) for supporting the superintendent. To Drayton, Stuart's success in this affair personified the imperial government's ultimate design to deny the local elite control over their own frontier affairs. He undoubtedly agreed with Henry Laurens's assertion that private negotiations for Indian land were "consonant with the Liberty of the British Subject." Given such a conviction, Drayton considered Stuart's interference in his Catawba land-lease scheme as an "intolerable intrusion" of American liberty, which nurtured within him a growing fear that the Crown's frontier policy represented a conspiracy against the colony's traditional spheres of self-government. The council attempted to assuage Drayton's feelings by grant-

---

24. South Carolina Council Journals, no. 37: 27–8, SCDAH; Stuart to Dartmouth, 26 February 1773, BPROCO 5/74, pp. 119–20.

25. Stuart to Dartmouth, 26 February 1773, BPROCO 5/74, pp. 119–20; South Carolina Council Journals, no. 37: 29–30, SCDAH.

ing him 3,000 acres in Craven County on the Wateree River. This generous offering failed to pacify him, however.[26]

Drayton's resentment toward his fellow councilors came to a head in August 1773 when he believed they were jeopardizing the welfare of the colony by attempting to force the assembly to rescind its £1,500 contribution to John Wilkes. Ever since the king reaffirmed the coordinate authority of the upper house in amending and passing money bills with his additional instructions of April 1770, the assembly had refused to allow the council to alter any part of a tax bill instructing it to reimburse the treasurer for the £1,500 sent to Wilkes. The council, in turn, refused to approve any tax bills.

The colony's financial problems finally reached a crisis late in the summer of 1773 when the general-duty law, which had been bringing substantial sums into the treasury since the passage of the last tax bill, was set to expire in September at the end of the legislative session. In early August one of the two colonial treasurers, Henry Peronneau, reported to the council that there was only about £10,000 left in the treasury, a deficiency due in part to the failure of local merchants to pay an estimated £130,000 owed to the government in import duties. If the government did not pass a new tax bill, he warned, the treasury would be depleted by October 1. Drayton immediately drafted a message from the council to Lieutenant Governor Bull claiming that the colony's £130,000 sterling debt would soon cause fiscal chaos and "give almost a mortal Wound" to its foreign credit unless the two houses quickly passed a tax bill. The councilors placed all the blame for this crisis on the Commons for continually creating revenue measures to which the councilors could not agree without violating the king's additional instruction regarding revenue bills and thereby "surrendering their rights as legislators." As a means of averting the emergency, the council advised Bull to order Attorney General Leigh to immediately sue local merchants for money owed to the treasury. To pressure the lieutenant governor into executing its suggestions, the council published their alarming letter in the local press.[27]

Instead of securing Bull's support, however, the councilors' tactless and provocative publication managed to only infuriate the lieutenant governor,

26. Henry Laurens to Elias Vanderhorst, 6 March 1772, *HLP*, 8: 215; Snapp, "William Henry Drayton," 647; Snapp, *John Stuart*, 149–52; South Carolina Council Journals, no. 37: 38–9, 48, SCDAH; Colonial Plats, 14: 268–9, SCDAH.

27. *SCG&CJ*, 17 August 1773.

who bristled at their attempt to force his position. Bull also thought little of the council's drastic suggestion to sue the local factors and curtly replied to his advisers that he would do whatever seemed necessary to him short of creating "any Inconveniences to the Persons concerned."[28]

The assembly also understood the council's political maneuverings and was not about to allow it to gain the upper hand in this showdown over control of the colony's revenue expenditures. In the August 16 issue of the *South Carolina Gazette*, the Commons House attempted to defuse the council's incendiary public announcement by reporting that the colony's financial situation was far from being as desperate as the governor's advisers insisted. The nearly £130,000 sterling due from "Gentlemen in Trade," the legislators maintained, should be regarded as actually in the treasury, in addition to £10,000 in gold and silver and various other forms of currency. However, the assemblymen did agree with the councilors that the failure to pass tax measures had jeopardized the colony's public credit; similarly, too, they absolved themselves of any responsibility in creating this economic emergency. The Commons justified its behavior in this dispute by claiming that it was simply looking out for the public's best interests, for had it passed a tax bill agreeable to the council, the lower house explained, it would have lost its most valuable privilege: the exclusive right of originating and framing all money bills. This self-serving defense had little influence on Bull, who understood that the lower house was intentionally impeding the passage of a revenue law in order to create an economic situation so grave that it would bring pressure on the Crown to withdraw the additional instruction giving the council equal authority with the assembly in amending and passing tax bills, rather than see the colony succumb to fiscal chaos.[29]

The council also understood the assembly's motive. Instead of surrendering to the lower house's unrelenting political pressure, most of the councilors decided to apply some coercion of their own by refusing to pass *any* legislation until the Commons drafted a General Duty Act that complied with the royal instructions. The assembly tested the council's resolve on this threat in late August when it sent to the upper house an innocent bill intended to discourage counterfeiting of the colony's currency. In dispatching the proposed

---

28. Maurice Crouse, *The Public Treasury of Colonial South Carolina* (Columbia: University of South Carolina Press, 1977), 125; Bull to Dartmouth, 26 August 1773, BPROSC 33: 294; Bull, *Oligarchs*, 190.

29. Crouse, *Public Treasury*, 124–5.

bill to the council for its concurrence, the assembly beseeched it to "expedite the passing" of this important measure so that the "public may not any longer be subject to the great Danger arising from the want of such a Law."[30]

This plea had no effect on the placemen councilors, who viewed the crisis as a perfect opportunity to compel the Commons to capitulate in their dispute over the province's appropriations process. When the bill came up for its third and final reading, the placemen deferred the deliberation of it sine die. Both Draytons, father and son, objected vehemently to this postponement of important legislation on the grounds that it was "fatal to the Freedom of our Country" because it put an "undue force" on the Commons into extending the still-pending General Duty Act and promoted further disunion between the two houses.[31]

The Draytons' protest might have fallen silent thereafter had Thomas Powell not published it in his gazette. Egerton Leigh, the council president, was upset with this publication of a portion of the upper house's journal without that body's consent. He summoned Powell to the council's chamber for questioning. In his defense, the printer explained that since no newspaper editor in the province had ever been called to answer for publishing any parts of the proceedings of either the governor, the council, or the assembly, he had readily complied with William Henry Drayton's request to print a portion of the upper house's journal. Herein the younger Drayton interjected and admitted to giving his protest to Powell. He further apologized to his colleagues for causing them any displeasure and accepted full responsibility for the incident. By accepting all the blame, Drayton was hoping to defuse the situation, knowing the council would not reprimand one of its own members—even though he had joined sides with the assembly in this dispute. The other councilmen, however, determined to establish their authority, ruled Powell guilty of high breach of privileges and contempt for publishing council proceedings. Enraged, Drayton challenged his colleagues' judicial expertise, angrily telling them they had no legal right to imprison the printer. The placemen refused to back down. At one point Drayton became so exasperated with Leigh, who issued the warrant committing Powell to jail, that he called the attorney general a "Damn Fool" to his face.[32]

30. Journals of the Commons House of Assembly, 39: 62, SCDAH.

31. *SCG*, 30 August 1773, supplement.

32. Ibid., 13 September 1773; Henry Laurens to William Manning, 22 May 1775, *HLP* 10: 126.

Drayton could no longer tolerate the placemen on the council. Their arrogance, monopoly of the colony's most lucrative posts, lack (in his view) of legal knowledge, and willingness to place the Crown's interests above the colony's were too much for him to accept. One of the placemen most responsible for the council's obstructionist policy was Leigh. To Drayton and many other South Carolinians, Leigh was the quintessential placeman, embodying everything the natives despised among the foreign-born officeholders. The attorney general was not apologetic about his status nor how he achieved it, openly bragging that "I am a downright *Placeman* . . . and that I owe more to the Royal Favor than any merit I possess can justly claim."[33]

Nine years Drayton's senior, Leigh had arrived in South Carolina in 1753 with his father Peter, who left his position as high bailiff of Westminster under charges of improper conduct to supersede Charles Pinckney as the colony's chief justice. Drayton's negative view of the Leighs, and of placemen generally, probably first developed that same year when he sailed to England with Pinckney, who undoubtedly voiced his disapproval at being replaced by a Britisher tainted with scandal. While Drayton spent the next ten years at school in England, twenty-year-old Leigh, described by Andrew Rutledge as a "genteel, well tempered Man," cultivated a brilliant career in South Carolina.[34] His father immediately admitted him to the Charleston bar despite his lack of formal legal training, and secured his appointment as clerk of the Court of Common Pleas in 1754. Through family connections and a dearth of educated men in the colony, Leigh quickly procured some of the most lucrative and treasured offices in the colony—surveyor general, councilor, judge of the vice-admiralty court and attorney general—within eight years after arriving in the province.

But Leigh's meteoric rise was superseded by an even quicker downfall. His public reputation began to decline during the Stamp Act crisis when he was the only member of the Charleston bar who opposed reopening the courts without stamped paper. Around this time he made rather questionable verdicts in several highly publicized court cases, which greatly offended local merchants. However, Leigh's most objectionable performance occurred in 1772 when he entered into an affair with his wife's young sister. The liaison

33. Jack P. Greene, ed., *The Nature of Colony Constitutions: Two Pamphlets on the Wilkes Fund Controversy in South Carolina by Sir Egerton Leigh and Arthur Lee* (Columbia: University of South Carolina Press, 1970), 63.

34. Andrew Rutledge to Peter Manigault, ca. 1753, Manigault Family Papers, SCL.

resulted in a pregnancy that Leigh tried to hide by boarding his sister-in-law on a ship bound for England. When she went into labor before the vessel departed, Leigh refused to allow her ashore. The young woman was forced to give birth without a midwife in attendance. The baby died within a week. As Leigh feared, the episode became public, thoroughly ruining his already tarnished public image. Henry Laurens wondered how "the wretch can hold up his head" in public. Isolated from Carolina society, Leigh became dependent on the Crown for his authority and stature in the province. To maintain good graces with His Majesty, he gave earnest and unquestioned support to the British government's colonial policies. In return, King George III rewarded Leigh with a baronetcy. This royal benefaction to a degenerate official who placed ministerial instructions above the colony's welfare only made provincials like Drayton even more disgusted with Leigh and the other English authorities.[35]

Drayton publicly protested the council's decision to incarcerate Powell in the printer's own weekly organ on the grounds that the group did not have the legal right to arrest him because there was no order, rule, or resolution preventing the publication of its proceedings. To his knowledge even the House of Lords had never punished a publisher for printing an excerpt from its journals. What was the use of a protest anyway, Drayton asked, if it could not be made public?[36]

Drayton's second public censure infuriated the placemen councilors, who quickly proposed a resolution reprimanding him for publishing a "false, scandalous and malicious" protest against the upper house. Drayton, who never believed his associates would prosecute one of their own, was shocked and unnerved. Before the councilors voted on the proclamation, he suddenly changed his story, this time denying that he ever submitted his dissent to Powell. However, he did admit to providing copies to four friends knowledgeable in the law for their opinion and advice, one of whom (Edward Rutledge), he recently learned, confessed to giving the protest to Powell.

Drayton had selected Edward Rutledge as his confidant knowing that as printer Powell's attorney, he would make use of the knowledge of Drayton's dissent. Additionally, Drayton's trust in Rutledge, who soon emerged as a

35. Henry Laurens to John Laurens, 19 November 1773, *HLP* 9: 153–4; Weir and Calhoon, "The Scandalous History of Sir Egerton Leigh," 47–74.

36. *SCG*, 2 September 1773.

leading figure in South Carolina's rebellion, reveals that Drayton was developing close personal ties with local revolutionaries. These alliances were strengthened by several marriages between friends and family members closely involved in the American cause. Twenty-four-year-old Edward Rutledge was courting and eventually married (in March 1774) Henrietta Middleton, the eldest sister of Arthur Middleton, an extreme patriot and leading member in the province's revolutionary movement. Drayton was already friends with Arthur and his family, as revealed when both Arthur and his father Henry served as cosigners and witnesses to some of Drayton's earlier financial transactions. This relationship with the Middletons was solidified familially in February 1774 when Charles Drayton married twenty-year-old Hester Middleton, another one of Arthur's many sisters. Further complicating the weave was the marriage in September 1773 of Drayton's longtime friend and vocal patriot Charles Cotesworth Pinckney to Arthur Middleton's seventeen-year-old sister Sarah. The alliance by marriage of these four families—the Draytons, the Middletons, the Pinckneys, and the Rutledges—would soon form one of the province's most influential power groups. Just as importantly, they brought William Henry Drayton even closer to those in the advance guard of America's struggle with the mother country and probably facilitated his radicalization.[37]

Drayton's recent admission that young Rutledge had published the protest without his knowledge convinced the other councilors to rescind their charge against their colleague. The fact that Rutledge was one of the ablest and most popular lawyers in the province certainly influenced them in their decision not to pursue the case against Rutledge. Absolved of any criminal behavior, Drayton was restored into the good graces of the council.[38]

Edward Rutledge's respect as a lawyer stemmed from his successful defense of printer Thomas Powell against Sir Egerton Leigh, a case that brought the running power struggle between the Commons and the council to a climax. Although he was only twenty-three and had just recently been admitted to the Charleston bar, Rutledge made an eloquent and intelligent defense of his client. Using arguments developed through a quarter century of debate over the relative power of the assembly and the council, Rutledge

37. James Haw, *John and Edward Rutledge of South Carolina* (Athens: University of Georgia Press, 1997), 55; Griffin, "The Eighteenth Century Draytons," 335–7.

38. *SCG&CJ*, 7 September 1773; *SCG*, 13 September 1773; Richard B. Clow, "Edward Rutledge of South Carolina, 1749–1800: Unproclaimed Statesman" (Ph.D. diss., University of Georgia, 1976), 25.

declared before a packed courtroom that the council did not have the authority to commit Powell to jail for the contempt of its authority because it was not an upper house of the legislature. Nor was the council comparable to the House of Lords since it was not composed of independent men as in the British upper house, but of men "dependent on the Will of the King." Consequently, the council was nothing more than a privy council, Rutledge concluded, endowed only with the authority to assist the governor with its advice. Judges Rawlins Lowndes and George Gabriel Powell, who presided over this "solemn hearing," agreed with Rutledge's argument and released the printer from jail.[39]

The council was furious with the justices' ruling, a decision they feared seriously undermined the council's authority because they believed it "absolutely and actually abolished one of the Branches of the Legislature." To protect its legislative power, the upper house naïvely requested assistance from the assembly in punishing Lowndes and Powell—who were also assemblymen—by having it waive the usual exemption from arrest of its members so that the council "may proceed to take Cognizance of their Breach of Privilege and Contempt" against it. Instead of handing over the two justices for the council to abuse, however, the assembly officially thanked Lowndes and Powell for their "able, upright and impartial decision." It further enraged the council by urging Lieutenant Governor Bull to suspend those councilors responsible for wrongfully arresting the printer and replace them with men who "really have at Heart the Service of his Majesty and Interest of the Province."[40]

The sagacious lieutenant governor refused to be drawn into the dispute, however, and deferred the matter to higher authorities. In a letter to Lord Dartmouth, Bull warned the secretary of state of the council's declining position. The assembly's frequent attacks against that body "have so much degraded [it] in the eyes of the People," explained Bull, that the councilors' situation has become "rather humiliating and obnoxious." The conflict between the two houses "is now at a great height and seems approaching to a crisis," he added. To avoid this disaster, the lieutenant governor implored His Maj-

39. Clow, "Edward Rutledge," 23–4; Petition of Charles Garth to the King's Most Excellent Majesty, 15 December 1773, BPROSC 33: 345; Journals of the Commons House of Assembly, 39: 85, SCDAH.

40. Journals of the Commons House of Assembly, 39: 78–9, SCDAH; South Carolina Council Journals, 39: 87–8; *SCG*, 15 September 1773, SCDAH.

esty for a "final determination" on the matter to end the "fruitless and acrimonious altercation" that was obstructing public business.[41]

Although Dartmouth despaired of ever restoring to the council its original authority, he considered unconstitutional any decision denying that body's right to serve as an upper house of the legislature. In January 1774 the secretary of state informed Bull that he would send the king's final decision on the matter in the next packet. But that important decision never came, as the ministry became preoccupied with suppressing the incipient rebellions in the northern colonies. Thus the assembly and the council continued fighting in "a spirit of Animosity" that Dartmouth believed left "little room to expect a return of that mutual confidence that is essential to the Peace and Welfare of Government."[42]

When Drayton returned to South Carolina early in 1771 with a more responsible demeanor and a commission to serve on the council, his future looked promising once again. However, one aspect of his personality which did not change during his year in England was his fondness for controversy, and the continual political discord in the province gave Drayton plenty of opportunities for debate. Indeed, 1773 turned out to be one of the colony's most contentious years prior to the Revolution, and Drayton's involvement in the political strife forced him to reassess his attitude toward South Carolina's future welfare. The placemen's behavior, in particular, convinced him that if harmony was to return to the province and the native elite were to have back much of their personal independence and political autonomy, the Crown had to replace the British-born officials with South Carolinians. Although Drayton was confident that Whitehall would remove these foreign officeholders once it fully understood the harm they were causing the colony, he continued his own efforts to emasculate the placemen's authority. In the process, though, he was quickly distancing himself from His Majesty's government and drawing himself into the ranks of his old enemies in the popular party.

41. Bull to Dartmouth, 18 September 1773, BPROSC 33: 308–9.
42. Garth Letterbook, 163, SCDAH; Dartmouth to Bull, 8 January 1774, BPROSC 34: 2–3; Drayton, *Memoirs*, 1: 103.

ABJURING THE CROWN

Drayton's shift toward the Whig camp accelerated during the next two years. A temporary appointment to the South Carolina bench early in 1774 did not slow this advancement; instead, Drayton became even more disgruntled with royal officials as he came to believe his judicial colleagues—all British placemen—were incompetent Crown yes-men who posed a danger to the liberties and welfare of South Carolinians. His patience with British authorities finally reached its limit later that year when Parliament passed the punitively motivated Intolerable Acts against Massachusetts. No longer able to give unquestioned support of the Crown's imperial policy, Drayton, in rather seditious and offensive language, called for the repeal of these coercive measures in a public letter to the Continental Congress. This derisive declaration offended the local placemen, who initiated with their young colleague a bitter and protracted political contest that nearly resulted in bloodshed. When the dust finally settled, Drayton was no longer a member of His Majesty's government, but a rising star in the local revolutionary movement.

In January 1774, though, Drayton believed he was a rising member of the royal government when the council appointed him to the South Carolina bench. An opening in the judiciary had occurred when assistant justice John Murray was killed in a duel. However, Lieutenant Governor Bull had difficulty filling the vacancy because Charleston lawyers were unwilling to abandon their practices for a post that only paid £300 annually, an amount much less than a lawyer could earn in a year. Anyone accepting this particular position, moreover, would almost certainly be replaced within a year by an Englishman. When Bull explained the predicament to the council on January 25, William Henry Drayton, "from a principle of public spirit," offered to fill the position. His fellow councilors reminded him that a trained lawyer from Britain would supersede him soon, but Drayton replied that he would not consider it a disgrace to be relieved by a "Gentleman who made the Law his particular study."

Drayton offered his services in this temporary position for at least three reasons. First, since Bull had done much to help further Drayton's career, it was only natural that he would want to extricate his beloved uncle from the quandary. Second, the backcountry circuits offered justices much public exposure and allowed them to expound their political views to the public from a position of authority, an opportunity that Drayton undoubtedly found appealing. Finally, as an ambitious young man, Drayton perhaps regarded this temporary position as an opportunity to prove his judicial skills—despite his lack of legal training—in hopes of receiving a similar permanent assignment in the future.

The council (particularly the placemen on it) also viewed Drayton's offer as an opportunity—one to rid themselves of a recalcitrant associate for at least three months of the year while he was riding the judicial circuit administering justice to backcountry bandits. They also hoped this temporary appointment to the bench might restore his attachment to the royal administration, and so "very readily and unanimously" approved him as a "fit person to be appointed to that office."[1]

The council's hope that Drayton's appointment to the bench would bring him closer to the royal fold backfired horribly. As with his service in the council, Drayton soon clashed with his associates in the judiciary. Neither awed by their legal learning nor self-conscious about his own judicial deficiencies, Drayton publicly questioned the legality of some of his colleagues' verdicts. He found Chief Justice Thomas Knox Gordon's judicial decisions and legal practices particularly offensive. In a case before the Charleston Court of Chancery, he openly protested Gordon's decision to let the governor cast a second and deciding vote, arguing that "no judge in the king's dominion had two voices on the same question." But the lawyer from Dublin refused to be corrected by a colonial with no legal training and stuck to his ruling. Attorney General Egerton Leigh was called in to settle the dispute

---

1. *SC&AGG*, 28 January 1774; South Carolina Council Journals 38: 12, SCDAH; Bull to Dartmouth, 11 February 1774, BPROSC 34: 9; Miscellaneous Records of South Carolina 32: 648, SCDAH.

and, according to Drayton, "at once silenced the learned Chief Justice." On another occasion Drayton charged Gordon with favoritism for admitting an Englishman into the South Carolina bar even though he lacked the required five years of legal training. The chief justice explained that "this gentleman came from England here *under a full persuasion that he had done enough*—and no man can pretend to say that the spirit and meaning of the rule has not been preserved." But Drayton firmly held to his charge, observing that "there are not wanting instances to shew this doctrine is not construed to extend to Americans." A much more serious criticism was Drayton's assertion that Gordon wrote judicial decisions in his chamber before even hearing the arguments, after which he would immediately "answer them from an opinion in his pocket."[2]

Gordon, who also served as a councilor, could not escape from Drayton's accusations in the upper house, either. Here the Carolinian "daily detected" the chief justice's "ignorance in the Law of Parliament." Nor were the associate justices exempt from Drayton's sharp comments. While on a tour of the upcountry circuit with Charles Coslett, for example, Drayton admonished his colleague on several occasions for making what he believed were grossly inaccurate judicial rulings.[3]

Gordon and Coslett were not the only royal officials Drayton believed were making decisions contrary to English law. In May 1773 Parliament passed the Tea Act to save the East India Company, one of Britain's largest businesses, from possible bankruptcy. The Tea Act was not so beneficial to Americans, though, who would still have to pay a duty on tea to England under the Townshend duties. They therefore viewed this measure as a clever trick to get colonists to pay an unconstitutional tax for revenue, income they feared the Crown would use to pay the salaries of royal officials, thereby making them independent of the colonial legislatures.

Believing that if Americans purchased the taxed tea, they would be admitting Parliament's right to impose taxes on them, radicals throughout the country quickly organized to oppose the legislation. Whig leaders in South Carolina beseeched their neighbors to resist this attempt to "raise a revenue out of your pocket *against your consent*—and to render assemblies of your rep-

2. The Answer of William Henry Drayton to the Remonstrance of Thomas Knox Gordon . . . , 3 October 1774, *DHAR*, 1: 43–5.
3. Ibid., 1: 78, 45.

resentatives *totally useless.*" In response, the Charleston Sons of Liberty and other radicals busied themselves disseminating propaganda and enacting a plan of opposition. Thus, when the *London* dropped anchor in Charleston harbor on December 1, 1773, with 257 chests of tea aboard, inhabitants of the capital were sufficiently aroused and vowed to prevent the landing of the offensive cargo. Three weeks later, however, the ship's officers caught the patriots off guard and quietly removed the tea under the cover of darkness and stored it in the dungeonlike basement of the Exchange in downtown Charleston. To prevent another such embarrassing event, the patriots on January 20 resolved to hold monthly general meetings to plot their strategy and generate a stronger protest.[4]

Although the many participants did not know it, these "General Meetings" held in the early months of 1774 marked one of the most important events in the coming of the Revolution in South Carolina. Gradually yet deliberately, the meetings assumed more and more permanency and eventually took on the qualities of a governing body. A forty-five member General Committee chaired by the extremist Christopher Gadsden conducted the chief business at the monthly gatherings. The committee was responsible for enforcing nonimportation and any other resolutions passed by the General Meeting. Entirely free of British control, this extralegal assembly soon became the voice of the people in South Carolina as well as the *de facto* legislature, performing many of the governing responsibilities that the assembly had been unable to carry out as a result of the impasse over the Wilkes fund controversy.[5]

The colonists' hostile response to the arrival of the East India tea, particularly Boston's destructive "tea party," alarmed the Crown. As the king and his cabinet saw it, Britain had a clear choice: either accept an act of anarchy and lose effective control of its colonies, or reassert British authority with a display of royal power. George III chose the latter approach, pressing Prime Minister North to be more resolute with the colonists. "I do not want to

4. *SCG*, 29 October 1773 and 6 December 1773; *SCG&CJ*, 1 February 1774; Walsh, *Charleston's Sons of Liberty*, 59; George C. Rogers Jr., "The Charleston Tea Party: The Significance of December 3, 1773," *SCHM* 75 (July 1974): 157–62.

5. William E. Hemphill and Wylma A. Wates, eds., *Extracts from the Journals of the Provincial Congresses of South Carolina, 1775–1776* (Columbia: South Carolina Archives Department, 1960), xvi; Poythress, "Revolution by Committee," 20–1; George E. Frakes, *Laboratory for Liberty: The South Carolina Legislative Committee System, 1719–1776* (Lexington: University Press of Kentucky, 1970), 119–21.

drive them [Americans] to despair," explained the king, "but to Submission, which nothing but feeling the inconveniences of their situation can bring their pride to submit to." Accordingly, between March and June 1774 Lord North steered through Parliament a series of four bills to punish and humiliate the recalcitrant Americans, especially the Bostonians. These measures closed the port of Boston, reduced the powers of self-government in Massachusetts, permitted royal officials to be tried in other colonies or in England when accused of crimes, and provided for the quartering of troops in the colonists' barns and empty homes. Quickly following on the heels of this offensive legislation was Parliament's passage of the Quebec Act, which the Americans considered just as horrifying, since it created a permanent civil government in the former French province without a popularly elected assembly and established Catholicism as the official religion. "[T]he die is now cast," wrote George III, "the Colonies must either submit or triumph."[6]

The Americans were not about to submit. By its establishment of a past record of retreat, the mother country encouraged, perhaps even enticed, the colonists to commit themselves to a position from which there was no escape. News of the Boston Port Act reached South Carolina in late May, and according to Bull, "raised an universal spirit of jealousy against Great Britain and of unity towards each other." The following week Charlestonians demonstrated their solidarity against what they termed the "crudest Policy that ever disgraced a British Senate" by refusing to celebrate the king's birthday, the largest annual celebration held in the colony. Although the Intolerable Acts had no direct effect on the province, South Carolinians believed it was part of a master plan by despotic ministers to bring, "one by one," the colonies into a "state of vassalage." One Carolinian warned his countrymen that "unless you unite in the most vigorous self-denying opposition," you will be "dragooned into . . . every Imposition of our Fellow Subjects, however arbitrary and cruel."[7]

In response to Parliament's passage of the Intolerable Acts, the South Carolina General Committee scheduled elections for representatives to a public meeting for July 6, 1774, to take steps necessary to preserve American liber-

6. Sir John Fortesque, ed., *The Correspondence of King George III* (London: Thomas Nelson, 1927), 3: 156, 130–1; David Ammerman, *In the Common Cause: American Response to the Coercive Acts of 1774* (Charlottesville: University Press of Virginia, 1974), 5–15, 130–2.

7. Bull to Dartmouth, 31 July 1774, BPROSC 34: 177; *SCG*, 6 June, 4 July, and 20 June 1774.

ties and to establish a union with the citizens of *"all our Sister Colonies."* This new extralegal assembly, described by the *South Carolina Gazette* as the "Largest Body of the most respectable Inhabitants that had ever been seen together upon any public occasion" in Charleston, met for three days to consider calls from Massachusetts to participate in a general nonimportation agreement and a Continental Congress. The mechanics and merchants could not agree on the "best means" to accomplish the first proposal, but there was widespread support for participation in a national congress to be held in Philadelphia in September. The delegates elected Thomas Lynch, Christopher Gadsden, Henry Middleton, and Edward and John Rutledge to represent South Carolina. Before adjourning, the assembly elected a ninety-nine-member General Committee and endowed it with the authority to perform any task necessary for carrying into effect the orders of the General Meeting. This enlarged General Committee held its first meeting on June 9 and thereafter continued to assemble every two weeks as the de facto government in South Carolina until March 1776, when royal rule ended.[8]

Although there is no evidence that Drayton attended the meeting held at Charleston in early July, he was greatly disturbed by the Intolerable Acts and longed to voice his protest against them. He had, of course, long been disgusted with Whitehall for appointing to local offices Crown sycophants over deserving Carolinians like himself. Thus when Parliament passed the five "tragic acts" against America, they "increased my alarms in [such] a progressive degree," he later wrote, that "it prevented my saying one word in favor of Administration." The "deliberate and systematic" nature in which Parliament passed these "series of oppressions" proved to Drayton that the king, his ministers, and the Commons were determined to either enslave America or bring it under an arbitrary government. Believing that the liberty and property of Americans were now at the "pleasure of a despotic power," Drayton would not allow even "an idea of *a risk of life itself*" to deter him from defending his "hereditary rights." Once the General Committee decided to send delegates to the Continental Congress, Drayton composed the twelve-thousand-word *Letter from Freeman of South Carolina to the Deputies of North*

8. *SCG*, 13 June, 1 July, and 11 July 1774; Christopher Gould, "South Carolina and the Continental Associations: Prelude to Revolution," *SCHM* 87 (January 1986): 30; Poythress, "Revolution by Committee," 47–51; Frakes, *Laboratory for Liberty*, 122–3.

America Assembled in the High Court of Congress at Philadelphia to offer a rationale for the delegation to follow in defending the American view of the British constitution.[9]

In writing the letter, Drayton followed the pattern set by the Declaration
of Rights of 1689. This political mimesis is not a reflection of a penchant for
precedent, but demonstrates that its author's cause for revolting against the
Crown is similar to the rationale for overthrowing James II during the Glorious Revolution. Like Parliament's 1689 proclamation, Drayton's loquacious
letter contained catalogues of grievances, rights, and resolves. Together they
offer a blueprint for the creation of a national government and constitutional
reform of the empire. As in his opposition to the South Carolina boycott five
years earlier, the English constitution and common law are still Drayton's
guide in formulating his arguments. The essay is littered with numerous references to the Magna Charta, the Petition of Right, the Act of Settlement,
colonial charters, and English statutes, to enable readers to "view the founda-
tions from which Americans build their claim of Rights and Liberties" (30).
Drayton also borrowed heavily from the ideas of such earlier English opposition writers as John Locke, Edward Coke, Robert Hooker, and William
Blackstone to support his assertions.[10]

Given his past opposition to the Whigs' 1769 nonimportation agreement
against Britain, Drayton was aware that people might misunderstand his
present protest and consider him "fickle and unsteady" in his political stand,
or, worse, that he was "influenced by disgust" at the Crown for bypassing
him for several royal positions in the local government (6). To correct any
idea that he had ever been "zealous for the [royal] prerogative," Drayton first
told his readers that the "*same Spirit* of indignation which animated me to
condemn popular measures in the year 1769 . . . actuates me in like manner,
now to assert my freedom *against the malignant* nature of the late five Acts of

9. Drayton, *A Letter from Freeman*, 5, 7–8. All subsequent citations to this work are given
parenthetically in the text.

10. Gerald Stourzh, "William Blackstone: Teacher of Revolution," *Jahrbuch fur Amerikastudien* 15 (1970): 193. The Declaration of Rights asserted that it was illegal to suspend or dispense
with the laws, collect taxes by prerogative, maintain a standing army without the consent of Parliament, interfere in parliamentary elections, tamper with juries, or impose excessive fines or
bail. The Petition of Right, a collection of public liberties exacted by the House of Commons
from Charles I in 1628, declared that no man shall be compelled to pay any tax, gift, loan, or
benevolence not voted by Parliament; that no free man shall be kept in prison unless upon a
specified charge; that soldiers and sailors shall not be billeted in private houses without the owner's consent; and that civilians shall not be subject to martial law.

Parliament" (5). It was his first principle, he explained, "not to proceed any further with any party than I thought they travelled in the *Constitutional highway*" (5). It was the British, through their constitutional innovation in recent measures passed against the American colonies, who were being untrue to the English constitution. In essence, Drayton was not revolting against the British constitution, but on behalf of it.[11]

According to Drayton, Parliament had swerved sharply off this legal lane with its passage of the Intolerable Acts, which he believed dwarfed the simple issue of taxation without representation resulting from the Stamp Act and Townshend duties. These coercive measures—"all unconstitutional, illegal and oppressive"—were a sweeping denial of the colonists' most treasured liberties. "The question now," exclaimed Drayton, "is not whether Great-Britain has a right to *Tax* America against her consent, but whether she has a constitutional right to exercise *Despotism* over America!" (7). In hopes of saving the colonies from "despotic" measures so "pregnant with horrible uproar and wild confusion" that they might compel Americans to "take up Arms against the Sovereign," Drayton created a blueprint for the reform of the British empire that denied Parliament's jurisdiction over the colonies (29, 4).

Of greatest concern to Drayton was Parliament's arbitrary removal of inherent liberties from the citizens of Massachusetts and Quebec, which he (along with many other Americans) feared could be taken away from the rest of the colonies too. If Whitehall could exercise despotic powers over one province, he asserted, "what fiction of argument shall prevent the same power being exercised over . . . all the Colonies in America, since the law considers them all but in one and the same light?" (22). To illustrate this point, Drayton graphically examined the one measure resulting from the Intolerable Acts that affected all the colonies: the Quartering Act, which allowed royal troops to billet themselves in private homes (with the owner's consent), barns, and public buildings. Not only was such a statute unconstitutional, he insisted, but it also encouraged frequent robberies, rapes, batteries, burglaries, and other assorted "barbarous cruelties." It was such "abominable vices and outrages" that had prompted Parliament to seek laws against the quartering of troops in 1628 in the first place, he exclaimed (28).

Some of Drayton's grievances against British imperial policy preceded the passage of the Intolerable Acts. He found particularly disturbing Parliament's

---

11. Gordon S. Wood, *The Creation of the American Republic, 1776–1787* (Chapel Hill: University of North Carolina Press, 1969; reprint, New York: W. W. Norton, 1972), 10.

persistent efforts to tax the American colonies without giving them representation in the House of Commons. Its assertion that the colonies were "virtually represented" was nullified in 1672, argued Drayton, when Parliament
granted representation to the County Palatine of Durham to justify taxing its
inhabitants (18). Legislation without the consent of the society "is no better
than a mere tyranny!" he underscored. (32). Equally tyrannical, according to
Drayton, was the Admiralty Court's power to issue general warrants to search
the property of any man not charged with a crime and Parliament's claim to
exercise "a power to bind the Colonies *in all cases* whatsoever," an authority
he believed it abusively and illegally flexed with its passage of the Intolerable
and Quebec acts (10–11).

In short, Drayton demanded that the British government treat Americans
equally under English law and denied that Parliament could exercise over the
colonies any powers which it could not exercise over Great Britain. "The
Parliament cannot there annihilate or constitute a Sovereign to Magna
Charta," Drayton argued, for "Magna Charta is such a fellow that he will
have no Sovereign." The colonists, as "subjects of English blood," automatically inherited all the rights of Englishmen both by blood and colonial charters granting them all the liberties, franchises, and privileges enjoyed in Britain. Relocation did not abrogate their rights as Englishmen, either, Drayton
added, because they all belonged to a composite whole. Anyone residing in
the British empire—whether or not they were of English descent—should
have the same rights as those living in England (slaves and Indians excluded,
of course). Drayton, for one, intrepidly vowed to oppose any attempt to "frit-
ter away" his birthright as an Englishman by an "artificial refinement" of
original judicial power, upon "principles of feudal sovereignty" (37).

Not all of Drayton's grievances involved English liberty. A complaint of a
more personal nature were the "troops of hungry placemen" overrunning
South Carolina (20). In part, Drayton was addressing this issue to refute preemptive accusations that he was writing the letter out of "disgust rather than
to principle" over recent news that the Board of Trade had nominated an Englishmen "regularly bred to the Bar" to replace him as assistant judge (6, n).
Drayton denied any disgust over this matter, or over previous snubs by the
Crown. His motivation for criticizing the Crown's policy of appointing
placemen to local offices, he maintained, was based on personal interest for
the colony's welfare—not his own. Previously, the Crown had filled the
council and judiciary with native men of independence. Now these important
positions were controlled by incompetent and ignorant "strangers from En-

gland," remarked Drayton, who, dependent upon the "smiles of the Crown for their daily bread," were more concerned in preserving their commissions than advancing the best interests of the province (18–19).

Previous historians have argued that the Crown's appointment of British dependents and fortune hunters to several local offices Drayton thought rightfully belonged to him explain his primary motive for abjuring the Crown and joining the patriot party. Granted, these rebuffs clearly offended Drayton, despite his repeated claims otherwise. Drayton felt that as an English-educated and financially independent man with vital interests in the welfare of his home province, he was just as qualified, and certainly more deserving, of many of the local positions held by placemen. Not only did he feel deprived of deserved rewards, but such deprivation threatened to undermine his local status. The Crown's scornful rejections incurred within him a feeling of inferiority and impotence and threatened his strong desire for fame and distinction. He naturally defended his honor and reputation as a gentleman of high social standing by angrily attacking the local placemen, whom he believed placed the royal prerogative above the welfare of the province.

However, these royal rebuffs were not enough to change Drayton from a loyal subject into a revolutionary; had they been, he would have joined the Whig party years earlier when these slights first occurred. Instead, the Crown's appointment of these placemen simply intensified within Drayton a feeling of Americanism and confirmed in his mind that the English were relegating Americans to second-class standing within the empire. Granted, these snubs and Drayton's subsequent quarreling with the foreign officeholders certainly made his road to revolution more volatile than most, but they did not serve as the most important catalyst transforming him from a royalist to rebel, as some historians argue. That Drayton switched allegiances only *after* Parliament passed the Coercive Acts, measures he believed flagrantly violated the English constitution and threatened to enslave Americans under a capricious and despotic government, strongly suggests that these punitive imperial acts, and not disgust with local placemen, was the most important factor causing his conversion.[12]

12. Robert M. Weir, "Who Shall Rule at Home: The American Revolution as Crisis of Legitimacy for the Colonial Elite," *Journal of Interdisciplinary History* 6 (spring 1976): 689–91; Timothy H. Breen, "Ideology and Nationalism on the Eve of the American Revolution: Revisions *Once More* in Need of Revising," *Journal of American History* 84 (June 1997): 30–5; Bertram Wyatt-Brown, "Honour and American Republicanism: A Neglected Corollary," in *Ideology and the Historians*, ed. Ciaran Brady (Dublin, Ireland: Lilliput Press, 1991), 52–3; Alan D. Watson,

*   *   *

Not content with merely uttering American grievances and asserting "ancient rights and liberties," Drayton devised a plan for restructuring the American political and judicial system that he believed would remedy many of the constitutional irregularities between the colonies and the mother country. He attributed much of the Anglo-American troubles to the lack of a permanent, independent, and middle branch of legislature—similar to the king's Privy Council—comprised of men "connected with the colonies by fortune" who would not be "subject to removal by [either] the *Crown* or [the] *People*." According to Drayton, this independent branch of government was an "essential part" of the English constitution to which the Americans had an "equitable right." Although he did not desire the creation of "Dignities, Lordships and Dukedoms" in America, Drayton nevertheless believed that a life peerage would give strength and stability to the colonial governments as effectively as an hereditary nobility did to that of Great Britain by creating a body of government independent of pressures and temptations from any source. But constitutional equity and effective government were not Drayton's only concerns in making this proposal. A more self-serving reason was his desire to protect the political power of local elites from both the "stretches of the Government party" and the "exuberances of Popular liberty" (4, 32–33).[13]

Another constitutional dilemma concerned Parliament's self-proclaimed right to tax and make laws for the colonies, a right Drayton denied altogether because America was not represented in the House of Commons. To solve the problem of representation, he proposed the creation of a national legislature, or "high court of assembly," in America with very limited authority. This body, with members selected from both houses of each colony, would have the power to collect and levy taxes to provide for the Crown's organization in North America and to pass legislation of a "general nature." These national laws would bind all colonies "in the same degree," Drayton explained somewhat enigmatically, but would not, he emphasized, impinge on each province's ability to regulate its internal policy (14–16).

As a jurist, Drayton was naturally concerned with the colonial judicial sys-

---

"Placemen in South Carolina: The Receiver Generals of Quitrents," *SCHM* 74 (January 1973): 27–30; Robert Barnwell Jr., "Loyalism in South Carolina, 1765–1785" (Ph.D. diss., Duke University, 1941), 18–9.

13. Bailyn, *Ideological Origins*, 278–83.

tem and sought to place it on an equal footing with that in Britain. He accordingly denied any legal authority to the governor and the council in each colony, just as the Crown and Privy Council in Britain were barred from any judicial power. Likewise, Drayton wanted American judges given life tenure in their posts just as their counterparts in England had enjoyed since 1701. A colonial judiciary consisting of independent judges chosen from natives was important to the protection of American liberties, according to Drayton. Undoubtedly influencing him in making this suggestion was the foreign placemen's control of the South Carolina judiciary, a circumstance that impressed upon him that an aggressive power in London ultimately controlled the institutions protecting his basic liberties.[14]

Drayton also attributed part of the present discontent in America to the lack of any constitutional courts of ordinary and chancery in the colonies, requiring Americans to present appeals to the distant king and Privy Council. This practice of conducting appeals in London was inconvenient, impractical, and a financial burden, maintained Drayton. He urged as a corrective measure the creation of courts of ordinary and of chancery in each province. However, Drayton did not advocate complete judicial autonomy for the colonies. These courts would direct appeals first to the respective upper legislative bodies and from there to the House of Lords, if required (33–36).[15]

As can be seen by this outline, Drayton's plan for national government was somewhat vague and lacking in detail. This was intentional. His objective in drafting the proposal was to encourage the Continental Congress to begin discussing the idea of a permanent American government. Because the Congress was composed of delegates from all the colonies, Drayton believed it was best able to devise a more detailed federal charter acceptable to most Americans. Despite the simplicity if his federal plan, it is much more than just a rudimentary restructuring of American government, offering as it does a complete reorganization of Great Britain's empire and the colonists' role in it. Drayton's blueprint would give Americans much greater autonomy, while dramatically limiting the ability of British authorities to meddle in American affairs. It would strip the king of all authority in the colonies, for example,

14. Carl J. Vipperman, "The Justice of Revolution: The South Carolina Judicial System, 1721–1772," in *South Carolina Legal History*, ed. Herbert A. Johnson (Spartanburg, S.C.: The Reprint Co., 1980), 239–40.

15. For a fuller discussion of Drayton's call for courts of ordinary and of chancery in America, see Joseph H. Smith, *Appeals to the Privy Council from the American Plantations* (New York: Columbia University Press, 1950; reprint, New York: Octagon Books, 1965), 210–2.

except his power to appoint individuals to royal offices, and limit the jurisdiction of the House of Lords to a legal role as a court of final appeals. In Drayton's model of the British Empire, Parliament would have no power to tax, legislate, "or in any shape to bind American Freeholders of the British Crown" (12). Its influence over the colonies was circumscribed to directing its foreign policy. In essence, Drayton was inviting Parliament to return to the same supervisory role it had exercised in the colonies before 1763.

According to Drayton, these fundamental changes in the traditional structure of the British Empire, along with an effective American union, were absolutely necessary if the colonists were ever to be secure in their liberty, property, and life goals from an increasingly aggressive and intrusive Parliament and royal ministry. Drayton believed his proposal to be a reasonable compromise to end the crisis between Britain and her American possessions. He knew the significant contributions the colonies had made to England's power and wealth and he feared the consequences to the empire if it lost America, with its three million inhabitants, vast territory, and profitable commerce. Thus he proposed what he hoped would be a practical solution. However, in making his proposal, Drayton was inviting Parliament and the ministry to return to the same supervisory role they had exercised in the colonies before 1763, a solicitation that leaders across the Atlantic were certain to reject with contempt. Although Drayton professed confidence in the Crown's willingness to eventually redress America's grievances, he cannot have been so naïve as to believe it would agree to his emasculating recommendations (which he hoped Congress would adopt). Given this, Drayton in making his proposal was perhaps attempting to advance the imperial contest to the next stage—civil war.

In a melodramatic peroration, Drayton claimed that America had played a significant part in making the British Empire the most powerful, glorious, and durable in recorded history. But instead of "parental tenderness," he wrote, "we experience a Step-Mother's severity—instead of justice, we receive marks of the most unfeeling ingratitude!" (44). Even the conquered island of Ireland received better treatment than America, complained Drayton. He therefore urged the delegates in Philadelphia to "boldly declare the Grievances and Rights of America" (47). If they did so, he had "entire confidence" that King George III would "preserve them from the Violation of their Rights." (14).

Drayton circulated his pamphlet far and wide. In addition to sending it to the fifty-five delegates meeting in Philadelphia's Carpenters' Hall, he shipped copies to Lords North, Shelburne, and the Earl of Dartmouth so that "they may see the State of Affairs in & the sentiments of America." Copies have also been found among the papers of Thomas Jefferson and George Washington. Despite *Freeman*'s wide dispersion, it is difficult to ascertain its influence on the Continental Congress. David Ramsay, a South Carolina physician, historian, and participant in the Revolution, maintained that the First Continental Congress virtually adopted the list of rights presented by Drayton as "The Bill of American Rights" sent to the king and Parliament. However, journal records of that assembly and published letters of its members do not mention any reference to Drayton's letter. This negligence is not a reflection of the delegates' views of the Carolinian's proposals, but rather a result of their inability to address formally the many suggestions made to them from all over America. Thomas Jefferson, Alexander Hamilton, and James Wilson all penned able (and familiar) arguments to the Continental Congress opposing parliamentary taxation and legislation over the colonies. Citizens from Suffolk County, Massachusetts, too, presented a set of resolutions (the Suffolk Resolves) to the Congress recommending outright resistance to the Intolerable Acts. Pennsylvania delegate Joseph Galloway also introduced a plan for imperial reorganization, which the congressmen addressed and narrowly defeated. Still, when the American Congress finally arrived at a compromise after five weeks of discussion, its general declaration denying Parliament any authority over the colonies except the right to regulate commerce was surprisingly similar to the one suggested in *Freeman*.[16]

Although *Freeman* did not receive the consideration from the Continental Congress that Drayton had hoped, South Carolina patriots appreciated his efforts and signified their approval with a "Public thanks." Even Henry Laurens, who had doubts about Drayton's recent conversion, admitted that the pamphlet was "not a bad thing & coming from a proselyte a good one." This acclaim and recognition greatly pleased Drayton, who, according to one local Crown officer, "publickly gloried" in being *Freeman*'s author. More importantly, though, the public letter to Congress signaled Drayton's official entrance into the American cause and revealed his intention to play an important role in it.[17]

16. Drayton to Dartmouth, 30 August 1774, BPROSC 34: 213–4; Drayton to Shelburne, 1 September 1774, Shelburne Papers, vol. 66, no. 623, CL; David Ramsay, *History of South Carolina* (Charleston: Walker, Evans, 1858), 2: 252.

17. Drayton to Shelburne, 1 September 1774, Shelburne Papers, vol. 66, no. 632, CL; *SCG*, 17 September 1774; Henry Laurens to George Appleby, 22 October 1774, *HLP*, 9: 599; Claim of Thomas Knox Gordon, American Loyalist Transcripts, 56: 419, NYPL.

Royal officials, on the other hand, were disgusted by *Freeman*, which they considered "full of the most seditious sentiments" and "altogether tending to excite a spirit of disaffection and rebellion in the Minds of his Majesty's subjects." One local placeman calling himself "Backsettler" was so upset with Drayton's "mad arguments" that he felt compelled to publish a thirty-six-page pro-administration pamphlet exposing the "imbecility" of *Freeman*. Perhaps the Crown officer most upset and disappointed by Drayton's public letter was his uncle, William Bull, who wrote Secretary of State Dartmouth that *Freeman* was "replete with sentiments so derogatory to the Royal Prerogative, the Authority of Parliament and the long established Constitution of Government in America, that it cannot fail to excite indignation." The lieutenant governor even considered removing his nephew from the council, but feared that such action would simply make Drayton a martyr in the "eyes of the discontented," whom "he has been courting with unwearied diligence." Instead, Bull forwarded a copy of *Freeman* to the secretary of state for his consideration. After reading this "very extraordinary performance," a perturbed Dartmouth notified Bull that higher officials would soon determine the proper discipline for "such conduct in a servant of the Crown."[18]

Drayton understood that his essay might "induce a letter of suspension" from the council. He therefore defended his allegiance in a letter to Lord William Shelburne, a member of the king's cabinet, in which he stressed the economic and social sacrifices he had made in supporting the British government during the nonimportation controversy. However, Drayton's ultimate allegiance was to the English constitution, not the Crown. Two days before writing Shelburne, he boldly proclaimed to Dartmouth that "having acquired my seat by the loyal sacrifice of a part of my fortune, I am content to lose it by the same steady adherence to the true principles of the Constitution."[19]

Two men who were unimpressed with Drayton's assault upon Britain's self-proclaimed authority over America were assistant judges Edward Savage and Charles Coslett, who claimed *Freeman* characterized foreign officeholders as

18. Claim of Thomas Irving, American Loyalist Transcripts, 56: 447–8, NYPL; Claim of Thomas Knox Gordon, ibid., 56: 419; *SCG*, 17 September 1774; A Backsettler, *Some Fugitive Thoughts on a Letter Signed Freeman, Addressed to the Deputies, Assembled at the High Court of Congress in Philadelphia* (South Carolina: 1774); Bull to Dartmouth, 31 August 1774, BPROSC 34: 210–1; Dartmouth to Bull, 2 November 1774, ibid., 34: 218.

19. Drayton to Shelburne, 1 September 1774, Shelburne Papers, vol. 66, no. 623, CL; Drayton to Dartmouth, 30 August 1774, BPROSC 34: 214.

"upstarts" who were dependent upon the "Pleasure of the Crown."[20] The two placemen confronted Drayton at his residence in Charleston on the morning of September 14 to find out if he was referring to them in his epistle. Drayton, seeing no reason why he should not "stand up for Freeman," told his two associates that his comments about placemen were of a general nature and not specifically directed against them. However, if they felt otherwise, he told Coslett and Savage that he was ready to give them the "*satisfaction which might be demanded of a Gentleman.*" Coslett, apparently surprised and shaken by this overture to a duel, replied that he did not feel the characterization applied to him because he owned a considerable estate back home in Ireland and was therefore far from "dependant upon the Smiles of the Minister." When Drayton exposed the absurdity of this assertion by asking the two Irishmen why they had traveled to the "far corners of the empire" for a lowly provincial post that paid a paltry £300 a year, Savage dropped all pretenses for their visit and loudly denounced the Carolinian as "a Publisher of Falsehoods, a Scoundrel, and no Gentleman." Drayton immediately realized that the true purpose of his colleagues' visit was to provoke a challenge and "frighten a Brother judge."

Coslett and Savage, whose political reputations had suffered considerably from Drayton's ceaseless public character assassinations, had a dual purpose in provoking this challenge with their nemesis: to redeem their honor and regain their prestige in South Carolina society; and to remove a political opponent by killing Drayton in a duel, thereby striking a blow at the American cause in the province. But Drayton did not easily frighten, nor did he tolerate aspersions on his honor. He therefore proposed that they immediately "settle the Affair like a Gentleman—by sword—a Gentleman's Weapon." However, disagreements over the particulars prevented this "honorable altercation" from occurring. Drayton persisted on "going alone to the Field," explaining that "I have long concluded never to be a Friend on such occasions, or to involve a Friend in the probable unhappy consequences." Judge Savage refused to meet Drayton on these terms. Before departing, however, the two Irishmen told Drayton that he would soon hear from them again. But Savage and Coslett would hear from Drayton first, via the *South Carolina Gazette.*

Drayton turned to the local press because he understood that leaders were dependent on the public at large for their personal honor and public career.

20. The following scene is taken from Drayton's published account in the September 17 issue of the *SCG.*

The detailed account of the preceding incident he published in the *Gazette* emphasized the foreign officeholders' "irregular" behavior while underscoring his own courageous stand against them. This public appeal about a private quarrel was a blatant attempt to influence public opinion in favor of himself. By publicly announcing his willingness to stand up to the unpopular placemen—even risking his life in this ritualized display of courage—Drayton was attempting to prove to his fellow Carolinians that he was a man of his word, a man of courage and principle, and thus deserving high political office. He was defending not only his honor but also his ability to claim power.[21]

Given the condescending attitude toward the common man that Drayton had displayed earlier, this open and shameless public pandering deserves further explanation. Early in the revolutionary movement, Whig leaders had recognized the importance of mass action as a tool of political opposition. In 1766, for example, the "meaner sort" played a significant role in South Carolina's successful resistance to the Stamp Act by ransacking the homes of stamp collectors and threatening to destroy the offensive paper if landed. Although Charleston's resistance to Britain's colonial acts was restrained compared to northern cities, the people were constantly ready to use more extreme measures in support of the American cause than most of its leaders desired. Following the mob's actions during the Stamp Act crisis, one patrician observer nervously noted that the "richer folks were terrified at a spirit which [they] themselves had conjured up."[22]

To keep a more watchful eye on the lower classes and diminish the chance of excessive violence, the revolutionary leaders gave the people a new direct role in shaping policy. During the 1769 crisis over the Townshend duties, the planters and merchants controlling the Whig party legitimized the role of the lower classes and augmented their authority within the resistance movement by allowing them equal representation in the extralegal "town meetings" and

21. Although Drayton's portrayal of this incident is skewed in his favor, it is probably generally accurate. In fact, Drayton boldly declared that his account of the episode was so true that neither Savage nor Coslett "will alter any material Part of what I have related as the Purport of the Conversation between us." He was right. Neither man denounced Drayton's version publicly in the newspapers or privately in their subsequent remonstrances against him.

For an excellent analysis of dueling in early America and its relationship to politics, see Joanne B. Freeman, "Dueling as Politics: Reinterpreting the Burr-Hamilton Duel," *W&MQ*, 3d ser., 53 (April 1996): 292–301.

22. *SCG*, 2 June 1766.

organizations created to enforce the boycott against British goods. With this taste of political power, the people lost some of their deferential and subordinate attitude. They were no longer content with simply being used as a pressure group or as puppets ready to perform to the whims of their aristocratic masters. Possessing their own interests and perspectives, the lower orders were quick to oppose their superiors when they found policy disagreeable. With these egalitarian developments, lowcountry aristocrats understood that political control could never again be exercised entirely on the basis of class prerogative or rightful privilege. Those desiring political influence in the revolutionary movement were now required to seek accommodation and acceptability from the public by catering to popular opinion. They therefore increasingly performed deeds and enacted programs intended to secure popularity.[23]

Whether he liked it or not, Drayton had to accept the democratic developments of the revolutionary movement if he wanted a prominent role in the American cause. Although he did not reveal his attitude toward these egalitarian tendencies at this time, Drayton's later writings and actions do suggest that he was willing to make some concessions to the common people in return for their support of the American cause. His highly injurious public debate over nonimportation in 1769 taught him that the lower classes could at times play an influential role in the Whig party. This realization does not necessarily reflect a changed attitude toward what Drayton believed was the common man's proper role in political affairs, just an awareness that popular approval could help him achieve a leadership role in the revolutionary government.

23. Arthur M. Schlesinger, "Political Mobs and the American Revolution, 1765–1776," *Proceedings of the American Philosophical Society* 99 (August 1955): 244–8; Gordon S. Wood, "A Note on Mobs in the American Revolution," *W&MQ*, 3d ser., 23 (October 1966): 638–9; Merrill Jensen, "The American People and the American Revolution," *Journal of American History* 57 (June 1970): 12–23; Pauline Maier, "The Charleston Mob and the Evolution of Popular Politics in Revolutionary South Carolina, 1765–1784," *Perspectives in American History* 4 (1970): 174–85; Mary C. Ferrari, "Artisans of the South: A Comparative Study of Norfolk, Charleston and Alexandria, 1763–1800" (Ph.D. diss., College of William and Mary, 1992), 73–95; Gordon S. Wood, *The Radicalism of the American Revolution* (New York: Knopf, 1992), 244–7; Jesse Lemisch, "The American Revolution Seen from the Bottom Up," in *Towards a New Past: Dissenting Essays in American History*, ed. Barton J. Bernstein (New York: Pantheon, 1968), 17–9; Walsh, *Charleston's Sons of Liberty*, 27, 30–6; Ronald Hoffman, "The 'Disaffected' in the Revolutionary South," in *The American Revolution: Explorations in the History of American Radicalism*, ed. Alfred F. Young (De Kalb: Northern Illinois University Press, 1976), 311–2.

Indeed, Drayton's aspiration for an influential position in the Whig party might have stemmed partly from a desire to help check the egalitarianism of the rebellion and ensure that the reigns of government remained firmly in the grasp of the wealthy and educated elite and partly from his continuing search for public distinction. The latter factor was the more influential, at least according to William Bull, who noted in a letter to Dartmouth in early 1775 that his nephew was "ever fond of appearing at the Tribunal of the Public." However, it must be stressed that Drayton's desire for fame was *not* a motivating factor in his joining the American cause, but merely in his desire to play a conspicuous role in the movement once he entered it. Drayton's letter to Congress and his later writings reveal that he was cognizant of the rebellion's importance not only for America, but for the entire world as a timeless example for all oppressed people. From his reading of classical authors such as Plutarch and Machiavelli, he knew that builders of empires and republics stood next highest to founders of religion in the annals of history. As he began to see the significance of the epochal events taking place around him, Drayton's desire for recognition became almost obsessive; he worked feverishly to secure influential berths in the revolutionary government so that he might build a "lasting monument" and earn the perpetual remembrance of posterity.[24]

Once Drayton joined the American cause, he immediately began selling himself to the people by taking every opportunity to publicly protest the Crown's imperial policies. This public pandering does not mean that Drayton was any less sincere in his support for the rebellion, just that he was not above using Britain's unpopular measures—or the placemen's equally unpopular attempts to enforce them—as a means to advance his position in the local revolutionary movement. By making resoundingly revolutionary speeches to the public and in the press, Drayton hoped to convince Whig leaders of his sincerity toward the American cause and the important contributions he could make to it, while at the same time transforming his public image among the common people as an elitist Crown supporter.

Edward Savage and Charles Coslett were not pleased to see Drayton's account of their private dispute in the Charleston newspapers. Having failed to seek satisfaction by sword, Coslett next attacked Drayton with a quill. He

---

24. Bull to Dartmouth, 22 February 1775, BPROSC 35: 23; Douglass Adair, "Fame and the Founding Fathers," in *Fame and the Founding Fathers: Essays by Douglass Adair*, ed. Trevor Colbourn (New York: W. W. Norton, 1974), 7–8.

sought the assistance of his fellow Irishman, Chief Justice Thomas Knox
Gordon, whom Drayton had earlier criticized for questionable decisions and
behavior both on the bench and in the council. The chief justice was eager
to assist Coslett, not only out of revenge but also because he believed that if
Drayton's conduct was "suffered to pass unnoticed" it would cause the royal
government to "soon fall into the lowest state of contempt."[25]

On September 21 Coslett and Gordon presented to Lieutenant Governor
Bull a brief yet caustic remonstrance maligning Drayton for his public letter
to the Continental Congress. This "impotent railer" has "so wantonly, so il-
liberally, and so falsely traduced" our character, complained the two judges,
that he portrays us as "totally unfit" for the office we hold. Specifically, the
two were upset with Drayton's accusation that they made decisions contrary
to the law from a "wicked and corrupt motive" to render themselves repug-
nant to the Crown. This characterization, claimed the Irishmen, had a "direct
tendency to raise groundless fears in the minds of his Majesty's subjects and
to alienate their affections from his sacred person." A man capable of such a
publication, they concluded, was not a proper person to serve the Crown.
They suggested that the lieutenant governor remove Drayton from office.[26]

The following day Bull presented Coslett and Gordon's remonstrance before the council for its consideration. Drayton promptly asked for a public
hearing on the merit of the charges made against him, but the lieutenant governor, ever aware of his nephew's desire for popular approval, refused his request. Forced to continue the dispute in the council, Drayton delivered a
lengthy defense before his colleagues in early October in which he asserted
that Coslett and Gordon, in making their charges, were only seeking to
avenge his earlier accusations that they were ignorant of the law and behaved
unprofessionally on the bench. Even their complaint against him reflected
these deficiencies, claimed Drayton, because it ignored the fundamental legal
right that a person is presumed innocent until proven guilty. In the same
breath, they have "accused me—evidenced against me—ascertained my
guilt—adjudged the nature of it—and in angry and passionate terms against
me, desired my condemnation and punishment!" Their behavior is "a more
violent prosecution than ever was exhibited in the Star Chamber!" Drayton
exclaimed, because it is based upon principles "arbitrary, oppressive and in-

25. Claim of Thomas Knox Gordon, American Loyalist Transcripts, 56: 420, NYPL.
26. The Remonstrance of Thomas Knox Gordon and Charles M. Coslett, 21 September
1774, *DHAR*, 1: 40–1.

imical to the liberty of the subject, to our happy constitution, and the American Freedom!" Since Coslett and Gordon's indictment was of such a "very criminal nature," Drayton requested a jury hearing on the matter. However, he still hoped the proceedings would not reach that stage and humbly implored his uncle to dismiss the Irishmen's baseless accusations against him.[27]

Coslett and Gordon considered ludicrous Drayton's "dilatory plea" for a jury trial. "Would Mr. Justice Drayton think it necessary before he discharged a bad servant to have the verdict of a jury for doing so?" asked the judges. He should not be so quick to ask for a trial in the first place, they added, for he might not get the desired verdict—"notwithstanding the gentleman's great popularity and the high degree of estimation he stands in with the public." Instead, the two placemen suggested the lieutenant governor, as the leading Crown representative in the province, should ascertain the conduct of one of the king's servants. Drayton's publication contained "indecent reflections" on both the king and his judges, they explained, by comparing the former to the Turkish Sultan and charging the latter with dishonesty and the "annihilation of popular rights." He is "sounding the trumpet of rebellion," cried Coslett and Gordon. Do not give up the king's prerogative to such a "special pleader," they told Bull, and decide for yourself "whether a man capable of such a publication is a proper person to serve his Majesty."[28]

Drayton's fall duties on the circuit courts prevented him from immediately answering Gordon and Coslett's rejoinder. Nevertheless, his judicial responsibilities gave him further opportunity to protest the Intolerable Acts and warn his fellow Americans of the impending danger to their liberties. In resoundingly revolutionary charges to grand juries of Camden, Cheraws, and Georgetown, Drayton "touched upon the nature and importance" of their "invaluable rights . . . which no time, no contract, no climate can diminish." However, Parliament's persistent efforts to impose taxes on Americans without their consent, he told the jurors, was seriously jeopardizing their rights. Without our "pious and unwearied endeavours to preserve these blessings,"

27. The Answer of William Henry Drayton to the Remonstrance of Thomas Knox Gordon and Charles M. Coslett, South Carolina Council Journals, 38: 215–7, SCDAH. The Court of Star Chamber, formally established under Henry VII in 1487, was a court at Westminster endowed with criminal and civil jurisdiction and the authority to inflict any punishment short of death. The court earned a notorious reputation with summary and iniquitous decisions accompanied by arbitrary and cruel punishments, excesses that eventually brought about its extinction in 1641.

28. The Reply of Thomas Knox Gordon and Charles M. Coslett, South Carolina Council Journals, 38: 231–7, SCDAH.

he warned, Americans can expect to fall under "a most cruel tyranny" similar to the one imposed by the Catholic Church—a despotism under which all Europe "groaned for many ages." Americans were now left with a clear and simple choice: "freedom or slavery!" Drayton admitted that other judges might consider his oration inconsistent with his duty to the British monarch, but "I know no master but the law," he proclaimed. "I am a servant not to the King, but to the Constitution." This conviction reveals that Drayton still considered himself a political conservative, defending the British constitution against threats to basic principles of English liberty. To him, the radicals were no longer in Charleston, but in London. Implying that the grand jurors should adopt a similar allegiance, Drayton instructed them to uphold the laws and rights within the constitution—"even at the hazard of your lives and fortunes."[29]

Drayton's judicial charges made a profound impression on his audiences. The grand juries of Camden and Cheraws presented as one of their grievances Parliament's claim to tax and make laws binding the American colonies "in all cases whatsoever" and pledged their lives and fortunes to defend the constitution. The grand jury in Georgetown even gave the judge an "elegant entertainment" where they drank numerous toasts to the king and to the success of Americans in defending their liberties. More importantly, Drayton's charges helped spread the patriot message and quash opposition from loyalists in those regions. To further circulate the revolutionary contents of his judicial address, Drayton ordered it published in the Charleston newspapers, another blatant attempt to further endear himself to the popular party and increase local enmity toward Parliament and the king's ministers.[30]

While Drayton's anti-administration speeches were rapidly making him a popular person among South Carolina patriots, they were turning him into a detestable figure among Crown officials in both Charleston and London. Associate justice Edward Savage was incensed with his colleague for inflaming the minds of a "rude and barbarous people" to the "highest pitch" with "virulent and seditious harangues." Lieutenant Governor Bull was so disturbed by his nephew's charges and the juries' replies that he sent the docu-

29. William Henry Drayton's Charge to the Districts of Camden and Cheraws, 5 and 15 November 1775, in Peter Force, ed., *American Archives: Consisting of a Collection of Authentick Records . . .* , *1774–1776* (Washington, D.C.: M. St. Clair Clarke and Peter Force, 1837–1853), 4th ser., 1: 959–62.

30. *SCG*, 12 December 1774; Force, *American Archives*, 4th ser., 1: 961; Alexander Gregg, *History of the Old Cheraws* (New York: Richardson, 1867), 216; Drayton, *Memoirs*, 1: 154.

ments to the British ministry for its consideration. An annoyed prime minister Frederick North presented them to the House of Commons on January 31, 1775. Two days later Secretary of State Dartmouth laid the same papers before the House of Lords. The king's ministers undoubtedly concurred with former governor Thomas Hutchinson of Massachusetts, who characterized Drayton's charges and the juries' presentments as a "publick nuisance."[31]

Drayton had scarcely left Charleston on his judicial circuit when William Gregory arrived from England with His Majesty's mandamus to replace Drayton as an assistant judge. Although he had expected Gregory's arrival, Drayton was still disappointed upon losing yet another royal post—especially one that brought him public respect and allowed him to propagate his views throughout the colony from a position of authority. Many South Carolinians were also upset with his displacement because it meant that British placemen would once again occupy all the province's top judicial positions—a sharp reminder that control over the institutions that protected their basic liberties lay not in Charleston, but in London. Lieutenant Governor Bull, on the other hand, was relieved to see Gregory's arrival, as he believed it would end the controversy between his nephew and the other judges and thus extricate himself from a delicate situation. Or so he thought.[32]

Drayton was not about to let the matter die so quietly, though. Anxious to resolve the charges against him before surrendering his commission, he pressed his uncle for a full public hearing on the chief justice's original complaint against him. Bull reluctantly set a hearing before the council for December 9. In anticipation of this trial, Drayton wrote and published a detailed and lengthy defense that simply repeated earlier complaints against his accusers and arguments defending *Freeman*. As it turned out, his efforts were for naught. The placemen councilors, suspecting that Drayton planned to use this public hearing as a vehicle to enlarge his reputation among the people while exposing them to further public insults, decided that it would be a waste of time and effort to further investigate the affair because the charges related to Drayton's competence was for a seat he no longer occupied. The council

31. Claim of Edward Savage, American Loyalist Transcripts, 57: 125–6, NYPL; *Journals of the House of Commons, 1547–1874*, 35: 85–6; *Journals of the House of Lords, 1509–1829*, 34: 301; Peter Orlando Hutchinson, ed., *Diary and Letters of His Excellency Thomas Hutchinson, Esq.* (London: Sampson, 1883), 1: 366.

32. Bull to Dartmouth, 19 December 1774, BPROSC 34: 225; Miscellaneous Records of South Carolina, 32: 144–5, SCDAH; Vipperman, "The Justice of Revolution," 239–40.

therefore issued a supersedeas officially ending the Carolinian's commission as an assistant judge.[33]

While Drayton was defending himself against written attacks by British placemen, Charleston was preparing itself against a possible invasion by the British navy. Ever since news arrived of the Crown's attempt to starve Boston into submission by blockading its port, inhabitants of the capital city had been in a "general and generous commotion" over the prospect of a similar fate. Although the British military presence in Charleston consisted only of an old, decrepit sixteen-gun sloop of war—the HMS *Tamar*—commanded by an even older second-rate captain and manned by an unstable and inefficient crew, Charlestonians still feared this situation could quickly change with London's increasingly hostile attitude toward the colonies. During the summer of 1774 city officials began fortifying the port and harbor, and the militia started augmenting its troops and holding more frequent drills. Officials in other parts of the colony were also forming and training companies of light infantry in case the rebellion spread into the interior.[34]

Whig leaders were also preparing for a possible confrontation with Great Britain. When Thomas Lynch, Christopher Gadsden, Henry Middleton, and the two Rutledges returned from Philadelphia on November 6 with details of the resolutions adopted by the Continental Congress, the General Committee wasted no time calling an election for another "General Meeting of the Inhabitants" to convene in Charleston on January 11, 1775. The purpose of the gathering was to consider the Congress's call for the creation of a Continental Association boycotting British goods, the scheduling of a second Continental Congress, and additional regulations "as shall be thought proper." As a result of Drayton's patriotic charges to the backcountry, voters in the Saxe-Gotha region (roughly present Lexington and Calhoun Counties) elected him to represent them in this convention.[35]

On January 11 Drayton and 205 delegates from across the province convened in Charleston, a meeting described by the *South Carolina Gazette* as

33. Drayton, *Memoirs*, 1: 152, 158–9; The Rejoinder of William Henry Drayton, *DHAR* 1: 55–70.

34. Charge of William Henry Drayton to the Districts of Camden and Cheraws, 15 November 1775, in Force, *American Archives*, 4th ser., 1: 959; John Griffiths III, "'To Receive Them Properly': Charlestown Prepares for War" (master's thesis, University of South Carolina, 1992), 39–57.

35. *SCG&CJ*, 15 November 1774; *JPC*, 7.

"the fullest and most complete Representation of the whole Colony that ever was, or perhaps ever will be obtained." After eight days of sometimes heated deliberation, the delegates finally agreed on four proposals: to send Christopher Gadsden, Thomas Lynch, and Edward Rutledge to the Second Continental Congress, to encourage all inhabitants to learn the "use of arms," to create new electoral districts in the backcountry, and to adopt Congress's intercolonial commercial boycott (or Association) against British goods. To enforce the Association and implement the resolutions of the continental and provincial legislatures, the delegates created a series of extralegal committees in villages, hamlets, and parishes throughout the colony. With the creation of this provincial legislature and the subsequent local enforcement committees, the revolutionaries managed to complete their usurpation of the royal government.[36]

Lieutenant Governor Bull desperately wanted to halt this rebellious activity, but with a lower house dominated by revolutionaries and a discredited and undermanned upper house unable to provide acceptable solutions to the problems of disloyalty, he realized that any efforts on his part would be futile. His position was further weakened by the fact that he was a "lame duck" executive, waiting for Lord William Campbell to replace him. Bull therefore made no real effort to contain the rebels, feeling that any action on his part would only create a "fruitless altercation" and expose himself to insults. Instead, he decided to simply remain an "unconcerned spectator" at his Ashley Hall plantation while "waiting with anxious impatience" for the arrival of Campbell. This partially explains why loyalists in the colony managed only an unorganized and feeble response to the patriots' defiance during this early stage of the rebellion. By the time Bull's replacement arrived in June 1775, the "king's friends" were in the "lowest state of despondency," according to one Crown officer, "expecting every moment to be drove from their occupations and homes and plundered of all they have earned."[37]

Ironically, while Drayton was helping to overthrow royal rule in South Carolina, he was also serving King George III as an official in the council. Not

36. *SCG*, 23 January 1775; *JPC*, 29, 18; Drayton, *Memoirs*, 1: 173.

37. Bull to Dartmouth, 4 January 1775, BPROSC 35: 3–4; Alexander Innes to Dartmouth, 3 June and 16 May, 1775, in B. D. Bargar, ed., "Charles Town Loyalism in 1775: The Secret Reports of Alexander Innes," *SCHM* 63 (July 1962): 131, 129; William Campbell to Thomas Gage, 1 July 1775, Thomas Gage Papers, CL; Carol R. Cunningham, "The Southern Royal Governors and the Coming of the American Revolution, 1763–1776" (Ph.D. diss., State University of New York–Buffalo, 1984), 262; Frakes, *Laboratory of Liberty*, 125.

surprisingly, Drayton's duplicity, coupled with Gordon's role in having the Carolinian removed from the bench, created a flammable atmosphere in the upper house. Tempers soon ignited in early February over the continuing feud regarding the assembly's contribution to John Wilkes. On the second of that month the Commons passed a Counterfeiting and Reviving Act with the intention of forcing the council to pass a Duty Act (which would expire at the end of the session) without the objectionable clause demanded by the king's additional instruction. If the upper house blocked the bill, it would deprive the colony of all its revenue. When the bill came up for its third and final reading, the placemen in the council still had not decided to pass or reject it. They further contrived a clever scheme to temporarily delay a decision on it until February 8 by using the pretense that enough members were not present to form a quorum—a technicality which had never before detained the passage of a bill. When the appointed day arrived the placemen again procrastinated on the same pretext. At this point Drayton became fed up with this stonewalling and entered into "a warm debate" with his colleagues in which he cast "many insults and indignities" against them, particularly his archnemesis Thomas Knox Gordon. But the Carolinian was simply wasting his hot breath. The motion to postpone the bill easily passed.[38]

Never content with voicing his dissent only privately, Drayton entered a virulent protest the following week in his favorite venue, the *South Carolina Gazette*. Drayton labeled the council's behavior "pregnant with mischief" because one of the absent members had left his important duties at the upper house to attend a frivolous dinner engagement. Such intentional obstruction was "wanton sporting" with the public welfare and could continue, Drayton exclaimed, "*de die in diem.*" This exposure of his colleagues' political gamesmanship compelled the council to pass—reluctantly—the Counterfeiting and Reviving Act, the first bill it had sent to the executive in more than five years and the last enacted under the royal government.[39]

The placemen on the council were infuriated with Drayton for forcing their hand on this decisive issue and quickly set into motion a new scheme to have him removed from the upper house. On February 11 Gordon delivered

38. Drayton, *Memoirs*, 1: 210; *DHAR*, 1: 71. According to Henry Laurens, Drayton "O'waced the Chief Justice" with a vulgar verbal assault. The term "whac" as used in the eighteenth century carried a connotation of vulgarism (Henry Laurens to John Laurens, 18 February 1775, *HLP* 10: 71, 8 n. 1). The Reviving Act continued thirty-seven acts for one additional year.

39. *SCG*, 13 February 1775; Drayton, *Memoirs* 1: 210–1, 234–5; Cooper and McCord, *Statutes at Large*, 4: 331–6.

in the council chamber a "violent invective" against the Carolinian, charging him with using his post as assistant judge to "excite a most dangerous Spirit of Sedition and Rebellion in the Minds of His Majesty's Subjects" and frequenting revolutionary assemblies where he "openly abated the designs of the Malcontents" by providing confidential information from the upper house "to disconcert the measures of Government." The other placemen agreed and "strongly supported" Gordon's motion.

Drayton was neither surprised nor offended by his colleague's motion. Indeed, the Carolinian told the council that he considered it an honor to be suspended from the group by men so "obnoxious to the whole people." Drayton was not apologetic about his annoying behavior toward the other councilors, either, openly admitting that he enjoyed attacking them as it served to "evince his attachment to his country." In any event, if his anti-administration conduct warranted his suspension, Drayton disdainfully told the placemen, then Gordon's ignorance of the law and malfeasance as chief justice certainly merited his dismissal as well.

Hereupon Gordon "clamorously interrupted" Drayton and presented the draft of an address penned by John Stuart—whose powers as councilor were supposed to be limited to Indian affairs—on behalf of the other placemen, officially proposing the Carolinian's suspension. In justifying its recommendation, the council maintained that Drayton had for a long time been guilty of "many insults and indignities" toward fellow councilors, as well as "outrageous breaches of privilege committed against this House." The council further explained that it had waited to make a formal complaint until it was "thoroughly convinced" that Drayton's conduct demonstrated a "determined purpose" to "destroy all Confidence of the people in this House" and "subvert the Constitution and unhinge Government." After reading the censure, Gordon called for a vote on the issue. With Drayton as the lone native in attendance, the measure easily passed. The council then sent its proposal to Lieutenant Governor Bull for his consideration.[40]

However, Bull was reluctant to suspend his nephew and dilatorily requested the council to provide him with the facts of the matter. Meanwhile, Drayton prepared a defense and submitted it to his uncle. In it, he explained that the upper house had fallen into contempt in proportion to the increase

40. Drayton, *Memoirs*, 1: 211–2; Claim of Thomas Knox Gordon, American Loyalist Transcripts, 56: 419–20, NYPL; Claim of Thomas Irving, ibid., 56: 447–8; South Carolina Council to William Bull, 11 February 1775, BPROSC 35: 32–3; *SCG*, 13 February 1775; *DHAR*, 1: 71.

of incompetent and dependent placemen appointed to it, not, he emphasized, as a result of his recent attacks on certain members of that body. In concluding, Drayton confidently asserted that the people would view his actions as a vigorous defense of the constitution, despite his accusers' charge that he had a determined purpose to subvert it.[41]

On February 22, the upper house brought forth the detailed report requested by the lieutenant governor. In addition to their previous allegations, the placemen accused Drayton of violating council rules of "decency and moderation" by throwing out "very illiberal charges and invectives" against a particular member, revealing its proceedings to revolutionary committees to which he belonged, denying the body to be an upper branch of legislature, and publishing antigovernment literature. Drayton had done such a superb job promoting himself to the people, the report concluded, that all these accusations "are facts of such public notoriety that your Committee apprehend they cannot be unknown to any intelligent person in Charles Town."[42]

The serious implications of these charges and the conspiratorial manner in which the placemen presented them finally motivated the other natives on the council—John Drayton and Barnard Elliott—to assist Drayton in his solitary stand against the foreign officeholders. Personal reasons had prevented them from joining the fray sooner. Elliott, although actively involved in the revolutionary movement and possessing a fiery and sometimes violent temper himself, was hesitant to aggravate the already volatile situation in the council out of respect for Bull, a close personal friend to whom he owed a substantial debt.

John Drayton, on the other hand, was nearly sixty years old and more interested in managing his large landholdings from his mansion at Drayton Hall than participating in politics. His keen interest in his plantations was, in part, an attempt to recover what he considered were exorbitant financial expenditures made by his ill wife, Margaret, who had spent nearly two years in Britain in an unsuccessful attempt to regain her health. During her convalescence she spent nearly £900, most of it on their spoiled and recalcitrant son Glen who was doing poorly at a preparatory school in Britain. When Mrs. Drayton refused her husband's demands to return Glennie home, John Drayton angrily responded by refusing to allow his wife to draw any further

41. *DHAR*, 1: 71–2; *SCG*, 13 February 1775.
42. South Carolina Council Proceedings, 22 February 1775, BPROSC 35: 39.

funds in his name. This punitive act forced Margaret to live the last months of her life in near poverty. She died in July 1772, away from her family, friends, and the splendor of Drayton Hall. Still, Drayton was exasperated over his late wife's extravagant expenditures and complained to his brother-in-law James Glen that his now-deceased sister had done him a "cruel injustice."[43]

If John Drayton's insensitive remark to Glen did not destroy their twenty-year friendship, his crass attempt to blackmail him to avoid repaying his brother-in-law the £2,600 reimbursement for the education of the Drayton boys in Britain certainly did. Matters came to a head in June 1773 when Glen was arrested for debt. He pleaded with Drayton to send the money owed him, pitiably adding that he could get no more coal until he had paid his long-overdue bill and that he expected similar treatment from every other person to whom he was indebted. These emotional appeals had little effect on the insensitive and self-centered Drayton, who was no longer concerned with meeting his financial obligations to Glen now that all his family members in Britain had either died or returned home by 1773. When Glen threatened to make a formal legal demand for the money, Drayton played upon his brother-in-law's love for the Drayton boys by informing him that such action would be "*very* injurious in its consequences to your nephews." Glen was shocked that Drayton could be so wicked as to use his "dearest nephews" as extortion to avoid paying the money spent on them. "My heart bleeds for you," Glen wrote his brother-in-law. "God Almighty be your Protector!" Such sentiments failed to move the hard-hearted Drayton, who never repaid the debts owed to his loyal and ever-generous in-law.[44]

While not busy cursing his deceased wife or blackmailing his charitable brother-in-law, John Drayton was preoccupied with wooing sixteen-year-old Rebecca Perry, whom he happily took as his fourth wife in March 1775. William Henry Drayton was not so pleased with this marriage as children from it would considerably reduce his already declining inheritance. He therefore strongly discouraged his father from entering the union, not mentioning his underlying selfish motives but emphasizing the scandal and embarrassment it would bring to the family. As Drayton feared, the age difference of more than

43. John Drayton to James Glen, 10 September 1773, Glen Papers, SCL; Griffin, "The Eighteenth Century Draytons," 202–4.

44. James Glen to John Drayton, 24 August 1774, John Drayton to James Glen, 8 December 1775, and James Glen to John Drayton, May 1775, all in Glen Papers, SCL; Griffin, "The Eighteenth Century Draytons," 311–4.

forty years between the prospective bride and groom provoked gossip among the South Carolina gentry. Even the fastidious Henry Laurens could not resist reporting this "droll coupling" to relatives in England. In the end, Drayton's forceful arguments had little influence with his father, who "would [only] please himself," Laurens noted.[45]

On February 22, 1775, John Drayton and Barnard Elliot set aside their personal interests and filed a vigorous and caustic dissent against the placemen's report calling for William Henry Drayton's suspension. Claiming it would be too time-consuming to address every objection in an account "Unparliamentary in almost every line," the native councilmen concentrated their dissent on two objections: first, that Drayton was correct in asserting that the council was not an upper branch of the legislature; and second, that the contents of his *Freeman* essay did not warrant suspension from the council. To dismiss him would only place the office of councilor upon a tenure of so arbitrary a nature that it could never again be considered "worthy the attention of an independent American."[46]

John Drayton's belated aid to his son in this controversy demonstrates at least some approval in the younger man's behavior. But this brief alliance probably did little to heal the estranged relationship between the two. Drayton was still angry at his father for largely disinheriting him and refusing him financial assistance when he most needed it. He responded by rarely visiting, conduct that caused the disheartened patriarch to lament that he was "very unhappy" with his eldest son. Drayton's resentment toward his father may help explain his decision to join the revolutionary movement. As one authority of the Revolution observed over thirty years ago, "[w]e must . . . eventually dissolve the distinction between conscious and unconscious motives, between the Revolutionaries' stated intentions and their supposedly hidden needs and desires." One of Drayton's "unconscious motives," or desires was his need for approval—to be noticed by both the king and his father. His trip to England in

45. *SCG*, 27 March 1775; Henry Laurens to John Laurens, 18 February 1775, *HLP*, 10: 72.

46. In making the assertion that the council was not an upper house, the natives were expressing their frustration at the Crown, who continued to ignore earnest requests for some sort of constitutional measure granting the council the right to serve as an upper house of the legislature. The king's silence on the matter, they argued, plainly revealed that he did not believe such a claim was warranted. The dissent by John Drayton, William Henry Drayton, and Barnard Elliot can be found in *SCG*, 27 February 1775; Drayton, *Memoirs*, 1: 240–2; and BPROSC 35: 40–3.

1770 and the publication of *The Letters of Freeman* the following year was at least in part an attempt to gain the approval of the former, while pursuing high political office and naming his first son John can be viewed as efforts to procure the blessing of the latter. There is no indication that the notice or the approval were ever given by either party. And as the Virginian Richard Henry Lee observed, "nothing can be more certain than allegiance and protection are reciprocal duties." When both these paternal authorities failed to reward, or even notice, his dutiful loyalty to them, Drayton must have felt a terrible sense of betrayal and resentment.[47]

Possibly the most important element in the reciprocal relationship between father and son was John Drayton. Psychological studies on such revolutionary personalities as Vladimir Lenin, Leon Trotsky, and Mohandas Gandhi show that revolutionaries frequently possess unresolved ambivalence toward their parents, specifically their fathers. According to this theory, the psychic relationship of revolutionaries to their fathers is characterized by intense feelings of both love and hatred. As young men, these types possess strong feelings of admiration for their fathers, but when privileges are withheld, the potential revolutionaries develop strong aggressive feelings toward their parents. This love/hate relationship in turn creates great internal conflict between basic drives and feelings of guilt. To free themselves of this internal psychic anxiety, the insurrectionists displace, or externalize, the personal conflict by projecting their feelings of hatred onto some overriding and denying authority (e.g., the king) and their love onto brother revolutionaries. In this way the hate for their father can be expressed with much less guilt.[48]

Granted, this psychological reductionism does not account for the great variety of revolutionary personalities. At least in Drayton's case, though, it may offer a partial explanation of the intense hatred he had for British authorities and the zeal with which he immersed himself in the American cause. Historians have recognized the importance of anger as a factor compelling

47. Gordon S. Wood, "Rhetoric and Reality in the American Revolution," *W&MQ*, 3d. ser., 23 (January 1966): 16; Robert M. Weir, "Rebelliousness: Personality Development and the American Revolution," in Jeffrey Crow and Larry Tise, eds., *The Southern Experience in the American Revolution* (Chapel Hill: University of North Carolina Press, 1978), 36; Bruce Mazlish, "Leadership in the American Revolution: The Psychological Dimension," in *Library of Congress Symposia on the American Revolution* (Washington, D.C.: Library of Congress, 1974), 121–31. Charles Drayton also paid few visits to his father. John Drayton to James Glen, 13 August 1772 and John Drayton to James Glen, 6 February 1773, Glen Papers, SCL.

48. Isaac Kramnick, "Reflections in Revolution: Definition and Explanation in Recent Scholarship," *History and Theory* 11, no. 1 (1972): 57–60.

men to jeopardize their lives and fortunes in risky revolutions. "It is just the recognition of this resentment that is so often missing from our accounts of the Revolution," remark Edwin Burrows and Michael Wallace, "so often buried beneath the weight of competing doctrine and interest that it becomes difficult to imagine the event as much more than a polite disagreement among gentlemen." But Drayton, like many Americans, was "boiling mad" at England for continuing to pass legislation robbing Americans of their personal dignity, their self-respect, and their autonomy. Some historians argue that without this hostility the colonists would not have rebelled against the mother country.[49]

Whether or not John Drayton's belated support of his son helped to breach the estrangement between the two, one thing is certain: it failed to help the younger Drayton's situation. In fact, the lieutenant governor believed Drayton and Elliott's report contained expressions and insinuations so disrespectful of the king that it possibly was another fact that merited their suspension. However, Bull prudently held off dismissing the only remaining natives on the council, afraid that such action would only incite further discontent among the people. The royal government in the province was so close to being nonexistent anyway, he explained to Dartmouth, that it did not matter who sat in the upper house. Nevertheless, Bull considered William Henry's earlier defense to be more a "proof and aggravation" of the charges against him than a refutation, and reluctantly sent his nephew a curt message on March 1 suspending him from the council.[50]

However, Drayton did not lament the loss of his council seat, which had become an impotent post by this time. Instead, he boasted that his suspension placed him in a "favorable light with the public" and added to his "little reputation." To further inflate his fame, Drayton published a garrulous and rather tiresome tirade against the placemen councilors, which simply repeated earlier complaints and accusations against them and questioned the council's right to sit as an upper house of the legislature.[51]

Nor was Drayton upset with the lieutenant governor for taking the place-

49. Edwin G. Burrows and Michael Wallace, "The American Revolution: The Ideological and Psychology of Revolution," *Perspectives in American History* 6 (1972): 294; Weir, "Rebelliousness," 38; Barnwell, "Loyalism in South Carolina," 18–9.

50. Bull, *Oligarchs*, 212; Bull to Drayton, 1 March 1775, *DHAR*, 1: 82; Bull to Lords Commissioners for Trade and Plantations, 8 March 1774, BPROSC 35: 29; Drayton, *Memoirs*, 1: 243.

51. Drayton to John Stuart, 29 June 1775, BPROCO 5/76, p. 329; *SCG*, 6 March 1775.

men's side in the dispute. His "respect and attachment" for his uncle was so strong, he said, that he refused to contest the suspension. Still, Drayton felt that he had done "nothing unbecoming an American" and wanted to clear his name and prove that he was "not a Criminal subject" as his accusers charged. To that end, he wrote Dartmouth explaining that his dismissal from the council was simply a vendetta Chief Justice Gordon held toward Drayton for questioning his judicial decisions and "daily detecting his ignorance in the law of Parliament." Once the ministry had examined all the facts related to the case, the Carolinian felt confident that it would see through "so superficial a gentleman" and overrule the suspension. Such posturing aside, Drayton knew that Whitehall would not grant him back his council seat. Nor did he want it, for he was already deeply immersed in the American cause.[52]

Drayton's decision to join the revolutionary movement was a fairly quick process, occurring in little more than two years from the time he took his seat in the council in April 1772 to the publication of his *Freeman* essay in August of 1774. Because there is no surviving correspondence surrounding Drayton's life at this time, it is difficult to determine how difficult the conversion was for him. That he changed sides so quickly suggests that he may not have gone through much anguish. Earlier evidence, too, lends credence to this conjecture. As noted in chapter 3, Drayton's loyalty toward the royal prerogative was probably quite limited as represented in his stand against certain elements of the local boycott in 1769, a position that demonstrated more a defense of individual liberties than support of parliamentary authority over the colonies. And though he received a position in the upper house in 1770, the Crown's appointment of placemen to two other offices he desired diminished much of the gratitude Drayton felt toward the British ministry. Intensifying his resentment over these slights was the fact that many of these placemen were Irishmen, whom Carolina's elite considered their social inferiors. Drayton became even more disgruntled with the Crown when he discovered that these "worthless poor rascals" ranked royal authority above the province's welfare. Thus when Parliament passed the Intolerable Acts threatening to, in Drayton's words, "exercise despotism over America," he claimed that he could no longer support Britain's imperial policy.[53]

52. Drayton to Dartmouth, 15 March 1775, *DHAR*, 1: 78–81.
53. Drayton later insisted that the passage of the Intolerable Acts was the deciding factor in his decision to join the American cause. See Drayton, "An Address to the Inhabitants of the

This assertion that Parliament's attack on Americans' constitutional rights was the deciding factor in his decision to switch allegiances is supported by a recollection from Charleston lawyer Alexander Garden, who observed that his friend was "too honest and proud in spirit" to "obey the dictates of a power daily encroaching on the liberties of the people," measures he believed were intended to "reduce them to submission" and which would have forced Americans to "lick the dust beneath the boot that spurned" them.[54] Certainly no bootlicker, Drayton publicly protested Britain's punitive measures and fought with its unpopular agents in the colony. This acrimonious conduct made him into one of the province's most zealous standard bearers of American interests and garnered him respect and approval from both the masses and Whig leaders—something he failed to secure from either the Crown or his father. In short, America's rebellion provided Drayton with a larger purpose in life, a new focus for his abundant energies and abilities, and hope for a future where the local gentry's control of provincial affairs and the colony's welfare were no longer threatened by either the Crown or its pretentious placemen.

Frontier Settlements," 6 December 1775, "Journal of the Second Council of Safety," SCHS *Collections* (Charleston: SCHS, 1859), 3: 56.

54. Alexander Garden, *Anecdotes of the Revolutionary War in America* (Charleston: A. E. Miller, 1822; reprint, Spartanburg, S.C.: The Reprint Co., 1972), 183.

REVOLUTIONARY JUGGERNAUT

With his last remaining tie to the Crown cut in March 1775, Drayton embraced the American cause with the enthusiasm of a recent convert. His enormous zeal, proven abilities, and patrician heritage soon earned him one top position after another in the nascent Whig government, so that by early June he had risen to become one of the "Five Rulers" of Charleston. In fact, until his appointment in late July to go on a mission to the backcountry, no other patriot held as much power, or wielded it with as much vigor, as did Drayton. As a member of all the important revolutionary assemblies and committees and serving as chairman of several, he displayed tremendous enthusiasm in obtaining crucial arms and ammunition for revolutionary forces at home and abroad, arousing patriotism within his fellow South Carolinians, crushing local opposition, spoiling British machinations, and helping plan the defense of the colony. However, Drayton did not acquire his enormous influence all at once. He first had to prove his loyalty to Whig leaders, like Henry Laurens, who remained suspicious about the authenticity of his recent conversion.[1]

Two weeks after his suspension from the council, Drayton was given a chance to further demonstrate his devotion to the American cause. This opportunity came in the form of a perceived attempt to break the Continental

1. Joseph Manigault to Peter Manigault, 4 June 1775, Manigault Family Papers, SCL. The other Rulers, according to Manigault, were Arthur Middleton, Charles Pinckney, William Tennent, and James Parsons.

Association. In March 1775, Robert Smythe, a Charleston merchant returned from London, asked the Committee of Observation (the authority created to adjudicate matters arising out of this boycott adopted by the Continental Congress) for permission to bring into the province his household furniture and two horses—personal articles he had used while residing in England. Uncertain about the legality of this request, the committee referred the matter to the parent General Committee, which decided that since the articles were previously acquired property that Smythe did not intend to sell, he could land them even though they came from England.

News of this decision spread rapidly through Charleston. The next day a large crowd gathered in "universal commotion" over the judgment. Many feared that if the ruling were implemented, it would brand South Carolina as a violator of the Continental Association and, more importantly, might destroy the nonimportation movement once it became generally known that Smythe had received preferential treatment. Spurred on by cries from the Sons of Liberty that "the Association was broken," hundreds of Charlestonians gathered along East Bay petitioning a reversal of the General Committee's ruling. Some fanatics even threatened to kill the horses if they were landed. With the public violently demanding strict adherence to the boycott, the General Committee reconvened on March 18 to reconsider its decision.[2]

In a room packed tightly with seventy committeemen and a crowd of excited townspeople, Christopher Gadsden opened discussion by moving to reverse the decision on the grounds that it violated the Association; that it would alarm and alienate the northern colonies, who would charge South Carolina with breaking the boycott; and, most importantly, that it angered the people. However, Edward Rutledge, Thomas Lynch, Rawlins Lowndes, and other conservatives countered Gadsden's oration by urging the General Committee not to surrender its authority to an intemperate populace. To do so would undermine that body's credibility, they argued, and therefore greatly weaken the revolutionary movement in the province. Moreover, if the committee adhered to the letter of the Association instead of its spirit, then the patriots could not import essential arms and ammunition from England.

Drayton strongly disagreed with this reasoning. In a protracted, demagogic speech addressed more to the civilian observers than his fellow committee members, he deliberately roused the audience's venomous passions by

2. Maier, "The Charleston Mob," 180–1; Richard Walsh, "The Charleston Mechanics: A Brief Study, 1760–1776," *SCHM* 60 (July 1959): 141–3.

reminding the General Committee that it was foremost a "servant of the public." As such, the committee's primary duty was to satisfy its constituents, who, he argued, were "always right on all public and general questions." According to Drayton, there was no difference between the townspeople's petition to the General Committee to reverse the Smythe decision and America's application to the king to rescind the Coercive Acts. Both appeals were built upon enormous popular agitation. If the committee refused to revoke its ruling because it feared that such a reversal would bring it into contempt, asked Drayton, could not the king make a similar argument against America's request? At any rate, it was ridiculous to believe that the public would suddenly lose respect for men who only did as they asked.

As Drayton saw it, the case was divided between adhering to the spirit, not the letter, of the Association and preserving unity among the populace. He believed the latter objective was infinitely more important because this unity "was the rock upon which the American political edifice was founded." Landing the horses threatened this solidarity, argued Drayton, because the people were "in commotion against it." Since the people are "ever in the right" on "all public and general questions," Drayton concluded obsequiously, the committee must obey their wishes.

Drayton's outburst drew cheers that could be heard throughout the heart of the city. The question was then put to a vote, and by only a single ballot, the committee rescinded the permission earlier granted to Smythe allowing him to import his horses and furniture. Drayton's agitating appeal was perhaps the critical factor compelling the committee to ultimately surrender to the popular will, as the deciding vote was certainly cast with the full knowledge of a waiting, potentially hostile populace. For the first time, popular pressure prevailed over the "men of property." Their ability to control the "many headed power of the people," Bull informed Dartmouth, was no longer certain.[3]

With this celebrated oration, and with Christopher Gadsden leaving soon to serve in the Second Continental Congress, Drayton became the people's new champion of American liberty. During the previous eight months he had managed to garner a substantial following in Charleston and portions of the backcountry by politicking demagogically on the people's ticket. This broad

3. David H. Villers, "The Smythe Horses Affair and the Association," *SCHM* 70 (July 1969): 137–48; *SCG*, 27 March 1775; Drayton, *Memoirs*, 1: 182–7; Bull to Dartmouth, 28 March 1775, BPROSC 35: 80–2.

public support, coupled with his enthusiasm, talent, and high social station, helped place Drayton in an ideal position to receive important berths in the Whig government.

Drayton's celebrated entrance onto the revolutionary stage came at an opportune time. The provincial congress was in the midst of rapidly creating an elaborate substructure of permanent committees to augment the effectiveness of the American cause in South Carolina. Motivating patriot leaders in this endeavor was the April 19 arrival of a British packet carrying news of a conciliatory gesture by Prime Minister North, offering the colonies the right to tax themselves in lieu of a parliamentary tax. South Carolinians readily dismissed the prime minister's proposals as "Neronian measures" conceived by a diabolical ministry to enslave them even further. Much more alarming was news of Parliament's address to the king in February declaring the colonies in open rebellion and urging His Majesty to enforce obedience to the laws of England. Many colonists considered Parliament's message a "cruel and unjust declaration of War against America." Realizing there was "little probability" of resolving the "present unhappy public disputes" with the ministry through "pacific measures . . . hitherto pursued," the General Committee felt it prudent to hasten the colony's preparations for what appeared to be an imminent showdown with the mother country.[4]

The General Committee's first acts following receipt of the distressing news of Parliament's declaration were the creation of three standing subcommittees—the Secret Committee, the Committee of Intelligence, and the Special Committee. Experienced, energetic, and dedicated men were needed to serve in these bodies. Drayton, who possessed an abundance of these and other important traits, was in obvious contention to receive a position on at least one, if not more, of these boards. His bold attack against the local boycott in 1769 had demonstrated a willingness to sacrifice everything for his beliefs, his singular service in the council showed him to be a dedicated public servant, and his ongoing dispute with local placemen revealed a concern with

4. *SCG&CJ*, 25 April and 9 May 1775; Drayton, *Memoirs*, 1: 218–20; Allan J. McMurry, "The North Government and the Outbreak of the American Revolution," *Huntington Library Quarterly* 34 (February 1971): 141–5. Claudius Caesar Nero, Roman emperor (A.D. 54–68), was a misanthropic man with a murderous streak who had his mother, wife, and aunt executed for various undeserved reasons. During a psychotic rage he kicked to death another wife who was pregnant at the time. However, Nero is most remembered for his cruel and sadistic persecution of Christians, whom he blamed for the fire that swept Rome in A.D. 64.

the economic and political welfare of his home province and the rights of its inhabitants. His brief stint as an associate justice displayed a remarkable understanding of the law, and his letter to the Continental Congress and charges to the grand juries exhibited a strong devotion to the American cause, an impressive ability to persuade others, and original ideas on creating a new system of American government. Recognizing the contribution Drayton's vigor, knowledge, experience, and skills could make to the revolutionary movement in South Carolina, the General Committee selected him to serve in the powerful position of chairman of all three subcommittees.

Even Drayton, who never underestimated his own abilities and who certainly felt deserving of top political appointments, had to be pleasantly surprised with his new assignments. As chairman of the three subcommittees, he immediately became the most influential member in the patriot party in South Carolina. Honored by his colleagues' trust in his abilities and devotion, Drayton vowed not to waste his broad powers. However, the General Committee was obviously unaware of Drayton's extreme political agenda, for had it known of the drastic measures he intended to promote, it certainly would not have placed him in such a powerful position of authority.

The most powerful of the three subordinate bodies was the five-man Secret Committee. Creating it on April 20, the General Committee assigned it to do whatever it felt necessary to place the colony in the best possible defensive posture and gave it virtually unlimited powers to fulfill this purpose. It also entrusted Drayton with the authority to select his own associates. Exploiting this privilege to its fullest, Drayton chose men much like himself—young, enthusiastic, and extremist in their views of Anglo-American relations. His first two choices were his brother-in-law Arthur Middleton, a wealthy planter and Cambridge graduate who was considered by patriots to be "worth his weight in Diamonds," and his lifelong friend Charles Cotesworth Pinckney, an influential planter and lawyer. Drayton thought so highly of Middleton and Pinckney that he nominated them to all three subcommittees. To fill the remaining positions on the Secret Committee, Drayton selected William Gibbes, who owned many schooners and stores that might prove valuable, and Edward Weyman, a glass grinder, cabinetmaker, and leading member of the Charleston mechanics.[5]

5. Poythress, "Revolution by Committee," 298; Peter Timothy to William Henry Drayton, 13 August 1775, in Joseph W. Barnwell, "The Correspondence of the Honourable Arthur Middleton," *SCHM* 27 (July 1926): 129; Drayton, *Memoirs*, 1: 221.

That Drayton, who only six years before had publicly proclaimed that mechanics had no business in political affairs, would select an artisan to serve with him on an important committee may appear odd. In choosing Weyman, though, Drayton was not acknowledging the craftsman's equality with the patrician class. He picked the cabinetmaker partly because Weyman had proven one of the most ardent opponents of British imperial policy and, just as importantly, because he hoped it would strengthen the attachment of the lower orders to himself and the American cause. Drayton understood that allowing the lower classes a greater taste of power might eventually threaten the established order, but if it advanced his circumstances and helped achieve a redress of grievances with Great Britain, it was a risk worth taking.

Under the guidance of its energetic leader, the Secret Committee wasted no time in utilizing its immense powers. On the night of its creation, the committee devised a daring plan to disarm their enemies and provide the patriots with the means of self-defense by raiding the province's stores of powder and guns. Encouraging them in this enterprise was news of similar activity by Whigs in Massachusetts. Not wanting to appear irresolute, Drayton and his colleagues took it upon themselves to bring South Carolina more in line with the patriotism of their northern counterparts. More conservative members within the party considered the plan a "useless" and "daring" insult to His Majesty's authority. However, they made only a "very faint" protest, fearing that stronger opposition might dampen the revolutionary spirit and perhaps create damaging divisions within the movement.[6]

Assisting the Secret Committee in the treasonous act were some of the province's most respectable men: Charles Pinckney, president of the provincial congress; Henry Laurens, chairman of the General Committee; Thomas Lynch, a delegate to the Continental Congress; and Stephen Bull, nephew of the lieutenant governor. In two separate raids, the rebels seized approximately 1,100 pounds of powder from the Hobcaw Point magazine (near the junction of Cooper and Wando Rivers) and over 500 pounds from Cochran's magazine on Charleston Neck. A third group, lead by Drayton, assembled at 11:00 P.M. at the statehouse to relieve the royal government of its guns. The robbers used neither masks nor disguises, but chose nighttime to avoid flagrantly insulting the authority of the beloved and much respected lieutenant governor. Drayton and his partners in crime had no problem breaking into the handsome two-story capitol building (which was "guarded" only by an

6. Alexander Innes to Dartmouth, 1 May 1775, BPROSC 35: 93–4.

elderly housekeeper), marching upstairs to the province's armory and happily relieving all eight hundred guns, and two hundred cutlasses from the Crown's possession. Thus in a matter of a few hours, the rebels managed to acquire the weapons and gunpowder necessary for the creation of their own military units. Coincidentally, just two days before in Lexington, Massachusetts, a similar event had resulted in the firing of the first shots of the Revolution.[7]

Lieutenant Governor Bull was shocked and outraged by such brazen assaults against his authority. In hopes of capturing the culprits, he offered a handsome £100 sterling reward for anyone providing information leading to the arrest and conviction of the men responsible for these "daring acts of violence." To widen the dragnet, Bull also ordered the assembly to investigate the seditious affair "without loss of time." In giving that directive, though, the lieutenant governor was essentially allowing the outlaws to investigate their own crime. The legislators, almost all of whom supported the patriots' actions—some had even participated in the raids—laughed at Bull's request. Not wanting to offend their friend, however, they "carried on the farce" and appointed a committee to examine the theft of public arms. After a "thorough investigation" lasting three days, the committee reported to the lieutenant governor that it was unable to obtain any hard proof relative to the robbery, but believed the "late alarming accounts from Great Britain" were the cause for "so extraordinary and uncommon a step."[8]

Drayton's Secret Committee continued taking "extraordinary and uncommon" steps toward revolution by devising a plan calculated to throw odium on the British administration, to vilify the Crown officers in the province, and to invigorate the ardor of the people. This was a vitally important task, for Charleston held one of the largest concentrations of king's friends in America. If the revolutionaries failed to subdue them, they had little chance of succeeding. After some discussion, Drayton and his fellow committeemen finally agreed that a public exhibition designed to excite the sight and senses of the multitude would be most effective in achieving the desired results. For this purpose, they constructed a large, moveable stagelike frame and furnished it with effigies representing the Pope, Lords Grenville and North, and

---

7. Drayton, *Memoirs*, 1: 222–3; Joseph Johnson, *Traditions and Reminiscences of the American Revolution in the South* (Charleston: Walker and James, 1851; reprint, Spartanburg, S.C.: The Reprint Co., 1972), 51–2.

8. Bull to Commons House of Assembly, 24 April 1775, Journals of the Commons House of Assembly, 39: 273, SCDAH; Committee Report on Raid of Provincial Armories, 27 April 1775, ibid., 39: 279; Drayton, *Memoirs*, 1: 224–5.

the Devil. Early one morning in late April, this "uncommon spectacle" was placed in an active site between the public market and St. Michael's Church. A large crowd soon gathered around the apparatus, wondering about its purpose. Their queries were soon answered, for no sooner did a royal official or an individual suspected of loyalist sentiments pass by, than the Pope immediately bowed with proportioned respect to them; the Devil at the same moment, hurled his dart at the Pope's head, causing the crowd to convulse with laughter. The stationary effigies of Lords Grenville and North, portrayed as attendants to the Pope, drew jeers from the people for the oppressive acts against America that they had steered through Parliament. After the performance was repeated throughout the day, the mob paraded the contraption through town and put the whole thing to flames amidst much festivity.[9]

Having sufficiently excited the sentiments of the urban masses, the patriots next placed their efforts on firing the emotions of those living outside the capital. With approximately two-thirds of the province's white citizens residing in the interior, such allegiance was crucial. Gaining these people's loyalty, however, would be difficult. Decades of indifference by the coastal elite toward the backcountry settlers' continual demands for greater legislative representation, courts, jails, schools, churches, bridges, and roads made many upcountry residents apathetic and even hostile to the patriots' cries of parliamentary abuse. Furthermore, the three provincial newspapers, all printed in Charleston, had very limited circulation outside the capital. Thus the General Committee on April 25 created the Committee of Intelligence for the purpose of informing the interior inhabitants of "all affairs and transactions as have any relation to the American cause." Membership in this committee included the triumvirate of Drayton, Pinckney, and Middleton, as well as the Reverend William Tennent, James Parsons, John Lewis Gervais, Roger Smith, and Thomas Heyward Jr.[10]

The day following its creation, the Committee of Intelligence penned a lengthy epistle to parish and local committees throughout the province. At least three similar dispatches followed during the summer of 1775. In trying to secure the backcountry's support, the committee sought to stir opposition

9. Wallace Brown, *The Good Americans: The Loyalists in the American Revolution* (New York: William Morrow, 1969), 236–7; Drayton, *Memoirs*, 1: 226–8.

10. Minutes of the General Committee, *DHAR*, 1: 107; *SCG&CJ*, 9 May 1775.

against what it considered the two main sources of sinister measures against the colonies—Parliament and the royal ministry—and to educate the frontiersmen on the progress of revolutionary activity in Charleston and elsewhere.[11]

With these objectives in mind, the committee informed the backcountrymen in explicit and excitable language of Parliament's recent "arbitrary" measures imposed upon the colonies: the "declaration of war" against America, the blockade of Boston, the dispatch of military reinforcements, and Prime Minister North's "conciliatory plan" allowing the colonies to tax themselves. These "humiliating terms," exclaimed the committee, were offered with "musket and bayonet at our breasts." There was no difference between this conduct and that of a thief, it added, who, "with a pistol at your head, demands your purse, with a blustering threat—*deliver, or I will blow your brains out!*" Even with North's offer allowing the colonies to tax themselves, Parliament still does not relinquish its self-proclaimed right to tax the colonies, the pamphlet continued. Instead, such proposals are "calculated to disunite the Americans, and to break a link in the great chain on this Continent now formed . . . in defense of American liberties." If Americans allow Parliament the unconstitutional right to raise enormous sums of money from the "sweat of our face," it warned, we will soon be as downtrodden as the poorest peasants in Germany and Ireland. It is therefore imperative that we unite and "resist the Iron hand of oppression," because "if we DIVIDE, we are LOST—we shall lie totally at the mercy of Administration and be obliged to pay a tax *as they please.*"[12]

The Committee of Intelligence's success in winning over the backcountry through these emotional epistles remains uncertain. Many frontiersmen would soon take up arms for King George III upon the outbreak of hostilities. On the other hand, an even larger number either remained neutral or fought with the Whigs, which suggests that the committee's communications may have converted or at least gained the sympathy of a significant number. Lord William Campbell, who would soon arrive to succeed Bull as chief executive, certainly thought the handbills were highly damaging to Administra-

11. Drayton claimed that he was the principal author of these essays, as well as of all correspondence and official documents for the committees he chaired. See William Henry Drayton to William Drayton, 4 July 1775, Gage Papers, CL. Extant Committee of Intelligence dispatches can be found in *SCG&CJ*, 9 May 1775; *SCG&CJ*, 18 July 1775 [also located in *DHAR*, 1: 107–16, and Robert Gibbes Collection, SCDAH]; and *SCG*, 7 September 1775, supplement.
12. *SCG&CJ*, 9 May 1775.

tion. He informed Dartmouth in late August that Drayton's Committee of Intelligence had "long taken uncommon pains to impress the minds of the people with the worst opinion of His Majesty's ministers," representing them as "capable of adopting the most ruinous measures." This "torrent of abuse" poured out through "flagitious publications," he complained, has "poisoned the minds of great numbers."[13]

In addition to corresponding with backcountrymen, the Committee of Intelligence exchanged information with revolutionary committees throughout North America. Although evidence is scant, it appears that Drayton and his associates were quite active in these intracolony communications. On June 6, 1775, for example, the committee sent a letter to its counterpart in New York, warning it to be on the lookout for North Carolina loyalists intent on obtaining weapons for Crown supporters residing in the southern frontier. The same day, the committee delivered to the North Carolina Committee of Intelligence copies of intercepted letters from General Thomas Gage to Governor Josiah Martin disclosing that those two Crown officials were "endeavouring to foment disturbances" among the interior inhabitants of their province. Drayton's committee did not ignore their southern counterparts, either, urging Whig leaders in Savannah to "keep a watchful eye" on their governor, James Wright, and their chief justice, the latter of whom it believed was engaged in "a very criminal correspondence . . . inimical to the Liberties of America."[14]

In May, South Carolinians received word of two acts by British leaders they considered hostile to American liberty, deeds that greatly diminished their hopes of ever reconciling with the mother country. The first of these, received on May 3, was an alarming message from Arthur Lee, a Virginian in London, informing the General Committee of a "black plan" by the ministry to sponsor both a slave uprising and an Indian war against the Carolinas. This

13. Campbell to Dartmouth, 31 August 1775, in K. G. Davies, ed., *Documents of the American Revolution* (Shannon, Ireland: Irish University Press, 1975), 9: 93–4.

14. South Carolina Committee of Intelligence to New York Provincial Congress, 6 June Convention, Records of the Continental Congress, Record Group 360, M247, reel 81, item 67, vol. 1, p. 21, National Archives and Records Administration; South Carolina Committee of Intelligence to the Committee of Wilmington, North Carolina, 6 June 1775, in William Bell Clark, et al., eds., *Naval Documents of the American Revolution* (Washington, D.C.: United States Government Printing Office, 1964–), 1: 618–9; South Carolina Committee of Intelligence to Committees at Newbern, North Carolina, and Savannah, Georgia, 4 July 1775, Gibbes Collection, SCDAH.

distressing news received some corroboration later that month by a rumor spread in the local press that the sloop of war soon to arrive with the new governor William Campbell was carrying 78,000 weapons to help carry out these uprisings. Still reeling from the shock of these horrifying reports, South Carolinians were further alarmed by reports of fighting having taken place in April in Lexington, Massachusetts, between colonial and British troops.[15]

With blacks outnumbering whites in the coastal region by more than three to one, rumor of a slave revolt, especially one incited by the Crown, was enough to throw lowcountry whites into paroxysms of fear and drive many firmly into the patriots' camp. "Words . . . cannot express the flame that this occasioned amongst all ranks and degrees," one royal official reported, "the cruelty and savage barbarity of the scheme was the conversation of all companies." These heightened fears of a slave rebellion prompted Drayton and his Special Committee, created on May 8, to earnestly investigate all reports of suspicious behavior by both blacks and whites. By June this inquest had uncovered a handful of individuals suspected of encouraging resistance among the human chattel. Evidence against them was scant and circumstantial, but this was no obstacle for Drayton and other extremists who, according to Henry Laurens, were determined to punish these men "for example Sake." In all, the revolutionaries imprisoned three white men, severely flogged and banished two slaves, and hanged and then set aflame before a large crowd the alleged ringleader, a free black fisherman and harbor pilot named Thomas Jeremiah. As expected, these gruesome public displays had the desired effect. Drayton cheerfully informed the South Carolina delegates at Philadelphia that their apprehensions of a slave revolt had "all passed over."[16]

Before their fears of a slave rebellion had "passed over," however, South Carolinians were further distressed by a widely circulated report that John

15. General Committee to Delegates for South Carolina at Philadelphia, 8 May 1775 (composed by William Henry Drayton), *HLP*, 10: 114 n. 2; William Campbell to Dartmouth, 31 August 1775, in Davies, *Documents of the American Revolution*, 9: 94; Alexander Innes to Lord Dartmouth, 16 May 1775, in Bargar, "Charles Town Loyalism," 128; Drayton, *Memoirs*, 1: 231; *SCG*, 29 May 1775.

16. William Campbell to Dartmouth, 31 August 1775, in Davies, *Documents of the American Revolution*, 9: 94; Henry Laurens to John Laurens, 18 June 1775, *HLP*, 10: 191; Committee of Intelligence to Delegates from South Carolina at Philadelphia, 4 July 1775, *DHAR*, 1: 118; Robert Olwell, "'Domestic Enemies': Slavery and Political Independence in South Carolina, May 1775–March 1776," *JSH* 55 (February 1989): 30–1; M. Foster Farley, "The South Carolina Negro in the American Revolution, 1775–1783," *SCHM* 79 (April 1978): 76–7; Weir, *Colonial South Carolina*, 200–3; Olwell, *Masters, Slaves, and Subjects*, 228–36.

Stuart, one of the strongest opponents of the Revolution in the lower South, was planning to send orders to the Cherokee and Catawba Indians for an attack upon southern frontier settlements. Sometime in May, the superintendent had met with headmen from the Catawba nation, giving them guns and ammunition to help maintain their allegiance to the king. Soon thereafter, Whig leaders learned that Stuart had received letters from General Thomas Gage, commander of British troops in North America. Already inclined to believe anything following Lee's shocking letter and the word of the fighting in Massachusetts, the patriots suspected that Stuart was part of a plot with the British military to bring the Indians upon them, a suspicion strengthened by the superintendent's refusal to show them his correspondence with Gage.[17]

Adding to the Carolinians' fear of an Indian uprising was the southern tribes' increasing hostility toward whites who continued to encroach on their hunting grounds. During the winter of 1774–1775, Creek Indians showed their displeasure by attacking frontier settlements in Georgia and the military units sent to protect them. One unfortunate militiaman who "fell into the hands of the Barbarians," reported the *South Carolina Gazette*, was found bound to a tree, castrated, his scalp and ears hacked off, a tomahawk imbedded in his skull, thirty arrows sticking from his body, and the barrel of a gun, "supposed to have been red hot," protruding from his anus. With the South Carolina frontier "not a little alarmed" over the savage attacks, the assembly implored Lieutenant Governor Bull to provide poor people in the backcountry with the arms and ammunition necessary to defend themselves against "those Savages in case of a rupture with them."[18]

With Stuart's gifts to the Catawbas and his secret correspondence with General Gage, South Carolinians suspected the superintendent of attempting to foment this break with the Indians. Some men considered Stuart so "obnoxious and dangerous" that they made plans to arrest him. Upon learning of this scheme, the superintendent fled in late May from his Charleston sickbed (he was suffering from malaria) to his Lady's Island plantation, barely escaping the "fury of a merciless and ungovernable Mob." From thence, he

17. Stuart to Dartmouth, 21 July 1775, in Davies, *Documents of the American Revolution*, 9: 53; Stuart to Drayton, 18 July 1775, and Stuart to Thomas Gage, 20 July 1775, Gage Papers, CL; Hamer, "John Stuart's Indian Policy," 352–3; John R. Alden, "John Stuart Accuses William Bull," *W&MQ*, 3d. ser., 2 (July 1945): 315–20; David D. Wallace, "Gage's Threat—Or Warning?" *SCHM* 47 (July 1946): 190–3; Snapp, *John Stuart*, 160–5.

18. *SCG*, 14 February and 31 January 1774; Commons House of Assembly to William Bull, 2 August 1774, Journals of the Commons House of Assembly, 39: 173, SCDAH.

went to Savannah. Some members of the General Committee wanted to send a posse to apprehend him, but cooler temperaments prevailed and the committee instead voted to refer Stuart's case to Drayton's Committee of Intelligence. Meanwhile, the superintendent tried to vindicate himself by presenting his official letter book before five leading Georgia Whigs. Unfortunately for Stuart, he unwarily produced a letter from his deputy Alexander Cameron, expressing confidence at the prospect of bringing down as many Indians as the superintendent should think necessary. With this new evidence, the South Carolinians' suspicions of Stuart turned to certainty.[19]

While Stuart was haplessly attempting to clear his name, Drayton's Secret Committee ordered John Joyner and John Barnwell—two members of the South Carolina provincial congress—to distribute throughout Beaufort and Savannah handbills designed to "inflame the minds of the people" against the superintendent. Among other things, the material in the circular accused Stuart of "calling down the Indians" upon the southern frontier, claimed the British government was sending him guns and ammunition to arm the Indians, and blamed him for the massacre at Fort Loudoun during the French and Indian War. The authors of this disparaging and inflammatory bulletin were none other than Drayton and his associates on the Committee of Intelligence, who were responsible for all Whig publications in the province. Drayton, who still resented Stuart's opposition to his Catawba land lease and the Indian agent's role in his recent suspension from the council, must have smiled as he thought of the terror the handbill would generate in his former adversary. Indeed, the committee's leaflet so enraged inhabitants throughout the region that Stuart once again feared for his safety. Still weak from his illness, the aging superintendent narrowly escaped falling into the hands of an "incensed mob" by boarding a vessel leaving for St. Augustine. There Governor James Grant of East Florida, upon observing that Stuart had a "good sweat" over his most recent escape, offered the Scotsman protection from the American rebels.[20]

19. Stuart to Dartmouth, 21 July 1775, BPROCO 5/76, pp. 307–12; Claim of Sarah Stuart, American Loyalist Transcripts, 56: 234–5, NYPL; Henry Laurens to John Laurens, 23 June 1775, *HLP*, 10: 189; Joseph Habersham to Philotheos Chiffelle, 16 June 1775, Gibbes Collection, SCDAH; Drayton, *Memoirs*, 1: 267, 289–91.

20. William Grant to Admiral Samuel Graves, 18 June 1775, and John Stuart to Dartmouth, 21 July 1775, in Davies, *Documents of the American Revolution*, 9: 177, 53–4; Arthur Middleton to Drayton, 4 August 1775, in Barnwell, "Correspondence of Arthur Middleton," 121. In early 1760 at the height of the French and Indian War, Cherokees attacked the British post of Fort

Stuart's flight to St. Augustine and his correspondence with Cameron proved conclusive evidence of his guilt in the eyes of South Carolina patriots. Before officially condemning him, however, the General Committee deemed it proper to allow the Scotsman the opportunity to make his defense. On June 21 it directed Drayton's Committee of Intelligence to demand from the superintendent an answer to the charge of inciting the Indians against the patriots and to request him to return to Charleston and appear before them in person. To encourage the Indian agent to comply with its behests and deter him from any possible mischief, the committee, in two separate dispatches, warned him that the Whig government had imprisoned his wife and daughter in their Charleston home and placed his £20,000 estate as security for the good behavior of the southern Indians. These threats "will make him quake," Drayton informed a cousin residing in East Florida, and "show him that we are serious."[21]

Stuart, worried about the safety of his wife and daughter, wrote the Committee of Intelligence in mid-July to alleviate the Whigs' suspicions that he had plans to incite the Indians. The superintendent informed the committee that he could not lawfully supply copies of his correspondence with Gage, but emphatically denied receiving orders from superiors that by even the "most tortured construction" could be interpreted to "spirit up or employ the Indians to fall upon the frontier inhabitants." This insistent denial that the colonists had any grounds for suspicion failed to diminish the conspiracy fears of Drayton and his committee, who yearned to have the superintendent brought back to Charleston to face Whig justice. But with Stuart safely residing under the protection of Governor Grant, there was nothing they could do against the Scotsman. The committee therefore decided to drop the dispute.[22]

Loudoun on the Little Tennessee River. Isolated and reduced to starvation, the garrison was forced to surrender on August 7. Three days later Indians slaughtered the weak and defenseless soldiers.

21. Committee of Intelligence to John Stuart, 21 and 29 June 1775, BPROCO 5/76, pp. 321–3, 325; William E. Hemphill, Wylma A. Wates, and R. Nicholas Olsberg, eds., *Journals of the General Assembly, 1776–1780* (Columbia: University of South Carolina Press, 1970), 32; William Henry Drayton to William Drayton, 4 July 1775, Gage Papers, CL.

22. Stuart to South Carolina Committee of Intelligence, 18 July 1775, BPROCO 5/76, pp. 153–4. Stuart's letter is more readily available in Force, *American Archives*, 4th ser., vol. 2: 1681–1682, and Drayton, *Memoirs*, 1: 292–6. See also Snapp, *John Stuart*, 165. Stuart and Drayton also exchanged a brief yet acrimonious correspondence in which the superintendent accused the Carolinian of circulating "injurious reports" that forced his departure from South Carolina and Georgia. Drayton smugly denied the charge. See *JPC*, 64; Drayton to Stuart, 29 June 1775,

Still, Whig leaders, roused by the recent outbreak of hostilities with the mother country and threatened by the reality of an Indian attack, were convinced of Stuart's guilt. To help counteract the superintendent's influence over neighboring Indians, they assigned Drayton in early July to draft a "talk" to representatives of the Catawba nation. The Catawbas were nervous over the increasing militancy in the province and came to Charleston to find out why the white warriors were "cleaning their guns" and "putting on their shot-pouches." In explaining the intricacies of American politics to the Indians, Drayton told the headmen in condescending terms that the "Great King" had some "bad men" who had persuaded him with "crooked talks" to force Americans at gunpoint to "pay four deer-skins for those goods which we used to buy for two." He explained that this tax will cause the tribes to "suffer in the same way" because it will force the colonists to charge them more for the same merchandise. However, the Americans are resolved "not to be cheated any longer," Drayton boldly told the headmen, and such defiant conduct could provoke the "Great King" to send his "red coats" to "try to take our money." The colonists expected the Catawba to join them in this contest since "your case and our case is just the same." But if they had any thoughts of allying with the Cherokees to attack settlers, the Carolinian warned, our soldiers will "set up the war-whoop" and "look upon you as enemies." Drayton's economic logic and threats had the desired effect. Two weeks later a company of fifty Catawba warriors enlisted in Captain Samuel Boykin's regiment, stationed near Camden.[23]

While Drayton and the Whigs were working to reduce the threat of an Indian attack from the west, they were also speedily preparing for a possible confrontation with Great Britain further east. South Carolinians were horrified by the arrival of reports on May 8 of fighting in Massachusetts between British troops and American militia. The "noise of the gathering Tempest of Civil War thickens in the gale," warned a local patriot, "and Horror stalks through our Western Continent with gigantic strides. . . . Our Parent State has already pronounced us rebels, and we may expect to be treated as such,

Gage Papers, CL; Stuart to Drayton, 18 July 1775, BPROCO 5/76, pp. 333–6; Stuart to Dartmouth, 21 July 1775, in Davies, *Documents of the American Revolution*, 9: 54.

23. Because of Drayton's devious land-lease scheme with the Catawbas in 1774, the Council of Safety wisely assigned Henry Laurens to read Drayton's speech to the headmen. Drayton's "Talk to the Catawba Indians," 4 July 1775, is found in "Journal of the Council of Safety for the Province of South Carolina, 1775," SCHS *Collections*, 2: 32–4, 63–4.

whether we submit or bravely oppose." Many South Carolinians decided to take the latter course of action. Just one week later, Henry Laurens observed from his home in Charleston that "daily & nightly sound of Drums & Fifes discovers a Spirit in the People to make all possible resistance against that arbitrary power complained of—upwards of one hundred Men besides the common Town mount guard every Night & Committees of observation, of Intelligence & of safety find employment everyday—in a word the People are resolved to do all in their power to resist against the force & stratagems of the British ministry." The patriots' military training and rapid assumption of governmental powers greatly alarmed the governor's secretary, Alexander Innes, who warned authorities in London that "if General Thomas Gage does not strike some successful blow within a few weeks, I have not a doubt that there will be a total change of Government here, and the very slight mask they now condescend to wear entirely thrown off."[24]

South Carolina patriots did indeed throw off their "slight masks." With the commencement of hostilities and reports that the ministry was in league with both the Indians and the slaves, Whig leaders felt immediate and resolute measures were crucial for promoting the public welfare. Accordingly, on May 8 they moved the opening date of the provincial congress up three weeks from June 20 to June 1 and created the Special Committee, consisting of eleven men instructed to form such plans they felt "immediately necessary" to execute the security of the colony.[25]

Under chairman Drayton's driving leadership, this powerful board quickly developed decisive proposals for the defense of Charleston and its harbor. These included plans for blocking up some channels in Charleston bar, equipping armed vessels, prohibiting the exportation of corn and rice, raising and paying a body of troops, and forming an Association (for boycotting trade with Great Britain) to be signed by inhabitants. However, fellow patriots apparently felt such measures were too extreme at this time. When Drayton presented the plan to the General Committee, several members were thunderstruck by it and charged that the Special Committee's scheme would usher in nothing less that an "immediate revolution." The parent board absolutely refused to consider the proposal, explaining to Drayton that procrastination was the more appropriate "line of conduct." As a compromise, though, the

24. *SCG&CJ*, 6 June 1775; Henry Laurens to John Laurens, 15 May 1775, *HLP*, 10: 119; Alexander Innes to Dartmouth, 16 May 1775, in Bargar, "Charles Town Loyalism," 128.

25. Drayton, *Memoirs*, 1: 231.

General Committee promised to present the plan to the provincial congress at its convening.[26]

On June 1 the provincial congress assembled in the Great Hall above the Exchange; its first act was to elect Henry Laurens as its president. Drayton continued his service as a representative for the Saxe-Gotha District. Every day for the next three weeks he and the other 204 congressmen met behind closed doors and adopted a policy of strict secrecy in their deliberations, conduct which caused "great apprehensions" among many Charlestonians. Generally, the congress's private proceedings followed the recommendations drafted by Drayton's Special Committee, including the formation of an Association boycotting trade with Britain.

From the very beginning there was great opposition to the Association. The main point of contention was a provision designating anyone refusing to subscribe to it as "inimical to the liberties of the Colonies" and ordering that all who did not sign be dealt with "according to sound policy." Drayton, as coauthor of the document, certainly supported this coercive stipulation. In fact, he may have been one of those "most furious" congressmen whom Joseph Manigault claimed wanted to imprison all opponents of the Association. This extreme attitude was a complete reversal from his earlier stand in 1769 when he had opposed the local boycott because of an identical provision. Given the enormous amount of abuse and financial injury Drayton received for his unpopular position, it is surprising that he would want others to suffer similarly. His reversal on this issue, however, can perhaps be attributed to new circumstances in both his personal life and the relations between America and Great Britain. Contrary to his earlier opposition to the Association, Drayton was now a prominent member of South Carolina's revolution; if it failed, he knew the British would target him for their vengeance. This horrifying understanding motivated him to do anything to ensure American success—even violate his most basic principles concerning individual liberties. Thus Drayton was willing to alter his political and constitutional principles to fit his personal changing circumstances. Contributing to Drayton's new outlook was the mother country's increasingly hostile policy toward the Americans, which gave rise to measures he believed threatened to enslave the colonists under an arbitrary and tyrannical government. Consequently, acts he once considered highly objectionable were now unavoidable if America was to break the chains of British tyranny. In the end, Drayton, Middleton,

26. Ibid., *Memoirs*, 1: 246–8.

Charles Cotesworth Pinckney, and other extremists managed to overrule their more fainthearted colleagues. Following a devotional service on June 4, members of the provincial congress signed the Association petition, in which subscribers pledged to unite themselves in defense of "our injured Country" and, if necessary, to "sacrifice our lives and Fortunes to secure her freedom and safety."[27]

The congress immediately instructed a committee of twenty-six men to gather signatures to the agreement from all inhabitants of the city and neighborhood—save Lieutenant Governor Bull, out of respect—and to report all those who refused to sign. Although "great numbers" of Charlestonians opposed subscribing their names to "so treasonable an engagement," according to one observer, "few dared refuse," for fear of retribution from the "fury of a desperate and vindictive mob." Within four days all men in Charleston except the king's officers and "a very few others" had signed the agreement. With the adoption of the local Association, South Carolinians had taken a giant step toward a clash with Great Britain.[28]

Two days later, on June 6, the provincial congress quickened its march by creating two regiments of infantry (1,500 men total) and one cavalry regiment (450 men and horses). To pay for the training of these soldiers and the general maintenance of the revolutionary government, the congress also voted to print £1 million worth of paper money. As financial backing for this currency, it prohibited the exportation of rice and corn for three months—another proposal made by Drayton's Special Committee—reserving the right for the Secret Committee to sell those staples to purchase items it considered "most conducive to the public good." Just before adjourning, the congress created a powerful thirteen-man Council of Safety to implement these and other measures it deemed expedient and necessary for strengthening, securing, and defending the colony while it was not in session. Drayton was one of the select baker's dozen chosen to wield this virtually unlimited power, while Henry Laurens was nominated to serve as chairman. Together, these thirteen

27. Joseph Manigault to Peter Manigault, 6 June 1775, Manigault Family Papers, SCL; Copies of the South Carolina Association can be found in *JPC*, 36; Drayton, *Memoirs*, 1: 285–6; South Carolina Provincial Congress Papers, SCL. See also Henry Laurens to Provincial Congress, 4 June 1775, *HLP*, 10: 173; Drayton, *Memoirs*, 1: 254.

28. Elizabeth Hasell to Gabriel Manigault, 6 June 1775, Manigault Family Papers, SCL; Alexander Innes to Dartmouth, 10 June 1775, in Bargar, "Charles Town Loyalism," 132; William Campbell to Dartmouth, 1 July 1775, BPROSC 36: 15; *SCG&CJ*, 9 June 1775.

men constituted the executive power of the province until the adoption of a permanent government in March 1776.[29]

The Council of Safety regarded public affairs so pressing that it held its first meeting on June 16, although the congress did not adjourn until the twenty-second. For the next five months, until the second provincial congress convened in mid-November, the councilors met nearly every day, often holding sessions early in the morning and then again at ten o'clock at night. Drayton proved one of the hardest working members. Some of the many duties he performed included surveying the town of Dorchester and preparing a plan for turning it into a defensive post in case of a British attack by sea; drafting numerous letters, correspondence, and speeches; and procuring munitions and powder for the newly raised troops.[30]

One of the most unique duties Drayton performed as a councilor was creating the emblems and mottos for the province's new currency. In all likelihood, the other council members selected Drayton to perform this unusual task because of his previous experience in designing emblematic devices, a talent he had displayed on the title page of *The Letters of Freeman*. Drayton's willingness to accept this assignment attests to his desire to have his hand in, and influence on, every aspect of the revolutionary movement in South Carolina.

Although a relatively minor duty, creating the emblems and mottos for the provincial currency was an important and effective means of propagating ideas and instilling support for the American cause within the populace. Making the most of this opportunity, Drayton designed symbols that reflected colonial grievances against Great Britain and America's imminent triumph against the mother country. The £50 note he created, for example, shows a woman representing the captive province of South Carolina, sitting under a palmetto observing the sun of freedom breaking through the clouds above the Charleston skyline. The slogan below it reads "Post Tenebras Lux"—

29. Drayton, *Memoirs*, 1: 255–6; *JPC*, 39, 41, 50–6. Also serving on the Council of Safety were Charles Pinckney, Rawlins Lowndes, Thomas Ferguson, Miles Brewton, Arthur Middleton, Thomas Heyward Jr., Thomas Bee, John Huger, James Parsons, Benjamin Elliott, and William Williamson.

30. Information on the work habits of those serving in the Council of Safety is found in Henry Laurens to Martha Laurens, 29 February 1776, *HLP*, 11: 131, and William Campbell to Dartmouth, 20 July 1775, BPROSC 35: 150. Drayton's activities in the Council of Safety are listed in its journals; see SCHS *Collections*, 2: 27–8, 31–4, 36–9, 48–50, 58.

"After Darkness Light." As a group, the emblems express the tyranny South Carolinians felt they were suffering under British rule, an oppression they would eventually unshackle, but only after a difficult struggle. Because of this persecution, the "friends of liberty" in the colony felt justified in resisting the mother country, an attitude symbolized by a hand drawing a sword, printed on the £10 bill. The inscription underneath it—"Et Deus Omnipotens"— reveals the patriots' belief that God is on their side. However, the emblem Drayton placed on the £5 note—a bundle of twelve arrows representing the united colonies—suggested that if Americans are to prevail, they must cooperate with one another. The device on the £20 bill—hands clasped in friendship holding palm fronds—conveys a similar message.[31]

If Drayton's Council of Safety duties were not enough, important matters originating in that body were continually referred to either the Secret Committee or the Committee of Intelligence or even directly to Drayton personally. The young patriot found sitting on so many boards and performing so many different assignments both exhilarating and exhausting. Writing to his cousin William Drayton in East Florida in early July, Drayton declared: "I tell you that being a member of the Congress, the General Committee, the Council of Safety, the Secret Committee, and the Committee of Intelligence, which last acts as a Secretary of State, and that all Reports, Resolutions, Letters and other papers are penned by me in each of these Departments, you may readily conclude that my time is not spent idly." Committee work alone had been keeping Drayton so busy the previous six weeks, in fact, that he felt himself a virtual prisoner in Charleston, unable to leave even for a day to attend to personal affairs at his plantation estate. "I am really almost jaded," he confessed to his kin.[32]

Perhaps another reason Drayton felt such fatigue is that his revolutionary activities left him little time for Dorothy and their two young children, John and Mary. His family probably resided with him in their Charleston townhouse much of the year, allowing Drayton some opportunity to visit with his loved ones. But given the numerous and time-consuming responsibilities as chairman of three revolutionary boards and as a member of several others, it is doubtful that he had much time or energy left to devote toward his wife

---

31. David C. R. Heisser, *The State Seal of South Carolina: A Short History* (Columbia: SCDAH, 1992), 8, 14–6. Why Drayton placed only twelve arrows, instead of thirteen, on the £5 bill is uncertain.

32. 4 July 1775, Gage Papers, CL.

and children. Although it is too strong to say that Drayton loved his new powers, exciting duties, and public distinction more than his family, his tireless devotion to the Revolution nevertheless reveals his willingness to jeopardize his relationship with them, particularly that with his wife, to further America's struggle for liberty. The marriage, already severely strained as a result of Drayton's earlier misconduct and dereliction, probably suffered further as he immersed himself ever more deeply into the American cause, which sometimes required his absence away from home for months or years at a time. This would perhaps explain why the young husband and wife, although only thirty-two and twenty-seven respectively, had no further children after he joined the patriot party in 1774.

Although Drayton was laboring hard for the American cause, there were some in the revolutionary movement who believed he and other "hot-headed young men" were too energetic and extreme. Royalists in the colony, too, considered Drayton "one of the most virulent Incendarys" in the province. The alarming events of the preceding month had produced varied reactions within the patriot party. Although all opposed the Intolerable Acts, they differed "in sentiment on the mode" of resisting them. At one end of the spectrum, according to Henry Laurens, were "Red-hot" zealots like Drayton, Arthur Middleton, Christopher Gadsden, Charles Pinckney, and Peter Timothy, who "foolishly talk[ed] of Arms." Aligned against these "desperate Incendarys" were conservatives such as Rawlins Lowndes, Miles Brewton, James Parsons, Thomas Heyward Jr., and Thomas Bee—all members of the Council of Safety—who, in Laurens's words, believed that "implicit obedience" to the Crown was the "Surest Road to a redress of Grievances." Falling between these two extremes were moderates like John Huger, Benjamin Elliott, William Williamson, and Laurens, who tried to adopt a safer middle course while still opposing British tyranny. Contention was so prevalent among Whig leadership that one local placeman cheerfully reported to Dartmouth that "nothing but Division, Riot, Anarchy, and Confusion reigns at present amongst them."[33]

Nowhere was this political division more evident than in the Council of

33. Laurens to Richard Oswald, 4 January 1775, *HLP*, 10: 22; Innes to Dartmouth, 3 June 1775, in Bargar, "Charles Town Loyalism," 131, 128, 134; Poythress, "Revolution by Committee," 124, 245–7; Raymond G. Starr, "The Conservative Revolution: South Carolina Public Affairs, 1775–1790" (Ph.D. diss., University of Texas, 1964), 85–6.

Safety, which was fraught with dissension and indecisiveness, resulting in a disinclination to action. Like the larger factional divisions among the patriot leaders, this body was composed of a relatively equal number of extremists, moderates, and conservatives. Because no contingent had a majority, it was nearly impossible for the group to forge and execute a comprehensive plan of defense against Great Britain. Fortunately for the revolutionary party, the more determined, more spirited, and less divisive General Committee, Secret Committee, and Committee of Intelligence—the latter two dominated by Drayton—were able to counter much of the Council of Safety's hesitancy. Moreover, as the movement progressed, the more conservative members grew increasingly reluctant to "draw back" for fear of hindering the cause.[34]

Despite the disparate political views among the Whig leaders, their incessant, intrepid attacks upon royal authority caused increasing alarm among the king's men in Charleston. "[T]his Province hardly falls short of Massachusetts in every Indecency, violence and contempt to Government," Alexander Innes exclaimed to authorities in London. Drayton, in fact, believed the colony had gone too far to retreat now. "*Peace, Peace* is now not even an Idea," he prophetically proclaimed exactly one year before America declared its independence. "A Civil War, in my opinion, is absolutely unavoidable. We already have an Army & a Treasury with a Million of money. In short a new Government is in effect erected. The Congress is the Legislative—the Council of Safety the Executive power—the General Committee, as Westminster Hall—and the District and Parochial Committees as County Courts. See the effects of oppression!" However, Drayton and his fellow Whigs were imposing an oppression of their own, at least against those who openly opposed the Association. Their determination to intimidate and crush all resistance within the capital was evident in their humiliating and sadistic punishment of Laughlin Martin and John Dealy, two men who not only refused to sign the petition but also were "hardy enough to ridicule [and] treat it with Contempt."[35]

This rowdy affair began when Martin and Dealy, both Catholic, entered the house of Thomas Nicoll (which also served as a tavern) and noisily announced to all in the room that they brought "good news" that the British were going to distribute arms to slaves, Catholics, and Indians. Upon hearing

34. Edward McCrady, *The History of South Carolina in the Revolution, 1775–1780* (New York: Macmillan, 1901), 30–1; Poythress, "Revolution by Committee," 245–7; Innes to Dartmouth, 3 July 1775, in Bargar, "Charles Town Loyalism," 135.

35. Innes to Dartmouth, 1 May 1775, BPROSC 35: 92; Drayton to William Drayton, 4 July 1775, Gage Papers, CL; *SCG&CJ*, 13 June 1775.

this, a Protestant named Michael Hubart replied that he considered it "bad news" if the Crown permitted "Roman Catholics and Savages" to massacre Christians. Offended by Hubart's remark, both Dealy and Martin soundly cursed the Protestant as a "false faced villain," drew their knives, and threatened to cut off his head if he did not beg forgiveness. Only when Hubart pleaded for his life did the two Catholics release him. Thereupon the two men had a drink, undoubtedly not the first that evening, and made a boastful toast to Drayton and his Secret Committee: "*Damnation to the Committee and their proceedings.*" Hubart immediately reported the incident to the Committee of Correspondence, which duly transferred the information to Drayton's Secret Committee for its consideration. After a brief deliberation, the committee gave its ruling, presented in Drayton's handwriting: "Secret, tar and feather him."[36]

The proper charge against the two men probably should have been "drunk and disorderly," but the rebel government wanted to establish complete control over all potential dissidents. Since the Whigs' legal control over provincial affairs was not yet absolute, and since the Association only called for condemnation and boycott, unofficial means were necessary to enforce the measure. This included use of a mob, which usually employed either attacks on property or tar and feathering. Accordingly, some of the townspeople set up a kangaroo court, with judge and witnesses, and tried Dealy and Martin for audaciously criticizing the Association and threatening members of congress. Although the verdict was never in question, the mock court deliberated nearly an hour before finding the two dissenters guilty of the charges against them. Dealy and Martin were then stripped of their garments and provided with "a Suit of Clothing of the true American Manufacture" (tar and feathers); thereafter, a "desperate and vindictive mob" carted the two badly burned loyalists through the streets of Charleston. Upon completing this degrading and painful punishment, the crowd placed the men aboard the ship *Liberty* (bound for Bristol) and banished them from the province. This sadistic form of street justice, the first of its kind in South Carolina, did much to cow loyalists in the capital. One Crown official who witnessed the tar and feathering of these two "poor wretches," informed superiors in England that

36. Drayton, *Memoirs*, 1: 273–4, 300–2; Richard C. Madden, "Catholics in Colonial South Carolina," *Records of the American Catholic Historical Society of Philadelphia* (March 1962): 30–4; Richard C. Madden, *Catholics in South Carolina: A Record* (New York: University Press of America, 1985), 7–14.

this "very *well-timed* piece of Justice" met with the "happiest effects, no one since daring even to think of refusing to swallow anything that may be offered."[37]

Soon after throwing Dealy and Martin to the angry Charleston mob, Drayton helped compose an address to Lord Campbell, who had finally arrived in Charleston on June 14 to replace Governor Bull, explaining the reasons for the provincial congress's defiant proceedings. One week later Drayton lead a fourteen-man delegation to the executive's residence in Charleston. With "all possible respect and politeness," Drayton bowed before the governor and informed him that the province had taken up arms against his authority. Campbell returned Drayton's bows as the Carolinian read the congress's declaration. "We declare, that no love of innovation—no desire of altering the constitution of government—no lust of independence—has had the least influence upon our Counsels," explained Drayton. However, when the "usual means of defence against arbitrary impositions have failed; mankind generally have had to recourse to those that are extraordinary—Hence, the origin of the Continental Congress—and hence the present representation of the people in this colony." Drayton emphasized to Campbell that they were not seeking independence, but only desired the "secure enjoyment of our invaluable rights." However, if the king's "wicked Counsels" continued their arbitrary actions against the colonies, he warned, it will "inevitably involve America in all the calamities of a Civil War." The patriots were confident in the justice of their cause and were willing to devote their "lives and fortunes" in preserving their constitutional rights because, as Drayton valiantly concluded, "we prefer Death to Slavery!"[38]

Despite all the courtesies displayed, Campbell was outraged by the "criminal nature" and "daring language" of the message. He wanted to answer it "in such terms as it merited," but felt that such a mordant reply would only further excite the "violent faction" that he believed was prepared to plunge the province into "open and actual rebellion." Instead, the Scottish nobleman suppressed his indignation, and after returning Drayton's bows, curtly replied

37. Laurent M. St. Georges, "Population Control and Guerilla Warfare as Decisive Factors in the American Revolution" (master's thesis, University of South Carolina, 1988), 33, 38; *SCG&CJ*, 13 June 1775; William Campbell to Dartmouth, 2 July 1775, BPROSC 35: 117–23; Innes to Dartmouth, 10 June 1775, in Bargar, "Charles Town Loyalism," 132.

38. Drayton, *Memoirs*, 1: 256–60; William Henry Drayton to William Drayton, 4 July 1775, Gage Papers, CL; "Address and Declaration of the Provincial Congress to His Excellency Lord William Campbell," 20 June 1775, *JPC*, 59–60.

that he knew of no representatives of the people of South Carolina except those constitutionally convened in the Commons House of Assembly. But Campbell soon discovered to his dismay that the Commons House was filled "almost to a man" with members of the Whig party and frequently worked in conjunction with the rebel government. This compelled the governor to strongly censure the "outrageous and illegal nature" of the assemblymen's "most dangerous Measures," acts he felt "indispensably bound" to warn them, "cannot fail of drawing down inevitable ruin on this flourishing Colony."[39]

Unbeknownst to the patriots, Campbell was reinforcing his verbal warnings with real action. Soon after arriving in Charleston, the governor was informed by "friends of the King" that the "intolerable tyranny and oppression" used by Whig leaders in enforcing their mandates had stirred up considerable opposition among many in the backcountry. Some frontiersmen even proposed creating their own "counter-Association" to demonstrate their distaste for Whig measures. Heartened by Campbell's arrival, leading loyalists from the Camden and Ninety-Six districts met secretly with the new governor to express their allegiance and to inform him that thousands more were ready to support whatever action he deemed appropriate for resisting the popular party. Campbell, realizing that he had "scarce a shadow of authority left" and no sign of receiving crucial military support from Great Britain in the near future, understood that these loyal frontiersmen were his only chance of gaining control of the colony. He therefore instructed them to quickly form and train several regiments of soldiers, promising them both "protection and reward" for this enterprise.[40]

As yet unaware of the governor's alliance with backcountry loyalists, revolutionary leaders in Charleston were more concerned with the intentions of

39. Campbell to Dartmouth, 2 July, 19 July, and 20 July 1775, in Davies, *Documents of the American Revolution*, 9: 33, 50; Campbell to the Provincial Congress, 21 June 1775, *JPC*, 65; Campbell to Commons House of Assembly, 10 July 1775, Journals of the Commons House of Assembly, 39: 290, SCDAH.

40. Campbell to Dartmouth, 19 August 1775, Historical Manuscripts Commission, *The Manuscripts of the Earl of Dartmouth* (London: Her Majesty's Stationery Office, 1895), 2: 354–5; Colonel Thomas Fletchall to William Campbell, 19 July 1775, ibid, 2: 355; Campbell to Dartmouth, 23 July 1775, BPROSC 35: 174; Campbell to Dartmouth, 19 and 20 July 1775, in Davies, *Documents of the American Revolution*, 9: 50; Cunningham, "Southern Governors," 270.

British officials elsewhere. In hopes of acquiring valuable intelligence enabling them to thwart parliamentary machinations, Drayton and his colleagues on the Committee of Intelligence took it upon themselves in late June to seize the royal mail expected any day. Immediately upon learning of the packet boat's arrival on the evening of July 2, Drayton, along with two fellow committee members, rushed to the post office before the postmaster delivered the mail. Upon reaching their destination they demanded to be allowed in, but Deputy Postmaster Jervais Henry Stevens "peremptorily refused" their forceful request. Hereupon Drayton "began to grow warm" and threatened to break down the door. Fearing personal injury, Stevens lost his nerve and reluctantly allowed them to enter the office. Drayton and his accomplices quickly appropriated twenty-six packets of letters written by Secretary of State Dartmouth to such men as Lieutenant Governor Bull, Chief Justice Patrick Tonyn (Florida), and Governors Campbell, Josiah Martin (North Carolina), and James Wright (Georgia). As he left the post office, Drayton told Stevens to inform his supervisor George Roupell that he, William Henry Drayton, had confiscated the letters. Since it was Roupell who had received the position of Postmaster General for the Southern Department over the Carolinian four years earlier, Drayton must have relished stealing the king's mail from under the Englishman's authority.[41]

After brazenly burglarizing the post office, Drayton carried the dispatches to the statehouse and summoned the Secret Committee. Upon reading them, the members made "such Discoveries of the Cruel designs of Government against us distressed Colonists," Laurens later reported, "as are exceedingly Shocking to humanity." At least to the patriots, the letters' contents made it clear that the British ministry fully intended to employ military force "for reducing the Colonies to the constitutional authority of Parliament." Fully understanding the importance of this information, the Secret Committee sent the dispatches to the Council of Safety, which ordered the Committee of Intelligence to "lose no time" in transmitting copies to its counterparts in North Carolina and Georgia as well as to the Continental Congress. Although Henry Laurens, along with some other patriots, thought Drayton

41. Drayton, *Memoirs*, 1: 309–10, 338–48, 357–8; Testimony of Jervais Henry Stevens, BPROSC 35: 159–61; William Moultrie, *Memoirs of the American Revolution, So Far as it Related to the States of North and South Carolina, and Georgia* (New York: David Longworthy, 1802; reprint, New York: Arno Press, 1968), 1: 59–60; Testimony of George Roupell, BPROSC 35: 139, 162–7.

acted excessively by confiscating the royal mail, he later admitted that the content "seems now to Sanctify the Act."[42]

About the same time Drayton raided the post office, his Secret Committee intercepted two letters from Governor James Wright of Georgia, to General Thomas Gage and Vice-Admiral Samuel Graves, both stationed in Massachusetts. In a message dated June 27, Wright anxiously informed the British general that the southern provinces were in dire straits. The powers of the governor are presently "executed by committees and mobs," he said, while the king's friends are left "naked and exposed to the resentment of an enraged people." The governor stressed that his position was especially precarious because South Carolina rebels controlled the port of Savannah and were inciting the local Whigs toward more violent conduct against his authority. The same day Wright implored Admiral Graves to quickly send a sloop of war, a military contingent, and money to pay for the construction of a fort, without which, he stressed, "neither law or government can be supported" here.[43]

In place of these letters, Drayton's Secret Committee forged others, painting a more optimistic picture of the royalist position and emphatically denying Wright's need for ships, troops, and money. The committee then mailed the letters to Gage and Graves with convincing facsimiles of Wright's signature and seal. The ruse worked admirably. Upon receipt of this forged document, Admiral Graves wrote to Governor Wright that he was extremely glad to find that, as he was not able to send a sloop of war to Savannah, "it has not, in your Excellency's opinion, been detrimental to the King's Interest within your Government." Governor Wright must have been confused and shocked upon reading this message, as he nervously waited in vain for a British warship to help him extinguish Georgia's rebellion. As a result of the Secret Committee's chicanery, the British sent neither troops nor vessels to Georgia during the summer of 1775.[44]

Drayton's Secret Committee caused Wright further aggravation later that summer when it organized a mission to commandeer valuable munitions sent to the governor from Great Britain. A serious and chronic problem facing the Whigs during the early years of the Revolution was an inadequate supply of

42. Henry Laurens to John Laurens, 14 July 1775, *HLP*, 10: 220; Drayton, *Memoirs*, 1: 338; "Journal of the Council of Safety," SCHS *Collections*, 2: 30–1.

43. Drayton, *Memoirs*, 1: 346–9.

44. Ibid., 310–1, 348–9; Graves to Wright, 22 August 1775, in Clark, *Naval Documents*, 1: 1204.

gunpowder. Most of the powder available in America in 1775 was left over from the Seven Years' War. Making matters worse, the few powder mills in the colonies were in ruins, the manufacture of explosive powder was all but a lost art, and the country was nearly destitute of ammunition and other war-like stores. Any chance of obtaining additional powder from Britain, more-over, had vanished with the outbreak of hostilities in April.[45]

Like the rest of the country, South Carolina was suffering from a severe shortage of gunpowder. Although Drayton and his fellow patriots had stolen sixteen hundred pounds from the royal magazines earlier that April, adding to about fourteen hundred pounds already in their possession, this amount was still not enough to supply all Whig troops throughout the province. Nearly half the soldiers in St. Peters Parish and Beaufort's militia companies, for example, did not have a single charge of powder in their horns. "Should a sudden Insurrection happen, or any other unfortunate Attack upon the People of this County," warned Colonel Stephen Bull of Beaufort, "I leave the Council of Safety to imagine the unhappy situation the numerous Inhabitants of this County would be reduced to." Reduced to either "fighting or submit-ting," David Ramsay later wrote, South Carolina patriots took "extraordinary methods" to procure additional gunpowder.[46]

In June 1775 Drayton's Secret Committee obtained intelligence from a "certain patriot gentleman" in Georgia that a ship from Great Britain was expected to arrive shortly in Savannah carrying several tons of gunpowder to be distributed by Governor Wright and John Stuart to the Indians as a means of keeping them attached to the Crown. This information aroused the com-mittee into immediate action. To reduce the king's influence among the Indi-ans, while at the same time filling the patriots' empty powderhorns, Drayton and his associates secretly commissioned captains John Barnwell and John Joyner—two members of the provincial congress from Beaufort—to use "all means in their power" to seize the military stores on board the English ship. So instructed, Barnwell and Joyner immediately assembled a force of forty well-armed men and sailed down the coast to the mouth of the Savannah River where they waited to intercept any vessel upon its arrival. Even this small military force frightened Governor Wright, who bemoaned to Vice-

45. Orlando W. Stephenson, "The Supply of Gunpowder in 1776," *American Historical Re-view* 30 (January 1925): 271, 281.

46. Bull to Laurens, 3 August 1775, *HLP*, 10: 271; Ramsay, *History of South Carolina*, 2: 137.

Admiral Graves that he did not have the power to prevent the South Carolinians from seizing the expected powder and doing "just what they please."[47]

Governor Wright's prediction proved true. The South Carolina patriots, with assistance from Georgia Whigs, outfitted a schooner and used it to successfully capture the British vessel *Philippa* without a fight when the ship neared the port of Savannah on July 8. After escorting the *Philippa* to Cockspur Island, the patriots unloaded the cargo—over 15,000 pounds of gunpowder and 700 pounds of lead bullets—and divided up the booty amongst themselves. The Georgians retained over 8,000 pounds of gunpowder, one-quarter of which they sent as a gift to neighboring Indian tribes in hopes of gaining their support. South Carolinian's share amounted to 5,200 pounds of gunpowder, six kegs of lead, and a small portion of the firearms.[48]

By chance, only a few days before the patriots had captured the *Philippa*, Drayton's Secret Committee had received an urgent letter from the South Carolina congressional delegation in Philadelphia entreating it to send all the gunpowder (even damaged material) the colony could spare for use in the siege of Boston. At the July 12 meeting of the Council of Safety, Drayton and Arthur Middleton both astonished and pleased their fellow councilors with a "double shot" of news: that the Continental Army was critically short of gunpowder; but patriots from South Carolina and Georgia, in actions just now being disclosed, had recently hijacked over seven tons of the explosive material. Because the call from Philadelphia was so pressing, the council agreed to send a delegation to Georgia asking them to help furnish the critical supply. To carry out this mission, it nominated Drayton and Miles Brewton, a wealthy and well-respected merchant and also a member of the Council of Safety.[49]

Wasting no time, the two emissaries immediately left for Savannah, where on July 15 they petitioned the Georgia provincial congress for as large a portion of the *Philippa*'s gunpowder as it felt able to contribute. A committee as-

47. Drayton, *Memoirs* 1: 268–71; Wright to Graves, 27 June 1775, in Clark, *Naval Documents,* 1: 764.

48. Drayton, *Memoirs* 1: 268–71; Sheldon S. Cohen, "The *Philippa* Affair," *Georgia Historical Quarterly* 69 (fall 1985): 344–51; Terry W. Lipscomb, *The Carolina Lowcountry: April 1775–June 1776* (Columbia, S.C.: SCDAH, 1994), 8; Jon R. Huford, "Enough Gunpowder to Start a Revolution," *Southern Studies* 23 (fall 1984): 315–8.

49. *LDC,* 1: 570; Drayton, *Memoirs,* 1: 272; "Journal of the Council of Safety," SCHS *Collections,* 2: 36; Lipscomb, *Carolina Lowcountry,* 8.

signed to consider the request soon reported back to the Carolinians that since the colony had a mere 12,700 pounds of gunpowder, they could only afford to donate 3,000 pounds. Both Drayton and Brewton earnestly objected, explaining that this paltry grant failed to "discharge the duty she [Georgia] owed to America and herself." The Georgia Whigs, who had just recently and somewhat hesitantly joined the American cause, did not want their more aggressive northern neighbors to view them as halfhearted patriots. Upon further reflection, they decided to increase their gift to two and a half tons, which appeased the Carolina agents. In addition to the gunpowder, Drayton and Brewton also managed to purchase all the saltpeter and sulfur (materials used in making gunpowder) available in Savannah, together with a considerable amount of blanketing.[50]

One week later the schooner *Polly*, laden with 5,025 pounds of gunpowder, left Charleston harbor "with all possible secrecy" and arrived in Philadelphia in late July. This timely delivery of explosive material, which amounted to nearly half of what the Continental Congress would receive from all other colonies combined through October, proved invaluable to General Washington's underequipped forces in their success in driving the British army out of Boston in March of the following year.[51]

As chairman of the Secret Committee, Drayton also sought to procure gunpowder through more conventional methods. In early May, his committee bought 1,450 pounds of gunpowder from James Leckie; in July it agreed to buy 20,000 pounds from another gunpowder manufacturer, Captain Isaac Caton, who promised to deliver it within four months. As a result of the Secret Committee's success in amassing this valuable material, the Council of Safety instructed it to procure other articles of war. The committee had equal fortune in this new endeavor, quickly purchasing all the muskets, balls, swan shot, and flints it could locate in Charleston. Drayton and his associates also secured important tools for constructing fortifications and employed gunsmiths and other craftsmen to clean and repair these items. Governor Campbell was shocked at how quickly the patriots were accumulating weapons of war. He informed Dartmouth that "by one means or other they have ammas'd great quantities of warlike stores, ammunition particularly,

50. "Journal of the Council of Safety," SCHS *Collections*, 2: 48–50; Drayton, *Memoirs*, 2: 272–3.
51. "Journal of the Council of Safety," SCHS *Collections*, 2: 54–5.

which they can easily do as there is no force by Sea or Land to prevent them."[52]

Despite Campbell's letter of alarm, the patriots were still wanting for "warlike stores." To supply this deficiency, the provincial congress offered lucrative bounties for those establishing iron bloomeries. Here Drayton saw an opportunity to both advance the colony's defenses and make a tidy profit. In July 1775 he obtained four thousand acres of land near present Spartanburg, a region rich in iron ore. He also invested £2,381 in a joint project with iron manufacturer William Wofford to build a bloomery. Later that summer he visited the uncompleted ironworks with Wofford. What Drayton saw there and heard from his partner must have disappointed him. Six months later he sold his interest in the venture to an industrial entrepreneur, Joseph Buffington.[53]

Drayton and his Secret Committee must receive most of the credit for causing Campbell and other royalists so much trepidation over the Whigs' accumulation of stores. Drayton, too, had to be somewhat surprised over the rapid advance of the rebellion in South Carolina during the spring and early summer of 1775. During this time, he and his fellow extremists on the committees he chaired took the lead in concentrating the public energies into a "firm and manly opposition," fully aware of the dire consequences their seditious deeds might have on their lives and fortunes.[54] Officials in London, through correspondence from Alexander Innes, already knew that Drayton was one of the most dangerous insurgents in South Carolina. Had affairs settled down in America and the Revolution not occurred, the British would certainly have targeted him as an early victim for their vengeance. However, by July 1775 Drayton firmly believed that war with the mother country was inevitable. Understanding the results failure in this conflict would have on his life made him even more determined to ensure American victory.

52. Ibid., 54, 58, 60; "Miscellaneous Papers of the General Committee, Secret Committee and Provincial Congress, 1775," *SCHM* 8 (July 1907): 132, 139; Agreement between William Henry Drayton and Isaac Caton, 28 July 1775, Gibbes Collection, SCDAH; Campbell to Dartmouth, 19 August 1775, *Dartmouth Manuscripts*, 2: 354–5.

53. South Carolina Royal Grants, 37: 192–9; *JPC*, 162–3, 249–50; William Tennent to Henry Laurens, 20 August 1775, *DHAR*, 1: 145; Ernest M. Lander Jr., "The Iron Industry in Ante-Bellum South Carolina," *JSH* 20 (August 1954): 337; Thomas Cowan, "William Hill and the Aera Iron Works," *Journal of Early Southern Decorative Arts* 13 (November 1987): 6–7; South Carolina Revolutionary Audited Accounts, "William Henry Drayton," #2030, SCDAH.

54. Drayton, *Memoirs*, 1: 274–5.

Owing partly to Drayton's aggressive actions, Britain's chances of quelling the insurrection in South Carolina and apprehending known rebels was considerably reduced. By August 1775 the Whigs, possessing an army, treasury, a legislature, and an elaborate substructure of permanent committees to carry out its measures, held control over affairs in Charleston. This substantial authority enabled them to subdue the king's friends and begin placing the capital in a defensive posture in case of an attack from Great Britain. Drayton, as one of the most zealous, energetic, and powerful firebrands within the revolutionary movement, played an instrumental role in these developments.

Many residents of the interior, on the other hand, still refused to support Whig measures despite the patriotic epistles sent throughout the region by Drayton's Committee of Intelligence. Decades of ill-treatment by the lowcountry oligarchy had brewed intense resentment among the backcountry inhabitants, many of whom remained unsympathetic to the patriots' cries of ministerial injustice. Whig leaders soon learned that Governor Campbell was desperately trying to organize and arm these disgruntled frontiersmen to help him gain control of the colony. It was this new crisis facing the revolutionaries to which Drayton next devoted his talents and energies.

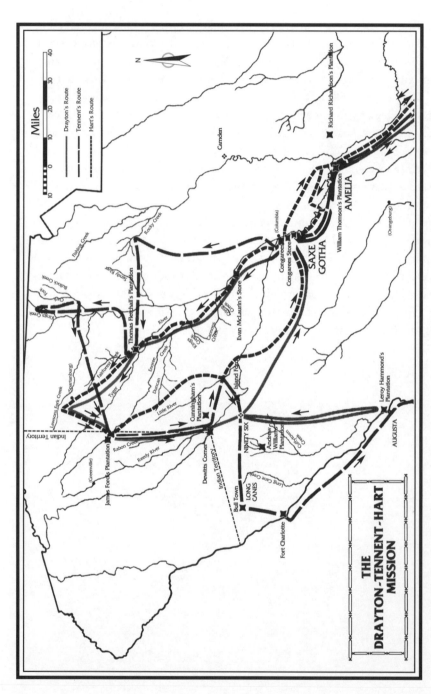

An approximation of the routes of William Henry Drayton, William Tennent, and Oliver Hart during their mission to win over backcountry settlers to the patriot cause in the summer of 1775.

Courtesy University of South Carolina Press

SUPPRESSING BACKCOUNTRY LOYALISM

During the first half of 1775, Drayton and his fellow revolutionaries accomplished the monumental task of establishing a separate form of government and silencing opposition in Charleston. The patriots had no time to rejoice in their achievement, however, as a new threat to their supremacy was developing in the colony's interior. Here a rapidly growing party of loyalists, led by influential men of high intelligence and determination, were forming themselves into military units and openly defying Whig measures. This development greatly worried lowcountry leaders, as recent events appeared to edge South Carolina closer to war with Great Britain. Realizing the dangers such a conflict would bring to a divided people, the Council of Safety appointed Drayton to lead a commission into the upcountry to, in one way or another, suppress the dissidents there. Although Drayton had confronted and conquered much adversity in his thirty-three years, this difficult and dangerous assignment proved to be his greatest challenge to date, requiring all of his energy, intellect, and guile.

Until the spring of 1775 the revolutionary movement in South Carolina had been confined primarily to the tidewater, and more specifically to the city of Charleston. The rest of the province remained largely indifferent, or even outright hostile, to the lowcountry's struggles with the British government. The question of loyalism in the South Carolina backcountry still remains largely unsolved. One reason for this is the complexity of the issue. A contemporary enigmatically described the backcountry allegiances in 1775 as a "wheel within a wheel." Another factor allowing this mystery to continue is insufficient evidence preventing historians from fully understanding individual or group motivation for choosing loyalism in the South Carolina interior. Therefore, any conclusions about its genesis and growth must be tentative.[1]

Recently, historians have revised the conclusions of earlier students of the subject who attributed backcountry loyalism to the region's distinct cultural, ethnic, social, and economic makeup; its isolation from the British policies which so offended lowcountry residents; its high number of recent German, Irish, and Scottish immigrants; and, most importantly, its frustrating and long-standing struggle with the coastal aristocracy for schools, roads, courts, jails, and political representation. Some of these recent studies still concede that the backcountry's large population of immigrants, who were immersed in the problems of pioneering and who were not engaged in large-scale commercial activities, were unlikely to support a movement opposing a king who had given them their land. Likewise, they maintain that hostility toward the lowcountry was another important factor contributing to loyalism in the interior, but unlike previous historians, contend that this resentment was not a direct result of the coastal elite's neglect of the backcountrymen's need for judicial, political, and religious institutions. Instead, this enmity, as Robert Lambert tentatively suggests, is now viewed as having several causes: a continuation of animosities stemming from the inland civil war of the late 1760s between farmers and the squatters and hunters terrorizing them; resentment by militia officers and justices of the peace who were temporarily deprived of their offices during this conflict; and the veterans of British military service dispersed throughout the backcountry population who were likely to "spring to the defense of royal authority" when it was challenged by backcountry rebels.[2]

1. Edward Musgrove to William Henry Drayton, 14 October 1775, *DHAR*, 1: 203; Robert S. Lambert, *South Carolina Loyalists in the American Revolution* (Columbia: University of South Carolina Press, 1987), 27, 29.

2. Lambert, *South Carolina Loyalists*, 27–8. The earlier group of historians includes Robert W. Barnwell Jr., "The Beginnings of the Revolution in the Back Country of South Carolina" (master's thesis, University of South Carolina, 1926), 1–34; Barnwell, "Loyalism in South Carolina," 91–4, 139–40; Wallace Brown, *The King's Friends: The Composition and Motives of the American Loyalist Claimants* (Providence, R.I.: Brown University Press, 1965), 219–20; Wallace Brown, *The Good Americans: The Loyalists in the American Revolution* (New York: William Morrow, 1969), 236–7. Recent revisions on loyalism in South Carolina are offered by Rachel N. Klein, *Unification of a Slave State: The Rise of the Planter Class in the South Carolina Backcountry, 1760–1808* (Chapel Hill: University of North Carolina Press, 1990), 79–84; Rachel N. Klein, "Frontier Planters and the American Revolution: The South Carolina Backcountry, 1775–1782," in *An Uncivil War: The Southern Backcountry during the American Revolution*, ed. Ronald Hoffman, Thad Tate, and Peter J. Albert (Charlottesville: University Press of Virginia, 1985),

Another important dynamic of backcountry allegiances was the tendency of neighborhoods and communities to coalesce around men of influence, particularly those who wielded economic, political, and military power, such as store owners, millers, militia officers, and magistrates. Many of these men had colonywide political and military ambition, and an important consideration for them in choosing or switching sides was the rank or office the Whig government offered them. As the following narrative reveals, several important backcountrymen switched to the loyalist party when they felt the provincial congress had not taken "proper notice" of them. When these men abandoned the American cause, many of their neighbors followed. Making it easy for them to join the loyalist party was a confidence that the patriots could not harm them. With the uncertainty of Whig authority on the one hand and the power of the British army and the broader community's sharing their hostility on the other, the backcountrymen felt themselves protected from any possible punishment resulting from their loyalism.[3]

In mid-1775, Crown officials—both inside and outside the province—began making a concerted effort to intensify this pro-British sentiment in the region. Drayton's Committee of Intelligence, for example, received information in early June that North Carolina governor Josiah Martin was planning an insurrection among the king's friends in the South Carolina backcountry. Later that summer, Whig authorities discovered that Governor Campbell was secretly encouraging prominent loyalists in the interior to organize armed companies of men to oppose the popular measures. And to dissuade any who had thoughts of joining the rebels, associate justice Edward Savage firmly pointed out the "dreadful consequences of Treason" to grand jurors in the region during his spring court sessions. This Crown activity prompted a horrified Henry Laurens to remark that "Administration & their Creatures" have left "no Stone . . . unturned . . . to disunite us poor distressed Americans."[4]

40–7; Rachel N. Klein, "Ordering the Backcountry: The South Carolina Regulation," *W&MQ*, 3d. ser., 38 (October 1981): 668–78; Lambert, *South Carolina Loyalists*, 27–9; and Richard M. Brown, *The South Carolina Regulators* (Cambridge, Mass.: Harvard University Press, 1963), 123–5.

3. Klein, *Unification of a Slave State*, 84–7; Ronald Hoffman, "The 'Disaffected' in the Revolutionary South," in *The American Revolution: Explorations in the History of American Radicalism*, ed. Alfred F. Young (De Kalb: Northern Illinois University Press, 1976), 311–2; Barnwell, "Loyalism in South Carolina," 91, 139.

4. North Carolina Delegates to the Presbyterian Ministers of Philadelphia, 3–8 July 1775, *LDC*, 1: 576 n. 1; Campbell to Dartmouth, 5 July 1775, BPROSC 35: 148–9; Drayton, *Memoirs*, 1: 323; Claim of Edward Savage, American Loyalist Transcripts, 57: 125–6, NYPL; Henry Laurens to John Laurens, 30 July 1775, *HLP*, 10: 258.

Facing the unthinkable prospect of fighting a war on two fronts if the backcountry remained loyal to the king, the Whig government made vigorous efforts to enlist the region in the revolutionary movement. One of the earliest of such attempts involved Drayton's Committee of Intelligence, which in the spring and summer of 1775 wrote and dispatched throughout the interior several epistles designed to gain the people's sympathy for the American cause. However, if the patriots were to have any chance in gaining the back-settlers' support, they had to win over local leaders, who, because of their prominent status, carried enormous influence over others in their community. To interest them in the Whig crusade, the General Committee appointed eighty-four prominent backcountrymen to local committees for enforcing the Association, officered seven of the twelve newly created provincial regiments with leaders from the interior, and gave the region 55 (out of 184) seats in the provincial congress—much more legislative representation than it had ever enjoyed under royal rule.[5]

These offerings succeeded in securing the support of many influential backcountry leaders, but there still remained large areas of resistance, especially along a band stretching from Charleston inland to Ninety-Six. One particularly strong concentration of king's friends was in the region between the Broad and Saluda Rivers, where reports indicated that possibly a majority of the inhabitants were "quite comfortable under British rule" and "passively, if not actively, disaffected from the American cause." Indeed, a militant loyalist party was forming under the guidance of Thomas Fletchall. Nothing is known of his origin except that he came to South Carolina around 1757 while in his early thirties and settled on Fair Forest Creek in what is today Union County. There he operated a gristmill and owned a substantial plantation worked by over a dozen slaves. He was also a colonel in the militia, a coroner, and a justice of the peace, positions that gave him respect and authority in the region. Despite his influence, Fletchall's ability to provide strong leadership was handicapped by extreme obesity (he weighed nearly three hundred pounds), which made travel difficult, and an overly cautious and vacillating temperament. Instead, more spirited and decisive men who had influence with the colonel provided the energy behind most of the party's forceful measures.[6]

5. Lambert, *South Carolina Loyalists*, 34.

6. Barnwell, "Loyalism in South Carolina," 94–5, 137; Brown, *King's Friends*, 220, 226; Memorial of Colonel Thomas Fletchall, American Loyalist Transcripts, 57: 223–39, NYPL; E. Alfred Jones, ed., *The Journal of Alexander Chesney: A South Carolina Loyalist in the Revolution and After* (Ohio State University, 1921; reprint, Greenville, S.C.: A Press, 1981), 66.

Because of Fletchall's authority in the region, the provincial congress tried to win his allegiance in January 1775 by appointing him to a committee to enforce the Association. However, by July the patriots obtained reports that suggested he was "not a friend to the cause of liberty" and was covertly taking an active part against the Whig government. To determine whether Fletchall chose to either "join the friends of the glorious cause of freedom" or preferred to "aid and abet the tools of despotism," the Council of Safety wrote him a strong letter on July 4 ordering him to sign the local Association petition and to encourage his regiment to do likewise. In compliance, Fletchall mustered the fifteen hundred men in the Upper Saluda Regiment and had his executive officer read the Association agreement to each company. "I don't remember that one man offered to sign it," Fletchall noncommittally reported to the council, "[and it] was out of my power to compel them to do so." Instead, said the colonel, "it was agreed amongst the people in general to sign a paper of their own resolutions." These resolves, drafted by thirty-three-year-old major Joseph Robinson, a man of considerable education in law and the classics and an influential resident of the Camden District, denied that the king had forfeited the colonists' allegiance or violated the British constitution. The signers of this "Counter-Association" petition pledged not to take up arms against the British monarch, to live in peace and true friendship with their neighbors, and to help defend against any Indian uprising or slave revolt.[7]

The Whigs' failure to curtail loyalism between the Broad and Saluda Rivers was quickly followed by a second reversal, this one occurring at the small village of Ninety-Six, near present Greenwood. To reduce the loyalists' fighting capabilities, the Council of Safety in late June ordered Major James Mayson to lead two companies of provincial rangers, commanded by Captains John Caldwell and Moses Kirkland, to seize Fort Charlotte (a lightly garrisoned post on the Savannah River approximately forty-five miles above Augusta) and remove its stock of powder and lead. After accomplishing the task without bloodshed, Mayson ordered Caldwell and his company to stay behind and occupy the fort while he and Kirkland delivered a large portion of the captured ammunition to the courthouse at Ninety-Six.

7. *JPC*, 24; Moultrie, *Memoirs*, 1: 45; Henry Laurens to Thomas Fletchall, 14 July 1775, "Journal of the Council of Safety," SCHS *Collections*, 2: 41; Thomas Fletchall to Henry Laurens, 24 July 1775, *DHAR*, 1: 123. A copy of Robinson's resolutions is in the "Journal of the Council of Safety," SCHS *Collections*, 2: 72–3.

Unbeknownst to Mayson, however, Kirkland had decided to change sides. His decision was motivated partly from resentment toward the provincial congress for giving the position of major in the rangers to Mayson, against whom he had a long-standing grudge based on both military rank and influence, and partly from a belief that the sentiment of the entire backcountry was strongly loyalist, as Fletchall's party was growing rapidly. After forsaking the patriot party, Kirkland sent a message to Fletchall informing him that if troops were sent to Ninety-Six to recapture the munitions from Fort Charlotte, they would face no opposition. Kirkland then ordered his men home, leaving the military supplies unprotected. However, the ever cautious Fletchall declined Kirkland's open invitation. Two of his younger and more assertive subordinates, Major Robinson and Captain Robert Cunningham, on the other hand, did not want to lose this golden opportunity and so volunteered to lead two hundred men to Ninety-Six. Cunningham, a native of Pennsylvania, was a popular and prosperous member of the Little River community, where he served as magistrate, deputy surveyor, and captain of militia. Like Kirkland, he was so exasperated when the congress overlooked him and appointed Mayson colonel that the Scotsman, according to Andrew Pickens, "immediately took to the other side of the Question." When he and Robinson arrived at the Ninety-Six courthouse on July 17 with their company of armed men, they had no trouble placing Mayson in jail and absconding with the supplies and ammunition they found in his possession.[8]

The loyalist movement had received a healthy dose of adrenalin with the addition of Moses Kirkland. Described in 1776 as a "stout corpulent man" between fifty and sixty years of age, Kirkland arrived in South Carolina from the north in the early 1750s and soon established himself as a man of wealth and strong persuasion. In addition to his prosperous 950-acre indigo plantation on Turkey Creek (in modern Edgefield County), he owned a sawmill, gristmill, ferry, and over three thousand acres of land. His success may have been due in part to his willingness to use questionable means. Not long after his arrival in the province, for instance, he was convicted of selling liquor to

8. Claim of Robert Cunningham, American Loyalist Transcripts, 54: 318–24, NYPL; Wilbur H. Siebert, *Loyalists in East Florida, 1774–1785* (Deland, Fla.: Florida Historical Society, 1929), 2: 315; Lambert, *South Carolina Loyalists*, 37; Andrew Pickens to Henry Lee, 28 August 1811, Andrew Pickens Papers, SCL; William Thomson to Henry Laurens, July 22, 1775, in Alexander S. Salley Jr., *The History of Orangeburg County, South Carolina: From Its First Settlement to the Close of the Revolutionary War* (Orangeburg, S.C.: R. Lewis Berry, 1898), 406; Drayton, *Memoirs*, 1: 317–8; "Journal of the Council of Safety," SCHS *Collections*, 2: 29.

the Catawbas and harboring runaway slaves. Later, in 1770, officials caught him red-handed in a scheme to steal land warrants from the township of Saxe-Gotha. Nevertheless, Kirkland's criminal record seems not to have diminished his reputation or influence, since his neighbors elected him to the assembly in 1768 and the governor appointed him deputy surveyor in 1774. Because of his authority in the region, the provincial congress in June 1775 gave Kirkland a captaincy in the rangers, hoping to attach him to its cause. Instead, the appointment only insulted the vain, egotistical planter, who felt that his prominence entitled him to a more prestigious command. A man of rough language and behavior, Kirkland would prove to be a deep thorn in Drayton's side during the patriot's mission to the backcountry.[9]

Kirkland's defection, along with the adoption of Robinson's Counter-Association and the seizure of powder from the patriots, swelled the loyalist ranks between the Saluda and Savannah Rivers. Whig rangers guarding Fort Charlotte were even deserting to the other party and back-settlers were refusing to accept provincial currency. The loyalist situation appeared so favorable, in fact, that some placemen believed if Governor Campbell entered the region and assumed command of Fletchall's party, he could overthrow the revolutionary government in Charleston. Alexander Innes, the governor's secretary, offered to assist in the venture by leading a portion of Fletchall's men to retake Fort Charlotte. Campbell rejected both proposals as too risky without military assistance from Great Britain. Until then, the governor felt he could "do no more" than provide encouragement to the "King's faithful Subjects."[10]

The governor's hesitation gave the Whigs time to act. On July 22, the Council of Safety received an encouraging letter from Colonel William Thomson, a well-respected planter from St. Mathews Parish and commander of a regi-

9. Robert L. Meriwether, *The Expansion of South Carolina* (Kingsport, Tenn.: Southern Publishers, 1940), 136–7; Memorial of Moses Kirkland, American Loyalist Transcripts, 57: 318–50, NYPL; Walter B. Edgar and N. Louise Bailey, eds., *Biographical Directory of the South Carolina House of Representatives* (Columbia: University of South Carolina Press, 1977), 2: 380–1; Jones, *Journal of Alexander Chesney*, 105; Brown, *South Carolina Regulators*, 128–30.

10. Drayton, *Memoirs*, 1: 323; James Mayson to Council of Safety, 18 July 1775, and James Mayson to William Thomson, 30 July 1775, "Papers of the First Council of Safety," *SCHM* (January 1900): 46, 71; Campbell to Dartmouth, 19 August 1775, BPROSC 35: 189–90; Affidavit of Elizabeth Simpson, 11 July 1775, "Journal of the Council of Safety," SCHS *Collections*, 2: 69–70; Barnwell, "Loyalism in South Carolina," 106–7.

ment of provincial rangers, insisting that if some men "of the most noted
Character" were sent into the backcountry to explain these "unhappy disputes" between Great Britain and America "in a proper Light," they might
be able to regain the allegiance of those "deluded" by Fletchall and Robinson. Heartened by this message, the Council of Safety commissioned Drayton and the Presbyterian preacher William Tennent to make a journey into
the upcountry to explain the nature of America's grievances to the people,
convince them of the necessity of a "general union" in order to "preserve
themselves and their children from slavery," identify areas and leaders of opposition, and most importantly, secure the allegiance and control of the backcountry militia by winning over its commanders. To help them accomplish
this task, the council authorized the commissioners to call upon the militia
and rangers for support and protection. Three days later, Henry Laurens,
president of the Council of Safety, drew up a second commission for the Baptist minister Oliver Hart to join Drayton and Tennent. Because the commissioners lived on the coast and thus knew relatively little about the men and
the conditions in the backcountry, the council appointed Colonel Richard
Richardson and the wealthy merchant Joseph Kershaw, two prominent and
influential men from the Camden District, to assist them on portions of their
journey.[11]

The Council of Safety used great care and thoughtfulness in selecting the
men for this important mission. Each one brought particular skills, knowledge, and experience necessary for its success. Drayton was an obvious
choice. He had proven himself a persuasive orator during the previous fall in
his revolutionary charges to the grand juries of Camden, Cheraws, and
Georgetown. Those speeches had brought him great popularity and respect
in those regions, as demonstrated when voters in the Saxe-Gotha District
elected him to the provincial congress. However, Arthur Middleton and
Peter Timothy believed that some "cool, dispassionate, timid, lukewarm
[and] disinterested" members of the council chose Drayton as a means to
temporarily remove a dangerous firebrand from the center of power.[12] Those
who favored moderate measures were undoubtedly disturbed by their young

11. Thomson to Laurens, 22 July 1775, in Salley, *Orangeburg County*, 405; "Journal of the
Council of Safety," SCHS *Collections*, 2: 58, 64.
12. Middleton to Drayton, 22 August 1775, in Barnwell, "Correspondence of Arthur Middleton," 134; Timothy to Drayton, 13 August 1775, *DHAR*, 1: 139.

colleague's aggressive actions, but if this was one of the council's reasons for selecting Drayton, it was merely tangential. Neutralizing loyalist sentiment in the backcountry was far too important a task to be used simply for political gamesmanship. In any event, it is possible that Drayton volunteered for this assignment simply to remove himself temporarily from the numerous responsibilities in Charleston that were leaving him, in his words, "almost jaded."

William Tennent, pastor of the Independent (Presbyterian) Church in Charleston, was also an obvious selection. As grandson of William Tennent I, the minister and educator who founded the Log College in 1736, his name alone carried respect and influence throughout North America. Tennent's education, experience, and credentials were as impressive as his family's reputation. He earned baccalaureate and master's degrees in religion from the College of New Jersey and a second graduate degree from Harvard. After receiving his license to preach in 1761, Tennent spent the next ten years in a slow migration southward, ministering to various Presbyterian churches in New York, Connecticut, and Virginia. By the time he finally settled down in Charleston in 1771 at the age of thirty-one, he possessed polished oratorical skills and a commanding presence. During the controversy surrounding the Tea and Intolerable Acts, the Presbyterian divine published essays in the local press to stimulate patriotism among South Carolinians. Tennent's revolutionary views may have arisen from his strong belief in both religious and civil liberty, which he considered inseparable. Nevertheless, his efforts in the American cause earned him the sobriquet "Firebrand Parson" among patriots in Charleston, who elected him to the provincial congress in 1775. That same year Whig leaders put his enthusiasm and persuasive skills to use by appointing him to Drayton's Committee of Intelligence. In selecting Tennent for the mission into the interior, however, the Council of Safety was influenced as much as anything by his Presbyterianism, because, as Colonel Thomson explained to Laurens, "a great many of those people are of his Religion."[13]

13. Middleton to Drayton, 22 August 1775, in Barnwell, "Correspondence of Arthur Middleton," 136; Thomson to Laurens, 22 July 1775, in Salley, *Orangeburg County*, 405. Information on Tennent was culled from Robert M. Weir, "William Tennent III" (1969), 1–7, manuscript in the William Tennent III Papers, SCL; Durwood T. Stokes, "The Clergy of the Carolinas and the American Revolution" (Ph.D. diss., University of North Carolina, 1968), 166–73, 266–7; George Howe, *History of the Presbyterian Church in South Carolina* (Columbia, S.C.: Duffie & Chapman, 1870), 1: 362–3, 366–7.

The backcountry was also filled with Baptists, which is why the council added the fifty-two-year-old Baptist minister Oliver Hart to the mission. It might have also selected Hart because, more than Drayton and Tennent, he identified with the class of people to whom the commissioners were sent— the self-made backwoodsmen. Born in 1723 to a poor family in Bucks County, Pennsylvania, Hart received only a limited education. He made his living as a carpenter until 1749 when, after hearing the Great Revival preachings of Jonathan Edwards, George Whitefield, and William Tennent I, he decided to join the ministry. The following year he came to South Carolina in response to an appeal from Charleston Baptists for a pastor. Upon his arrival, Hart quickly set about an active career promoting religion in the province. In 1751 he organized four churches into the second Baptist Association in America. Five years later he established a plan through that organization to help train ministers. Hart also made numerous trips into the backcountry, preaching to the religiously starved frontiersmen. Through these and other efforts he became the recognized leader among South Carolina Baptists. Despite his prominence, however, Hart may not have been the best choice for the assignment. At fifty-two, he lacked the stamina necessary for such a physically grueling journey. He also did not possess Drayton's self-confidence or Tennent's magnetism—two vital characteristics necessary to persuade others. Nevertheless, Hart's influence with the Baptists and his common heritage with the simple woodsmen convinced the council that he would make a valuable addition to the mission.[14]

Drayton, Tennent, and Hart did not ride together, but took separate routes in order to cover more area. Several times, two commissioners traveled with each other, but on only three occasions were all three together. Thus much of their mission is a tale of three independent and unique expeditions, with varying efforts and results. Before departing, the genteel commissioners exchanged their patrician clothing for the plain garments of the backwoods-

14. Loulie L. Owens, *Oliver Hart, 1723–1795: A Biography* (Greenville, S.C.: Baptist Historical Society, 1966), 7–16, 41; Loulie L. Owens, "Oliver Hart and the American Revolution," *Journal of the South Carolina Baptist Historical Society* 1 (November 1975): 5, 13; Loulie L. Owens, "South Carolina Baptists and the American Revolution," *Journal of the South Carolina Baptist Historical Society* 1 (November 1975): 31, 34; Loulie L. Owens, "A Nail in Time," *Sandlapper* 9 (January 1976): 17; Durwood T. Stokes, "The Baptist and Methodist Clergy in South Carolina and the American Revolution," *SCHM* 73 (April 1972): 88–91; Leah Townshend, *South Carolina Baptists, 1760–1805* (Florence, S.C.: Florence Printing, 1935), 122–5.

men in an attempt to portray themselves as "men of the people." Still, they expected a hostile reception. Drayton, for one, carried with him at all times a pair of pocket pistols and a sword for his personal safety.[15]

Drayton traveled with Tennent during the first leg of the journey into the "disaffected country." They left Charleston at 6 A.M. on August 2 in Tennent's four-wheeled chaise and headed north along the Cooper River. After covering thirty miles by sundown—a rapid pace by eighteenth-century standards—they stopped for the night at Thomas Broughton's large plantation estate. They spent the second night at a tavern, but failed to get much sleep "owing to the noise of a Maniac occasionally there." The following evening was no better for the two men as they endured "a sick and sleepless night" after eating some green corn at the home of Tacitus Gaillard, a friend and member of the provincial congress. Tennent and Drayton could not catch up on their sleep during the day, either, as their chaise rumbled along "the worst Road I ever saw," in the words of the Presbyterian minister. By the evening of August 5, the two wearied travelers had finally covered the 130 miles that brought them to their first destination, the Congaree Store—a trading post in the German settlement of Saxe-Gotha near present-day Columbia.[16]

The next morning Drayton and Tennent dispatched notices to community leaders inviting them to assemble the inhabitants for a speech that evening. To the commissioners' "great mortification," not one German appeared at the scheduled gathering. Those who attempted to organize the meeting explained to Drayton that their countrymen feared the king would take away their land if they joined the patriots. Moreover, the Germans were upset with the provincial congress for placing a body of rangers near their settlement, believing it was a crass attempt to terrify them into signing the Association agreement. When a rumor spread through the township that Drayton and Tennent had come to unleash this cavalry upon them, no amount of argument could induce the Germans to "come near" the commissioners. Drayton and Tennent were greatly disappointed with this early failure; the envoys still had "some hopes of success," but admitted to the council that "they are but small in this quarter."[17]

15. Drayton, *Memoirs*, 1: 378 n.

16. William Tennent Diary (1775), pp. 1–2, William Tennent III Papers, SCL.

17. Drayton, *Memoirs*, 1: 325–6; Drayton and Tennent to Council of Safety, 7 August 1775, *DHAR*, 1: 128.

To steer the obstinate Germans into hearing their message, the commissioners employed a crafty combination of coercion and deception. First, they ordered the two German companies from Colonel William Thomson's rangers to muster near the Congaree Store on Wednesday, August 9. To ensure that their order was obeyed, the emissaries threatened officers refusing to assemble their companies with loss of their commissions. They next employed two German clergymen to gather their congregations for religious services on August 11 and 13—without notifying them that the Whig delegates would also attend. In the meantime, the commissioners began a campaign of economic warfare against the settlers by posting an announcement that the provisional government would not allow anyone to sell or purchase goods at the Congaree Store or in Charleston without a certificate indicating they had signed the Association petition. To enforce this measure, Drayton urged Whig leaders in Charleston to station guards at the entrances into the capital. The General Committee approved of their colleagues' economic pressure and appointed a committee on August 14 to "take proper measures" for enforcing the resolution.[18]

On Sunday morning (August 6), Tennent went to Colonel Thomson's ranger camp at "the Congarees" (near modern Columbia) to perform a religious service for the troops. Drayton took advantage of the gathering to lecture the soldiers on the nature of the Anglo-American dispute and their "duty and obligation" to oppose any British troops landing in the colony. Afterwards, several of the men complained about the insufficient pay and provisions allotted to them by the Whig government, but the commissioners had little sympathy for the soldiers' plight. Drayton explained to them that since they were not serving under "an established and quiet Government," they could not, "in honor or conscience," request more than "absolute necessaries." However, he suggested that if they considered it a hardship to go abroad to procure their provisions, the council could save them this trouble by deducting a portion of their pay in exchange for supplying all their essentials. A few of the soldiers expressed their gratitude to Drayton and Tennent, who then departed the camp satisfied that they had redressed the soldiers' grievances.[19]

18. Drayton and Tennent to Council of Safety, 7 August 1775, and Drayton to Council of Safety, 9 August 1775, *DHAR*, 1: 129, 135; *SC&AGG*, 25 August 1775.

19. Drayton and Tennent to Council of Safety, 7 August 1775, *DHAR*, 1: 129–30; Drayton, *Memoirs*, 1: 326–7; Thomson to Council of Safety, 9 August 1775, in Salley, *Orangeburg County*, 415.

However, the commissioners were gravely mistaken in making such an assumption. About midnight they were awakened by the "most alarming intelligence" that a mutiny had erupted among the rangers, who threatened to "quit the camp" in the morning and disband. After seeking the advice of Captain Joseph Kershaw and Colonel Thomson, Drayton and Tennent agreed that the best approach to the crisis was simply to allow the soldiers to cool overnight. Their forbearance had the desired effect, as the men "appeared quiet" the next morning. Colonel Thomson marched his regiment to the Congaree Store, where Drayton "dealt plainly" with them on the previous night's disorder. He told them that nobody would be punished, hoping that such leniency "would work a reformation in them." However, if any soldier had ideas of deserting, Drayton quickly warned, the provincial government would offer a large reward for their return to Charleston "dead or alive." For those who remained loyal, on the other hand, he promised that the "gentlemen from below" would reward them with "all kinds of favors and acts of friendship" when these "troubles were over." As a token of this goodwill, and to demonstrate his sympathy with the soldiers' dilemma, Drayton permitted them to purchase supplies from local residents, who were anxious to sell their surplus goods, and urged Thomson to provide his recruits with "snug and comfortable" huts. He then disbanded the regiment until August 18, when it was to repair a new camp in Amelia Township, located about thirty miles south of the Congaree Store.[20]

The following day Colonel Thomson informed the council that Drayton's discourse had solved the problem of provisions "to the full satisfaction of the Rangers," who he felt were now "content, & perfectly disposed to do their duty." In his reply four days later, Henry Laurens expressed hope that the regiment's new disposition was "the effect of a true sense of their Duty & not the transient product of an harangue." No matter how Drayton quelled the incipient mutiny, his prudent intervention at this critical juncture prevented a probable catastrophe; had he failed to hold together this group of ill-provisioned enlisted men, who—unlike the aristocratic Whigs in Charleston—were largely without ideological motivation, the patriots' attempt to neutralize loyalism in the region would have suffered a crippling setback.[21]

20. Drayton and Tennent to Council of Safety, 7 August 1775, *DHAR*, 1: 130–2; Tennent Diary, 3; Drayton to Thomson, n.d., in Salley, *Orangeburg County*, 422–3.

21. Thomson to Council of Safety, 9 August 1775, in Salley, *Orangeburg County*, 415–6; Laurens to Thomson, 13 August 1775, *HLP*, 10: 302; Drayton, *Memoirs*, 1: 329.

Immediately after dealing with this emergency, the commissioners were confronted with a new one when they received intelligence that Moses Kirkland, whom the patriots now considered a "rebellious, seditious son of a bitch," was on his way to Charleston to meet with Governor Campbell. Drayton and Tennent immediately issued orders for his arrest and advised the council of his approach. If Kirkland was allowed to continue his journey, they warned, "evil consequences" would arise because he was very active in "poisoning the minds of the people." Apparently this warning arrived too late, for at about the same time the council received the letter, it obtained an alarming report from Whig leaders in Georgia that Kirkland, with Governor Campbell's encouragement and support, was planning an assault on Augusta. The council sent a brief notice to Drayton informing him of this disturbing development and conferring upon him the power to do anything he felt necessary to apprehend Kirkland. "[F]or God's sake," Middleton wrote Drayton, "as you come down, sweep the Chimney of the State or we shall shortly have a *Bonfire!*" However, Drayton was confident there was "no foundation" in this report, explaining almost boastfully to Colonel Thomson that "the heads of the [loyalist] party . . . will not attempt anything of that sort while I am in this part of the Country." Instead, he felt the non-Associators' primary target, if they were to attack, would be Fort Charlotte.[22]

While Drayton and Tennent were confronting resistance and resolving emergencies near the Congaree Store, Oliver Hart was traveling leisurely through the Piedmont preaching to fellow Baptists. Although the council had appointed him last, Hart was the first commissioner to leave for the interior. Early on the morning of July 31, he loaded copies of the Association agreement into his saddlebag, mounted his horse, and departed alone on a course paralleling the Cooper River to Moncks Corner. From here Hart slowly proceeded northwesterly until stopping on August 4 at a predominantly Baptist settlement above the confluence of the Congaree and Wateree Rivers.

After winning strong encouragement from community leaders regarding his intended business, Hart went to the Congaree Baptist Church on Sunday and preached to a "good Congregation" on John 8:36—"If the Son sets you free, than you will be really free." He then cleverly tied in this sermon on

22. Middleton to Drayton, 12 August 1775, *DHAR*, 1: 137 ("bitch" is not spelled out in the published account but is in the original, which is located in the Gibbes Collection, SCDAH); Drayton and Tennent to Council of Safety, 7 August 1775, *DHAR*, 1: 133; Drayton, *Memoirs*, 1: 396; Middleton to Drayton, 12 August 1775, in Barnwell, "Correspondence of Arthur Middleton," 126; Drayton to Thomson, [15 August?], in Salley, *Orangeburg County*, 422.

freedom with a talk on the "subject of the Times." The parishioners wholly approved of Hart's speech; not necessarily as a result of his oratorical or persuasive skills, but primarily because their pastor, Joseph Reese, was a vigorous patriot who had already converted his congregation to the American cause. Seeing the influence Reese had over his followers, Hart prevailed upon his fellow minister to assist him in the "grand Design of this Excursion." When Reese eagerly accepted his request, Hart viewed it as "favourable Providence." On August 7, the two Baptist divines left the region for the residence of Colonel John Chestnutt (near Congaree Store), where they joined Drayton and Tennent.[23]

With the delegates finally together for the first time, they conferred and plotted their routes and schedules. It was agreed that the mission would have a greater chance of success if they split up and made three separate journeys. Drayton (accompanied by Kershaw) gave himself the difficult assignment of tackling the troublesome Dutch Fork region between the Broad and Saluda Rivers, the only part of the province where loyalists reportedly outnumbered patriots. Oliver Hart was to assist Drayton in this task, but not accompany him. Tennent had a much easier job. He was to proceed north across the Broad as high as Rocky Creek and preach to the Scotch-Irish in the region, who, according to Drayton, were "numerous and ready to sign the Association." After completing their individual assignments, the commissioners planned to meet on August 17 at the residence of Colonel Fletchall on Fairforest Creek. Hart left on his mission with Reese early the following morning, while the others remained in the Congarees three more days to attend to unfinished business.[24]

While the two Baptist ministers were traveling north along the Saluda River, Drayton and Tennent crossed the Congaree and rode five miles to an election at John Adam Summer's plantation on Crim's Creek to thwart "some evil disposed persons" intending to "do what mischief lay in their power." Upon arriving there, however, the commissioners were pleasantly surprised to learn that the men refused to vote until the patriots had enlightened them on public affairs. Inspired by the voters' interest, Drayton and Tennent "harangued

23. "Oliver Hart's Diary of his Mission through the Backcountry" [typescript], Oliver Hart Papers, SCL, p. 1.

24. David Ramsay, *The Revolution in South Carolina* (Trenton, N.J.: Isaac Collins, 1785), 1: 67; Drayton and Tennent to Council of Safety, 7 August 1775, *DHAR*, 1: 129.

the meeting in turns until every Man was convinced," the Presbyterian minister later wrote. Even those intending to disturb the election "cheerfully" signed the Association petition and "begged Pardon for the words they had spoken to the People." Thereafter, the men formed themselves into volunteer militia companies under command of the provincial congress.[25]

Exactly what Drayton and Tennent said at this meeting to persuade their listeners to sign the Association agreement and form militia units is not known because they did not record their speeches. Fortunately for posterity, Andrew McJunkin, an eyewitness to one of the gatherings, did make some notes. According to this self-avowed patriot, the commissioners deliberated in a "calm, persuasive and Christian-like manner" upon the English constitution, the dangers of a Roman Catholic colony in Canada, the ministry's repeated attempts to tax the colonies without allowing them representation in Parliament, and the people's legal right to self-government. Throughout their speeches, the two emissaries reinforced their arguments with "touching allusions to the privations and sufferings" endured by the first settlers in America "for the sake of civil and religious liberty." These stirring discourses, McJunkin remarked, "had the effect of arousing many of the people to a proper appreciation of the rights of man."[26] In all likelihood, the commissioners delivered the same speeches, with slight variations to meet changing circumstances, at all their meetings throughout the backcountry.

Drayton and Tennent's patriotic speeches brought them even greater success the following day in their scheduled appearance before Colonel Thomson's rangers in Amelia Township. The "falling tears from the audience" during their orations, boasted Drayton, "showed that their hearts were penetrated, and that we might hope for success." All but fifteen soldiers subscribed to the Association; those who refused promised to sign later in the week after further examining the issue. Drayton's dressing down of the regiment the previous week and his economic warfare against inhabitants of the region undoubtedly contributed to the soldiers' willingness to sign their names to the document. Nevertheless, Drayton was overjoyed with these two triumphs in as many days and confidently wrote the council, "I have now no doubt of success in the Dutch settlements."[27]

25. Drayton to Council of Safety, 9 August 1775, *DHAR*, 1: 134. The election was for representatives to the provincial congress. See *JPC*, 56–7; Tennent Diary, 3.

26. James H. Saye, ed., *Memoirs of Major Joseph McJunkin: Revolutionary Patriot* (Richmond, Va.: *Watchman and Observer*, 1847; reprint, Greenwood, S.C.: *Index-Journal*, 1925), 5.

27. Drayton to Council of Safety, 9 August 1775, *DHAR*, 1: 134.

Drayton's letter "afforded great Satisfaction" among council members. Most pleased were conservatives like Miles Brewton and Rawlins Lowndes, who, according to Arthur Middleton, were using the commissioner's success to urge the council to extend the length of the mission in hopes of making a "retrograde progress" in the colony's revolutionary movement during Drayton's absence. Indeed, Lowndes's frequent attempts at either delaying or preventing the adoption of aggressive measures earned himself the nickname "Rawlinus postponator" among extremists in the party. Because of the conservatives' obstructionist tactics, Drayton's friends in the council (Middleton and Pinckney) urged him to make rapid progress in "adjusting matters" in the interior, for they "most earnestly" needed his assertive leadership in Charleston.[28]

Spurred by these reports, Drayton and Kershaw left the Congarees on August 9 and traveled toward the troublesome Dutch Fork region. Their first stop was at a German church about ten miles up the Saluda River, where on Friday, August 11, Drayton spoke to the congregation on the righteousness of the American cause. Unlike his previous speeches, however, this one blended biblical texts with secular matter to correspond with the spiritual environs. Despite this clever packaging of the patriot message, only one parishioner signed the boycott agreement. Drayton's failure to gain more subscribers, he soon learned, was the result of some "very active" loyalists who were "perverting" the people's minds. Even those fifteen soldiers in Thomson's regiment who had earlier agreed to subscribe now reneged on their promise. Fed up with the Germans' obstinacy, Drayton decided to implement measures that he felt confident would "go sufficiently home to the Dutch sensibilities." He therefore announced that from now on no miller who was a subscriber to the Association could grind wheat or corn for non-Associators. This declaration gave an "immediate shock" and raised a "general alarm" among the people, Drayton happily reported to the council. He expected this economic pressure, along with some "other operations," to have a "desirable effect" against the intractable Germans.[29]

These high expectations were quickly dashed the next day when Drayton failed to procure even one subscriber at a meeting of approximately one hun-

28. Middleton to Drayton, 22 August 1775, Middleton to Drayton, 12 August 1775, and Timothy to Drayton, 13 August 1775, in Barnwell, "Correspondence of Arthur Middleton," 134, 127–9.

29. Drayton, *Memoirs*, 1: 363; Drayton to Council of Safety, 16 August 1775, *DHAR*, 1: 141. A copy of this letter is also in the Miscellaneous Collection, CL.

dred Germans at Evan McLaurin's Spring Hill estate (located about ten miles up the Saluda River from present Columbia). This failure owed largely to the efforts of McLaurin and several other loyalist leaders in the community, who "threw a damp upon the people" before his arrival. Realizing that no amount of argument or economic pressure could sway the inflexible Dutch Fork residents, Drayton thought it best to save himself the "mortification" of proselytizing to a people who he concluded were "obstinate and would not hear." So he quickly departed the "stiff-necked" Germans and proceeded to King's Creek. Here the commissioner dejectedly wrote the Council of Safety that "the Dutch are not with us."[30]

Hart and Reese were facing similar opposition from inhabitants residing between the Tyger River and Fairforest Creek. Here lived Colonel Thomas Fletchall and the Reverend Philip Mulkey, a faithful loyalist and one of the most active and respected Baptist preachers in the backcountry.[31] These two prominent men had "so fixed" their neighbors "on the Side of the Ministry," Hart complained, that "no argument on the contrary Side seemed to have any Weight with them." Most settlers in the region, in fact, had already signed Robinson's Counter-Association, "a jejune incoherent Piece," according to Hart, which he feared would "delude the people" into measures having "bad consequences."

The Baptist minister saw the effects the Counter-Association had on its subscribers on the evening of August 11 while he and Reese were speaking before a group of about thirty people in the Fairforest Baptist Church. During Reese's discussion of national affairs, several "extremely obstinate" loyalists cried out that they "wished 1,000 Bostonians might be kill'd in Battle" and that all the salt in North American cities would suddenly disappear. "On the whole," Hart despondently wrote in his diary that night, "they appear to be obstinate and irritated to an Extreme." The commissioner was further disheartened on Sunday when John Newton, an assistant of Joseph Reese who had just made a tour of the region, gave him an account of the "distracted State of the Frontier Inhabitants." The people "wear the most alarming Faces," he told Hart, which led him to believe that there was the "greatest appearance of a Civil War"—unless prevented by "some remarkable Interpo-

30. Drayton to Council of Safety, 16 August 1775, *DHAR*, 1: 141; Memorial of Isabella McLaurin, American Loyalist Transcripts, 53: 320, NYPL.

31. Hart Diary, 2. Mulkey was pastor of the Fairforest Baptist Church. Bob Compton, "The Fairforest Church," *Journal of the South Carolina Baptist Historical Society* 1 (November 1975): 47–50; Townshend, *South Carolina Baptists*, 125.

sition of Providence." Of course, no divine intervention occurred—at least not of a positive nature. Instead, the backwoodsmen's ire was further inflamed the following day when Joseph Robinson read to them Lord John Dalrymple's *Address of the People of Great-Britain to the Inhabitants of America*, a sixteen-thousand-word "Ministerial Piece" designed to discourage colonists from rebelling against the mother country. Governor Campbell had earlier sent copies of this paper to loyalist leaders in the backcountry for them to use against the commissioners' propaganda. Colonel Fletchall was undoubtedly responsible for staging this presentation for his neighbors.[32]

Essentially, the "Address" argued that the Continental Congress was rapidly leading the colonies on a path to war with the strongest military power on earth, a conflict which America had no hope of winning because the closing of trade with Great Britain would ruin the country's economy, its slaves would revolt or run away at the first appearance of the enemy, and it lacked a single walled town, disciplined regiment, warship, or even an independent treasury. Therefore America's "destruction is inevitable," the address forewarned. If by some miracle the colonies did achieve independence, the young and vulnerable nation would fall prey to "all the miseries of foreign, civil, and domestick war." Why risk such calamity, it asked, when the colonies already reaped so many advantages from living under the infinite generosity of His Majesty: the most extensive personal liberties in the world, military protection, and "vast bounties" on major industries such as flax, hemp, timber, naval stores, and indigo. However, the essay's concluding statement about American lawyers proved most harmful to the patriots' mission in the backcountry in its assertion that "there are men among yourselves against whom you ought to be equally on your guard. It is hard that the charge of our intending to enslave you should come oftenest from the mouths of those lawyers who, in your Southern Provinces, at least, have long made you slaves to themselves."[33]

Robinson's long-winded yet foreboding address "fix[ed] the Minds of all disaffected Persons," according to Hart, who despondently added that Colonel Fletchall now "has all those people at his beck and reigns amongst them like a little King." The Baptist minister was so frightened by the frontiersmen's nearly fanatical loyalism resulting from Dalrymple's essay that he felt

32. Hart Diary, 2–3.

33. John Dalrymple, *The Address of the People of Great-Britain to the Inhabitants of America* (London: T. Cadell, 1775), 3–4, 6, 15, 19–20, 26, 59–60.

compelled to begin writing his journal entries in code. No longer holding any hope of persuading these people to "have a suitable Regard to ye interest of America," Hart remained at Mulkey's residence (which bordered Fletchall's) "doing nothing" except anxiously awaiting the arrival of his fellow commissioners.[34]

Meanwhile, Tennent and Richard Richardson, a leading backcountryman assisting the commissioners, were having considerable success propagating the American gospel to the Scotch-Irish settlements above the Broad River. On Friday, August 11, the Presbyterian minister spoke for an hour on the "State of the Country" to a "pretty large Congregation" at the Jackson Creek Meeting House, where he managed, after "much pains," to convert the "chiefs" in the community. He hoped these men would use their influence to persuade those still "obstinately fixed against the proceedings of the Colony" to follow their example. Later that afternoon, the commissioners assembled a company of nearby provincial rangers, who followed their commander's lead and enthusiastically signed the Association agreement. After a "fatiguing but successful day," Tennent and Richardson rode five miles to the home of Robert Allison, owner of a small farm near the Enoree River, where they reposed for the night.[35]

Following a brief delay while their horses were reshod the next morning, Tennent and Richardson continued northward through heavy rain until evening, when they reached Rocky Creek. On Sunday the thirteenth Tennent preached to a large gathering at the Rocky Creek Meeting House on the many rewards of accepting the gospel. After apologizing to the parishioners for having to address the subject of his mission on the Lord's Day, he proceeded to "harangue at large" on the Anglo-American conflict. During his rousing discourse, the commissioner almost succumbed to the suffocating summer heat. Tennent's suffering and perseverance did not go unrewarded, however, as the entire congregation signed the petition, "fully convinced of the Necessity of it," the minister happily noted.[36]

Following this successful meeting, Tennent and Richardson rode ten miles through more torrential rain before stopping for the night. "If we can stand

34. Hart Diary, 3–4.
35. Tennent Diary, 4–5.
36. Ibid., 5.

this we need fear nothing," the Presbyterian minister wrote in his journal before retiring. He was soon to endure even greater suffering, for the "Inclemency of the Skies" was unequal to the "fury of the little Inhabitants" of his bed. When he awoke the next morning after a restless night's sleep, Tennent was shocked by the "blood & slaughter" throughout his calico shirt and sheets, presumably from some type of bedbug. Exhausted but undeterred, Tennent labored hard with Richardson the following three days, enlisting over four hundred men to serve in five volunteer companies under the command of the Council of Safety. The "Ministerial Heroes were much chagrined" at our success, boasted Tennent, "but there was no recall." Afterwards, the two commissioners traveled westward to meet their fellow emissaries at Fletchall's on Fairforest Creek.[37]

Drayton and Kershaw were having a much more difficult time gaining adherents to the American cause. After they had dejectedly left the implacable Germans in Dutch Fork on August 16, the two rode a course paralleling the Broad to King's Creek, where two days later they addressed "a pretty large gathering" at the local meeting house. The audience was "generally satisfied" with their speeches, according to Drayton, and lined up to sign the Association pact. However, just when success was nearly in the patriots' grasp, Robert Cunningham and several others belonging to Fletchall's party stepped into the meetinghouse and announced that they desired to give a different account of the dispute between America and Britain. Drayton was openly frustrated by this unexpected opposition. He tried to influence the loyalists with kindness by inviting them to dinner. After eating, Drayton spoke to them seriously but politely regarding the business at hand. But his benevolence and eloquence failed to dissuade his opponents. "[T]hus I was to be made a public disputer in spite of my teeth," Drayton later reported to the Council of Safety. When the people reassembled, Thomas Brown, an outspoken Crown supporter from Georgia who had recently joined Fletchall's group after being beaten and burned by patriots in Augusta, pulled from his jacket a copy of Dalrymple's "Address," and, in his heavy Scottish burr, read the protracted essay from beginning to end. When he finished nearly two hours later, Drayton "applied ridicule where I thought it would have effect,

37. Ibid., 5–6.

the people laughed heartily and Cunningham and Brown could not but grin—horribly."[38]

Although Drayton reported that he had beaten the loyalists "out of the field," they apparently succeeded in foiling his efforts. Nowhere in his letter of August 16 to the council did Drayton mention anyone subscribing to the Association, even though he claimed there were many ready to sign it before Brown's speech. The loyalist's success in discouraging any potential subscribers is markedly reflected in Drayton's report, in which he warned that Brown was "as dangerous a man as any in this Colony" and would not "stick at anything to throw our affairs into utter confusion."[39] Indeed, Brown's desire for vengeance, coupled with a considerable education and boundless energy and courage, made him a valuable acquisition to Fletchall's party. In the forthcoming weeks Brown would do much to heighten the hostility of upcountry men toward the Charleston Whigs.

Following his failure at King's Creek, Drayton must have felt somewhat apprehensive as he left the next day to confront Colonel Fletchall at his home near the falls of Fairforest Creek. Adding to his concern was a recent dispatch informing him that Hart had been "rather ridiculed" by Fletchall and his crew. Arthur Middleton was also discouraged after reading about these developments and seriously doubted that the commissioners would "meet with much more success" in their mission. He urged Drayton and Tennent to "come down soon," explaining that their "harangues" would be much more useful in the senate chambers, where he said the Council of Safety was "doing nothing but repairing two or three bastions to amuse the people." But the emissaries were not going to quit so soon, at least not before they had their chance to convert the "great and mighty nabob Fletchall." So great was the colonel's influence in the region, that if the commissioners could induce him to sign the Association agreement, they might accomplish their mission in one swift stroke—or so they hoped.[40]

38. Drayton to Council of Safety, 16 August 1775, *DHAR*, 1: 142; Drayton, *Memoirs*, 1: 365–7; Edward J. Cashin, *The King's Ranger: Thomas Brown and the American Revolution on the Southern Frontier* (Athens: University of Georgia Press, 1989), 26–30; Gary D. Olson, "Loyalists and the American Revolution: Thomas Brown and the South Carolina Backcountry, 1775–1776," *SCHM* 68 (October 1967): 207–8; Barnwell, "Loyalism in South Carolina," 112–3.

39. Drayton to Council of Safety, 21 August 1775, *DHAR*, 1: 149.

40. Drayton to Council of Safety, 16 August 1775, *DHAR*, 1: 143; Middleton to Drayton, 22 August 1775, in Barnwell, "Correspondence of Arthur Middleton," 134; Middleton to Drayton, [30 August?] 1775, Drayton, *Memoirs*, 1: 398; Tennent to Laurens, 20 August 1775, *DHAR*, 1: 145.

When the commissioners arrived together at Fletchall's residence early in the morning of August 17, however, they were discouraged to find him surrounded by his zealous lieutenants—Cunningham, Brown, and Robinson. "These men," Drayton soon noticed, "manage Fletchall as they please, when they have him to themselves." So after breakfast, Drayton and Tennent carefully steered the colonel outdoors away from his more aggressive subordinates and doggedly engaged him in a three-hour private conversation. "We endeavoured to explain everything to him," Drayton reported to the Council of Safety four days later. "We pressed [reasons] upon him. We endeavoured to show him that we had confidence in him. We humored him. We laughed with him. Then we recurred to argument, remonstrances and entreaties to join his countrymen and all America. All that we could get from him was this: He would never take up arms against the King, or his countrymen; and that the proceedings of the Congress at Philadelphia were impolitic, disrespectful and irritating to the King."[41]

Discouraged but not defeated, the commissioners next tried to trick the colonel into allowing them to speak directly to the troops under his command. They charged him with communicating with Governor Campbell—implying that there was something nefarious in such correspondence. Fletchall admitted the charge, but swore that there was "no harm in it" and that he would "not take up arms against his country." Drayton and Tennent then asked him to prove his neutrality by mustering his regiment for them on August 23 at James Ford's plantation on the Enoree River. The colonel, whom Campbell had instructed to preserve peace and avoid provoking the Whigs until British reinforcements arrived, agreed to the commissioner's request.[42]

When the three men returned to the house that evening, Fletchall informed Cunningham, Brown, and Robinson of his decision to allow the patriots to address the regiment. His captains were collectively "open-mouthed against the measure," Drayton reported, and vehemently urged their commander to reconsider. Fearful that Fletchall might change his mind, Drayton and Tennent joined the discordant din to try to keep the colonel to his word. Hereupon an abusive verbal storm erupted between the two parties. At one point the belligerent Brown tried to pick a fight with Drayton by calling him a traitor to the king and a false patriot. The Scotsman's accusation infuriated

41. Drayton to Council of Safety, 21 August 1775, *DHAR*, 1: 150.

42. Tennent to Laurens, 20 August 1775, and Drayton to Council of Safety, 21 August 1775, *DHAR*, 1: 145, 150; Campbell to Fletchall, 1 August 1775, *Dartmouth Manuscripts*, 2: 355.

the Carolinian, who had no quarrel with the king, only with his "wicked ministers" and with Parliament. "I almost lost my caution" at this point, he later wrote, "[b]ut thank God I did not even appear to do so." Nevertheless, Drayton "severely checked" Brown for his insulting allegations. This only succeeded in igniting another round of verbal fireworks. A duel between the two men seemed imminent until Fletchall finally ended the caustic quarrel by ordering his pugnacious colleague to bed.[43]

With things "wearing so unfavorable an appearance" following this near calamity at Fletchall's, the commissioners agreed that "vigorous measures" were now "absolutely expedient" if they were not to lose the backcountry to the loyalist cause. Because most of the upcountry opposition appeared to come from backwoodsmen who disliked the Charleston oligarchy but cared little about the dispute with Great Britain, the commissioners believed that this threat to the revolutionary movement could be defused by seizing the twelve most influential leaders. "If a dozen persons are allowed to be at large," Drayton warned the council, "our progress has been in vain, and we shall be involved in a civil war in spite of our teeth." However, he wanted to make certain he had his colleagues' full support before executing this provocative plan. Drayton therefore asked the council to provide him with specific "orders on the subject," along with "proper authority" to carry out the kidnappings. He admitted that capturing the loyalist chiefs would result in "some commotion" in the "disaffected parts," but was confident that by implementing "prompt and vigorous measures," he could quash "every appearance of insurrection."[44]

Drayton's confidence in his ability to crush any armed attempt that Fletchall might make owed to the fact that he could bring forces to bear on the latter's regiment from three sides. To the north were Colonel Thomas Neel's regiment, Captain Ezekial Polk's rangers (which Drayton augmented with a brief recruiting campaign after the miserable meeting at Fletchall's), and Thomas Polk's regiment from North Carolina. To the south he could depend on a good portion of Andrew Williamson's regiment between the Saluda and the Savannah, while to the east were several regiments in the middle portion of the province. With such military might at his fingertips, Drayton confi-

43. Drayton to the Council of Safety, 21 August 1775, *DHAR*, 1: 151; Tennent Diary, 6.
44. Lewis P. Jones, *The South Carolina Civil War of 1775* (Lexington, S.C.: The Sandlapper Store, 1975), 60; Drayton to Council of Safety, 21 August 1775, *DHAR*, 1: 153.

dently told the council that he planned to remain in the backcountry until he saw "every spark of insurrection extinguished."[45]

While waiting for the council's reply, the agents continued on their separate errands, agreeing to meet at Ford's 750-acre plantation on the Enoree on August 23 for the muster of Fletchall's regiment. Drayton, Hart, and Reese continued in a northwesterly direction toward Lawson's Fork near present-day Spartanburg. Tennent traveled north toward the New Acquisition District with a new companion, Joseph Alexander, a Presbyterian minister from Bullock's Creek. Richardson and Kershaw felt they had little influence in these regions, so they returned home.

While on his way to New Acquisition, Tennent received several frightening reports that he felt revealed the loyalists' true intentions. The first of these was an account of a "horrid scheme" to seize the powder and arms from Fort Charlotte. The second was a report that Joseph Robinson had visited the governor in Dorchester, northwest of Charleston, and returned with blank commissions to raise a royal army in the backcountry in preparation for a "dismal campaign" against the Whig government. Most menacing, however, was the rumor that Alexander Cameron (deputy superintendent to the Cherokees) was preparing to send three thousand Cherokee warriors to join the king's forces against supporters of the revolutionary government. Upon hearing of these "infernal designs," Tennent hastily dispatched this information to the Council of Safety. "There is all the appearance of a hellish plot," he warned. "In short, your friends in town are preparing a great dish of blood for you." The Presbyterian minister hoped these distressing developments would finally awaken the conservatives in Charleston from their "lethiferous slumber."[46]

Tennent was never one to relax his support for the American cause. The minister hurried northward to Bullock's Creek, where he formed several volunteer companies to help counter the loyalists' menacing designs. With these new units, plus those the commissioners had earlier formed on Crims Creek and between Rocky Creek and Sandy River, Tennent felt confident that they were "hemming in the dissidents on all sides." Nevertheless, he still feared "some harsh designs" from loyalist leaders who, he believed, "seem deter-

45. Barnwell, "Loyalism in South Carolina," 115–6; Drayton to Council of Safety, 21 August 1775, *DHAR*, 1: 153.

46. Tennent to Laurens, 20 August 1775, *DHAR*, 1: 145–6; Affidavit of Jonathan Clark, 21 August 1775, ibid., 1: 147–8.

mined if possible to bring the people to draw blood before they have time to be enlightened." In a letter to Drayton informing him of the enemy's dangerous maneuverings, Tennent warned his colleague to "be upon your guard."[47]

When Drayton received this intelligence while at Lawson's Fork, he immediately dispatched an express to the commanding officer at Fort Charlotte warning him of the planned assault against his compound, and another to Major Andrew Williamson, commander of the Orangeburg regiment, directing him to send thirty militiamen to reinforce the forty soldiers already stationed in the garrison. However, Drayton believed Cameron's plan involving the Cherokee posed the greatest danger and warranted his personal attention. He met with Richard Pearis, an influential yet opportunistic and unscrupulous Indian trader, and convinced him to deliver a "short talk" to the Cherokee nation inviting six of their headmen to meet him in Amelia Township in twelve days for a "face to face" discussion on the colonists' "Quarrel with the Great King." To help Pearis gain the Cherokees' favor, the commissioner requested from the Council of Safety £80 worth of shirts, coats, blankets, linen, and paint for him to give as gifts to the Indians.[48]

After addressing these emergencies, Drayton, accompanied by Hart and Reese, rode from Lawson's Fork to the residence of Captain William Wofford on the fork of the Tyger River to join a large meeting of residents who had gathered to hear about the troubles in the lowcountry. Many from the "other party" attended, but fortunately for the commissioners, none of its contentious leaders were present to oppose them. Reverend Reese began the assembly with singing and praying, generating an atmosphere similar to a religious revival. With the audience in a cheerful spirit, Drayton spoke to them for more than an hour on the state of affairs in the nation. The crowd listened attentively, according to Hart, and afterwards more than seventy responded to the altar call to sign the Association pact. In fact, the men were so "active and spirited" in the patriots' favor that they insisted on being formed into a provincial regiment. Realizing an armed unit here could place a "severe

47. Tennent to Laurens, 20 August 1775, and Tennent to Drayton, 18 August 1775, *DHAR*, 1: 145–7; Tennent Diary, 6–9.

48. Beverly T. Whitmire, "Richard Pearis, Bold Pioneer," *Proceedings and Papers of the Greenville County Historical Society* (1962–1964): 75–85; John Bennett, "Historical Notes," *SCHM* 18 (January 1917): 97–8; Claim of Richard Pearis, American Loyalist Transcripts, 26: 362–82, NYPL; Drayton to the Kings, Warriors & Beloved Men of the Cherokee Nation, 21 August 1775, BPROCO 5/77, pp. 143–5; Affidavit of Richard Pearis, 11 November 1775, Simms-Laurens Collection, roll # 2, SCL; Drayton to Council of Safety, 21 August 1775, *DHAR*, 1: 152–3.

check" on Fletchall's followers, Drayton accepted their eager offer and ordered the quartermaster at Fort Charlotte to supply them with a small quantity of lead and powder.[49]

Despite the increasing number of troops at his disposal, Drayton was still worried about the approaching meeting with Fletchall's regiment. "I am not without some apprehension that some violence will be used against us," he wrote the council, for "it is my firm belief that Brown, Cunningham, and Robinson will do everything in their power to bring things to extremities. . . . They are clearly of opinion they can beat the whole Colony." Drayton was so concerned over his own and his colleagues' safety, in fact, that he directed Major Andrew Williamson to have his troops ready to come to their rescue if they were captured.[50]

Drayton's apprehension over the regimental muster proved warranted. When he, Tennent, and Hart arrived at Ford's plantation on the twenty-third, Colonel Fletchall and his "Gang of Leaders" met them "double Armed" with pistols, swords, and rifles. They were also brandishing "dark Designs" upon their brows. "Much venom appear[ed] in Cunningham's countenance," Drayton nervously observed, while Brown's looks were "utterly against him." The commissioners were equally distressed by the small size of the gathering. Of the approximately 1,200 to 1,500 men in Fletchall's regiment, only about 250 soldiers assembled at Ford's estate. Drayton and Tennent were certain that the "heads of the party" had discouraged their men from attending the muster.[51]

The hostile reception and poor turnout did not deter Drayton from delivering a spirited speech. Afterwards, Moses Kirkland rose up and opposed the commissioner and the provincial congress in "virulent, reflecting and opprobrious terms." Drayton, who "resented personal reflections"—particularly from a vulgar and crude frontiersman—interrupted Kirkland with a scathing verbal assault of his own. Hereupon a "wild altercation" erupted between the two men, which so aroused the emotions of each party that a "terrible riot" appeared imminent. Kirkland was on the verge of assaulting Drayton when Colonel Fletchall and the commissioners stepped in and separated the two

49. Drayton to Council of Safety, 21 August 1775, *DHAR*, 1: 152; Hart Diary, 5. The volunteer companies organized here became known as the Spartan Regiment.

50. Drayton to Council of Safety, 21 August 1775, *DHAR*, 1: 153; Andrew Williamson to Council of Safety, 22 August 1775, in Salley, *Orangeburg County*, 424.

51. Tennent Diary, 9–10; Drayton to Council of Safety, 21 August 1775, and Drayton and Tennent to Council of Safety, 24 August 1775, *DHAR*, 1: 151, 156.

hotheads. Once things settled down, Tennent gave a "most solemn & impressive discourse" lasting over an hour. To counter, Thomas Brown read Dalrymple's loquacious address to the regiment. However, so few of the soldiers appeared to listen to it that the commissioners did not think it worthwhile to say even one word in response.[52]

Still, the commissioners were "painfully indignant" over Kirkland and Brown's offensive and disruptive behavior. "Imagine every indecency of language," they wrote the council, "every misrepresentation, every ungenerous, and unjust charge against the American politics, that could alarm the people, and give them an evil impression of our designs against their liberties, and the rights of Great Britain; imagine all you can on these points, and you will not exceed what we heard . . . from Kirkland and Brown." What particularly incensed Drayton and Tennent was that the loyalists succeeded in foiling their attempt to convert those attending the muster. Of the 250 soldiers present, only seventy signed the Association petition; most of these, moreover, were previous subscribers who only added their name a second time to "give a good example."[53]

With only mixed results to show for their efforts in the region between the Enoree and Broad Rivers, the commissioners decided to take their stump-speaking tour to a more appreciative audience. However, the Reverend Hart did not continue the campaign, but returned to Charleston following the meeting at Ford's plantation. Although the commissioners' letters do not explain this peculiar development, evidence in Drayton and Tennent's travel accounts suggests that they might have lost confidence in the Baptist minister. On several occasions they mention that the opposition party had "ridiculed" or "browbeaten" their colleague during public meetings. Since the mission was apparently winding down anyway, Drayton and Tennent might have felt Hart's services were no longer required and so suggested that he return home. Hart's own travel account reveals that he was growing weary of traveling through the frontier and becoming discouraged over his lack of success in convincing people to "stand up for liberty." Instead of preaching the revolutionary gospel to large gatherings, Hart spent much of his time simply tarrying in people's homes. Disappointed and jaded, the Baptist minister left

52. Hart Diary, 5; Tennent Diary, 9; Drayton and Tennent to Council of Safety, 24 August 1775, *DHAR*, 1: 157.

53. Drayton and Tennent to Council of Safety, 24 August 1775, *DHAR*, 1: 157.

Ford's on August 23 and made a slow trip back to Charleston, where he arrived on September 6.[54]

While Hart was riding back to the capital, Drayton and Tennent were traveling south along Rabon Creek toward DeWitt's Corner. Since they had already proselytized through the heart of loyalist country, the two remaining commissioners planned to make only a few more stops—at Ninety-Six, Augusta, and Amelia—before returning home. Much of the region west of the Saluda already supported the provincial congress, so Drayton and Tennent expected a much easier time during this last leg of their journey. However, Fletchall and his crew had different plans for the patriots.

On Sunday August 27, Drayton and Tennent spoke to a "considerable meeting" at the village of Ninety-Six. According to the Presbyterian minister, the listeners departed "fully convinced" of the virtues of the American cause. Afterwards, the commissioners received a message from nearby Long Canes settlements requesting them to come speak there. Since Drayton had an impending conference with the Cherokee, Tennent accepted the solicitation.[55]

After an unpleasant trip riding through heavy rain and sleeping in wet and drafty log cabins, Tennent finally arrived at Boonesborough Meeting House near the upper portion of Long Cane Creek on August 31. Here the minister spoke to a large gathering for over two hours "to good effect," he boasted. Apparently so, for later that day he raised three companies of volunteers among the residents to serve under Captain Andrew Pickens, Colonel Champness Terry, and James McCall. Afterwards, Tennent traveled to the Bull Town Meeting House (located about fifteen miles from the Indian Line), where on September 2 he received an eager welcome by the largest assembly he had yet seen during the mission. Inspired by such an enormous and anxious audience, Tennent gave an exceptionally "animated and demonstrative" discourse on the "American dispute" lasting nearly three hours. "Its Effect was very visible," the minister proudly noted in his diary, "the people holding a profound Silence for more than a Minute after I was done." Once the stunned listeners had recovered from the protracted yet enlightening speech, most eagerly lined up to sign the boycott agreement.[56]

While Tennent was succeeding in the Long Canes settlements, Drayton

---

54. Drayton to Council of Safety, 16 August 1775, *DHAR*, 1: 143; Tennent Diary, 13; Hart Diary, 5–8.

55. Tennent Diary, 12.

56. Tennent to Council of Safety, 1 September 1775, *DHAR*, 1: 165; Tennent Diary, 14–5.

had acquired several affidavits asserting that Kirkland was organizing attacks against Augusta and Fort Charlotte. Alarmed but not completely surprised by this news, the commissioner hurried toward Augusta. When he arrived at Captain Leroy Hammond's Snow Hill plantation opposite the town on August 29, he drew upon his plenipotentiary powers to initiate a three-pronged military operation to thwart Kirkland's "evil intentions." Acting like a general in his "theater of operations," Drayton ordered Major Andrew Williamson to march three hundred men to Harden's Ford (about thirty miles upriver from Augusta); directed Colonel William Thompson to post his regiment along the Ridge; and commanded Colonel Richard Richardson to station his three hundred recruits at the confluence of the Enoree and Broad Rivers to act as a check against Fletchall, just in case he had notions of assisting Kirkland. As an added deterrent, Drayton distributed a circular letter throughout the Ninety-Six District declaring that Kirkland was endeavoring to "violate the public peace" and warning that anyone who joined him would be "deemed public enemies to be suppressed by the sword." Afterwards, Drayton notified the council of these developments and sent an express to Tennent instructing him to proceed with all speed to Fort Charlotte to help ready the garrison for a possible assault against it.[57]

Back in Charleston, the councilors read "with horror" the commissioners' reports regarding their recent military maneuvers. Even more alarming to them was Drayton's earlier proposal to capture the top dozen loyalists in the backcountry. Was it not possible, they asked Drayton, that removing "twelve active mischievous men" might reveal the enemy to be a Hydra, thereby creating "twice as many heads to bring on their four thousand adherents, with fury, to rescue their first leaders, or to revenge their cause?" According to Arthur Middleton, the council vigorously debated whether to support Drayton or recall him to Charleston. While some of the moderate members believed his actions would set the frontiersmen to "cutting one another's throats," his more assertive supporters argued that he had so far confronted each crisis boldly yet prudently. If the council failed to support Drayton, they added, the backcountry would certainly fall under loyalist control. Perhaps

57. Jones, *South Carolina Civil War of 1775*, 60; Drayton to the Council of Safety, 30 August 1775, and William Henry Drayton, "Printed Circular—Ninety-Six District, South Carolina," 30 August 1775, *DHAR*, 1: 162–4; Tennent Diary, 15. The Ridge is a high portion of ground located northeast of Augusta between the headwaters of the Little Saluda and the fork of the Edisto.

the deciding factor was the councilors' inability to formulate alternative measures that would avert a confrontation while still frustrating the proceedings of such "evil-minded persons." So on August 31, by a narrow margin of four votes to three—with two of the four in danger of being reversed—the council agreed to empower Drayton to "take every decisive step and to use every vigorous measure" he thought necessary to promote the public welfare. In vesting him with this broad power, however, the executive body cautioned the commissioner to "premeditate every important step, and weigh probable consequences" before implementing any plan.[58]

In a separate dispatch, Middleton informed his friend of the details of the proceeding. Charles Drayton, too, apprised his older brother of important political and military developments in Charleston and urged him to accomplish his mission "without bloodshed." With this news, Drayton realized that the body that had sent him on this dangerous mission now hesitated to support him. Nevertheless, he still believed his plan to capture the leading loyalists was the surest and safest means of defeating the enemy. He therefore disdainfully told his fellow councilors that if they lacked confidence in his ability to successfully handle this emergency, they should "put it in other hands." But Drayton also understood that if a war did erupt in the backcountry, his associates would probably attribute it to his recklessness. Their confidence in him would subsequently wane, thus seriously jeopardizing his political future. Realizing the council was carefully scrutinizing his every move, Drayton, from this time on, sent painstakingly detailed reports, frequently providing supporting documents to justify his actions and constantly reassuring his colleagues that he was acting with utmost caution and circumspection.[59]

Meanwhile, Tennent had followed Drayton's urgent instructions and arrived at Fort Charlotte on September 3. He examined the stone structure and, to his disappointment, found it "much out of repair."[60] Hereupon the commissioner assembled the apathetic troops and exhorted them about the

58. Drayton, *Memoirs,* 1: 396–8.

59. Charles Drayton to William Henry Drayton, 16 September 1775, in Barnwell, "Correspondence of Arthur Middleton," 136–7; Drayton to Council of Safety, 11 September 1775, *DHAR,* 1: 175.

60. Fort Charlotte, constructed in 1766, was a square fortification with brick and stone walls ten feet high and one hundred feet long on each side. Each corner had a bastion. Inside were barracks capable of housing several hundred troops and a well for water. Nora M. Davis, *Fort Charlotte on the Savannah River and Its Significance in the American Revolution* (Greenwood, S.C.: Daughters of the American Revolution, Star Fort Chapter, 1949), 7–8.

"goodness of their Cause," a speech which they "seemed to take very kindly," Tennent privately noted. He then ordered Captain John Caldwell, the commandant of the fort, to erect platforms for the cannon, clear the surrounding corn fields (to provide maximum visibility of the approaching enemy), and place the horses out of harm's way. The threat of an impending assault and the "madness of the Opponents of Liberty" weighed heavily on the minister's mind that night, robbing him of any sleep.[61]

Despite his exhaustion, Tennent rode fifty-five miles the next day to meet with his fellow commissioner at Leroy Hammond's residence. When he arrived there on the evening of September 4, Drayton told him the situation had grown so critical that he felt it necessary to send Tennent to Charleston to provide a first-hand account of the "whole Matter" to the Council of Safety. Moreover, Kirkland's hostile intentions had forced Drayton to change his tactics from persuasion to intimidation. Therefore Tennent's "presence in the country," Drayton explained to the council, "will not be of any advantage in the way of expounding our political texts to the people." When Tennent arrived at the capital in mid-September, he informed the executive board that it must send at least two thousand troops to the backcountry to crush the loyalists' "dangerous conspiracy" and "save an effusion of innocent blood."[62]

Unbeknownst to Tennent, Drayton's military maneuvers and threatening declaration had already defused Kirkland's scheme to attack Augusta and Fort Charlotte. Drayton immodestly reported to the council on September 11 that when word had spread throughout the Ninety-Six District of his "prompt and decided measures," all but a few of Kirkland's most devout followers had abandoned him. Deserted by his adherents, and with an armed band of angry patriots after him, Kirkland had sent his brother to Drayton with an offer of surrender in exchange for "reserving his life." But Drayton had refused to grant any concessions to the traitor, and replied that he would only make terms with him on an "unconditional surrender to a due course of law." Fearing for his life, Kirkland had fled in disguise to Charleston, where Governor

61. Tennent Diary, 16–7.

62. By this time, Hart was already on his way to the capital, but was probably not informed of the military maneuvers. Tennent Diary, 16–8; Tennent to Council of Safety, 10 September 1775, *DHAR*, 1: 169.

Campbell gave him asylum aboard the HMS *Tamar* anchored in Charleston harbor.[63]

Confident after his success in foiling Kirkland's plot, Drayton implemented his plan to defeat the loyalist faction by capturing their remaining leaders and frightening their followers. He first dispatched a posse of twelve men, divided into three parties of four men each, to bring Moses Kirkland, Robert Cunningham, and Thomas Brown back to him "dead or alive." Next he decided to place an intimidating military presence near Fletchall's district. He ordered Colonels Thomson and Mayson and Major Williamson to meet him with their regiments at Ninety-Six courthouse. Drayton commenced his march on September 6 with a hastily assembled company of 124 local militiamen and four cannon. This show of force struck such fear into the king's men in the region that many went to Drayton to "make peace." Moreover, during the march his posse of "notorious horse thieves" captured nine "heads" of the opposing party, but the principal leaders—Cunningham, Brown, and Kirkland—escaped by being "continually on the wing." Soon after his arrival at Ninety-Six on September 8, Drayton was joined by a party of 84 Georgians and 141 soldiers from North Carolina. These additions, along with Thomson's, Mayson's, and Williamson's regiments, brought the total number of soldiers under Drayton's command to nearly one thousand.[64]

Instead of cowing the men in Fletchall's quarter, Drayton's "acts of violence so incensed our People," wrote Brown, that he and Cunningham, in a matter of only five days, managed to assemble approximately 1,200 armed men at O'Neal's mill, about ten miles above the Saluda River across from Ninety-Six. Colonel Fletchall soon joined them with an additional 250 recruits. According to Brown, the loyalists were a formidable force, consisting chiefly of men with previous military experience and "violent resolutions." This ragtag army was so bent on fighting, in fact, that a mutiny nearly broke out among the ranks when the fainthearted Fletchall arrived to assume command of the legion. Only with "extreme difficulty" were Brown and Cun-

63. Drayton to Council of Safety, 11 September 1775, *DHAR*, 1: 173; Drayton, *Memoirs*, 1: 382. At this time, Kirkland was still on his way to Charleston. Whig authorities captured him later in the year as he was traveling north to confer with General Thomas Gage about assistance for the king's friends in the South Carolina backcountry.

64. Thomas Brown to William Campbell, 18 October 1775, p. 2, Henry Clinton Papers, CL; Drayton to Council of Safety, 11 September 1775, *DHAR*, 1: 173.

ningham able to prevent their men from drumming the craven colonel out of the camp.[65]

On the afternoon of September 10, Drayton obtained word of this gathering but had no idea of its strength. Assuming it to be small, he detached one hundred horsemen to disperse the enemy. When the cavalrymen returned later that afternoon, they informed the commissioner of the true size of Fletchall's force, and—even more shocking—that it was planning to attack at 2 A.M. Drayton hurriedly gathered Colonel Mayson, Major Williamson, and Captain Hammond to formulate a response to this threat. They considered three proposals: retreat to Colonel Thomson and his rangers posted at the Ridge, defend Ninety-Six, or launch a preemptive strike. Drayton and his military advisers quickly dismissed the idea of a retreat, fearing that it would dishearten and disgrace their men and encourage the loyalists. Likewise, they rejected the second proposal because the courthouse at Ninety-Six was not bulletproof and the prison, which apparently was bulletproof, could only accommodate about a third of their men. This left them with only one course of action: attack!

Drayton hurriedly divided his forces, stationing a small guard in the local prison, a regiment of rangers at Island Ford on the Saluda under Major Mayson, and one hundred men in a defensive position about halfway between. In a conspicuous demonstration of his willingness to sacrifice his life for the American cause, Drayton then joined the lead force on the Saluda River to "head the attack." However, with the council's recent letter urging him to act with caution still fresh in his mind, Drayton wisely waited to signal the charge until Fletchall's hostile intentions became obvious. It is fortunate that he did, for half an hour after the loyalists were to have commenced their assault, the commissioner received "certain accounts" that the alarm was false. Drayton called off the attack, but kept the troops at their posts as a precaution.[66]

Having so narrowly avoided an undesirable bloody conflict, Drayton decided to ease tensions between the two factions by offering the loyalists a neutrality. One reason he desired to make peace is that the loyalist army was half again as large as his own. In addition, if he involved the colony in a civil war, even

65. Brown to Campbell, 18 October 1775, p. 3. Brown claimed that 2,200 men joined the loyalists' forces, but this was a gross exaggeration. Drayton's estimate of 1,200–1,400 men was closer to the truth. Drayton to Council of Safety, 17 August 1775, *DHAR*, 1: 188.

66. Drayton to Council of Safety, 11 September 1775, *DHAR*, 1: 173–4.

accidentally or reluctantly, it would firmly establish his reputation as an impetuous zealot in the minds of his colleagues, who might never again trust him with an influential post. Successfully completing the mission without bloodshed, on the other hand, would garner him greater respect among his peers and, he hoped, an expansion of his authority in the Whig government. His political future aside, Drayton felt confident that he could accomplish his objective just as well with a truce, because he believed such an action would foment disunion among the loyalist leaders, which in turn, would create confusion among their adherents who would not know who to follow. Thus the loyalist party would simply "moulder away." Neutrality was "infinitely preferable to our having put a part of those people to the sword," Drayton later explained to the council, because a clash of arms "would not only have laid the foundation for lasting animosities," but might also provoke authorities in London to quickly send a strong body of troops to crush the revolutionary government in South Carolina.[67]

Drayton was confident that the loyalists would accept a peace offering because he knew they were far from united in their aims and leadership. While many were ready to follow Cunningham, Robinson, and Brown in aggressive measures, others wished to be allowed to remain neutral. From conversations with Fletchall, Drayton knew the colonel was inclined to side with the latter, at least until British troops arrived in the backcountry. To compel these pacifists to join him at the bargaining table, while at the same time stack the deck in his favor, Drayton cleverly inserted two wild cards into the game designed to take advantage of these disparate positions among his opponents.[68]

On September 13 he issued a proclamation to those north of the Saluda stating that no harm would come to them as long as they chose to "behave peaceably." He blamed the present discontent on certain "tools of administration" in the region, men of "low degree . . . totally illiterate," who he said were practicing "every art, fraud and misrepresentation" to thwart the "virtuous efforts of America." The commissioner explained that so far in his efforts to oppose this "hellish plan," he had used his "utmost patience and industry" to "gently . . . persuade men to a peaceable conduct." Drayton strongly denied that he had raised troops with intentions of forcing people to sign the

67. Drayton to Council of Safety, 17 September 1775, *DHAR*, 1: 190; Drayton, *Memoirs*, 1: 398–9.
68. Drayton to Council of Safety, 17 September 1775, *DHAR*, 1: 187–8; Barnwell, "Loyalism in South Carolina," 118.

Association petition. "We abhor the idea of compelling any person to associate with us," he explained. At the same time, though, he threatened to "prosecute military measures with the utmost rigor" against "every person in arms" opposing measures of the provincial congress. To prove that this was no idle threat, Drayton sent to Colonel Richardson a letter designed to be intercepted by Fletchall's men, ordering the colonel to attack the loyalists from the rear, and directing Colonel John Thomas to burn the houses and destroy the plantations of all non-Associators who were absent from their homes.[69]

Having thus set the table, Drayton sent a message to the loyalists on September 16 inviting their leaders to his camp for negotiations. Drayton's moves, as he had expected, caused division among the loyalists. When Brown read Drayton's invitation to his men, they were "raised to such a Pitch of Fury," he later wrote Campbell, "that it was with the utmost difficulty we restrained them from attempting an attack in the Indian mode upon their camp that very night." Fletchall, on the other hand, was so "struck with terror," Brown added, that the "poor Bastard . . . went so far as to acquaint Drayton that it was his opinion we would submit to any terms." But the colonel felt he had no other choice but to accept Drayton's offer because his regiment was desperately low on ammunition.[70]

In any event, Brown and Cunningham suspected treachery on Drayton's part and refused to enter his camp. However, they had no objection to Fletchall's attending with some "Officers of inconsiderable consequences as messengers." So the colonel brought with him six men "as ignorant and illiterate as himself," in Brown's judgment. Having little confidence in these men or in Fletchall, Brown and Cunningham drafted instructions for them to follow in negotiating with the patriots: they should demand the release of all prisoners, the end of trade restrictions against non-Associators, the dissolution of extralegal bodies, the disarming of the rebel troops, a promise not to arrest the governor, and the return of all arms and ammunition seized by the provincial congress. In short, Brown and Cunningham called for an end to the revolutionary movement. But these instructions were wasted on Fletchall, who was so apprehensive about the meeting with Drayton, according to

69. "Declaration of William Henry Drayton," 13 September 1775, *DHAR*, 1: 180–3; Drayton to Council of Safety, 17 August 1775, ibid., 1: 188. Brown to Campbell, 18 October 1775, p. 5.

70. Brown to Campbell, 18 October 1775, pp. 4–6; Intelligence Contained in Mr. Cameron's Letter of November 8, 1775, BPROCO 5/77, p. 163.

Brown, that he had "such frequent recourse to the Bottle as to soon render himself *non compos*." Without mentioning a "syllable" of the instructions, the uncomprehending colonel signed the terms Drayton dictated and prevailed upon the other loyalist delegates to "follow his example."[71]

By the terms of the Treaty of Ninety-Six, the loyalist deputies and the people they were authorized to represent declared that their refusal to sign the Association pact was due not to an "unfriendly principle or design," but only to a desire to "live in peace and tranquility" with their neighbors. Furthermore, they promised never to join or give any aid or comfort to British troops sent into the colony and recognized the provincial congress's authority to arrest and punish any person who criticized or opposed its proceedings. In return, the Whigs promised that non-Associators could return to their homes and live there unmolested as long as they observed the agreement. Those who did not consider themselves bound by the treaty, on the other hand, "must abide by the consequences." By this agreement the loyalists also gained the removal of the restrictions on trade with Charleston, though this provision was not specifically mentioned in the treaty.[72]

The Treaty of Ninety-Six was a pragmatic solution for both parties. Drayton and Fletchall were satisfied because it allowed them to avoid a battle that neither wanted. The agreement also rescued Drayton from a difficult predicament, for there was danger that the Council of Safety might revoke the grant of additional powers it had so narrowly conferred on him if fighting on a large scale should break out. Drayton's colleagues in Charleston were pleased with the treaty, too, as it appeared the loyalist threat was extinguished. Those back-settlers who were neutralist in their sentiments were also satisfied with the agreement because it granted their wish to be left alone. Finally, the pact appeased non-Associators, who secured a resumption of trade with Charleston.

In all, Drayton was pleased with his handiwork. "I make no doubt but that the affair is now crushed," he boasted to the Council of Safety. The "spirit

71. Brown to Campbell, 18 October 1775, pp. 7–8. Philip Mulkey and Robert Merrick denounced the negotiations as a farce and refused to endorse the treaty. In all fairness, the deputies Fletchall selected to accompany him—Benjamin Wofford, John Ford, Thomas Greer, Evan McLaurin, the Reverend Philip Mulkey, and Robert Merrick—while not leaders of the first rank, were men who had influence and respect in their communities. See Barnwell, "Loyalism in South Carolina," 119.

72. The Treaty of Ninety-Six is printed in *DHAR*, 1: 184–6; Drayton, *Memoirs*, 1: 400–3; and *SCG*, 3 October 1775. See also Drayton to Council of Safety, 17 September 1775, *DHAR*, 1: 189–90.

of discord is gone forth among them, and there is now a great quarrel between Fletchall and his men." Indeed, Brown, Cunningham, and other stal-
wart loyalists considered the treaty a "shameful and disgraceful" surrender
and cursed Fletchall for betraying them. Some even offered to follow Brown
and Cunningham in continuing active opposition. After careful deliberation,
though, the two captains decided that war was a matter for Governor Campbell to decide and sent their men home.[73]

Nevertheless, Cunningham was dissatisfied with neutrality and vowed not
to heed the treaty. When Drayton was informed of this, he wrote the loyalist
a letter on September 21 with the intention of drawing from him an expressed statement of his continued hostility as a means to justify his arrest.
The cunning commissioner skillfully accomplished this by asking Cunningham if there was any truth to the rumor that he refused to observe the peace
pact of September 16. So that he could not weasel his way out of the question,
Drayton remarked that he would assume a refusal to reply as a confession of
guilt. Cunningham thought the question unfair, but as it was his determination not to "deceive either party," he boldly, though unwisely, confessed that
he had no intention of complying with the "false and disgraceful" document.
Thereupon Drayton sent a copy of Cunningham's confession to the Council
of Safety, which immediately issued orders for his arrest.[74]

While Drayton was cleverly luring Cunningham into his trap, the danger
from the Cherokee was becoming critical. The council had been greatly
alarmed by Drayton's letter of August 21 informing them of Alexander Cameron's alleged intention of joining three thousand Cherokee warriors to the
loyalist army. Adding credibility to this rumor was the Cherokees' indignation with the Whigs for driving their friend John Stuart from the province
and stealing the powder and ammunition from the *Philippa* that was intended
for them. Even if the rumor proved false, the patriots could not afford to assume that the Native Americans would remain passive. The council therefore
instructed Drayton to expedite his meeting with the Cherokee headmen—"a
matter of great moment [that] requires your immediate attention."[75]

73 . Drayton to Council of Safety, 17 September 1775, *DHAR*, 1: 189; Edward Musgrove to
Drayton, 14 October 1775, ibid., 1: 201–2; Brown to Campbell, 18 October 1775, pp. 8–9; Barnwell, "Loyalism in South Carolina," 120–1.

74. Drayton to Cunningham, 21 September 1775, *DHAR*, 1: 191–2; Cunningham to Drayton, 6 October 1775, Drayton, *Memoirs*, 1: 405–6, 417–8.

75. Drayton to Council of Safety, 21 August 1775, and Affidavit of Jonathan Clark Concerning Cameron and the Cherokee Indians, 21 August 1775, both in *DHAR*, 1: 152–3, 147–8; An-

When Drayton finally arrived at the Congarees on September 25, nearly three weeks after the appointed date, he found Richard Pearis, Escuy the Good Warrior, and three Cherokee headmen waiting for him "in the utmost anxiety and impatience." After apologizing for his extreme tardiness, the commissioner read his speech to them, with Pearis acting as translator. He began by explaining that the colonists were arming themselves not to attack the Indians, but to protect themselves from the king's "unjust and wicked" ministers who were trying to steal their money and property, enslave their wives and children, and kill them "whenever they please." Drayton next cleverly played upon the Indians' ethnicity to raise serious doubts among them concerning their security under royal rule. "If they use us, their own Flesh and Blood in this unjust way," he exclaimed, "what must you expect: you who are red people; you whom they never saw; you whom they know only by the hearing of the ear; you who have fine lands? You see by their treatment of us, that agreements even under hand and seal go as nothing with them. Think of these things my Friends, and reflect upon them day and night." If this was not enough for the Native Americans to contemplate, Drayton made an appeal to their economic interest, asserting that because the "men about the Great King" take our money "violently against our consent and good liking," we will have to raise the price of trade goods. Now that you "see plainly" that "our interest in this quarrel is the same," he continued, we should "support and assist each other against our common enemies." Near the end of his speech, Drayton finally addressed the issue in which the Cherokee were most interested: powder and lead. The commissioner was sorry to inform the headmen that he had no ammunition to give them, but promised that the council would shortly provide them with all the "friendly aid, assistance and supplies in [its] power." As a token of this pledge, Drayton removed his coat and handed it to the Indians, saying, "For my part in this unhappy time, I will be content to wear an osnaburg split shirt."[76]

---

drew Williamson to Council of Safety, 12 July 1775, "Journal of the Council of Safety," SCHS *Collections*, 2: 55–6; "Copy of a Talk from the Cherokees to Mr. Cameron," 8 August 1775, Simms-Laurens Collection, roll #2, SCL; Council of Safety to Drayton, 15 September 1775, *HLP*, 10: 386–8.

76. Laurens to Drayton, 21 September 1775, *DHAR*, 1: 192; "A Talk from the Honourable William Henry Drayton to the Beloved Men, Head Men & Warriors of the Cherokee Nation at the Congarees," 25 September 1775, can be found in Alexander Salley, ed., *Documents Relating to the History of South Carolina during the Revolutionary War* (Columbia: State Co., 1908), 14–20; Drayton, *Memoirs*, 1: 419–26; and Force, *American Archives*, 4th ser., vol. 3: 789–91. The original is in the Gibbes Collection, SCDAH. See also Tom Hatley, *The Dividing Paths: Cherokees and*

Knowing that his speech and token gift had little chance of winning the Cherokee away from the British as long as Cameron resided among them, Drayton wrote the Indian agent the following day ordering him to leave the Cherokee nation for, as he put it, "we look upon you as an object dangerous to our welfare." Any attempt to hide amongst the warriors, he warned, will only bring "danger to . . . your Person and the People in your charge." Following through with his threat, Drayton directed Pearis to have Cameron killed or taken prisoner. The Indian trader apparently obliged the commissioner and supposedly offered a "considerable reward" to anyone who shot the Scotchman "from behind a bush." But with Cameron living amongst thousands of devoted Cherokee warriors, it is perhaps superfluous to add that he was never shot or captured.[77]

Although Cameron eluded Drayton's grasp, the summer 1775 backcountry mission as a whole was highly successful. The commissioners formed numerous volunteer companies throughout the region, adding over six hundred men to the patriot forces.[78] Drayton's Treaty of Ninety-Six gave the provincial government nearly three months of valuable peace, allowing them to augment their forces, train and supply their new recruits, and develop a successful plan to eventually crush the remaining elements of resistance in the backcountry. Invaluable to the success of such a campaign was the vast amount of information the commissioners accumulated about backcountry loyalism: where exactly it existed, who its leaders were, how much public support it had, and how well its troops were supplied. The commissioners obtained similar information concerning patriot support in the region.

Equally vital to the Whig cause in the backcountry was the Machiavellian strategy Drayton used in the latter part of his mission, which effectively

South Carolinians through the Era of Revolution (New York: Oxford University Press, 1993), 186–8.

77. Drayton to Cameron, 26 September 1775, BPROCO 5/77, pp. 147–9, and in Henry Clinton Papers, CL; "Intelligence Contained in Mr. Cameron's Letter of 8 November 1775," BPROCO 5/77, p. 159; Cameron to Stuart, 21 July 1775, ibid., 141–2; Cameron to Drayton, 16 October 1775, ibid., 151–3; Henry Laurens to Edward Wilkinson, 29 October 1775, BPROCO 5/77, pp. 155–6; John Lewis Gervais to Cameron, 27 June 1775, ibid., 135–6; John L. Nichols, "Alexander Cameron, British Agent among the Cherokee, 1764–1781," *SCHM* 97 (April 1996): 95–101; John P. Brown, *Old Frontiers: The Story of the Cherokee Indians from the Earliest Times to the Date of their Removal to the West, 1838* (Kingsport, Tenn.: Southern Publishing, 1938), 122–3; Grace S. Woodward, *The Cherokees* (Norman: University of Oklahoma Press, 1963), 84–5.

78. Barnwell, "Loyalism in South Carolina," 126.

annulled several of the most belligerent and committed loyalists, particularly Moses Kirkland and Robert Cunningham. Through the Treaty of Ninety-Six, Drayton also managed to divide the opposition against itself, thus removing much of the leadership and unity necessary for the loyalists to effectively challenge the patriots. Drayton's aggressive and decisive actions also prevented the enemy from capturing Fort Charlotte and its important storage of powder and lead. Consequently, Fletchall's army lacked the ammunition necessary to attack Drayton's force in September, despite having an enormous numerical advantage.

Further evidence of the success of Drayton's mission comes from men who lived in the region. Soon after the signing of the Treaty of Ninety-Six, leaders throughout the backcountry wrote congratulations to the commissioner for his successful handling of Fletchall and his followers. John Prince, a resident of the district between the Broad and Saluda Rivers, reported to Drayton that his treaty had silenced the loyalist "chiefs" in the region and turned their followers into "impotent wretches." The "scales seem turned very much now," hailed Edward Musgrove from the Enoree River, "and you are much applauded for acting at Ninety-Six." Major Andrew Williamson reported to the Council of Safety in mid-October that "from the best intelligence I can learn since Mr. Drayton went from hence, I have the pleasure to acquaint your Honors, that every thing seems in perfect tranquility, both here and on the other side of the [Saluda] river. Volunteers are there and here forming." Whig leaders were impressed by the success of Drayton's militant strategy and continued to follow it throughout the remainder of 1775. This aggressive policy contributed to the patriots' eventual victory in the backcountry by converting some loyalists and keeping the neutralists passive.[79]

Drayton and his fellow commissioners accomplished these important feats in the face of enormous physical hardship: drenching rain, swollen streams, suffocating heat, rough roads, uncomfortable sleeping accommodations, sickening food, and unruly horses sometimes carrying their riders "with the greatest rapidity & danger." Compounding the physical challenges was the mental anxiety of entering hostile territory and agonizing over the frustrations of awakening the backcountry to British abuses. In spite of these difficulties and discouragements, Drayton and his fellow proselytizers never mentioned quitting before completing their mission.

79. Prince to Drayton, 25 September 1775, Musgrove to Drayton, 14 October 1775, and Andrew Williamson to Council of Safety, 16 October 1775, *DHAR*, 1: 193, 201, 207, respectively; Jones, *South Carolina Civil War of 1775*, p. 59.

When Hart and Tennent returned to Charleston, the provincial congress thanked them for the "important services" they had rendered during their "late progress into the Back Country."[80] The two ministers took very different paths thereafter. Tennent continued his service in the revolutionary government, sitting with Drayton in the congress and the Committee of Intelligence. He devoted most of his energy, however, to working for the disestablishment of the Church of England in South Carolina, which the legislature accomplished in January 1777, just months before Tennent's untimely death from an unknown fever.

Oliver Hart, on the other hand, quietly exited the revolutionary stage following his evangelistic mission into the backcountry. His lack of success in converting frontiersmen to the American cause probably convinced him to stick to the easier task of spreading the gospel. Still, when the British closed in on Charleston in 1780, Hart felt his patriotic activities during the summer of 1775 might make him a target of loyalist retribution. He therefore left for Pennsylvania, thence to Hopewell, New Jersey, where he became minister of the local Baptist church. Although Hart longed to return to Charleston, and made at least one attempt to do so, he never again set foot in South Carolina. He died in Hopewell in December 1790.[81]

After his meeting with the Cherokee headmen on September 26, Drayton hurried back to the capital to reinvigorate the province's revolutionary movement, which, according to Middleton and Timothy, had stalled during his absence.[82] However, before leaving the Congaree Store, Drayton, never one to miss an opportunity to advance his reputation, sent to the Charleston newspapers his treaty with Fletchall and a self-promotional synopsis of his mission. Consequently, when the commissioner arrived in the capital in late September, he received an enthusiastic welcome from the city's patriots. Governor William Campbell was not so pleased to see Drayton's return and sarcastically informed his counterpart in East Florida that the "famous Mr. Drayton has returned from his backcountry expedition in triumph." To consolidate his victory over the entire province, Drayton broadcast the docu-

80. *JPC*, 167.

81. Owens, *Oliver Hart: A Biography*, 17–23.

82. Indeed, during the months of July and August, the Whig government in Charleston concerned itself primarily with equipping and training its army. Not until early September when news came that the British warship HMS *Scorpion* was arriving soon to confiscate the irreplaceable ammunition and cannon from Fort Johnson did patriot leaders become more active in preparing the city's defenses. See Griffiths, "'To Receive Them Properly,'" 122–31.

ments related to the treaty in printed circulars throughout the interior. He also ordered them printed in the London press to show the king, his ministers, and the British people that South Carolinians were united behind the American cause.[83] By these actions, Drayton secured his position as the most prominent patriot in South Carolina and one of the most reviled rebels in the eyes of Great Britain. Nearly intoxicated with his popularity and supremely confident following his success in quelling loyalism in the backcountry, Drayton next devoted his energies toward duplicating those achievements in Charleston.

83. *SCG*, 3, 17, October 1775; *SC&AGG*, 29 September–6 October 1775; Campbell to Patrick Tonyn, 15 October 1775, Simms-Laurens Collection, roll #2, SCL. Henry Laurens obligingly sent the Treaty of Ninety-Six and Drayton's "Declaration" to the London *Public Advertiser* and the London *Evening Post*. Drayton to Council of Safety, 17 September 1775, *DHAR*, 1: 190; Henry Laurens to John Laurens, 26 September 1775, *HLP*, 10: 428.

PUSHING FOR INDEPENDENCE

When Drayton triumphantly returned to Charleston in late September, he was pleasantly surprised to find all vocal opposition to Whig authority silenced within the capital. The patriots had begun their final push for complete control of the city on July 22 when the General Committee publicly branded the remaining non-Associators, nearly all Crown officers, as men "inimical to the Liberties of America," confiscated their arms, confined them to the limits of Charleston, and made sure they felt ostracized from the rest of the community. To further intimidate the king's friends, the Whigs on August 12 gave George Walker, the royal gunner at Fort Johnson, a "new suit of Cloathes" made of tar and feathers for openly uttering the "most bitter curses and imprecations" against the American rebellion. Afterwards a mob of about five hundred people, most of them newly recruited soldiers, carted Walker through town for five hours while pelting him with rocks. The mob made numerous stops during this cruel procession to present the burned, bloodied, and nearly blind gunner to the home of every leading Tory as an example of what awaited them if they opposed Whig authority in any way. In a final act of sadism, the patriots then pumped water on and into Walker for an hour before throwing him off Beale's Wharf into the harbor.[1]

1. Drayton, *Memoirs*, 1: 313–7, and 2: 21; *SC&AGG*, 1 September 1775; James Simpson, American Loyalist Transcripts, 54: 205–7, NYPL; Arthur Middleton to Drayton, 12 August 1775, and Peter Timothy to Drayton, 13 August 1775, in Barnwell, "Correspondence of Arthur Middleton," 125–9; Memorial of George Walker, American Loyalist Transcripts, 52: 90–1, 99–100; Narrative of George Milligan of his Experiences in South Carolina, 15 September 1775, in

As the Whigs had anticipated, this "barbarous outrage" struck abject fear in the loyalists, some of whom sought safety aboard HMS *Tamar* anchored in Rebellion Road. Governor Campbell implored the assembly to enforce the laws and protect His Majesty's servants since the "powers of government," he explained, "are wrested out of my hands." However, the Whig-controlled Commons replied that it was not in its power to "prescribe limits to popular fury" when individuals "wantonly step forth and openly condemn measures universally received and approved." These people "must abide by the consequences!"[2]

One reason the revolutionaries had been so intent on subduing all opposition in the capital was word of the impending arrival of more British warships to reinforce the *Tamar*. Their fears were realized on September 7 when HMS *Cherokee*, an armed sloop of war, arrived in Charleston harbor. The Whigs were further alarmed one week later by a double measure of disturbing news: on August 23 King George III had declared the American colonies in open rebellion, and Governor Campbell had recently received a letter from Dartmouth informing him of His Majesty's scheme to subjugate the rebellious American colonies, a plan that involved sending troops to South Carolina in the fall. Arthur Middleton reacted to these horrifying facts by calling for the immediate arrest of Governor Campbell, but strong opposition headed by Rawlins Lowndes blocked that provocative proposal. Still, the threats galvanized the Whigs to implement other, equally inflammatory measures. "We are putting our town in a posture of defense," boasted a Charleston patriot, "and are all determined to oppose whatever troops may come here." The patriots demonstrated their resolve on the morning of September 15 when 150 crack troops led by Colonel Isaac Motte easily captured Fort Johnson, a 21-gun bastion located on a promontory of James Island and the only remaining military installation still controlled by the English in South Carolina. If the British were going to try to subdue Charleston by sea, they would now have to run a gauntlet of fire from Fort Johnson's formidable array of heavy cannon.[3]

Davies, *Documents of the American Revolution*, 11: 112; Campbell to Dartmouth, 18 August 1775, *Dartmouth Manuscripts*, 2: 353–5.

2. Drayton, *Memoirs*, 2: 19, 21.

3. *SCG*, 7 September 1775; Drayton, *Memoirs*, 2: 29–38, 51–3; Dartmouth to Campbell, 5 July 1775, BPROSC 35: 141–4; South Carolina Council to Dartmouth, 15 September 1775, ibid., 264–5; "News from South Carolina," 15 September 1775, *Virginia Gazette*; Moultrie, *Memoirs*, 1: 88–9; Isaac Motte to Council of Safety, 15 September 1775, *HLP*, 10: 382; Griffiths, "'To Receive Them Properly,'" 124–46.

The Whigs' seizure of Fort Johnson and rumors that they were plotting to take the governor hostage convinced Campbell that his influence and power were "all gone" and that even "his person was in jeopardy." He therefore dissolved the assembly in the afternoon of the fifteenth, took the provincial seal, and fled to the *Tamar*, vowing never to return until he could "support the King's authority" and "protect his faithful and loyal subjects." With Campbell's flight from Charleston, all pretense of royal government in South Carolina came to an embarrassing end. The revolutionary congress now assumed complete administration of the province while the governor and his placemen could only sit by as impotent spectators.[4]

Whig leaders had little time to rejoice in their seizure of Fort Johnson and Campbell's flight from the capital. On September 18 HMS *Scorpion* arrived in Charleston harbor to join the *Tamar* and the *Cherokee*. Alarmed by the arrival of this most recent British gunship, the Whigs moved quickly to strengthen their defensive posture by adopting a proposal to blockade the entrance to Charleston harbor by sinking old schooners in the two main channels—the Ship Channel and Lawford's Channel. To help ensure that the British men-of-war would not interfere, the General Committee considered erecting bastions on Haddrell's Point and Sullivan's Island to compel the king's ships to depart. Opinion in the executive body was so divided on this point, however, that the measure passed by only one vote. Still, Thomas Bee and other conservatives were so afraid that this scheme would provoke the *Tamar* and *Cherokee* into firing upon "this now flourishing town" that they implemented a scheme to undermine the committee's decision by taking their case before the people. By using "very unfair means," according to one Whig leader, they managed to persuade 368 townspeople to sign a petition opposing the measure until the "sense of all the inhabitants of Charleston should be fully known." The General Committee wisely chose not to oppose the popular will and complied with the petition.[5]

The radicals were frustrated by the conservatives' latest obstruction against aggressive measures. One extremist wrote Christopher Gadsden, still in Philadelphia, imploring him to return and inject new spirit into a people

4. Drayton, *Memoirs*, 2: 39; General Committee to Campbell, 29 September 1775, and Campbell to Laurens, 30 September 1775, in *SCG*, 30 October 1775.

5. Henry Laurens to John Laurens, 23 and 26 September 1775, *HLP*, 10: 422, 426–7; Drayton, *Memoirs*, 2: 54–8; Thomas Ferguson to Christopher Gadsden, 5 October 1775, *DHAR*, 1: 200–1; William Campbell to Patrick Tonyn, 15 October 1775, Simms-Laurens Collection, roll #2, SCL.

who he claimed were "more inclined to lay down their arms than defend their country."⁶ But Gadsden would not return to South Carolina until early February 1776. Fortunately for the South Carolina rebellion, Drayton arrived in Charleston at this pivotal juncture to reinvigorate the revolutionary party.

When Drayton entered the Council of Safety chambers in early October, he led his fellow extremists in a concerted effort to impress upon their faint-hearted colleagues the importance of fortifying the town. The capital must be defended at all costs, he declared, for "if the enemy makes good their landing in Charles Town, it is but too probable they will remain there entirely upon the defensive, in order that the war may be drawn into length, to ruin us by our expenses, and depreciation of our currency; to tire us out by our new manner of living and great fatigues, and, above all else, to allow time for discontents among ourselves—thus to break our combination even without their attacking us." With Drayton's forceful leadership, the radicals managed to push the reluctant council to enact measures designed to repel the impending British attack. On October 5 it established two committees: one to prepare a plan of entrenchments across Charleston neck and the other to furnish a plan of defense for the capital.⁷

The council appointed Drayton chairman of the latter committee and assigned Arthur Middleton, Thomas Ferguson, and Charles Pinckney to assist him in the task. Although these men had either little or no military training or experience, their comprehensive sketch for the defense of the capital was so effective that the Whig leaders used it, with only minor modifications, as the blueprint for their successful defense of Charleston against the British in June 1776. Drayton and his fellow commissioners were aided by the works of John Müller, one of the foremost military engineers of the time. The plan they devised called for the construction of two redoubts—one on Cummings Island (six twenty-six-pound cannon) and another on Sullivan's Island (four twenty-six-pound cannon)—to keep enemy ships out of range of downtown Charleston. Ships carrying only six- and nine-pounders attempting to pass between such heavy cannon, the commissioners argued, "cannot long sustain so superior a weight of metal." If for some reason an invading vessel managed to pass these two positions, a battery of ten twenty-six-pounders at Haddrell's point would cover the northern channel entrance into the harbor while cannon at Fort Johnson on James Island would cover the southern channel. As a

6. Thomas Ferguson to Gadsden, 5 October 1775, *DHAR*, 1: 200–1.
7. Drayton to Council of Safety, early October 1775, *DHAR*, 1: 205; Drayton, *Memoirs*, 2: 58.

final line of defense, batteries at the northeast and southern parts of the town would also engage the enemy. Any attacking British fleet exposed to such a barrage would receive "considerable damage," according to the commissioners, with "but little loss to ourselves." If the enemy did land in Charleston, they suggested the town's militia and regulars retreat to Dorchester, "a place of great security," taking with them the powder magazines, government records, and printing presses. Having once established this defensive post, the committee recommended that the patriots then attack the enemy in Charleston by "surprise, storm or regular siege."[8]

The warlike measures in the committee's report provoked a "long and warm debate" in the Council of Safety when Drayton delivered it to that body on October 13. Most councilors adamantly refused to put the town and harbor in an "offensive posture," but were willing to build fortifications for its inhabitants to retreat to in the event of an attack. Drayton accepted this compromise, content that his colleagues would "insensibly be led from one thing to another, far beyond what they originally intended." With this agreement, the council appointed two committees to supervise the construction of the proposed fortifications. Drayton was made chairman of one panel to oversee the construction of a twelve-gun redoubt on James Island west of Fort Johnson. He and his fellow commissioners charged with erecting the battery proceeded with such spirit that "energy quickly replaced languor" among the revolutionaries, and "one fortification followed another in happy succession."[9]

The increasing militancy in the colony compelled the General Committee on September 30 to summon the second provincial congress on the first day of November, a full month ahead of schedule. When the legislators met on the appointed day, their first act was to elect Drayton as their president. The congress's selection of Drayton was undoubtedly due in part to his enormous popularity among patriots in the colony following his recent successful mission into the backcountry. His nomination may have also been at attempt on the part of moderate and conservatives to muzzle the most militant member of the revolutionary movement as legislative tradition circumscribed the

8. "Report of the Committee for Forming a Plan of Defence for the Colony," *DHAR*, 1: 203–6. Sometime in 1775 Drayton ordered a copy of Müller's *Treatise on Artillery*. See Records of the Continental Congress, reel 51, vol. 7, p. 12, National Archives and Records Administration.

9. Drayton, *Memoirs*, 2: 58–60; *DHAR*, 1: 206.

president from participating in debates on the floor. If this was their motive, it was a futile effort, as events will reveal. The reasons for his election as president aside, Drayton was immensely proud of this "great, unsolicited and unexpected honour" because, as he told his colleagues, it not only reflected their "confidence and esteem" in him but also meant he ranked among the "ambitious and designing men" whom the king and Parliament said had "deceived and misled" the people.[10]

Elated with the lofty appointment, Drayton took full advantage of his position as president to push for more aggressive measures, much to the consternation of the conservatives. Early in the session, for instance, he took a "vigorous part" in an important debate concerning a proposal to attack the British vessels in the harbor. Henry Laurens, Rawlins Lowndes, and James Parsons, realizing that Drayton's speeches carried greater influence from the president's chair than from the floor, protested his participation on the grounds that he was acting contrary to legislative custom. Drayton replied that he had the right to speak since he was also an elected representative and appealed to the house for a vote. The congress supported the president, who continued using his influential position to promote his extreme views.[11]

Only hours after Drayton took the president's chair, the congress obtained word that Major Andrew Williamson had apprehended Robert Cunningham and had brought him to town. Drayton, who certainly had not forgotten Cunningham's hostile behavior and abusive language during the backcountry tour, must have relished charging the loyalist with "high crimes and misdemeanors against the Liberties of this colony" and ordering him to jail. One person who was not pleased with Cunningham's arrest was his brother Patrick, who quickly raised sixty well-armed men to rescue Robert. This large posse failed to free Cunningham, but did succeed in ambushing a company of provincial rangers near Mine Creek on November 3 and escaping with the thousand pounds of powder and two thousands pounds of lead they were escorting to the Cherokees to fulfill Drayton's September pledge. When the promised powder and ammunition never materialized, the Indians were greatly disappointed and accused the patriots of having told "a great many Lies" about giving them ammunition. Some young braves even threatened to attack settlers residing west of the Saluda. To placate the Cherokees, Drayton sent Richard Pearis (the Indian trader who had acted as interpreter during

10. Drayton to Provincial Congress, 27 March 1776, *JPC*, 267.
11. *JPC*, 81, 112; Drayton, *Memoirs*, 2: 70.

Drayton's talk with the Cherokees) to explain the loss of provisions, with the promise that the congress would immediately forward any goods recaptured. To recover the ammunition, the president ordered Colonel Richard Richardson to assemble several backcountry regiments preparatory to an attack against Patrick Cunningham's faction.[12]

Unbeknownst to Drayton, however, Pearis had forsaken the revolutionary cause in early November upon learning that the Whig government had selected his rival George Galphin to be their Indian commissioner, a position he claimed Drayton had promised to him for bringing the Cherokee headmen to the Congarees. To get even, the Indian trader made a disparaging deposition to backcountry leaders against Drayton, accusing him of attempting to use the powder sent by the Council of Safety as a gift to the Cherokees in return for land, and of intending to employ the Indians to massacre non-Associators on the frontier.[13]

As both president of the provincial congress and one who had just spent two dangerous and difficult months suppressing loyalism in the interior, Drayton felt duty-bound to "quiet the minds of the misguided people" in the interior from the "perversed" charges of an "infamous Traitor." In a declaration to backcountry residents, he carefully explained that Pearis's charge accusing the council of delivering ammunition to the Cherokee with the purpose of slaughtering non-Associators was "absurd in its very nature" because if the Indians were "let loose" upon the frontier they must indiscriminately massacre Associators and non-Associators alike since there is "no mark to distinguish either to the Indians." Instead, he said, the council sent the powder to the Cherokee to "cultivate a good correspondence" with them and to undermine their relations with the British. And besides, he added, the quantity of ammunition promised to the Indians was only "sufficient to keep them quiet, not sufficient to enable them to make war." In a second address to the frontier settlers, Drayton detailed the "unprincipled" motives behind Pearis's

12. *JPC*, 83, 101–4, 107; *SC&AGG*, 8 December 1775; Andrew Williamson to Edward Wilkinson, 6 November 1775, *DHAR*, 1: 209–10; Edward Wilkinson to Andrew Williamson, 7 November 1775, Simms-Laurens Collection, roll #2, SCL; Drayton to Richard Pearis, 8 November 1775, ibid.

13. Affidavit of Richard Pearis to Evan McLaurin, 11 November 1775, Simms-Laurens Collection, roll #2, SCL; Claim of Richard Pearis, American Loyalist Transcripts, 36: 362–82, NYPL; Council of Safety to Andrew Williamson, 2 December 1775, *HLP*, 10: 526; William Henry Drayton, "An Address to the Inhabitants of the Frontier Settlements," 6 December 1775, "Journal of the Second Council of Safety," SCHS *Collections*, 3: 53–7.

"poisonous" deposition and disdainfully dismissed the "barefaced misrepresentations" as only a few among many directed against him by the "malignant party" in a nefarious attempt to intimidate him into inaction.[14]

If anything, Pearis's public attack incited Drayton to even more determined action. He soon set upon a provocative scheme to strengthen the radicals' political position by attempting to draw the British into making an attack on patriot forces. Most Whig leaders, aware that their military was not ready to fight, were wary of engaging the enemy. In early November, though, word reached Charleston that the British had bombarded Bristol, Rhode Island. This "cruel cannonade," together with the British military buildup in the colonies, the king's proclamation of August 23 ordering civil and military officers to "exert their utmost endeavours" to suppress the American rebellion, and Campbell's threats of hostile action—all "sunk deep into the minds of the people" the "disagreeable necessity" of removing the British military presence in the colony. Accordingly, on November 9 President Drayton ordered Colonel William Moultrie, commander of the 2d South Carolina Regiment of Foot, to fire on any British ship that attempted to cross the harbor bar. Considering that Great Britain and the American colonies were still at peace and trying to resolve their differences, Drayton's order was a bold, provocative measure. The next day he thought it proper to warn Captain Edward Thornbrough, captain of the *Tamar* and commander of the British forces in South Carolina, of his order to Moultrie and the "shedding of blood" that would follow any attempt by the British to violate it.[15]

Captain Thornbrough, an elderly man marked by a pusillanimous nature, ignored the president's thinly veiled challenge to pass Fort Johnson. Undeterred by the British captain's timidity, Drayton devised a cagey plan to provoke an attack on the colony. On October 19 the Council of Safety had appointed Drayton and Thomas Heyward Jr. commissioners to obstruct the passages of Marsh Channel and Hog Island Creek, two narrow channel approaches to Charleston that were outside the range of the guns of Fort Johnson. They easily and quickly sunk two schooners in Marsh Channel. But the council considered the obstruction of Hog Island Creek the riskier venture and assigned the patriot warship *Defence*, a brigantine captained by Simon

14. "Declaration to the Inhabitants of the Back Country," 19 November 1775, *JPC*, 137–9; "An Address to the Inhabitants of the Frontier Settlements," 6 December 1775, "Journal of the Second Council of Safety," SCHS *Collections*, 3: 53–7.

15. Drayton to William Moultrie, 9 November 1775, and Drayton to Edward Thornbrough, 9 November 1775, *JPC*, 112–3.

Tufts and the only patriot vessel that possessed mounted broadside cannon, to act as cover. As this operation was to be performed in full view of the *Tamar* and *Cherokee*, Drayton hoped the British, once realizing what the Americans were up to, would attempt to interfere. To ensure that hostilities did erupt, the president planned to board the *Defence* to direct events. By provoking the English into being the aggressors, Drayton hoped to rally public sentiment, thereby forcing the provincial congress and other public councils to "make a bolder stand" in the American cause.[16]

Drayton was not to be disappointed. About two o'clock on Saturday, November 11, the plan was put into operation when the *Defence*, with its four hulks in tow, dropped down Hog Island Creek with the ebb tide in full view of the British warships. As the *Defence* approached its destination, the *Tamar* fired six shots at the patriot vessel. Although all shells fell short of their target, the fainthearted Captain Thornbrough, feeling he had "done as much as his duty required," halted his fire. The *Tamar*'s attack was not nearly as spirited as Drayton had hoped, so to provoke Thornbrough to greater belligerence, the president ordered Captain Tufts to open fire directly at the British warship. The two nine-pounders discharged missed their target, but still had the desired result. Roused at the insult, the *Tamar* fired four ineffective shots of its own, which the *Defence* promptly answered with a single blast.

As nightfall put an end to the naval battle, the patriots busily proceeded with sinking the four hulks. Meanwhile, Governor Campbell urged Captain Thornbrough to quietly and carefully warp the *Tamar* and the *Cherokee* as close to the patriot warship as they dared, then open fire. When they completed the maneuverings at 4 A.M., the two British gunships fired their broadsides at the *Defence*. Soldiers at Fort Johnson responded by discharging several twenty-six-pounders at the *Tamar* and the *Cherokee*, but finding the British warships at the extreme limit of their guns' range, they ceased firing. Residing at a safe distance, Captain Thornbrough continued his cannonade for another three hours. The cacophonous roar of the ships' cannons awakened the slumbering townspeople, who rushed to the wharves to watch the battle. Fortunately for Drayton and the seventy other men on board the *Defence*, only three of the more than 130 shots fired by the British warships were hits, and these only caused minor damage to the ship's sails. Although the British cannonade produced no serious damage to the vessel or any casualties to its crew, it did force the patriots to withdraw prematurely and to bungle

16. Drayton, *Memoirs*, 2: 71.

the sinking of the fourth hulk. Soon after the bloodless battle ended, the *Defence* moored at Beale's Wharf. Here Drayton disembarked triumphantly amidst the plaudits of the numerous spectators. When asked if the *Defence* was damaged by the British guns, Drayton replied with a smile, "None, excepting one shot, that struck her between wind and water."[17]

Indeed, Drayton had much to smile about. His order to Captain Tufts to fire on the British warships had begun the fighting between South Carolina and Great Britain. As he had hoped, this conspicuous confrontation caused an enormous amount of popular excitement and fired the members of congress into a "fit temper" for planning vigorous measures. By committing the province to open rebellion, Drayton had cleverly outmaneuvered his political opponents into escalating the hostilities from a verbal conflict to a physical one. A frustrated Henry Laurens admitted that Drayton and his fellow extremists "have Step by Step, by ways & means which are too mighty for me, gained the ground which they had in view" and "plunged us into desperate measures." Pleased with his victory over the conservatives, Drayton proudly proclaimed the Battle of Hog Island Creek as "an event of the highest moment to the southern part of the United Colonies." His judgment of the battle's importance was not overestimated, for it clearly demonstrated that the American rebellion had become continental in scope and impressed upon the Crown that even the more conservative colonies were protesting its policies by force of arms.[18]

Over the next several weeks the provincial congress worked feverishly to adopt and implement the desperate measures Drayton so earnestly desired. However, his proposals did not pass without strong opposition from moderates like Rawlins Lowndes, James Parsons, and Henry Laurens, who viewed some of Drayton's "mad schemes" as "too rash." In the end, their efforts could not overcome Drayton's determination to force warlike preparations upon the province. Through skillful parliamentary maneuverings and powerful and eloquent arguments voiced from the president's chair, Drayton managed to convince a majority of the congress to "breast the crisis" facing them

---

17. Ibid., 2: 70–4, 114; *JPC*, 119; *SCG*, 14 November 1775; "Journal of H. M. Sloop *Tamar*, Captain Edward Thornbrough," in Clark, *Naval Documents*, 2: 1015–1016; Harold A. Mouzon, "*Defence*, A Vessel of the Navy of South Carolina," *American Neptune* 13 (January 1953): 29–33; "Diary of Captain Barnard Elliott," *Charleston Yearbook* (1889): 176–7; Lipscomb, *Carolina Lowcountry*, 16–7; Griffiths, "'To Receive Them Properly,'" 179–83.

18. Drayton, *Memoirs*, 2: 74; Laurens to William Manning, 14 November 1775, *HLP*, 10: 509; Drayton to Georgia Council of Safety, 13 November 1775, *JPC*, 123.

by passing measures of "greater preparation." Following on Drayton's declaration that Charleston "ought to be defended to the last extremity," they ordered the construction of six additional batteries, requisitioned the ship *Prosper* as a frigate of war, and commanded every man able to shoulder a rifle to
"appear completely armed" for daily training exercises.

Even Drayton's cautious brother Charles, who heretofore had been reluctant to take a determined stand on the Anglo-American crisis, was moved by
the martial spirit and applied to the provincial congress requesting to form a
volunteer company of foot soldiers. What role Drayton had in his brother's
decision is uncertain, but he certainly must have been pleased with the request and undoubtedly used his influence as president to push the legislature
to create the 4th Regiment of Artillery and to commission Charles as one of
its captains. To help outfit this and other battalions, the congress offered lucrative premiums to individuals producing gunpowder, iron, lead, steel, and
gun locks. Near the end of the session, the legislators created a "Second
Council of Safety," comprising essentially the same members as the first, to
manage the colony's affairs once the congress adjourned.[19]

The adjournment took place on November 29, to last until February 1,
1776. As a sign of solidarity and respect, Rawlins Lowndes delivered a speech
on behalf of the entire congress thanking Drayton for his "unwearied attendance" as president and for the "diligence and propriety" with which he had
discharged the duties of that "important station." Indeed, without Drayton's
strong and skillful leadership, the conservatives would have undoubtedly defeated many of the radicals' proposals designed to provide the patriots with
the best means of defending the capital against Britain's looming assault.[20]

While Drayton and the congress were busily making preparations for war,
Major Andrew Williamson was quickly assembling troops with the purpose
of recapturing the gunpowder stolen by Patrick Cunningham earlier in November. Over 550 officers and men from twenty-five companies responded
to a muster he scheduled at Ninety-Six. However, this force did not compare
to the size of Cunningham's faction, which, encouraged by the procurement
of additional ammunition and the rumor of an approaching Indian uprising

---

19. *JPC*, 118–24, 127–9, 132, 143–4, 160–3; Drayton, *Memoirs*, 2: 74–7; Laura P. Frech,
"The Career of Henry Laurens in the Continental Congress, 1777–1779" (Ph.D. diss., University of North Carolina, 1972), 55–68.

20. *JPC*, 167.

against non-Associators, grew to between 1,900 and 2,400 men. On November 19 this large force, described by a modern authority as "more of a posse than an army," crossed the Saluda River at the Island Ford, marched into Ninety-Six, and quickly surrounded the Whigs' hastily constructed stockade. For the next three days the opposing armies sniped at each other, inflicting approximately thirty-seven casualties altogether, including five deaths. These first fatalities in South Carolina's struggle against the British would prove to be a small yet symbolic portent.[21]

Drayton's calculating and determined efforts in suppressing the most belligerent and committed loyalist leaders during his recent mission into the backcountry now began to bear fruit. Only one member of the opposing party who had signed the Treaty of Ninety Six—Evan McLaurin—participated in the November uprising. As a result, the loyalists were without a leader capable of directing them and every captain felt he had a right to take matters into his own hands. Confusion ensued among the officers, and the rank and file quickly lost confidence in them. The loyalists, despite their overwhelming numerical advantage, were therefore obliged to capitulate, Campbell explained to Dartmouth, "for want of a Leader of either consequence or knowledge enough to direct their Enterprise." On November 21 Cunningham's men raised a white flag and asked for a truce. The patriots, who were down to less than thirty pounds of powder, accepted the offer. The next morning delegates from both sides hammered out the details of the cease-fire agreement (the Second Treaty of Ninety-Six) in which the two parties agreed to immediately suspend hostilities, destroy their forts, return all prisoners, disperse their troops, allow each side unhindered communication with their respective authorities in Charleston, and bind all their troops to the agreement.[22]

The same day, Drayton, unaware of this agreement, wrote the military commanders throughout the province to muster one-third of their regiments and "hold them in constant readiness at a minute's warning." Four days later the congress was still in the dark concerning the "late affair" at Ninety-Six, and fearing the worst, it directed Drayton to prepare "proper instructions" for Colonel Richard Richardson to use in a campaign to "crush" the enemy.

21. Lambert, *South Carolina Loyalists*, 49; Joseph Robinson, American Loyalist Transcripts, 26: 402–10, NYPL.

22. Campbell to Dartmouth, 1 January 1776, Clinton Papers, CL; Drayton, *Memoirs*, 2: 121; reproductions of the Second Treaty of Ninety Six, 22 November 1775, can be found in *DHAR*, 1: 214–5, and Drayton, *Memoirs*, 2: 148–9.

Congress assigned Drayton this responsibility not only because he was president but also because the intelligence he had accumulated during his tour of the interior made him the best qualified person to draft such instructions. During the backcountry mission Drayton had met with military leaders in the region (in some cases even establishing regiments and assigning commands), and therefore knew which commanders could be trusted and which companies had sufficient ammunition, provisions, and training to participate in such an extended and dangerous campaign. His directive to Colonel Richardson was a blueprint for conducting the operation, specifying which regiments to draw from, how to conduct the march, which individuals to apprehend, and how to respond to a variety of possible predicaments, from a mutiny to an overpowering enemy.[23]

By the end of November, over four thousand troops had flocked to Richardson's standard and were quickly moving westward across the Broad and Saluda Rivers toward the loyalists' main camp at the Great Cane Break on the Reedy River in Cherokee country. More than six hundred of these men came from volunteer companies Drayton and Tennent had established during their backcountry trip—a solid testament to the success of their mission. As Richardson slowly marched westward, his rangers swept the region for loyalist leaders. Two of their most important catches were Richard Pearis and Colonel Thomas Fletchall, the latter of whom they found hiding in a hollow sycamore tree. Pearis's capture pleased Drayton particularly. Soon after being incarcerated in the Charleston jail, the Indian trader wrote Drayton, asking permission to speak before the Council of Safety so he could "give you satisfaction in respect to my past conduct." The president, still indignant at Pearis for his earlier betrayal of the American cause and disparaging deposition against him, ignored the turncoat's humble plea. Instead, Drayton ordered Colonel John Thomas and the four hundred militiamen under his command to burn Pearis's plantation and home and bring his wife and children back to Charleston to be placed under house arrest.[24]

On December 21 a detachment of the patriot army surprised the principal enemy camp at the Great Cane Break. The dismayed and dazed loyalists offered only fainthearted resistance. In the ensuing skirmish the patriots killed several of the enemy and captured nearly 140 others. Loyalist commander

23. *JPC*, 103, 144, 153.

24. Pearis to Drayton, 13 January 1776, Gibbes Collection, SCDAH; Richard Pearis, American Loyalist Transcripts, 26: 370, NYPL.

Patrick Cunningham fled during the chaos, yelling for every man to "shift for himself"—another telling example of the poor state of that side's leadership following Drayton's backcountry trip. Whigs troops quickly captured Cunningham and escorted him to Charleston. Other opposition leaders not apprehended—Thomas Brown, Joseph Robinson, Evan McLaurin, and Alexander Cameron—soon fled to East Florida, where there was a British sanctuary. The Whigs' victory at the Battle of the Great Cane Break marked the end of organized backcountry resistance, at least until the British occupation in 1780. "The knot is broke," exulted Henry Laurens, "and we shall be watchful to prevent a re-union."[25]

Although there was no longer a threat of an attack from the interior, there still remained considerable danger of an invasion from the sea. To prepare for such a confrontation, the Second Council of Safety used its extensive authority to increase military readiness in the capital. As one of its first acts, the council on December 2 appointed Drayton chief commissioner to design and erect a four-gun battery on Haddrell's Point (on Sullivan's Island), a favorable position from which to drive off the *Tamar* and *Cherokee*. Upon completing the design, Drayton gave it to his friend Charles C. Pinckney, who on the night of December 19 directed a motley crew of soldiers, slaves, and "gentlemen volunteers" to build the battery. The men worked with such spirit that by dawn they had built the platforms and mounted the four cannon. Exhausted, yet excited by their achievement, the soldiers eagerly opened the garrison's embrasures and saluted the British ships with their eighteen-pounders. The men-of-war immediately moved to a safe distance, thereby giving the patriots entire command of the cove.[26]

Drayton met with less success in his efforts to help build a navy to drive away the British warships. Although Charleston had a thriving trade, South Caro-

25. Marvin L. Cann, "Prelude to War: The First Battle of Ninety-Six, November 19–21, 1775," *SCHM* 76 (October 1975): 197–214; Olson, "Loyalists and the American Revolution," 216–9; Lambert, *South Carolina Loyalists*, 45–6; Andrew Williamson to Drayton, 25 November 1775, Richardson to Laurens, 22 December 1775, and Richardson to Laurens, 2 January 1776, *DHAR*, 1: 216–9, 242–4, 246–8, respectively; *SCG*, 24 November–8 December 1775; Henry Laurens to John Laurens, 6 December 1775, *HLP*, 10: 542–5; Laurens to North Carolina Provincial Congress, 2 January 1776, "Journals of the Second Council of Safety," SCHS *Collections*, 3: 142.

26. "Journal of the Second Council of Safety," SCHS *Collections*, 3: 40, 61, 98; Moultrie, *Memoirs*, 1: 114–5; Drayton, *Memoirs*, 2: 163–4; Zahniser, *Charles Cotesworth Pinckney*, 42.

lina possessed few ships of its own in 1775. By December, the patriots' fledgling navy consisted of only four warships—the *Hawke*, the *Hibernia*, the *Defence*, and the *Prosper*—and only the latter two possessed mounted broadside cannon. Adding to the colony's lack of ships was the equally troubling problem of a shortage of trained seamen and a captain for the *Prosper*, the newest gunship. To address these problems, the Council of Safety on December 7 assigned Drayton to investigate the state of the colony's navy and report on the most effective and quickest means of manning it. His findings must have been worse than originally thought, for one week later he offered his services in the colony's naval department. This may seem like a rather surprising proposition considering that Drayton had no seafaring experience except two voyages to England. But what the eager patriot lacked in nautical know-how, he more than made up with his tremendous self-confidence, energy, and desire to further the American cause in any way.[27]

Concern over the wretched condition of the Whig navy was not Drayton's only motive in volunteering for naval service. He also aspired to military glory. Drayton had already served in all the Whig government's most important offices, from committee chairman to president of the provincial congress. The only other way he could advance the American cause in South Carolina, while at the same time satisfying his ravenous appetite for fame, was a military command. His craving for combat had first manifested itself in September when he led patriot forces in a standoff with Fletchall's army near Ninety-Six; his brief taste of sea warfare against the British in November—and the enormous public praise he received from participating in it—intensified his relish for military distinction.

The council accepted Drayton's offer on December 15 by assigning him to command the *Prosper*, the patriots' largest and most heavily armed gunship. Evidently the council felt that anything less than the command of the *Prosper* would be beneath Drayton's dignity. The assignment undoubtedly pleased Drayton, who viewed it as an opportunity to provoke a stronger opposition to the British military presence in South Carolina while augmenting his popularity and power within the revolutionary movement. Others were not so satisfied with Drayton's appointment, however. Colonel William Moultrie, for one, felt it was absurd and perhaps even harmful to the American cause to

27. Heyward Stuckey, "The South Carolina Navy and the American Revolution" (master's thesis, University of South Carolina, 1972), 3–4; *JPC*, 128, 146, 157; "Journal of the Second Council of Safety," SCHS *Collections*, 3: 64, 69–70, 86.

give such a highly specialized and influential naval post to a landsman who "did not know any one rope in the ship from another." Even Drayton's son felt it necessary to explain that his father's appointment was intended to stimulate recruiting for the struggling navy. On the other hand, the conservative councilors must have welcomed Drayton's offer as it removed the ever active and impetuous firebrand from their chambers and directed his energy to the less conspicuous duty of outfitting naval vessels. As for Drayton, he had hopes of using the *Prosper* to drive the British warships from the province.[28]

Realizing he knew nothing about sailing, Drayton wasted no time finding able officers to help command his ship. On the same day he received his naval commission, Drayton procured commissions for three experienced seamen—Stephen Seymour, Jacob Milligan, and Thomas Sherman—to serve as his lieutenants.[29] Drayton also promptly launched a campaign to recruit a crew. In the December 22 issue of the *South Carolina & American General Gazette* appears the advertisement headed "Good Births" [*sic*] and reading:

> The Honourable William Henry Drayton, Commander of the Colony Ship of War *Prosper*, hereby invites all able-bodied Seamen and Land-men to enter on board the said Ship. He assures them, that they shall meet with good Treatment, and that they shall in their Commander find a Friend. And for their further Encouragement, It is hereby notified, That to every such Person entering on board the said Ship a Bounty of Ten Pounds will be paid and also Twenty-One Pounds per Month Wages. And that on the 20th of November last, the Congress Resolved, That they will make Provision for the support of all Persons who may be maimed and disabled in the Public Service of the Colony by Sea or Land; and also of the Families of such as may be killed in the said Services.

Because there were few trained seamen in South Carolina, Drayton also sent recruiters on recruiting expeditions to Georgia, Pennsylvania, New York, and New England to enlist seamen for the South Carolina navy. By liberally spending over £200 of the Whig government's money, his agents managed to recruit fifty-four seamen in Georgia alone. Evidently these campaigns failed to procure enough men to sufficiently operate the *Prosper*, however, be-

28. *JPC*, 128, 146, 157; "Journal of the Second Council of Safety," SCHS *Collections*, 3: 82–8; Moultrie, *Memoirs*, 1: 111; Drayton, *Memoirs*, 2: 162; Stuckey, "The South Carolina Navy," 20–1. The *Prosper*'s armament consisted of at least twenty cannon: eight twelve-pounders, eight sixes, several four-pounders, and some swivels (Drayton, *Memoirs*, 2: 81).

29. "Journal of the Second Council of Safety," SCHS *Collections*, 3: 90.

cause in mid-January the council ordered sailors from the brigantine *Comet* on board Drayton's warship.[30]

While Drayton was busy procuring a crew, he was also outfitting and arming his vessel. He quickly purchased an anchor, cable, rigging, a sail, tackle, pumps, furniture, kitchen items, carpenter's tools, pitch, turpentine, and tar—essentials for maintaining a sailing vessel. To turn his vessel into a warship, he armed the *Prosper* with over twenty cannon: eight twelve-pounders, eight six-pounders, and between four and ten four-pounders. The Council of Safety completed the outfitting of the warship by supplying its captain and crew with cutlasses and the necessary shot and powder.[31]

Much to his disappointment, Drayton never got to fire the powder or unsheathe the cutlasses. Whig officials largely ignored the *Prosper*, leaving it to serve as a guard ship for Charleston harbor. This was certainly not the service Captain Drayton had in mind for his warship when he armed it with cannon and shot and warned his crew that the congress would provide for their families should they die in battle with the enemy at sea. He desperately wanted to fulfill the congress's original purpose in outfitting the vessel: to capture or sink the British warships lying in Rebellion Road. The Council of Safety finally gave Drayton this opportunity on January 22, 1776, when it ordered him and Simon Tufts, captain of the *Defence*, to use their "best endeavours to take or destroy" the enemy vessels. However, the order was soon postponed when Drayton requested a hearing on the matter. What he told the council is not recorded in its journals, but apparently Drayton felt that his vessel was not up to the task, because he and Tufts never executed the order to attack the British warships. The problems afflicting the *Prosper* were partially explained by Charles C. Pinckney, who described Drayton's ship as a heavy, clumsy craft. More recently, naval historians have further determined that the small schooner, which Drayton unwisely outfitted with more than twenty heavy cannon, must have been "cranky and unseaworthy," lacking the stability necessary for a fighting ship. By late February it became obvious that the

30. "Journal of the Second Council of Safety," SCHS *Collections*, 3: 64, 90, 131–3, 174, 259; *JPC*, 157; John Rutledge to Robert Cochran, 31 December 1775, "Journal of the Massachusetts Council," 16 February 1776, and Massachusetts Council to Robert Cochran, 17 February 1775, in Clark, *Naval Documents*, 3: 326–8, 1316, and 1333 respectively; South Carolina Council of Safety to Georgia Council of Safety, 13 February 1776, *HLP*, 11: 99; Thomas Sherman to Drayton, 7 January 1776, and Joseph Habersham to Drayton, date unknown, *DHAR*, 1: 253, 258–9.

31. "Accounts of the ship *Prosper*," Gibbes Collection, SCDAH; "Journal of the Second Council of Safety," SCHS *Collections*, 3: 110, 116, 155, 183.

Prosper was unfit for sea duty, so the council ordered Drayton to transfer thirty of his men to the *Comet* and ten to the *Defence*. In June 1776, the guns and ammunition from the *Prosper* were removed and dispersed to several batteries and redoubts around Charleston. With the ship stripped of its crew and guns, the Whig government ordered it to be sold at auction.[32]

Given the amount of time, manpower, and money devoted to outfitting the *Prosper*, Drayton and the council had to have been disappointed with the project's failure. The British press, on the other hand, was elated with the *Prosper*'s demise and could not resist poking fun at Drayton's unsuccessful naval command. The *Gentleman's Magazine* lampooned his captaincy in the following lines:

> Self-created from nought, like a mushroom we see,
> Spring an able Commander by land and by sea;
> Late of Tories the prince, and his country's great foe,
> Now the Congress's Chairman, a split-shirted beau;
> All titles of honour and profit do wait on
> Judge, General, Counsellor, Admiral Drayton,
> Who never smell'd powder, nor handled a rope,
> But infallible more than Lord Peter the Pope;
> Who makes flesh and blood of his bread and his wine,
> While Drayton of schooners makes ships of the line,
> Makes all laws of mechanics and nature knock under,
> Can cram in an eggshell a twenty-four pounder;
> Can burn in an instant the whole British navy,
> And eat up an army without salt or gravy.[33]

This satirical poem marked the final insult to Drayton's brief and ignominious service as captain in the South Carolina provincial navy.

32. Moultrie, *Memoirs*, 1: 111; "Journal of the Second Council of Safety," SCHS *Collections*, 3: 206–9, 221, 258, 270; Charles Pinckney to Eliza L. Pinckney, 29 June 1776, *DHAR*, 2: 8; Harold A. Mouzon, "The Ship *Prosper*, 1775–1776" *SCHM* 59 (January 1958): 10; "Diary of Captain Barnard Elliott," *Charleston Yearbook* (1889): 208; Hemphill et al., *Journals of the General Assembly*, 85–6; *SC&AGG*, 25 September 1776. The *Prosper* was eventually sold to Thomas Sherman, who renamed it the *Liberty*. A British privateer captured the ship on March 29, 1777, when it was carrying a cargo of rice and tobacco bound for Bordeaux. See Thurman T. Morgan, "The Fate of the Ship *Prosper*," *SCHM* 93 (July 1992): 202–4.

33. *Gentleman's Magazine* (London) 46 (June 1776): 279. Drayton had spent nearly £2,000 sterling on supplies, equipment, and wages in outfitting his vessel ("Accounts of the Ship *Prosper*," Gibbes Collection, SCDAH).

* * *

Drayton therefore must have been relieved to assume his more familiar duties as president when the provincial congress opened its second session on February 1, 1776. One week later, John Rutledge, Henry Middleton, and Christopher Gadsden returned from Philadelphia with a resolution passed in the Continental Congress the previous November allowing South Carolina to establish a government that, in the Congress's judgment, will "best produce the happiness of the people" and most effectively "secure peace and good order" in the colony during America's present dispute with Great Britain. This offer was quite timely, as "everything was running into confusion," observed William Moultrie; the "affairs of the province," he explained, had simply become "too unwieldy" for the various revolutionary governing bodies to manage. In granting South Carolina this permission, however, the Continental Congress stressed that Whig leaders should not consider the new government as preparatory for independence, but merely as a temporary administrative body for the maintenance of public order until the royal government should resume its authority.[34]

Despite that stipulation, Drayton still saw the resolution as a golden opportunity to advance the idea of independence. After thanking Middleton, Rutledge, and Gadsden for their "important services" performed in the Continental Congress, he launched into a vituperative tirade against the British ministry. "When the hand of tyranny, armed in hostile manner, was extended from Great Britain to spoil America of whatever she held most valuable," the president told the three delegates, "it became your business to ascertain the rights of America—to point out her violated franchises—to make humble representation to the King for redress." But King George III has been "deaf to the cries of his American subjects," he exclaimed, forcing the colonists to erect forms of government independent of and in opposition to regal authority. "Worthy Delegates!" Drayton concluded "It is the judgment of your country, that your conduct, of which I have just marked the grand lines, in the American Congress, is justifiable before God and man, and that, whatever may be the issue of this unlooked-for defensive civil war, in which, unfortunately, though gloriously, we are engaged—whether *independence or slavery*—all the blood, and all the guilt, must be imputed to *British*, not to American counsels."[35]

34. *JPC*, 181–2; *JCC*, 3: 326–7; Moultrie, *Memoirs*, 1: 125.
35. Drayton to Second Provincial Congress, 8 February 1776, *JPC*, 179–80 (italics mine).

With this bold—and, to some, horrifying—speech, Drayton became the
first leading figure in South Carolina to openly call for independence. Motivated by his stirring oration and the colony's unwieldy affairs, the provincial
congress later that day appointed a committee (with Drayton serving as a
member) to consider the Continental Congress's resolution that they establish a new government for the colony. On February 10 Laurens submitted
the committee's report favoring such a new government. Agreeing that the
"present mode of conducting public affairs is inadequate to the well governing the good people of this colony," the legislature proceeded the next day to
ballot for members to draw up a constitution. To ensure that this committee
created a charter that was to be only temporary while the Anglo-American
dispute continued, they stacked the panel with conservatives and moderates
like Lowndes, Laurens, and Bee, and elected John Rutledge to chair it. The
only radicals on the eleven-man board were Arthur Middleton and Christopher Gadsden. Their leader, Drayton, was conspicuously excluded from the
constitutional committee.[36]

Omitted from this panel, Drayton devoted his time and energy to presid-
ing over the colony's day-to-day legislative and administrative affairs. Although he knew that the new government was meant to last only until
America and Great Britain resolved their dispute, Drayton nevertheless used
his powerful position as president to push the delegates to continue passing
legislation making such a reconciliation more and more unlikely. They accordingly elected Thomas Lynch, John and Edward Rutledge, Arthur Middleton, and Thomas Heyward Jr. to represent South Carolina at the next
meeting of the Continental Congress. The provincial congress, along with
the Council of Safety, also purchased one thousand rifles, obtained additional
armed vessels to protect the ports of Beaufort and Georgetown, established a
commissary department to supply the troops with rations, established hospi-
tals with medical provisions, increased military recruiting and training in
both the army and navy, and employed a professional military engineer—
Joseph Ferdinand Sebastian DeBraham—to supervise work on the numerous
fortifications under construction around the capital.

All this preparation for war prompted many men to remove their wives,
children, and "other valuables" to safety in the country. This mass exodus left
Charleston, "always heretofore lively and busy at this Season," wrote merchant Josiah Smith, "now [a] Melancholy [sight] to behold, houses shut up,

36. *JPC*, 181–5; Drayton, *Memoirs*, 2: 172–3.

and Wharves and Stores all empty, Trade not carried on, Places of Worship almost deserted, Scarce a Woman to be seen in the Streets, Men continually on Military Duty, and no other Musick but Drum and Fife." Certainly these were not the actions of men intent on peace. "Every day leads us . . . deeper & deeper into Warlike preparations," Henry Laurens nervously noted to a friend. These "uncommon resolutions to oppose any Encroachments on their Privileges" prompted one outside observer to proclaim that South Carolinians "have gone to greater Expence than any other[s] considering their Situation." Indeed, by early March the Whig defensive position stretched from the eastern tip of James Island all the way to the northern shore of Sullivan's Island, a distance of twelve miles. Charleston was therefore "really very strongly fortified," according to one resident, "and must occasion bloody work to be taken by Sea."[37]

Although South Carolina was rapidly preparing for war, its southern neighbor was hesitating to support the American cause. Georgia patriots had failed to send delegates to the First Continental Congress and had refused to join the Continental Association. Whig leaders in South Carolina were disheartened by Georgia's "seeming apostasy" and feared that a break in America's unity would seriously jeopardize its chances of successfully resolving the dispute with Great Britain. Their concerns grew in early January 1776 when they learned that Georgia had shipped several cargoes of merchandise to Britain in violation of the Association. In response, the Council of Safety later that month ordered Colonel Stephen Bull of Beaufort to hold two hundred men "in constant readiness" to fly to Georgia's assistance "upon the first call." The affair rested until February 16, when President Drayton sent Rawlins Lowndes, James Parsons, and Thomas Savage to Savannah to induce Georgia to cooperate in "paying the strictest obedience" to all the resolves of the Continental Congress, particularly those relative to nonexportation. To "give weight" to the behest, Drayton sent along a letter strongly urging Georgia's congress to establish a provincial Association.[38]

When the South Carolina delegation returned on March 1, they reported

37. *JPC*, 193, 204, 209, 212, 214, 222, 232–3; "Journal of the Second Council of Safety," SCHS *Collections*, 3: 247, 250, 255–69; Henry Laurens to William Manning, 27 February 1776, *HLP*, 11: 122; Haw, *John and Edward Rutledge*, 65; Anonymous letter written in Charleston, 14 February 1776, Clinton Papers, CL; Griffiths, "'To Receive Them Properly,'" 247–69.

38. "Journal of the Second Council of Safety," SCHS *Collections*, 3: 126–8, 135–7; Drayton, *Memoirs*, 2: 202; *JPC*, 191–3. The one exception to Georgia's pattern was St. John's Parish, which sent Lyman Hall to the First Continental Congress.

that the Georgia patriots wanted to adopt the Continental Congress's resolves but complained that opposition in the province was too great—a fact
revealed when scarcely three hundred militiamen answered a recent call to
arms issued by Whig leaders. Even Archibald Bulloch, president of the Georgia provincial congress, dejectedly admitted that there were "but few righteous souls among them." Unless South Carolina "interfered in a forcible
manner," the Georgia Council of Safety reported, "exportation [of more
goods to Britain] would speedily take place." Judging such action as "detrimental to the interest of America," Drayton ordered Colonel Stephen Bull
and Colonel Charles C. Pinckney to lead a force of 350 men to Savannah to
prevent loaded vessels from proceeding with their cargoes and to capture
every person in Georgia "dangerous to the liberties of America." With assistance from forty Georgia patriots, the Carolinians took possession of the capital without bloodshed. Georgians thereafter "acceded to the resolutions of
Congress," one disgusted loyalist wrote, "but it was owing to the threats of
the Carolina men that they did it at all," he added. With opposition to American measures quashed in Savannah, the "true friends of liberty" there has-
tened to implement more vigorous means of public defense.[39]

While Drayton was aiding the American cause in Georgia, the Committee of
Eleven (the group created by the South Carolina provincial congress to draft
a new state constitution) presented its plan for a new government on March
5. Leading conservatives managed to successfully block progress on this "very
important business" until March 21 when word arrived that Parliament and
the king had declared the colonies in open rebellion and that American property, vessels, and persons were therefore subject to seizure. This stunning
news silenced nearly all opposition to a new form of government. Five days
later the congress adopted the constitution.[40]

Much to Drayton's disappointment, the new charter did not establish a
separate form of government. Most South Carolina patriots were "ready to
spend their Blood and Fortunes" in defense of American liberty, but were
"shocked at the bare idea" of independence from Great Britain. Instead, the
new plan of government reflected the timidity of its drafters who still hoped

39. Drayton, *Memoirs*, 2: 201–14 ; *JPC*, 218–9; Thomas Taylor to J. Morrison, 3 January
1776, in Robert S. Davis Jr., ed., "A Georgia Loyalist's Perspective on the American Revolution:
The Letters of Dr. Thomas Taylor," *GHQ* 81 (spring 1997): 126.

40. Henry Laurens to John Laurens, 22 February 1776, *HLP*, 11: 118; Drayton, *Memoirs*, 2:
177–8.

for reconciliation with the mother country. In the preamble, the provincial congress justified its creation of a new government by explaining that Governor Campbell's "utmost efforts to destroy their lives" and his flight from the capital with the provincial seal and the royal instructions made it "indispensably necessary" for it to regulate the "internal polity" of the colony. And although the mother country had "traduced and treated" South Carolinians as rebels, the congress still desired "an accommodation of the unhappy differences" between Great Britain and America.[41]

With this hope in mind, the congress made no radical changes in the operating structure of the established government; to do so would have caused problems upon the expected reinstatement of British control. Accordingly, the old Commons House became the new General Assembly, whose members were elected by the people—the only government officials popularly voted into office. A legislative council of thirteen members, selected by the General Assembly from its own membership, replaced the royal council. Jointly, the General Assembly and legislative council elected a president, who replaced the royal governor. The president was granted power to veto legislation, but the power to prorogue and dissolve, so abused in the previous five years by the royal executives, was withheld. A seven-member Privy Council, consisting of the vice-president and six others chosen jointly by the General Assembly and the council, served as an advisory board to the executive. Courts and law remained virtually unchanged, although now judges held their positions for life on the condition of good behavior.

The congress also carefully composed the constitution to ensure that the coastal elite retained absolute control of the government. Although the low-country contained less than half the white population, the congress allotted the region 126 delegates, while giving the upcountry only 76. Moreover, the constitution prevented the unpropertied masses from participating in provincial politics by requiring voters to own at least one hundred acres of land, or a town lot or house worth £60. All officeholders, additionally, had to own five hundred acres of settled land and ten slaves, or property valued at £1,000 sterling.[42]

On March 26 the provincial congress adopted the constitution under a

41. Unidentified letter written in Charleston, 14 February 1775, Clinton Papers, CL; *JPC*, 258.

42. The South Carolina Constitution of 1776 can be found in *JPC*, 256–63 and Drayton, *Memoirs*, 2: 186–97.

"grand & most decent solemnity." President Drayton crowned the momentous event by signing his name to the document. With this act South Carolina became only the second colony to officially establish an independent form of government, following the lead of New Hampshire, which had adopted a temporary constitution two months earlier. Although the congress never submitted the document to the people for ratification, Henry Laurens boasted that it was "attended by the acclamations of the People without noise or confusion." South Carolinians were not the only people cheering the establishment of their new government. Massachusetts firebrand John Adams observed that South Carolina's constitution "has aroused and animated all the continent. It has spread a visible joy, and if North Carolina and Virginia should follow the example, it will spread through the rest of the colonies like electric fire." In closing the proceedings of the pivotal session, President Drayton humbly thanked the members for honoring him with a position "the highest any man can receive" and prayed that their recent conduct would help to forever preserve America's liberties. Having written itself out of existence, the second provincial congress adjourned, and "in the twinkling of an eye" wrote Laurens, reconvened the same day into the first General Assembly.[43]

The new legislature's first order of business was to elect officers for the new government. Dominated by moderates who were "still afraid to admit what they were doing," the assembly chose John Rutledge as president and Henry Laurens as vice-president—two men who at that time strongly opposed American independence—and only selected moderates to the legislative council. Drayton's aggressive behavior as president deterred the assembly from seriously considering him for any of these positions. Nevertheless, it could not ignore his zeal, talents, popularity, and past services, and so rewarded him with the office of chief justice, the government's third highest post. The General Assembly and legislative council, additionally, appointed him to the Privy Council, while voters in Saxe-Gotha reelected him to the legislature. Thus Drayton was in the unique position of having a voice in all three branches of government, giving him considerable opportunity to influence public policy.

43. John Adams to James Warren, 11 April 1776, in Samuel E. Morison, ed., *Sources and Documents Illustrating the American Revolution, 1764–1788, and the Formation of the Federal Constitution*, 2d ed. (Oxford, U.K.: Clarendon Press, 1929), 146; Drayton to Second Provincial Congress, 27 March 1775, *JPC*, 267; Henry Laurens to John Laurens, 28 March 1776, *HLP*, 11: 194–5.

On March 28 Drayton and the other newly appointed officers were sworn into their respective berths during a specially convened session of the General Assembly. Afterwards, members of the two houses, preceded by President Rutledge and Vice-President Laurens, marched out onto Broad Street where they then made a "solemn procession" from the statehouse to the Exchange in front of a line of provincial troops and a crowd of bystanders. The ceremonious cavalcade evoked an assortment of emotions. Some "gazed at them with a kind of rapture," remarked an eyewitness, while others shed "tears of joy." When the procession reached the Exchange, Thomas Grimball, sheriff of Charleston, announced the officers of the new government amidst the "heart-cheering plaudits of the people." Cannon from the city's bastions and battleships fired thirteen shots—one for each American colony. Some people were so moved by the event that they "vowed never [to] give up this Government." Having devoted nearly all his energy toward achieving this goal, Drayton, for one, pledged to commit "every moment" of his time to ensure that the new government remained intact.[44]

The winter of 1775–1776 proved a watershed in South Carolina's revolutionary movement. During this brief time, the Whig government matured from a precarious, de facto makeshift to a stable, official administration. In a variety of ways Drayton proved the most significant catalyst in this metamorphosis. He helped prepare a successful plan for the colony's defense, roused the people and politicians to increase military preparedness, planned Richardson's successful military campaign against backcountry loyalists, provided aggressive and influential leadership as president of the second provincial congress, and helped strengthen the Whigs' position in Georgia. Drayton was not successful in all his endeavors, though. His service as ship's captain, for example, was a disappointment. However, this setback failed to dampen his desire to secure American independence, as his behavior in the forthcoming months was to reveal.

44. John Adams to Mrs. Adams, 17 May 1776, in Force, *American Archives*, 4th ser., vol. 6: 488–9; Drayton, *Memoirs*, 2: 243; *SC&AGG*, 3 April 1776; Drayton to Second Provincial Congress, 27 March 1775, *JPC*, 267.

William Henry Drayton. This engraving by B. L. Prevost is from
an original portrait done by Pierre du Simitier in Philadelphia
in 1779, the year of Drayton's death.
Courtesy South Caroliniana Library, University of South Carolina, Columbia

Balliol College, Oxford, ca. 1770. Trinity College is to the right.
Courtesy Balliol College, Oxford

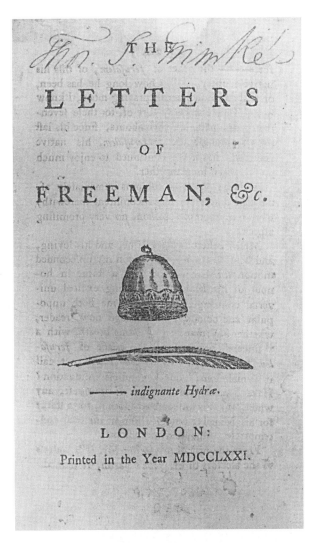

THE

LETTERS

OF

FREEMAN, &c.

—— indignante Hydræ.

LONDON:

Printed in the Year MDCCLXXI.

Title page of Drayton's *Letters of Freeman*, published in London in 1771
Courtesy South Caroliniana Library, University of South Carolina, Columbia

A View of Charles Town, Thomas Leitch, 1774
Collection of the Museum of Early Southern Decorative Arts, Winston-Salem, N.C.

Drayton Hall
Courtesy Drayton Hall, Charleston, S.C.

Original die of the South Carolina State Seal, designed by
William Henry Drayton and Arthur Middleton, 1776.
Courtesy South Carolina Department of Archives and History, Columbia

Arthur Middleton and family, 1772, by Benjamin West
Courtesy Middleton Place, Charleston, S.C.

Henry Laurens by John Singleton Copley, 1782
*Courtesy National Portrait Gallery, Smithsonian Institution. Transfer from
the National Gallery of Art; gift of Andrew W. Mellon, 1942*

The British attack against Fort Moultrie on Sullivan's Island, June 28, 1776, as depicted in a 1783 engraving by Pocock.

PRESERVING INDEPENDENCE

Drayton exerted himself during the next two years in a variety of roles to keep South Carolina and all of America on a straight path toward independence. As a privy councilor and assemblyman he continued to advocate aggressive military measures; as chief justice he enthusiastically championed independence; as a private citizen he publicly opposed attempts at reconciliation; and as a commissioner of various kinds he raised troops, concluded a treaty with the Indians, and confronted a crisis in a neighboring colony. However, Drayton's most lasting achievements during this time were his participation in designing a state seal, creating a new state constitution, collecting materials for a history of the Revolution in South Carolina, and devising a plan of federal government.

South Carolina's new legislature met for less than two weeks. The eleven acts it passed during this brief session were as conservative as the members who dominated the body. Of these measures, only two were war-related: one to prevent sedition and another to deter desertion. Before President Rutledge adjourned the session on April 11, he urged the assemblymen to use all their influence and authority to fully explain to their constituents Parliament's "various unjust and cruel" measures against the American colonies, the "indispensable necessity" of establishing "some mode of government" in the province, and the many privileges that their new constitution guaranteed them. To remove any apprehensions the people might have about the new government, the president also directed the delegates to emphasize that "this constitution is but temporary."[1]

Drayton took President Rutledge's instructions to heart—except the last one. When the courts reopened on April 23, the new chief justice took this opportunity to lead the forces for independence in South Carolina in a series of patriotic charges to the state's grand juries.[2] In them, Drayton explained the principal causes leading to the "late Revolution" in the government, argued the people's right to create a separate constitution, and enumerated the benefits resulting from that "happy and necessary establishment" (277).

In justifying the creation of the new state charter, Drayton launched into an uncharacteristic attack on George III. In earlier criticisms against the Crown, Drayton had regarded the king as sacrosanct and protected him behind "wicked ministers." Now, however, he began placing equal blame on His Majesty for Britain's offensive colonial policy. The shift in Drayton's attitude can probably be attributed to the King's Proclamation of August 23, 1775, declaring the colonies in an "open and avowed rebellion," and his refusal to receive the colonies' Olive Branch Petition offered earlier in July. Encouraging the Carolinian to castigate the British monarch was Thomas Paine's pamphlet *Common Sense*, which, when it was published in January 1776, was the first full-scale attack on the king in the colonies. Like Paine, Drayton understood that a symbolic execution of George III was essential to convert the colonies into free and sovereign states.[3] In placing equal blame on the king for the policies of his reign, the chief justice was cleverly getting the people to think of independence rather than reconciliation; if George III was just as culpable as his ministers and Parliament, there was no hope that

1. Drayton, *Memoirs*, 2: 247–52.

2. Drayton's April 23, 1776, judicial charge can be found in *SC&AGG*, 8–22 May 1776; Drayton, *Memoirs*, 2: 259–74; Force, *American Archives*, 4th ser., vol. 5: 1025–1032; and *DHAR*, 2: 277–89, from which the succeeding parenthetical citations are taken. A portion of his charge is also in the *Remembrancer* (London), 1776, part 2: 320–30.

3. The Olive Branch Petition, so named for its suppliant tone, was passed by the Second Continental Congress on July 5, 1775. This document begged George III to intervene on behalf of the colonies against Parliament and offered to end armed resistance if he withdrew the British troops and revoked the Intolerable Acts. The king not only refused to receive the petition, he also declared the colonies in "open and avowed rebellion" and dispatched an army of twenty thousand troops to crush the American rebels.

For an analysis of Thomas Paine's attack against King George III and its possible influence on Drayton, see Winthrop D. Jordan, "Familial Politics: Thomas Paine and the Killing of the King, 1776," *Journal of American History* 60 (September 1973): 294–308.

Americans would ever have their grievances redressed. "Almost with the commencement of his reign," Drayton exclaimed, "his subjects felt causes to complain of government." Building to his climax, he continued, "The reign advanced—the grievances became more numerous and intolerable—the complaints more general and loud—the whole Empire resounded with the cries of injured subjects! At length, grievances being unredressed and ever increasing; all patience being borne down; all hope destroyed; all confidence in royal government blasted! Behold! the Empire is rent from pole to pole!—perhaps to continue asunder forever!" (278).

As evidence, the chief justice listed the "catalogue of oppressions" enacted by the king and Parliament to "arbitrarily enslave" America: claiming a right to bind the colonies "in all cases whatsoever," laying duties "at their mere will and pleasure" upon all colonies, suspending the legislature of New York, annulling the charter of Massachusetts, restricting America's trade and commerce, sending armed forces to America in time of peace, and establishing both an arbitrary government and the Roman Catholic religion in Quebec (279). If these oppressive measures were not enough, Drayton reminded his audience that the king, in concert with his generals, governors, and Indian agents, had instigated the "savage nations" in the southern colonies to indiscriminately massacre men, women, and children, had armed slaves against their masters, and had even armed brother against brother and son against father. "Oh, Almighty Director of the Universe!" the chief justice cried, "what confidence can be put in a Government, ruling by such engines, and upon such principles of unnatural destruction . . . it has no parallel in the registers of tyranny!" With the colony suffering from such a variety of "enormous injuries" resulting from the king's repressive colonial policy, Drayton explained, members of the provincial congress found it unavoidably necessary to create a new form of government "for the good of the people" (281).

One important precedent giving South Carolinians this right of "Revolution" had been established in 1719, according to the chief justice, when their ancestors cast off the proprietary authority for no other purpose than to "preserve their inalienable rights."[4] Because King George I had accepted Caroli-

---

4. In the years immediately prior to 1719, Carolina suffered from a variety of problems: a major war with the Indians, a staggering debt, increasing danger from the Spanish in Florida, a loss of much of its trade with the Indians to the French in Mississippi, and an incompetent and offensive chief justice. The proprietors refused to send aid, nor did they allow the colony to work out its own solutions to its difficulties. Instead, they further aggravated the colonists by attacking some of their most cherished laws. Fed up, the Carolinians renounced the government of the

na's plea to assume direction of its affairs, Drayton continued, he not only "admitted the legality of that Revolution," he also vested in us, through our forefathers, "a clear right to effect another Revolution" (278).

Drayton drew his strongest justification for rebellion, however, from England's Glorious Revolution of 1688, in which Parliament had removed James II from the throne for breaking the "original contract" between the king and the people (282). That "famous resolution" also supports the "edifice of Government which we have erected," argued the chief justice, because George III and his representatives in the colonies have abused the Americans "at least as grievously" as James II "injured the people of England" (282, 286). Both rulers had irrevocably violated the constitution and failed in their role as protector by suspending the operation of government, breaking election laws, levying money without the consent of the representatives of the people, and maintaining a standing army in time of peace; the royal governor was also guilty of fleeing the subjects under his care. "From such a result of injuries, from such a conjecture of circumstances," Drayton boldly announced, "the law of the land authorizes me to declare . . . that George the Third, King of Great Britain, has abdicated the Government, and that the Throne is thereby vacant; that is, he has no authority over us, and we owe no obedience to him!" (286).

Realizing the impact this declaration would have on much of his audience, Drayton tried to allay their anxiety by pointing out some of the "great benefits" resulting from such a change of government: security of their property and natural rights from British tyranny, encouragement of their trade and manufacturing, and, generally, the promotion of their happiness by allowing the poorest man, through virtue and merit, to "arrive at the highest dignity." Who would not be satisfied with a government "calculated to make the people rich, powerful, virtuous and happy?" he asked (287). To discourage those who still hoped for reconciliation, Drayton warned that even the "most express" acts of Parliament could not give Americans their security because they are "as cheaply repealed as made." Nor will a change of ministry avail us, he added, because the "rapid succession" of ministers during the present reign have continually imposed the same "ruinous policy" against America. "In short," the chief justice announced, "I think it my duty to declare . . .

Lords Proprietors in November 1719, elected their own governor, and beseeched King George I to place the colony under his immediate protection. Touched by the Carolinian's plight, the king appointed veteran Francis Nicholson royal governor of the colony the next year.

that true reconcilement never can exist between Great Britain and America" (288–89).

Reconciliation was also impossible, Drayton maintained, because "the Almighty created America to be independent of Britain" (289). The "fortitude with which America has endured these civil and military outrages," he explained, "the union of her people, as astonishing as unprecedented, when we consider their various manners and religious tenants; their distance from each other; their various and clashing local interests; their self-denial; and their miraculous success in the prosecution of the war; I say these things all demonstrate that the Lord of Hosts is on our side!" (280). In concluding his charge, the chief justice urged his listeners to "beware of the impiety" of ignoring the "Almighty hand now extended to accomplish his purpose"; for "our piety and political safety are so blended," he asserted, "that to refuse our labors in this divine work, is to refuse to be a great, a free, a pious and a happy people" (289).

Drayton's revolutionary charge of April 23, 1776, is ranked among the most outstanding speeches in American history, a production "replete with learning, eloquence, and the strongest patriotism," in the words of one nineteenth-century literary scholar.[5] However, his address had a much more important legacy. By depicting the British monarchy as both despicable and dispensable, the chief justice helped South Carolinians make the painful break with the mother country. In its presentment, the grand jury not only expressed its "most unfeigned joy in the happy Constitution," but also maintained that it was "a sacred duty for every citizen to maintain and defend [it] with his life and fortune" (290–291). Even the moderate patriot Henry Laurens read the chief justice's charge with "satisfaction and pleasure" (276).

Drayton's patriotic address was printed in newspapers throughout America and also in London. Governor John Rutledge sent a copy of it to the Continental Congress, where, according to Arthur Middleton, it helped inspire the delegates to declare American independence. Just a week after the "epochal declaration," Middleton informed him in allegorical prose: "The plant [independence] which you have been nursing has thriven amazingly, its roots have reach'd this place & sprung up in full vigour. I send you the fruit [Declaration of Independence] you plucked from 12 of the Branches

5. Frank Moore, ed., *American Eloquence: A Collection of Speeches and Addresses, By the Most Eminent Orators of America; with Biographical Sketches and Illustrative Notes* (New York: D. Appleton, 1857), 1: 49.

[states] & have the pleasure to tell you that the 13th [New York] is in full Blossom. My Sentiments upon the subject you shall have soon, in the meantime enjoy the delicacies of this forbidden fruit, if it has any." Prominent patriots outside of Congress also read Drayton's judicial address with much satisfaction. Thomas Paine, who rarely paid tribute to a fellow author, was impressed with the "elegant masterly manner" in which the chief justice argued for independence, and remarked that it was "of the first rank in America." Perhaps nobody was more pleased with the charge than Drayton himself, who later boasted that it was "the first public declaration in America that my countrymen owed no allegiance to the King of Great Britain." Although his boastful assertion is grossly inaccurate, Drayton's revolutionary charge of April 23, 1776, certainly marked him as one of the earliest and most vocal advocates for independence in America.[6]

While Drayton was using his position as chief justice to plant the idea of independence firmly in the minds of Americans both at home and abroad, he was also trying to make it a reality as a privy councilor. As the linear heir of the royal council, the seven-man Privy Council's chief responsibility was to advise the president. The body's powers expanded tremendously in April 1776 when the General Assembly dissolved the Council of Safety and vested that group's extensive authority in the Privy Council and president while the legislature was out of session. This gave the executive supreme command over military stores, forts, regular land and naval forces, and the militia; his capacity as commander-in-chief meant the "automatic involvement" of the Privy Council in his military and emergency powers. Unfortunately the council's journals during its first years of existence have not survived, making it impossible to provide details of its activities during this decisive period. Scant evidence from personal papers of a few of its members does suggest, however, that it was engaged in many wartime activities in 1776 and 1777. With President Rutledge, for instance, it acted as a Board of War and Admiralty, making important decisions concerning the colony's land and sea defenses. These included requisitioning privately owned ships into state service

6. Middleton to Drayton, 10 July 1776, *LDC*, 4: 432; Moncure D. Conway, ed., *The Writings of Thomas Paine* (New York: G.P. Putnam's Sons, 1894), 1: 215. See also Owens Aldridge, "Thomas Paine and Comus," *Pennsylvania Magazine of History and Biography* 85 (January 1961): 73; Hezekiah Niles, comp., *Principles and Acts of the Revolution in America* (Baltimore: William Niles, 1822; reprint, New York: Burth Franklin, 1971), 111.

to drive away British cruisers from South Carolina's coast, organizing work on fortifications around the capital, and appointing staff officers for the South Carolina Continentals. Although the Privy Council was dominated by conservatives, Drayton certainly did not let this deter him from urging the executive to initiate aggressive measures.[7]

Determined action became absolutely necessary during the spring of 1776 when Whig officials learned that the British were mounting an expedition against the southern colonies, where reportedly there was widespread loyalist support in the backcountry. As early as October 1775, William Campbell had encouraged the ministry to subjugate the capital of South Carolina. In a letter to Secretary of State Dartmouth, the exiled governor wrote that "Charles Town is the fountainhead from which all the violence flows. Stop that and the rebellion in this part of the continent will, I trust, soon be at an end." Crown officers in North Carolina, Virginia, and Georgia also insisted that with a timely display of military force, the loyalists could restore and maintain the king's authority in the region. Convinced of the idea, the home government informed Campbell in December that it would send an expedition headed by Admiral Peter Parker to the southern colonies. Charleston, the only city in the southern colonies, was the logical military target.[8]

Although Whig leaders knew of Britain's hostile plans, the arrival of Admiral Parker's squadron off Charleston in early June threw the city into pandemonium. Men frantically dashed about the city looking for horses, carriages, and boats to send their families and valuables into the country. Drayton most likely sent Dorothy and their children Mary and John to their plantation estate in the country, if they were not there already. Meanwhile, President Rutledge and the Privy Council quickly implemented the defensive plan Drayton had helped devise the previous October by ordering the public records and newspapers removed to Dorchester, incarcerating royal officers and those suspected of disaffection, and summoning the backcountry militia for assistance. As militia from the interior arrived in the capital, they collided

7. Richard G. Stone Jr., "The Privy Council of South Carolina, 1776–1790: A Study in Shared Executive Power" (Ph.D. diss., University of Tennessee, 1973), 2, 71, 86–7, 94, 128; Adele S. Edwards, *Journals of the Privy Council, 1783–1789* (Columbia: University of South Carolina Press, 1971), ix–xii; Haw, *John and Edward Rutledge*, 102–4.

8. Campbell to Dartmouth, 19 October 1775, and Dartmouth to Campbell, 23 December 1775, BPROSC 35: 277, 306–9, 312; Eric Robson, "The Expedition to the Southern Colonies, 1775–1776," *English Historical Review* 66 (July 1951): 542–51.

with refugees fleeing the town. Those men remaining behind (including slaves) redoubled their efforts toward improving Charleston's defenses.[9]

Adding further motivation to their labors was the arrival on June 4 of Major General Charles Lee, an Englishman whose celebrated reputation as a soldier of fortune was surpassed only by his excessive vanity and arrogance. However, these character flaws did not deter the Continental Congress, which was desperately in search of experienced military officers, from placing him in charge of the entire southern army and sending him to Charleston to command the military operations there. Soon after arriving in the capital, Lee, whom Carolinians soon recognized to be an "odd fish," began examining the garrisons around the city. The most important of these outposts to Charleston's defense was Fort Sullivan, a half-completed bastion on the southwestern tip of Sullivan's Island, which commanded the approach to the harbor. This was one of two redoubts Drayton's committee on fortifications had urged the Council of Safety to build the previous October to keep enemy ships out of range of downtown Charleston. Despite the fort's unfinished state, its commander, Colonel William Moultrie, had confidence that its walls of spongy palmetto logs and sand would absorb the impact of the British cannonballs and that its thirty-one cannon and 380 defenders were ample to repel the redcoats. Although General Lee had a contrary assessment of the fort—labeling it a "slaughtering pen" for its lack of a secure avenue of re-treat—and recommending its abandonment, President Rutledge and the Privy Council indignantly rejected the general's proposal, fearing such an act would humiliate and dishearten the troops and citizens. Lee was deeply in-sulted at having his military judgment questioned and overruled by local ci-vilians, but he swallowed his pride and made a last-minute effort to strengthen Moultrie's fort.[10]

General Lee had a similar opinion of the battery on Haddrell's Point de-signed by Drayton the previous December. The general's first question upon seeing the fort was: "What damned fool planned this Battery?" When the captain commanding the bastion informed him that it was Chief Justice

9. Drayton, *Memoirs*, 2: 277–9; Moultrie, *Memoirs*, 1: 140; Frances R. Kepner, ed., "A Brit-ish View of the Siege of Charleston, 1776," *JSH* 11 (February 1945): 97–8.

10. William Henry Drayton, "Battle of Fort Moultrie," *DHAR*, 2: 10; Drayton, *Memoirs*, 2: 282–3; Moultrie, *Memoirs*, 1: 141; Middleton to Drayton, 14 September 1776, *LDC*, 5: 166; John R. Alden, *General Charles Lee: Traitor or Patriot?* (Baton Rouge: Louisiana State University Press, 1951), 124. For a much more critical view of Lee's actions surrounding Fort Sullivan, see Grif-fiths, "To Receive Them Properly," 317.

Drayton's design, Lee replied: "he may be a very good Chief Justice, but he is a damned bad engineer, for if the enemy had the planning of it, they could not have fixed it in a better place for the reduction of Fort Johnson." He then ordered workers to demolish the outpost and transfer its guns for service elsewhere. Drayton was deeply offended by Lee's criticism. "Every idea of his must be right," he griped to a friend, "and, of course, every contrary idea in every other person must be wrong." Drayton neither forgot nor forgave Lee for the slight; thereafter, he took every opportunity available to publicly disparage the English commander's military ability. His complaints aside, the general wisely ordered the remaining Charlestonians to tear down the stores and houses along the wharves and refortify the redoubts. Their efforts put the capital in the "best posture of defense," reported one patriot, and put the citizens in "high spirits" with "little fear" of the impending British assault.[11]

When Admiral Peter Parker and Major General Henry Clinton confidently approached Charleston on the morning of June 1 with nine warships carrying 280 guns and 2,200 British regulars, they reportedly boasted that they would "Breakfast at Sullivan's Island, dine at Fort Johnson & sup in Charles Town." However, "delays of various kinds" intervened, General Clinton later complained, changing British tactics from a *"coup de main* to something too much like a formal siege." Finally, on the morning of June 28, Parker ordered his squadron toward Sullivan Island. At 10:30 A.M. a resounding roar echoed through the harbor as the bomb ketch *Thunder* opened fire on Fort Sullivan with its 8 ten-inch mortars. While the small ketch had the garrison's attention, the 50-gun ships *Bristol* and *Experiment* and the 28-gun ships *Active* and *Solebay* advanced to make one of the fiercest cannonades in the annals of eighteenth-century naval warfare. As described by one eyewitness, "The first five vessels continued a very heavy cannonade, one of the most fierce ever known, without ten minutes intermission in the whole, in which by the most moderate calculation they could not have fired less than twelve thousand times, till nine o'clock at night, when they ceased, lying the whole time within four hundred yards of the fort." Even the battle-hardened veteran General Lee remarked that he never in the whole course of his military service had seen or heard "so dreadful a cannonade." The rain of British

11. Richard Hutson to Isaac Hayne, 24 June 1776, "Letters of the Honorable Richard Hutson," *Charleston Yearbook* (1896): 320–1; Drayton to Henry Laurens, 1 November 1777, *HLP*, 12: 1; Drayton to Francis Salvador, 24 July 1776, *DHAR*, 2: 28; John Laurens to Gabriel Manigault, 5 April 1776, Manigault Family Papers, SCHS; A. Winyon to Captain John Bowie, 28 June 1776, John Bowie Papers, NYPL.

shells proved ineffective, however, as they generally buried themselves in the sand or sunk into the spongy palmetto logs and failed to explode. On the other hand, the troops within the besieged bastion fired nearly a thousand rounds from their eighteen- and twenty-four-pounders with such "dreadful execution" that it left the British warships in the "most miserable, mangled situation you can possibly imagine," wrote one British sailor. After making the necessary repairs to their vessels, the British dejectedly departed Charleston harbor in late July to join the main British army in New York.[12]

The departure of the damaged British warships had a tremendous impact throughout the province. More than Paine's *Common Sense* or Drayton's charges to the grand juries, the victory at Sullivan's Island galvanized South Carolinians behind the cause of liberty. After the attack upon the island, "there were few men here who had not lost all inclination for renewing our former connexion with your King & his Ministers," Henry Laurens informed his son John. On the other hand, those who supported the royal government were "ashamed of their opposition to the struggles of an infant people for their dearest rights," wrote David Ramsay, and "retired into obscurity." A consensus finally began to emerge among the colony's leaders. The majority were now determined to secure America's independence.[13]

The patriots' resolve was immediately tested when the Cherokee launched an attack against some frontier settlements that coincided with the British assault on Charleston. Despite earlier efforts by Drayton and other Whigs to procure the Cherokees' loyalty, they had been unable to "gain the least ground" amongst them, William Campbell happily reported to authorities in July 1776. Not only were the Native Americans united with the British, he added, but they were "all in the best disposition possible" to make war against the rebels. As part of its strategy for reducing the South, Britain planned to utilize the loyal Cherokee simultaneously with Admiral Parker's attack by sea. In preparation for the assault, Stuart supplied the Indians with five thousand pounds of powder and lead. When the British fleet of gunships arrived off

12. Henry Laurens to Martha Laurens, 17 August 1776, *HLP*, 11: 253; Henry Clinton to George Germaine, 8 July 1776, in Davies, *Documents of the American Revolution*, 12: 163; Lipscomb, *Carolina Lowcountry*, 28; Extract of a Letter from Charleston, 3 July 1776, in Clark, *Naval Documents*, 5: 905; Robert Pringle to John Pringle, 13 August 1776, in Mary Pringle Fenhagen, ed., "Letters and Will of Robert Pringle (1702–1776)," *SCHM* 50 (July 1949): 148–9; Anonymous letter, n.d., and William Falconer to Anthony Falconer, 13 July 1776, *DHAR*, 2: 16–7, 20.

13. Henry Laurens to John Laurens, 14 August 1776, *HLP*, 11: 227–8; Ramsay, *History of South Carolina*, 1: 157.

Charleston in late June, Cherokee warriors raced through the southern back-country from Virginia to Georgia, destroying property and "massacring . . . men, women and children, indiscriminately."[14]

The South Carolina government quickly responded by sending a punitive expedition of nearly nineteen hundred men led by Colonel Andrew Williamson into the Cherokee nation to "obtain satisfaction for their cruel outrages." To lure volunteers to the campaign, the General Assembly offered substantial rewards of £75 for each Cherokee scalp and £100 for each prisoner taken alive. With such monetary inducements, Williamson's men "march[ed] forth against the Savages with all the alacrity and cheerfulness you can conceive," wrote one Charleston patriot, "and with a full determined resolution to extir-pate the whole tribe." However, revenge and money were not the only fac-tors motivating the Americans to massacre the Cherokee. Greed for land was an equally important catalyst. No better individual example of this land hun-ger can be found than in Drayton, who urged regimental commanders to "make smooth work as you go," to be sure "you cut up every Indian corn-field, and burn every Indian town—and that every Indian taken shall be the slave and property of the taker; that the nation be extirpated, and the lands become the property of the public. For my part, I shall never give my voice for a peace with the Cherokee nation upon any other terms than their re-moval beyond the mountains." The chief justice's call for Cherokee genocide was heard throughout the southern colonies as patriot forces (totaling six thousand men) from Georgia to Virginia swept through the Cherokee nation with little resistance, burning one town after another, scalping live Indians, killing women, even the lame, and destroying every means of sustaining life with "a savagery equaling and a thoroughness surpassing their enemies." By October the Cherokee were effectively subjugated. Those natives not killed or captured were driven further west into the mountains where they were forced to survive on nuts, roots, insects, and reptiles.[15]

14. Campbell to the Lords of Trade, 8 July 1776, BPROSC 36: 61–2; "An Ordinance Ap-pointing Commissioners . . . to Conclude a Peace with the Cherokee Nation," 13 February 1777, Cooper and McCord, *Statutes at Large*, 4: 391.

15. John Rutledge to South Carolina Legislature, 19 September 1776, and General Assembly Journals, 22 September 1776, in Hemphill, et. al., *Journals of the General Assembly*, 64, 103; Ex-tract of a Letter from Charleston, 21 July 1776, in Force, *American Archives*, 5th ser., vol. 1: 481; Drayton to Francis Salvador, 24 July 1776, and Andrew Williamson to Drayton, 22 August 1776, *DHAR*, 2: 29, 32; William Henry Drayton to John Bowie, 5 June 1776, and Malcolm Brown to John Bowie, 10 June 1776, John Bowie Papers, NYPL; Drayton, *Memoirs*, 338–71; David D.

Driven to destitution, Cherokee headmen met with Governor Rutledge and the Privy Council on February 3, 1777, in Charleston, where they "sued in the most submissive terms" for peace. The council set a date for formal parleys at DeWitt's Corner (near present Due West, South Carolina) on May 7, 1777, and invited delegates from Georgia, North Carolina, and Virginia to attend. The president and councilors appointed Drayton, who had experience dealing with the Cherokee, to lead the South Carolina commission to conclude a peace treaty with them "upon such terms as may be just and Equitable."[16]

Until then, Drayton wanted to devote his energy and enthusiasm to military service. This desire may partially be attributed to the exhilaration following the defeat of the British at Sullivan's Island. Another element may involve envy and Drayton's continual drive for fame. Soon after the naval battle, the fort was christened in honor of its commander, Colonel William Moultrie. Realizing this tribute immortalized the colonel, Drayton perhaps came to view military service as a means to achieve similar recognition. If nothing else, an appropriate military title would enhance his status as a gentleman. Moreover, the legislature and courts were closed, leaving the energetic patriot with much time on his hands. He therefore asked Vice President Laurens on July 7 for a military command, explaining that "while I have no occasion to wear my gown, I ought to wear a sword." But with Drayton's belligerent action in Hog Island Creek still fresh in his mind, Laurens refused the chief justice's offer "to be active in the defense of my country."[17]

Instead of entrusting Drayton with a military command, Laurens assigned him the relatively innocuous task of designing a "Great Seal" for the new state government. Arthur Middleton, who was serving in the Continental

Wallace, *The History of South Carolina* (New York: American Historical Society, 1934), 2: 166; Hatley, *Dividing Paths*, 185–203; Chapman J. Milling, *Red Carolinians* (Chapel Hill: University of North Carolina Press, 1940), 307–19; Woodward, *Cherokees*, 89–99; Brown, *Old Frontiers*, 153–7; James Mooney, *Historical Sketch of the Cherokee* (Chicago: Aldine, 1975), 36–41; O'Donnell, *Southern Indians*, 34–58.

16. Drayton, *Memoirs*, 2: 360 n.; John Rutledge to Richard Caswell, 10 May 1777, William L. Saunders and Walter Clark, eds., *The Colonial and State Records of North Carolina, 1662–1790* (Raleigh: P. M. Hale, 1886–1907), 11: 417. The other South Carolina commissioners at De-Witt's Corner were Andrew Williamson, LeRoy Hammond, and Daniel Horry. Georgia sent three delegates—Jonathan Bryan, Jonathan Cochran, and William Glascock. North Carolina and Virginia were unable to send delegates before the scheduled date of the treaty.

17. Drayton to Laurens, 7 July 1776, *DHAR*, 2: 23.

Congress at the time, was asked to assist in the project. The president and the council selected the two firebrands for this assignment because of their previous experience in designing mottos and emblems. Drayton had proven his skill by designing the provincial currency. Middleton, too, had an interest in slogans and insignias, which he liberally peppered throughout his correspondence. Drayton chose to design the obverse of the seal while Middleton drew the reverse.

The designs on both faces of the Great Seal celebrated the new state's "baptism of fire and blood" at the unfinished fort on Sullivan's Island. In the center of the obverse Drayton placed a palmetto tree (representing Fort Moultrie, as it came to be called) supported by twelve spears (the United States) which, with the tree, are bound together in one band as a symbol of unity and triumph.[18] On the tree are two shields, one bearing the date March 26—South Carolina's adoption of a separate government—and the other inscribed with the date July 4, the date of America's independence. Following through on this theme, Drayton placed at the bottom the motto "Meliorem Lapsa Locavit, 1776" (Having Fallen, It Has Set Up a Better), an unmistakable allusion to the downfall of royal rule in both South Carolina and America, and its replacement with a separate and improved form of government. Lying prostrate under the palmetto is a fallen English oak, with its roots above the ground and its branches cut—a reference to Sir Peter Parker's fleet of British ships, made of English oak, defeated by the palmetto fort on Sullivan's Island. Immediately above the tree is the legend "South Carolina," and on the opposite part of the circle, "Animis Opibusque Parati" (Prepared in Mind and Resources).

For the reverse of the seal, Middleton drew a woman dressed in a transparent garment, confidently standing on a seashore strewn with the swords and daggers of the enemy. She represents Hope overcoming recent dangers and difficulties. In her right hand is a laurel signifying the honors Colonel Moultrie and his officers and men received after defeating the British. Behind Hope is the sun, rising in full splendor over the sea—an intimation to the rising glory of America in general and South Carolina in particular. The legend "Dum Spiro Spero" (While I Breathe I Hope) is inscribed across the top of the seal.

Drayton and Middleton submitted their designs to the Privy Council in October 1776. After making a few slight alterations, the council turned the

18. Why Drayton included only twelve spears instead of thirteen remains a mystery.

designs over to the engraver, George Smithson, who delivered the finished seal to state officials the following May. To this day, Drayton and Middleton's basic designs are still used in South Carolina's official seal. The original dies have been preserved and are conspicuously displayed at the South Carolina Department of Archives and History in Columbia.[19]

While Drayton was busy designing the seal, he heard word in late July of Richard Henry Lee's motion in the Continental Congress for separation from Great Britain. As one who had been anxiously awaiting this moment for more than a year, Drayton could hardly contain his excitement when he wrote to a friend, "God speed the passage of it." He did not have long to wait. On August 2 a courier from Philadelphia arrived in Charleston bringing news of Congress's declaration of American independence. Patriots throughout the city received this announcement with the "greatest joy." To celebrate the momentous occasion, President Rutledge, Vice President Lowndes, Chief Justice Drayton, all civil and military officers of the state, and a crowd of thousands gathered around the Liberty Tree on August 5. There they listened to Major Barnard Elliott, Drayton's former colleague in the royal council, read the Declaration of Independence. When he finished, the gathering burst into boisterous applause and huzzahs.[20]

After devoting all his energy during the preceding year toward realizing American independence, Drayton was determined to ensure its preservation. He soon had his opportunity when two brothers—General Sir William Howe, the senior military officer in North America, and Admiral Lord Richard Howe, the recently appointed commander of the Atlantic squadron—arrived in New York just days after the signing of the Declaration of Independence with commissions from the king to effect a reconciliation with the Americans. However, the commissioners were hamstrung in their ability to negotiate a settlement by instructions forbidding them to reveal the Crown's terms until a colony had restored its royal officials, surrendered its fortifications, and established a loyal legislature. In hopes of coercing the Americans to accept this humiliating capitulation, the Howes brought with them 150 ships and 15,000 troops to add to the 20,000 redcoats already in America.

But the Continental Congress, its fortitude strengthened by its recent ep-

19. Heisser, *State Seal*, 4, 7–8, 27; Alexander S. Salley Jr., *The Seal of the State of South Carolina* (Columbia, S.C.: State Co., 1907), 3, 8; Drayton, *Memoirs*, 2: 372–6; *Public Ledger* (London), 11 February 1778.
20. Drayton to Francis Salvador, 24 July 1776, *DHAR*, 2: 29; Drayton, *Memoirs*, 2: 315.

ochal declaration, was not influenced by this overt threat. At the peace conference held on Staten Island on September 11, the American delegation, consisting of John Adams, Benjamin Franklin, and Edward Rutledge, told Lord William Howe that "a return to the domination of Great Britain was not now to be expected." The Howes were undeterred by the delegation's unwillingness to negotiate a compromise, however. In a brief public letter published September 19, they beseeched the "misguided Americans" to "reflect seriously upon their present condition" and decide whether it was "consistent with their honour and happiness" to die in an "unjust and precarious cause," or return to their allegiance and secure a "free enjoyment of their liberty and properties upon the true principles of the constitution."[21]

Drayton was incensed by the British commissioners efforts to, in his words, "decoy [Americans] into Slavery."[22] In late October he responded with an acrimonious public letter under the signature of "a Carolinian." If the Howe brothers really wanted to restore public tranquility, Drayton began, why did Admiral Richard come "Clothed in all his Terrors" to "intimidate and coerce?" (7). Not only were their designs malevolent, he continued, but their proposal would not "confirm to us our Rights by the Law of Nature" because it would simply "cover us with Infamy, chill the Sap, check the Luxuriance of our imperial Plant [and] deprive us of our natural Equality with the Rest of mankind." In short, Drayton said, "your Excellencies invite men of common Sense to exchange an independent Station for a servile and dangerous Dependence!" (2). The Carolinian considered it "a Matter of Wonder" how the commissioners could "appear so lost to Decency as to hold out Subjection as the only Condition of Peace," especially submission to a government that "is absolutely abandoned to Corruption!" (3). "Did not your Excellencies blush and *shrink within yourselves*," asked Drayton, "when you asked Men who had been almost ruined by your *gracious* Master, to aban-

21. "Proceedings of His Majesty's Commissioners with the Congress for Restoring Peace between Great Britain, and the Revolted Colonies in North America," in Robert Beatson, ed., *Naval and Military Memoirs of Great Britain, 1727–1783* (London: J. Strachan, 1790), 6: 427–8. See also Ernest and Gregory Schimizzi, *The Staten Island Peace Conference: September 11, 1776* (Albany: New York State American Revolution Bicentennial Commission, 1976), 3–5; Ira Gruber, *The Howe Brothers and the American Revolution* (New York: Atheneum Press, 1972), 73–101; Paul L. Ford, "Lord Howe's Commission to Pacify the Colonies," *Atlantic Monthly* 77 (June 1896): 758–62.

22. William Henry Drayton, *To Their Excellencies Richard Viscount Howe, Admiral; and William Howe, Esq; General, of His Britannick Majesty's Forces in America* (Charleston: David Bruce, 1776), 3. Subsequent citations from this document are in parentheses in the text.

don the honourable and natural Station of Independence, and stoop to kiss
his Hand now daily BATHED in, and which ever must continue *stained* by the
Blood of a Friend! a Brother! a Son! a Father!"(8).

Here Drayton further revealed his belief that George III was ultimately
responsible for Britain's actions against America, for, as he explained, Parliament is "absolutely under the King of Great Britain's Direction" (5–6). This
bodes badly for the new country, he warned, because it is obvious that the
king has "not one generous thought respecting America" (7). If His Majesty
really wished to conciliate his colonial subjects, Drayton continued, he would
have repealed the acts when Americans first voiced complaints against them,
or at least have vested the Howes with "competent powers" to accomplish
their task. Instead, he turned a "criminally deaf ear to the Cries of the injured" and was now trying to "terrify them into Silence. . . . [H]aving burnt
their Towns—refrained their Trade—seized and confiscated their Vessels—
driven them into enormous Expenses—sheathed his Sword in their Bowels—
and adorned the Heads of their Aged, Women and Children, with a Cincture
made by the scalping Knife of his Ally the Indian Savage—you now tell these
injured People, that 'the King is graciously pleased to direct a Revision'! His
very mercies are Insults!" (6–7). With such a nefarious ruler at the helm of
the British Empire, Drayton boldly announced, "the Allegiance of America
to the King of Great Britain, is *now utterly out of the Question*" (5).

This caustic public letter to the Howe brothers probably had little effect
on the Continental Congress and other Whig leaders in America, who were
already unwilling to listen to any British peace proposal that did not include
provisions for American independence. Nor did it influence the Howes, who
had resigned themselves to a military solution to force the rebels to accept
reconciliation under British terms. Still, the pamphlet served as effective war
propaganda by inciting popular agitation against the king and his peace commissioners. It also advanced Drayton's reputation as a passionate and gifted
polemicist. Given his desire for fame, that might have been an underlying
factor motivating the Carolinian to make such a public response. Whig leaders across America were so impressed by Drayton's address to the Howes, in
fact, that when Great Britain made another peace overture in 1778, the Continental Congress asked him to pen a reply.

At the same time Drayton was excoriating George III and the peace commissioners, he was encouraging Americans to remain resolute in their support of
independence. When South Carolina's courts reopened for their fall session

on October 15, the chief justice delivered a hastily written and highly disorganized charge to the Charleston grand jury on "The Rise of the American Empire." Despite its chaotic construction, this judicial address offered further insight into Drayton's evolving view of the Revolution and its place in history. Before the Continental Congress began moving toward declaring America's independence, Drayton had almost exclusively used constitutional and historical arguments to justify the rebellion. But as the ideal of an independent America began to take shape, he began linking traditional religious beliefs to sanctify the cause of liberty. His conjoining of patriotic and theocratic ideas was hardly unique at the time; Whigs everywhere started adopting a millennial interpretation of the imperial crisis in 1776. What set Drayton's use of Providence apart from most others, however, is that he wielded it more as a dramatic than a theological construct, and by the April charge he was more explicit than most regarding the connection—"our piety and political safety are so blended."[23]

The reasons for this sudden shift in Drayton's view are uncertain, but several hypotheses seem plausible. It is likely that the Reverends Oliver Hart and William Tennent, both of whom had used an amalgam of piety and eighteenth-century political discourse in preaching the gospel of Revolution in their recent mission into the backcountry, influenced him to integrate Providence into his interpretation of the Anglo-American conflict. In fact, it was at a meeting with Dutch Fork residents in August 1775 that Drayton had first put biblical quotations in his patriotic orations. By the following April his millennial view of the Revolution had evolved to the extent that he felt confident enough to announce that "The Almighty created America to be independent of Britain." Accelerating the development of this providential interpretation of the rebellion were a series of American military victories during the first half of 1776, including General William Howe's evacuation of Boston in March and Colonel William Moultrie's decisive defeat of Parker's seemingly omnipotent expeditionary force in June. These victories were clear signs to Drayton and many other patriots that God favored the "righteous Americans" over the "despotic British." Although there is no reason to doubt Drayton's convictions on this subject, one suspects that the chief justice, knowing that colonial religious tradition made Americans predisposed

---

23. William Henry Drayton, Charge to the Grand Jury of Charlestown, 23 April 1776, *DHAR*, 1: 289; Lester H. Cohen, *The Revolutionary Histories: Contemporary Narratives of the American Revolution* (Ithaca, N.Y.: Cornell University Press, 1980), 79.

toward viewing the world in millennial terms, must have understood that such a cosmic interpretation of the Anglo-American conflict would be a powerful and effective means of selling the Revolution.[24]

Accordingly, Drayton began the October judicial charge by cheerfully informing the jurors that "by the Hand of God," America's revolution had set them free from British tyranny.[25] Until now, the chief justice asserted, the people of Great Britain had been God's select agents to advance his providential plan. However, because Britain's American policy since 1763 had been calculated to "surprise, deceive, or drive the People into Slavery," Providence no longer smiled on that kingdom (5). According to the Carolinian, God was making use of British tyranny to fashion and arrange those materials for his end, for "if we consider the Manner in which Great Britain has conducted her irritating and hostile Measures," he said, "we cannot but clearly see that God has darkened her Counsels; and that with a stretched out Arm, he himself has delivered us out of the House of Bondage, and has led us on to Empire" (6). By releasing the colonists from British oppression, God demonstrated his special mercy on the virtuous Americans—proof that he was destroying the ruling powers of evil to inaugurate the blessed millennium (22). "The Almighty setteth up; and he calleth down," explained the chief justice. "He breaks the Sceptre, and transfers the Dominion. He has made a Choice of the present Generation to erect the American Empire" (3). As proof of America's chosen status, Drayton reminded his audience of recent victories against the British at Lexington, Bunker Hill, and Sullivan's Island. "Such a Series of Events is striking!" he exclaimed. "It surely displays an over ruling

24. Drayton, Charge to the Grand Jury, 23 April 1776, *DHAR*, 1: 289; Ruth H. Bloch, *Visionary Republic: Millennial Themes in American Thought, 1756–1800* (Cambridge: Cambridge University Press, 1985), 57.

25. William Henry Drayton, *A Charge on the Rise of the American Empire, Delivered by the Hon. William Henry Drayton, Esq., Chief Justice of South Carolina to the Grand Jury for the District of Charleston* (Charleston: David Bruce, 1776), 2. Subsequent citations to this work are made parenthetically in the text. Drayton's charge can also be found in *SC&AGG*, 21 and 28 November 1776; *New England Chronicle*, 25 July 1777; *Remembrancer* (London), 1777, pp. 327–42; and Force, *American Archives*, 5th ser., vol. 2: 1049–1059. The present analysis of the charge draws from Bloch, *Visionary Republic*, xiii–xiv, 6–7, 54–85; Cohen, *Revolutionary Histories*, 49–79; J. F. Maclear, "The Republic and the Millennium," in Elwyn A. Smith, ed., *The Religion of the Republic* (Philadelphia: Fortress Press, 1971), 183–216; Stephen J. Stein, "An Apocalyptic Rationale for the American Revolution," *Early American Literature* 9 (winter 1975): 211–25; and Nathan O. Hatch, "The Origins of Civil Millennialism in America: New England Clergymen, War with France, and the Revolution," *W&MQ*, 3d. ser., 31 (July 1974): 407–30.

Providence that has confounded the British Counsels, to the End that America should not have been at first shackled" (8).

Drayton's view of the Revolution was not limited nationally. He clearly saw America's epochal struggle for liberty as a crusade for all mankind, not just for one nation (11). The American Empire "attracts the Attention of the Rest of the Universe," the chief justice told the jurors, "and bids fair, by the Blessing of God, to be the most glorious of any upon Record" (10). And because America "attracts the Eyes of the World," Drayton added, "she deserves our whole Attention" (14).

However, the chief justice understood that many Americans were reluctant to give their "whole attention" to the revolutionary movement because they feared defeat in a war with Great Britain. To instill hope among the apprehensive, Drayton enumerated Britain's many weaknesses: a £5-million debt; a cessation of trade with America, its principal trading partner; a manufacturing industry at its "last Morsel"; a precarious public credit; an undermanned army and navy; a military unaccustomed to the "sudden vicissitudes" of the American climate; an untenable supply line from Britain to America between "inveterate Enemies" (France and Spain) who were "watching for the critical moment" to "swallow up" England's Caribbean islands (13).

The United States of America, on the other hand, possessed "all the Resources for the War," Drayton remarked optimistically: a strong unity, a dedication to the war based on principle, and a military force willing to follow its leaders into battle, able to withstand the harsh climate, and possessing convenient sources of supplies and widespread public support (13). Not to mislead his audience into thinking victory would be easy, though, Drayton told them that "we ought to expect Difficulties, Dangers and Defeats." Enduring this crucible was a necessary prelude to glory, an unavoidable price for achieving something new and desirable. "What, shall we receive Good at the Hand of God, and shall we not receive Evil?" asked Drayton. Remember that Job's perseverance in the face of "every calumny" eventually elevated him to the "height of human felicity." If America, too, "behaves worthy of herself," the chief justice promised, "even our defeats will operate to our benefit" (14).

Now that Congress had declared America's independence, Drayton stressed that there could be no turning back. He called upon his fellow Carolinians to exert themselves in this "important Operation directed by Jehovah himself." Refusing to do so would be to "impiously question the unerring Wisdom of Providence." (3). Drayton was not reluctant to use fear as a motivating force, either, as he warned any who might "treacherously or pusillanimously" seek the return of regal government with vengeance from a "Brutus" among their ranks (23). In concluding his charge, Drayton implored his audience to always remember that "the American Empire is composed of States that are, and of Right ought to be, free and independent" (23).

The grand jury took the chief justice's charge to heart. In its presentments, the jury congratulated the Continental Congress for declaring America's independence from Great Britain, and ordered Drayton's "excellent charge" published so that others could benefit from its contents. Copies of the address were printed in newspapers from South Carolina to Massachusetts. Although it is impossible to determine the precise contribution of Drayton's apocalyptic charge, it certainly strengthened the fortitude of those who already supported independence, alleviated some of the fears among the apprehensive, and helped to subdue the remaining loyalists in the state.

Despite Drayton's efforts at kindling enthusiasm for the American cause in South Carolina, the new government lacked a sufficient number of troops to defend the state in case of a large-scale invasion. Whig leaders expected the British to redirect their military operations from the North to the more temperate South in the ensuing winter months. The Privy Council in late October therefore decided to send a "gentleman of character" to North Carolina to solicit the aid of fifteen hundred militiamen. The man it selected for this important mission was none other than William Henry Drayton. His position as chief justice and some recent success he had enjoyed recruiting troops in Virginia in June made him the top choice.[26]

Armed with a letter from President Rutledge, Drayton addressed the North Carolina provincial congress on November 20 in Halifax. Here he informed the legislators that South Carolinians were unable to defend Charleston against the anticipated British assault because they had to place much of their militia in the backcountry to control the "numerous and internal Enemy" still residing there. The North Carolinians were alarmed by Drayton's report. Realizing that their fate was "intimately and immediately connected" with South Carolina's, they agreed to raise two battalions of volunteers for their sister state. Drayton thanked the congress and assured it that

26. John Rutledge to William Henry Drayton, 6 November 1776, *DHAR,* 2: 42–3. I was unable to find any additional information concerning Drayton's recruiting campaign in Virginia during the summer of 1776. See *Virginia Gazette,* 15 June 1776; Charles Lee to Edmund Pendleton, 25 May 1776, "Charles Lee Papers," NYHS *Collections,* 5: 38.

the South Carolina government would pay the soldiers "more than equal to the labor of any common man," provide them with rations "more than sufficient for any appetite," and room them in "comfortable and roomy" barracks. However, South Carolina officials evidently failed to live up to the promises made by its chief justice. One disappointed North Carolina officer stationed in Camden complained to Governor Richard Caswell in March 1777 that his men had not collected any pay for more than a month and that they owed no thanks to the South Carolina government for the "plenty of good beef and pork" they were enjoying because they had to import it from home. "This is the most miserable part of God's creation, both men and lands," he concluded. Fortunately for South Carolina, the feared British attack did not occur, thus saving it from having to use these disgruntled troops.[27]

Because of Drayton's success in recruiting the North Carolinians, the General Assembly, believing that a union between Georgia and South Carolina would tend to "promote their strength, wealth, and dignity, and secure their liberty, independence and safety," sent the chief justice to Savannah to sell the idea to the Georgians. However, this self-proclaimed altruism was not the sole factor motivating the South Carolina assembly to make this fantastic proposal. Speculators north of the Savannah River pushed for a union with Georgia because they believed it would increase the value of land there. Whig officials, too, hoped that annexing Georgia would resolve, possibly to their advantage, the outstanding dispute between the two colonies over their western boundaries and settle troublesome differences in their legal, political, and financial institutions.[28]

Perhaps the most important factor encouraging South Carolina to seek this union was trepidation over Georgia's lack of enthusiasm for the Ameri-

27. John Rutledge to President of North Carolina Congress at Halifax, 6 November 1776, Saunders and Clark, *Records of North Carolina*, 10: 892–3; "Journal of the North Carolina Provincial Congress," 21 November 1776, ibid., 10: 928; Robert Howe to the North Carolina Provincial Congress, 7 November 1776, *DHAR*, 2: 43–4; Abraham Shepperd to Richard Craswell, 16 March 1777, Saunders and Clark, *Records of North Carolina*, 11: 431–2.

28. William Henry Drayton to Humphrey Wells, 8 May 1777, Gibbes Collection, SCDAH; Kenneth Coleman, *Colonial Georgia: A History* (New York: Charles Scribner's Sons, 1976), 175; David R. Chesnutt, "South Carolina's Expansion into Colonial Georgia, 1720–1765" (Ph.D. diss., University of Georgia, 1973), iv, 62–5; Frances Harrold, "Colonial Siblings: Georgia's Relationship with South Carolina during the Pre-Revolutionary Period," *GHQ* 73 (winter 1989): 712–23; Ulrich B. Phillips, "The Course of the South to Secession," *GHQ* 21 (March 1937): 18–9.

can cause. This concern had been driven home the previous year when Drayton, while serving as president of the provincial congress, had to send troops to Savannah to enforce the Continental Association. The strong loyalist presence in Georgia compelled one Savannah Whig to complain that "there never was a State existed that had so little Honesty or patriotism among its members as the State of Georgia." As Georgia was South Carolina's first line of defense against attacks from East Florida, patriot leaders in the Palmetto State were deeply distressed over their neighbor's lack of support for the American cause. By annexing Georgia, South Carolina hoped to bring its devotion to the Revolution more in line with the rest of America.[29]

The General Assembly was encouraged to pursue its annexation scheme the following winter (1775–76) when several native South Carolinians were elevated to top positions in Georgia's newly created revolutionary government. The most prominent and powerful of these transplanted Carolinians was Archibald Bulloch, who served as president of the provincial congress. Whig leaders in South Carolina thought Bulloch and other native Carolinians might desire a union with their former home province. This idea was partially confirmed in late 1776 when conservatives in Georgia, dissatisfied with how the radical party was running the government, made it known to their northern neighbor that union with South Carolina was preferable to radical rule. The South Carolina General Assembly responded by unanimously resolving to send William Henry Drayton and John Smith as commissioners to exploit that sentiment.[30]

Although some Georgians favored the idea of consolidation with South Carolina, Drayton knew there were many "designing men" who opposed it and would strive to "pervert" and "scandalize" this "most salutary proposition." Nevertheless, as he continued to study the idea, Drayton became convinced that it was just, practical, and advantageous to both states in particular, and America in general. Holding the South Carolina–Georgia junction

29. Harold E. Davis, "The Scissors Thesis, or Frustrated Expectations as a Cause of the Revolution in Georgia," *GHQ* 61 (fall 1977): 247–8; Coleman, *Colonial Georgia*, 269–70; Joseph Clay to Edward Telfair, 10 August 1777, "Letters of Joseph Clay, Merchant of Savannah, 1776–1793," Georgia Historical Society *Collections* (Savannah: Morning News, 1913), 8: 37–8.

30. Chesnutt, "South Carolina's Expansion," iii–vi, 51, 62–3, 206–11; Edward J. Cashin, "'The Famous Colonel Wells:' Factionalism in Revolutionary Georgia," *GHQ* (Supplement 1974): 137–56. No information seems to be available on John Smith.

"much [to] heart," he vowed not to allow any "discouraging obstructions" to dampen his ardor for realizing it.[31]

Speaking before the Georgia convention in late January, Drayton confidently argued for over an hour that nature, climate, soil, products, and kindred interests all "pointed out" that the two states should unite. All their longstanding jealousies, rivalries, and disputes would then cease. Agriculture, internal trade, and foreign commerce would rapidly improve. Carolina planters would extend their improvements into Georgia, resulting in higher land prices there. Carolina merchants would bring added trade opportunities to Georgia, instead of monopolizing commerce in the region as they were presently doing. Moreover, Georgia's currency, which was of inferior value to South Carolina's, would be placed on "an equal footing" with its northern counterpart. With the combined resources of the two states, they could clear the entire Savannah River, which would "occasion an immense increase" in the economic growth of the entire river-valley region. Savannah's commerce, too, would increase "almost without imagination," although it would lose the seat of government. However, by maintaining only one established government, both the government and public defense would improve, yet at a reduced expense. Should Georgia refuse the proposal, Drayton warned, South Carolina would ruin Savannah by quickly planting a rival town on the river to attract all its commerce. On the other hand, if the two states merged, South Carolina would use a portion of its vast wealth to assist Georgia in discharging its public debt. South Carolinians, furthermore, would not take up large tracts of land in Georgia as some feared. Rather, what South Carolina desired on the whole, Drayton concluded, was to promote the general welfare by a union based on justice and equity.[32]

After completing his overture, Drayton delivered it in written form as a basis for discussion. The convention agreed to consider the proposal the next day, but refused the commissioner's request that he be allowed to participate in the debate. As a compromise, it did permit Drayton to attend as a private citizen. This was little consolation to the Carolinian, as Button Gwinnett, a leading radical recently returned from signing the Declaration of Indepen-

---

31. William Henry Drayton's Speech to the Georgia Convention, in Salley, *Documents Relating to the Revolution*, 12–4; John Lewis Gervais to Henry Laurens, 29 July 1777, John Lewis Gervais Papers, SCHS.

32. William Henry Drayton to Humphrey Wells, 8 May 1777, Gibbes Collection, SCDAH.

dence, came forward as champion of an independent Georgia. His reference to a clause in the Articles of Confederation prohibiting states from entering into any treaty, confederation, or alliance without the consent of Congress had great influence upon the delegates. Drayton must have writhed as he could only sit by and take notes on what he considered were "gross misrepresentations" of his proposal. He certainly yearned to point out that Congress had not yet adopted the Articles and therefore the clause outlawing a union between two states was not binding. Later that afternoon the convention politely rejected the proffered union. Dejected, Drayton left the assembly and returned home.[33]

When Drayton returned to Charleston, he was confronted with a serious personal dilemma. The General Assembly, motivated by a perception that leading loyalists had significantly contributed to the series of American military disasters in the latter half of 1776, began debating an ordinance in January requiring all royal officials still in the state to abjure the Crown and swear allegiance to the Continental Congress on penalty of banishment or "Death as a Traitor."[34] Unlike previous measures imposed on royal officials, the Abjuration Act, as it was called, would also target William Bull. Drayton secretly warned his uncle that the assembly would likely pass this ordinance.

Considering the ramifications this proposal might have on his uncle, Drayton found himself in a "truly disagreeable" situation. On the one hand, he certainly did not want any abuse directed at the sixty-seven-year-old lieutenant governor, who only wanted to live out his remaining years in peaceful retirement on his Ashley Hall plantation. On the other hand, Drayton felt it "absolutely necessary" to expel all resident Crown officers and other dissidents. Drayton's predicament was an "ironic reversal" of the situation Bull had confronted two years earlier when he had to decide whether or not to suspend his nephew from the royal council. In March 1775, Bull had reluctantly put duty first. Now, Drayton would do the same.[35]

33. Walter G. Charlton, "Button Gwinnett," *GHQ* 8 (June 1924): 146–58; Drayton to Humphrey Wells, 8 May 1777.

34. "An Ordinance for Establishing an Oath of Abjuration and Allegiance," 13 February 1777, Cooper and McCord, *Statutes at Large*, 1: 135–7.

35. William Henry Drayton to Stephen Bull, 8 February 1777, *DHAR*, 2: 75; Bull, *Oligarchs*, 252; Geraldine Meroney, "William Bull's First Exile from South Carolina, 1777–1781," *SCHM* 80 (April 1979): 91–2; Geraldine Meroney, *Inseparable Loyalty: A Biography of William Bull* (Norcross, Ga.: Harrison, 1991), 125.

Divided over his loyalty to his uncle and his country, Drayton was extremely hesitant to participate in the debate over the proposed loyalty oath. But given his assertive leadership in the American cause, and his recent threats against loyalists in the latest jury charge, Drayton felt that he could not remain silent on the question without exposing himself to criticism. After anxiously waiting for everyone to voice opinions on the matter, he finally rose before the assembly "deeply impressed" with a feeling he had "never before experienced." The chief justice sorrowfully told his colleagues that the time had come when the public welfare compelled them to adopt measures that might affect the "tranquility of [his] nearest relations," particularly that of his uncle, whom he owed the "greatest obligations" and the "most respectful affections." He realized that his support of expulsion would invite reproach as "an ingrate—a man void of natural affection." But the first duty of all men was to their country, Drayton reasoned. Failure to follow this principle could seriously jeopardize America's fight for independence. After the chief justice finished his solemn speech, the assembly voted on the measure, which passed with only five members opposing it.[36]

Anticipating such an outcome, Drayton had earlier conspired with his cousin Stephen Bull and President Rutledge to devise a plan that would allow the lieutenant governor to resign his commission "without incurring blame in the eyes of posterity." But Bull refused to abjure the Crown. To do so, explains one biographer, "would deny the meaning of his lifetime of pubic service and make a lie of the oaths he had taken as an officer of the Crown." Bull was not too disheartened over his banishment anyway, as Britain's recent military successes in the North indicated to him that the war would not last much longer. Expecting to return within a year, he and his wife Hannah sailed for England in early May 1777. Drayton, who certainly felt guilty for supporting the expulsion of his beloved uncle, was perhaps more despondent over Bull's banishment than was the lieutenant governor himself. Drayton would certainly have been even more depressed if he had known at the time that he would never see his uncle again. Bull remained in exile much longer than he had anticipated and did not return until after the fall of Charleston in May 1780. Following the war, he left for England again, unable to live under a government independent from Great Britain. He died in July 1791.[37]

36. Drayton to William Bull, 8 February 1777, *DHAR*, 2: 75–6.
37. Drayton to Stephen Bull, 8 February 1777, *DHAR*, 2: 76–7; Meroney, *Inseparable Loyalty*, 126.

While the Bulls were sailing across the Atlantic toward Europe, Drayton was riding through the backcountry to DeWitt's Corner to meet with the Cherokee for the formal negotiations agreed to earlier in the year. On May 7 some six hundred tribesmen met the American delegation, and for the next two weeks hammered out a treaty in which the contracting parties pledged to "bury the hatchet" and reestablish "universal peace and friendship" among one another. The defeated and destitute Cherokee had little choice but to make peace on American terms. By the articles of the agreement, they relinquished all land east of the Unicoi Mountains (the present-day counties of Greenville, Pickens, Oconee, and Anderson), and promised to release all captives and captured property, as well as to deliver up any loyalists who had assisted them in the war. For its part, South Carolina promised to renew trade with the Native Americans and to evict all squatters from Cherokee territory.[38]

While Drayton was negotiating with the Cherokee, some leading residents of Georgia, upset with how their state's government was managing its affairs, encouraged him to renew his annexation scheme. During the first half of 1777 conditions in Georgia had deteriorated significantly as a result of currency inflation, bitter political factionalism, incompetency and malfeasance among its governing officials, and disastrous military expeditions. Savannah merchant Joseph Clay predicted that by year's end there would be "a necessity to sell every estate in the State, for God Almighty seems to have doomed us for destruction." Some Georgians, according to John Wereat, were already fleeing to East Florida as a result of "being oppressed & plundered of their little means of subsistence," while many more "talked seriously" about moving to South Carolina. The incompetency of those officials who "misrule the State" convinced Wereat that Georgia "shall in a short time be joined to Carolina," a circumstance he believed was "infinitely preferable" to its present situation "when neither Liberty or property are secure." Opposition to such a union received a heavy blow in May 1777 when Button Gwinnett—the principal obstacle to annexation—was killed in a duel with Lachlan McIntosh.[39]

38. *SC&AGG*, 26 June 1777.

39. Joseph Clay to Edward Telfair, 10 August 1777, "Letters of Joseph Clay," Georgia Historical Society *Collections*, 8: 37–8; John Wereat to George Walton, 30 August 1777, in Lilla M. Hawes, ed., "The Papers of Lachlan McIntosh, 1774–1779," Georgia Historical Society *Collections*, 12: 71; George Lamplugh, "'To Check & Discourage the Wicked and Designing': John Wereat and the Revolution in Georgia," *GHQ* 61 (1977): 295–307.

With Gwinnett dead and Georgia reeling from an array of political, economic, and military problems, Drayton was convinced that the time was ripe to launch a new campaign for the absorption of South Carolina's southern neighbor. Since his earlier attempt at winning over Georgia's legislature to the efficacy of the union had failed, Drayton decided to bypass the government this time and take his case directly to the people. To this end, he composed and distributed throughout the state broadsides and petitions for the union that the citizens might address to their legislature. Drayton even went to Augusta to personally oversee the distribution of this literature. However, he did stay clear of Savannah, where threats were made to tar and feather the chief justice if he meddled in Georgia's affairs.[40]

In urging the Georgians to seriously consider union with South Carolina, Drayton's petition highlighted some of the "blessings" South Carolinians enjoyed as a result of their stable, well-managed government: a strong defense, prosperous trade, healthy manufacturing, and enormous wealth. He then contrasted this pleasant picture with the misery Georgians were suffering because of their discordant and malfeasant administration: an economy destitute of trade and commerce, a pitifully small militia unable to defend the state, and incompetent and unscrupulous officials squandering the treasury and imposing "bare-faced frauds" upon the public. To alleviate these problems, Drayton beseeched the citizens to call on their elected representatives to reconsider South Carolina's overture as the surest means of relieving their fears, increasing their strength, advancing their prosperity, securing their liberties, and insuring their safety.[41]

Drayton's petitioning campaign had the desired effect according to Georgia officials, who angrily remarked that it was "daily exciting animosities" against the government. In response, Governor John-Adam Treutlan issued a proclamation on July 15 offering a £100 reward for the capture of Drayton and any other person who was "UNLAWFULLY endeavouring to POISON the Minds of the good People of this State against the Government thereof."[42]

---

40. For evidence of Drayton's authorship of these petitions and broadsides, see John Lewis Gervais to Henry Laurens, 29 July 1777, and John Wells Jr. to Henry Laurens, 23 June 1777, *HLP*, 11: 413, 388; and James Wright to George Germaine, 8 October 1777, Georgia Historical Society *Collections*, 3: 247.

41. "Form of the Remonstrance and Petition of the Inhabitants in the State of Georgia," *DHAR*, 2: 81–3.

42. "Minutes of the Executive Council, May 7 through October 14, 1777," *GHQ* 34 (March 1950): 31. Treutlan's Proclamation is in the Gibbes Collection, SCDAH.

Drayton was "not a little hurt" by Treutlan's bounty, according to a friend. He promptly unsheathed his ever ready pen and composed a caustic "public reprehension" to the governor and the executive council. In it, Drayton labeled Treutlan's announcement a "compound of nonsense and falsehoods . . . illegal and void in itself." To prove its unlawfulness, the chief justice used his extensive knowledge of the law to cite judicial cases and parliamentary rulings declaring that private individuals had a right to petition. Only you, remarked the Carolinian, as "traitors or simpletons" would "traduce petitioning, and order petitioners to be apprehended." Drayton was so confident of the proclamation's illegality that he promised to pay for the defense of anyone arrested under it. In any event, he denied exciting animosities among the inhabitants "even for an hour"; rather, many were already so troubled with the crisis in Georgia that they urged him to renew his consolidation plan. Considering the wretched situation in Georgia, Drayton explained, he felt compelled to make "friendly and pressing recommendations." In fact, he considered Treutlan's administration such a "disgrace and detriment to the American cause" that he was inclined to believe Georgia's officers were "concealed Tories" who sought to "burlesque Government" to the point that the people "might be sick of an American administration" and therefore strive to return under British domination merely for the sake of "endeavoring to procure something like law and order." Drayton laughed at Treutlan's attempt to silence him with his "amusing production" and intrepidly concluded that he would continue to promote union between the two states "to the utmost" of his power. Despite this boast, Drayton discontinued his efforts to, in the words of one Georgian, "reduce Georgia to a state of vassalage to South Carolina."[43]

Instead, Drayton was forced to direct his attention toward a more serious problem at home. The British, after failing to capture Charleston in June 1776, left South Carolina alone for nearly three years. So much tranquility reigned in every part of the state, observed a contemporary, that the "bulk of the people were scarcely sensible of any revolution or that the country was at war." Many Carolinians took advantage of this peace to augment their wealth rather than contributing to the state's military defenses. South Carolina soon became the chief supplier of goods to the war-ravaged North, and merchants,

43. John Wells Jr. to Henry Laurens, 7 August 1777, *HLP*, 11: 431; William Henry Drayton, *To His Honour, John Adam Treutlan, Esquire, Governor and Commander in Chief of the State of Georgia . . .* (Charleston: David Bruce, 1777); *DHAR*, 2; 84–7.

planters, farmers, craftsmen, and wagoners all benefitted from this lucrative trade. Business so flourished in the state that "at no period of peace were fortunes more easily or more rapidly acquired," wrote David Ramsay. Self-absorbed in this "lust of wealth and pleasure," many South Carolinians became more interested in preserving their fortunes than their liberties.[44]

The Whig government did little to excite the passive citizens toward action. President John Rutledge, according to William Tennent, intentionally relaxed the "nerves of the state" with "*lullaby notes*" which the minister claimed had "put the people to sleep" and pacified the General Assembly from initiating "vigorous or determinate" measures. An exasperated Drayton observed that even when the legislature made "gentle recommendations," the people still ignored them. This civil and political languor left Charleston's defenses in utter disrepair.[45]

Drayton was infuriated with the people's growing apathy. When the courts reopened for the fall session on October 21, 1777, he decided to use his obligatory charge to the grand jury to reinvigorate his fellow Carolinians. He began by attempting to both shame and inspire his audience into stronger action by recounting in detail the North's enormous effort and sacrifices made in opposing the British at White Plains, Trenton, Princeton, Brandywine, and Bennington. "Oh! that I could give as good an account of the *public vigour of our people*," the chief justice lamented. Instead, he could only chastise them for placing the pursuit of "private gains" above "public defense." To continue such conduct, Drayton warned, will only invite the British to "turn their steps this way and seize your country as a rich and easy prey." What calamities shall we have to suffer before we are finally forced to renew our efforts in the Revolution? asked the chief justice. Will we have to "be driven from this beautiful town—to be dispossessed of this valuable seat of trade—to see ourselves flying we know not whither—our heirs uselessly sacrificed in our sight, and their bodies mangled with repeated stabs of bayonets? Tell me, do you mean that your ears shall be pierced with the unavailing shrieks of your wives, and the agonizing screams of your daughters under the brutal vi-

44. Ramsay, *History of South Carolina*, 1: 151, 164.

45. William Tennent, "Historic Remarks on the Session of Assembly. . . . September 17, 1776," Newton B. Jones, ed., "Writings of the Reverend William Tennent, 1740–1777," *SCHM* 61 (October 1960): 190; William Henry Drayton, Charge to the Grand Jury of Charleston, 21 October 1777, in Niles, *Principles and Acts*, 97; H. Roy Merrens, ed., "A View of Coastal South Carolina in 1778: The Journal of Ebenezer Hazard," *SCHM* 73 (October 1972): 185.

olence of British or Brunswick ruffians? Rouse, rouse yourselves into activity capable of securing you against these horrors."[46]

If these imaginable atrocities were not enough to motivate his neighbors into action, Drayton thought, then perhaps pride in their past achievements might be. "We were the first in America who publicly pronounced Lord North's famous conciliatory motion inadmissible," the chief justice reminded his audience. "[W]e raised the first regular forces upon the continent, we first declared the . . . causes of taking up arms—we originated the councils of safety, we were among the first who led the way to independence by establishing a constitution of government—we were the first who made a law authorizing the capture of British vessels without distinction—we alone have defeated a British fleet—we alone have victoriously pierced through and reduced a powerful nation of Indians, who urged by Britain, had attacked the United States." Unless these "brilliant proceedings" are "supported with propriety," Drayton cautioned, "they will appear as the productions of faction, folly and temerity; not of patriotism, wisdom and valor" (96).

In hopes of stimulating South Carolinians to "strive to rival the *vigour of the North*," the chief justice next enticed them with the thought of immortality. The present work of creating an American empire, he told the jurors, provides every man an opportunity to place his name in "indelible characters" along with the "great names of antiquity." This "unexampled opportunity" is rapidly passing, Drayton noted, but it was not too late, nor too difficult, to acquire a place on this "most illustrious list." Planters can send slaves to labor on the public works, he said; those without black chattel can donate their own energy toward constructing forts and batteries; and anyone knowledgeable in the present dispute can instruct those "ignorant of the importance of the public contest." To set an example and "raise a *spirit of emulation*" among his countrymen, Drayton promised to donate his last year's income to needy families in the frontiers whose husbands and sons could not adequately support them because they were stationed in Charleston (96–97). If everyone devoted themselves toward America's noble cause with "unwearied application, unabating vigor, and a readiness to make the greatest sacrifices," Drayton concluded, "posterity will have no just cause to reproach our conduct" (97).

Drayton's chiding yet inspiring speech had the desired effect among his

---

46. Drayton, Charge to the Grand Jury of Charleston, 21 October 1777, in Niles, *Principles and Acts*, 95. Subsequent citations to this work are given parenthetically in the text.

audience. In their presentment, the jurors bemoaned the capital's lack of military readiness and urgently called for measures "remedying this evil." Just a week later Drayton happily reported to Laurens, then serving as president of the Continental Congress in York, Pennsylvania, that "[a]t last we are in earnest about fortifying our town." For his part, the chief justice offered to "take up the Spade" and serve as commissioner of fortifications. He volunteered for this duty not only to counter the "langour of our People," he explained, but also to refute General Charles Lee's judgment against him in the "affair of the Western battery." His motivations aside, Drayton used his new position to push the government to enact additional measures for Charleston's defense. He made a motion in the Privy Council, for example, urging the government to confiscate all able-bodied slaves belonging to those banished by the Abjuration Act and use them on the public works. Drayton was somewhat surprised when his more conservative colleagues agreed to the proposal. Apparently his judicial charge had inspired even the timid councilors.[47]

Drayton's charge to the Charleston grand jury demonstrates that he had an appreciation of the momentous events of his own day and an understanding of the possibility for immortality to those playing an active and conspicuous role in them. Animated by this realization, as well as by a great love of the past, Drayton began collecting documents for a work on a history of the Revolution in South Carolina. His motive in this endeavor, he wrote Henry Laurens, was to ensure that "our Star shall be as brilliant as any in the new constellation, by particularly placing its Revolution in the same page with that of its Sister Planets." Given Drayton's obsession with public recognition, one suspects that he was also writing this history in an attempt to make his mark as an historian of the Revolution and, by giving himself a prominent part in the story, to prevent the actions of other patriots from overshadowing his resplendent role in the American cause.[48]

When Drayton started this project is uncertain, but by November 1777 he had made considerable progress in gathering documents pertaining to the Revolution in South Carolina from the Stamp Act to the end of the Cherokee War. Evidence suggests that he made requests from patriot leaders throughout America for general information about events in other states, too. Joseph Reed, secretary to George Washington, sent the Carolinian a summary of

47. *SC&AGG*, 13 November 1777; Drayton to Laurens, 1 November 1777, *HLP*, 12: 1.
48. Drayton to Laurens, 1 November 1777, *HLP*, 12: 2–3.

important events that occurred in Pennsylvania and Massachusetts while he was serving as a member of the Philadelphia committee of correspondence in 1774 and 1775. However, Drayton was "much in the dark" on affairs in the Continental Congress. To fill this gap in his narrative, he wrote Laurens beseeching him to "snatch an hour or two from mere Congress business" to procure some information on the affairs up North. Drayton particularly wanted details on the battles of Bunker Hill, Long Island, White Plains, Brunswick, Brandywine, and Germantown, including troop strengths and the number of casualties suffered in each conflict. Drayton also asked Laurens to encourage his son John, who was serving as an adjutant to General George Washington, to collect "many interesting circumstances" about the commander of the Continental Army. Whether or not Laurens provided the materials Drayton requested is unknown. However, the lack of such information in both Laurens's extensive correspondence and Drayton's surviving manuscripts leads one to believe that he did not honor the chief justice's request. Laurens was extremely busy with his duties as president of the American Congress and was likely insulted by Drayton's request to take time out from "mere Congress business" to go hunting down official documents for Drayton's newest pet project.[49]

While Drayton was collecting material for a history of the Revolution, he was also helping to formulate a new state constitution. Congress's declaration of independence forced South Carolina to replace its 1776 constitution, which stated that its people were still striving for reconciliation, with a permanent framework of government in accordance with its new autonomous status. Because the South Carolina legislative journals from October 1776 to August 1779 are no longer extant, it is difficult to determine Drayton's precise role in the constitutional debate. Other evidence, however, suggests that he had an enormous influence in its creation. In fact, Laurens asserted that the chief justice was "almost Father & Mother of that production." Similarly, a modern authority on South Carolina's 1778 constitution has declared that it was "basically written" by Drayton. Whether or not these grandiose claims are true, what is known for certain is that the chief justice sponsored or cosponsored several radical revisions: disestablishing the Anglican church, replacing the legislative council with a larger, popularly elected senate, abolish-

49. "A State of Affairs Drawn Up by J[oseph] Reed & Delivered to William Henry Drayton," n.d., NYHS *Collections* (1878): 269–73; Drayton to Laurens, 1 November 1777, *HLP*, 12: 2–3.

ing the president's veto and limiting the executive to one term in office, and barring relatives of the president from serving in the Privy Council. Drayton's support of the first revision, the disestablishment of religion, does not necessarily reflect a desire for religious equality. His support for this measure was more than likely an attempt to woo the populous backcountry residents, most of whom belonged to dissenting faiths, to the American cause. Likewise, his champion of a larger, popularly elected senate was a measure he hoped would lure more people to support the Whig party. The measures restricting the president's powers, on the other hand, reveal his continuing fear of a strong central authority.[50]

Drayton and the other legislators finally completed work on the new constitution in March 1778 and submitted it to President Rawlins Lowndes for his signature. In certain respects the new constitution was a considerable improvement over the first. It expanded suffrage by reducing property qualifications from one hundred acres of settled land to fifty acres or a town lot taxed the equivalent of fifty acres. It disestablished the Anglican church, guaranteeing equality to all Protestant sects. The charter also allowed the people to elect the senators. The president no longer had the veto power, moreover, and was ineligible for reelection until the end of four years after his term of office had expired. Finally, the creation of probate courts in all six interior judicial districts and the distribution of representation based on a district's taxable wealth and number of white inhabitants pleased many residents of the backcountry.[51]

Although the new constitution extended the suffrage and made the government more democratic, Drayton and the other lowcountry aristocrats who drafted the constitution assured their continuing control of political affairs by raising property qualifications for all officeholders. Candidates for governor, lieutenant governor, and the Privy Council, for example, had to own estates worth at least £10,000 sterling currency or more. Senators had to possess a freehold valued at £2,000 sterling, while assemblymen had to own five hundred acres and ten slaves or a town lot of equivalent value. These

50. Hemphill, et. al., *Journals of the General Assembly*, 143, 148–9; Henry Laurens to John Laurens, 16 May 1778, *HLP*, 13: 309; Paul A. Horne Jr., "The Evolution of a Constitution: South Carolina's 1778 Document," SCHS *Proceedings* (1988), 7–13. Members of the new constitutional committee were Rawlins Lowndes, John Mathews, Christopher Gadsden, Thomas Bee, Thomas Heyward, Charles Pinckney, Paul Trapier, Alexander Moultrie, and John Edwards.

51. Although this provision provided for a much more equitable representation, backcountry settlers were still upset because it was not to go into effect until 1785.

property qualifications for officeholding made it virtually impossible for the lower classes to overthrow the *ancien régime.* Nonetheless, the constitution of 1778 provided an effective form of government during the remainder of the Anglo-American crisis.[52]

While South Carolina was drafting a new state constitution, the Second Continental Congress was writing a similar document for the independent American states. As early as July 1775 Benjamin Franklin introduced a plan for an American confederation. The idea was premature, however, and his suggestion was rejected. But as independence loomed and prospects of an extended war increased the following summer, the need to create a legitimate central authority capable of conducting war, borrowing money, regulating trade, and negotiating treaties became crucial. In June 1776 Congress therefore appointed a committee, headed by the reluctant revolutionary John Dickinson of Pennsylvania, to draw up a plan of perpetual union.

The Articles of Confederation, which the Congress finally adopted in November 1777, allowed each state to retain its "sovereignty, freedom and independence, and every power, jurisdiction and right" not expressly delegated to the United States Congress. The only prerogatives entrusted to Congress included the "sole and exclusive right and power" to regulate foreign affairs, initiate war, declare peace, fix weights and measures, regulate Indian affairs, establish a post office, send and receive ambassadors, coin money, and mediate boundary disputes between the states. As extensive as these powers may appear, the new U.S. Congress lacked the critical ability to raise troops, levy taxes, or even regulate trade. To run the war, it could only lay assessments on the states, hoping they would comply. The Articles also made no provisions for an executive branch. Instead, it authorized Congress to establish committees to manage the financial, diplomatic, and military affairs of the United States. Nor did the Articles include a national system of courts by which the national government could compel allegiance to its laws. Consequently, the union was little more than a "league of friendship" among thirteen independent state republics under an emasculated federal government.

The Continental Congress, believing its plan of confederation was "the

52. South Carolina's 1778 constitution is reprinted in Francis N. Thorpe, comp., *The Federal and State Constitutions, Colonial Charters, and Other Organic Laws of the State, Territories, and Colonies now or Heretofore Forming the United States of America* (Washington, D.C.: Government Printing Office, 1909), 3248–57.

best which could be adapted to the circumstances of all," dispatched the Articles to each of the state legislatures for ratification. In an accompanying circular letter, it beseeched the states to rise above "local attachments" and to review the constitution "with a liberality becoming brethren and fellow-citizens surrounded by the same imminent dangers, contending for the same illustrious prize, and deeply interested in being forever bound and connected together by ties the most intimate and indissoluble."[53]

This plea for quick and unamended ratification of the Articles was quickly dismissed by William Henry Drayton. "The American confederacy should be the effect of wisdom, not of fear, an act of deliberation, not of hurry," he explained.[54] "Millions are to experience the effects of the judgment of those few, whom the laws permit to think and to act for them in this grand business. Millions—posterity innumerable, will bless or curse our conduct! Their happiness or misery depend upon us—their fate is now in our hands! I almost tremble, while I assist in holding the important balance!" (98). Inspired by the magnitude of this responsibility, Drayton took time away from a variety of public and private business in early January 1778 to study the Articles with "liberality . . . decency and respect" (98). His examination of the national charter uncovered so many ambiguities and flaws, however, that he felt compelled to draft an alternate constitution, which he believed was "more likely to form a beneficial confederation" (114, 98). Accompanying his proposal was the most elaborate critique of the Articles that has been preserved.[55] As such, Drayton's production represented an important contribution to the debate over the creation of America's first national government, and now distinguishes him as one of the leading constitutional theorists of his day. Just as importantly, his analysis of the Articles of Confederation provides valuable insight into his vision of the proper role of the federal government and its relation to the states.

Drayton delivered his fifteen-thousand-word essay with "profound humility" before the South Carolina General Assembly on January 20, 1778. Be-

53. *JCC*, 9: 933.

54. William Henry Drayton, "Speech Upon the Articles of Confederation Delivered Before the General Assembly on January 20 1778," in Niles, *Principles and Acts*, 115. Subsequent citations to this speech are given parenthetically in the text. A portion of this speech in Drayton's hand is located in the William Henry Drayton Papers, Pennsylvania Historical Society, Philadelphia.

55. George D. Harmon, "The Proposed Amendments to the Articles of Confederation," *South Atlantic Quarterly* 24 (July 1925): 309.

cause the Articles would have an enormous impact on millions of Americans for generations, the chief justice wanted "every appearance of doubt . . . carefully eradicated out of it" (100). The Carolinian conceded that the present Continental Congress clearly understood the meaning of the Articles, but he feared that future Congresses would attempt to interpret beyond the letter of the law. Any doubts and inaccuracies within the document, Drayton underscored, will only encourage men to "obstinately contend for and persist in opposite constructions" (99).

One perceived ambiguous clause Drayton wanted Congress to clarify was found in section four of Article VI, which allowed the federal government to stipulate the number of gunships each state could maintain in peacetime but which failed to specify whether or not a state could issue a new commission if the number of vessels in its navy fell below the quota established by Congress. More troubling to Drayton, though, was the "dangerous inaccuracy" in Article VI, which prohibited states from entering into a conference, agreement, or alliance with any king, prince, or state. Such a ban was intolerable to the Carolinian, who was still smarting from his failure to annex Georgia to South Carolina. He wanted one state to be able to aid another without the prior consent of Congress in the case of an Indian war. Likewise, Drayton wanted repealed the first section of Article IX, forbidding Congress from making commercial treaties with foreign nations if such negotiations hindered the states' ability to impose duties on other countries. Failure to give the national government precedence in such instances would impose an "intolerable clog to foreign negotiations" (99). Drayton also found distasteful section two of Article V, prohibiting congressional delegates from serving in a paid federal office, a clause which he believed was "utterly impolitic" because a congressman "may be most capable of the station" since he possessed the "secrets of Congress." Instead, he wanted the delegate to vacate his seat upon accepting a commission and prevent him from seeking reelection during the time he held it (101).

In addition to finding so many ambiguities, Drayton also thought the Articles were replete with harmful defects. One of the most egregious, according to him, involved the first section of Article IV, which entitled free inhabitants of each state—paupers, vagabonds, and fugitives from justice excluded—to all the privileges of free citizens in the several states. This right is "absolutely inadmissable," the chief justice exclaimed. "Would the people of *Massachusetts* have the free *Negroes* of Carolina, eligible to their general court?" he asked. Only free white inhabitants of one state should be entitled to the "privileges and immunities" provided to the same in the other states (100, 110).

An exception Drayton wanted to make to this provision were those who refused to "take up arms in defence of the confederacy," particularly the Quakers, who he said had "sagaciously found a few words" in the Bible justifying their passive opposition to military service. Those who were unwilling to defend their civil rights, he believed, should not have an equal opportunity to participate in them. The conviction in fall 1777 of twenty-one Pennsylvania Quakers accused of engaging in communications prejudicial to the American cause convinced Drayton that the Society of Friends was a "dangerous body" that Congress should expel from the country just as Jesus had cast out the money changers from the temple (111).[56]

A danger of another sort, Drayton believed, was the provision in Article V allowing each state—no matter the amount of wealth or population it possessed—to have one vote in Congress. He considered this form of representation unfair to the more populous states, who he thought should have a vote in Congress in proportion to their populations. If each state was to have the same political leverage in Congress, he remarked, "let each contribute the same sum." More importantly, he feared that equal representation might lead to the development of political regions similar to England's rotten boroughs, a "fatal disease," he said, that has "long been consuming the vital vigor of the English constitution" (113). To prevent America from contracting this lethal disorder, the chief justice recommended that Congress base a state's representation on its importance to the confederation. In determining a state's importance, he divided the country into three classifications based upon the requisition of 1777. Those states whose requisition totaled less than $300,000 would have three votes. These included New Hampshire, Rhode Island, New York, New Jersey, Delaware, North Carolina, and Georgia. States that contributed between $300,000 and $800,000—in this case Connecticut, Pennsylvania, Maryland, and South Carolina—would be allowed to have six votes. The remaining two states, Virginia and Massachusetts, would have nine votes since their requisition exceeded $800,000. This plan would create a Congress of sixty-nine delegates, who would by a majority determine the passage or rejection of legislation. However, the real barometer of a state's importance, according to Drayton, was the actual amount of financial aid it sent to Con-

56. Don Higginbotham, *The War of American Independence: Military Attitudes, Policies and Practices, 1763–1789* (Macmillan, 1971), 275–6.

gress. To encourage each state to contribute its quota, he suggested that Congress increase or decrease its representation in accordance to the amount actually paid.

Drayton was also "absolutely against" the taxing methods set forth in the Articles of Confederation, which required states to pay their quotas based on the value of land, buildings, and improvements. This arrangement was "unequal, injurious and impolitic," he asserted, because it was unrealistic to expect assessors to appraise such lands and other property equally. Instead, the chief justice suggested that Congress use capitation to measure the amount of taxes each state should pay to the confederation because a state's "true riches and strength" were its people, not its land and property. Drayton proposed a decennial census of white inhabitants as "the best means of enabling Congress to wield the strength of America with equal justice to the several states" (110). By specifying that only whites should be counted to assess taxes, the slave-owning Carolinian removed blacks from being used to determine the amount of money a state had to pay Congress. Thus large slave states like South Carolina would not have to relinquish to the central government some of the vast wealth produced by their numerous bondsmen.

Drayton was equally concerned with Congress's failure to elaborate on the Articles' terse provision establishing a continental navy. "Never was so important a subject more expeditiously dispatched," he complained (113). Preceding the eminent naval historian Alfred T. Mahan by more than a century, Drayton argued that America "must be a great naval power" because both history and experience showed that the maritime nations have had the "greatest influence" upon world affairs. To help create and maintain a powerful navy, he recommended that Congress require each state to establish a "naval seminary" to educate and train five seamen for every thousand white inhabitants (108). Such a plan would not only curtail the "evil" and "oppressive" practice of impressment, Drayton argued, but would also allow America, within a quarter century, to have twice the number of seamen than Britain ever had during its "most formidable hour" (113).

One of Drayton's most important concerns involved state sovereignty. Although Article II allowed each state to retain "every power, jurisdiction and right" not delegated to Congress, he still believed the other clauses placed so many "great and humiliating restrictions" upon the states that "scarce a shadow of sovereignty remain[ed] to any" (98). Drayton realized it was necessary to restrict some of the state's sovereignty, "but I would do this with a *gentle* hand," he said (98). However, Drayton's assault upon many of Congress's powers was anything but gentle. For instance, he did not want congressional delegates to regulate disputes between the states, as stipulated in Article IX, because he felt the process was "full of delays." Instead, he felt Congress should select judges known for their "knowledge in the law of nations" to preside over these interstate disputes (101–2). Similarly, Drayton strongly opposed the clause in Article IX giving Congress the "sole and exclusive right and power" to regulate the alloy and value of coin and to fix the standard of weights and measures, two things each colony had been doing successfully for years (102).

The Carolinian also could not "see the shadow of a good reason" why Congress should have the power to appoint all naval and army officers, except regimental commanders, in the service of the United States. He believed it was more appropriate for the states to select all officers necessary to complete their respective military quotas because they were better able to "penetrate into the characters and abilities of candidates" within their own "spheres of action" (112). The only military officers Drayton wanted Congress to appoint were an "admiralissimo" and "generalissimo" to command the entire army and navy respectively, and major-generals to supervise the several military departments. Nor did Drayton want Congress to have authority over land and naval forces, as stipulated in Article IX, because he assumed it would allow a body of troops to occupy a state entirely independent of the local civilian authority. Drayton did not want the state's civil authorities to "absolutely direct" all troops within its borders, but he did at least want the executive to have the power to act as the "representative of Congress" for military affairs. To prove the sagacity of his proposal, Drayton related President Rutledge's decision in June 1776 to overrule General Charles Lee's bid to abandon Fort Sullivan, a judgment he believed saved Charleston from certain capture by the British. The Carolinian wished for a continuance of that command that had saved South Carolina, a command which he believed was inseparable from the civil power.

Although Drayton vehemently censured the Articles for giving "almost all the important powers of government" to Congress (98), his loudest complaint, ironically, was that it failed to provide the central government with the authority to require the states to furnish their quota of men and money. To underscore the necessity for such a clause, he reminded the delegates that in 1777 when America was in its "hour of . . . most pressing necessity," the states still neglected their military quotas with impunity. Drayton claimed that if each state had provided its designated proportion of soldiers the previous year, the

American army could have defeated and captured the British forces in the country with little bloodshed. The chief justice was distressed over this exclusion because he believed that man was "so selfish and ungenerous a being" that he would "throw his load upon the shoulder of his neighbor" whenever he could. To ensure that each state shouldered its allotted burden, Drayton would give Congress the authority to penalize any state that defaulted in its pecuniary or military quota by an amount equal to the original requisition.

Drayton most likely had the northern states in mind when he contrived the above recommendation. He was distrustful of their "levelling principles" and certainly would have agreed with Edward Rutledge's assessment that they were a politically cunning group intent on "destroying all Provincial distinctions" and making the other states "subject to the Government of the Eastern Provinces."[57] Heightening Drayton's suspicions of northerners was his pessimistic view of human nature and his realization that there was in America a distinct South and a North with opposing interests. As he explained,

> When I reflect, that from the nature of the climate, soil and produce of the several states, a northern and southern interest in many particulars naturally and unavoidably arise, I cannot but be displeased with the prospect, that the most important transactions in Congress may be done contrary to the united opposition of *Virginia*, the two *Carolinas* and *Georgia*. States possessing more than one half of the whole territory of the confederacy, and forming, as I may say, the body of the southern interest . . . the honor, interest and sovereignty of the south, are in effect delivered up to the care of the north. Do we intend to make such a surrender? I hope not! (104)

To prevent the North from "abusing the confidence of the South," Drayton proposed changing the number of votes required to pass all major legislation from nine to eleven (104). Previous historians have incorrectly charged that this proposal conflicts with his apportionment scheme whereby states would be given either three, six, or nine votes in Congress.[58] However, Drayton wanted to give states only one vote each on "important" decisions: declaring war, entering treaties or alliances, ascertaining military quotas for the states, equipping a naval force, levying a general tax, declaring treason, ad-

57. Edward Rutledge to John Jay, 29 June 1777, in Edmund C. Burnett, ed., *Letters of Members of the Continental Congress* (Washington, D.C.: Carnegie Institute, 1921–1936), 1: 517–8.

58. Paul A. Horne Jr., "William Henry Drayton and the Articles of Confederation," SCHS *Proceedings* (1990): 26. M. E. Bradford also erroneously asserts that Drayton wanted the South to have a veto on "all legislation." "No Master But the Law," 129.

mitting a new state into the union, and appointing a commander for the army and navy (107, 114). This alteration would, in effect, give the South the ability to veto measures related to any of these issues if only two states from the region objected. On the other hand, because Drayton would have given the South the power to utilize its veto only on these few legislative matters, one must question the extent of his desire to protect the southern interest, especially considering that these issues were not pregnant with sectional tension. Nevertheless, he urged Congress to accept the measure by reminding it that the States General of Holland, a "government [that] is accounted a wise one," required a unanimous vote for the passage of important legislation. Although this stipulation "causes their proceedings to be slow," the Carolinian conceded, "yet it secures the freedom and interest of its respective states. Is not this our great aim?" he asked (104).

Drayton had many "great aims" in proposing his alterations to the Articles of Confederation. His primary goal was to protect all of America from tyranny, not just the South or an individual state. He believed the best means of doing this was to organize a confederation allowing the central authority responsibility only over general or national affairs, while providing the states with the power to control local matters. He provided his own interpretation of what constituted national and local concerns. And to help make certain that neither governing agency overstepped its boundaries, he clarified perceived ambiguities within the Articles that, he felt, might lead to use of authority not originally intended. Thus Drayton was not interested in unlimited state sovereignty. Had he been, the Carolinian would not have suggested giving Congress the power to enforce its decisions. He simply believed that local authorities were better able to cope with regional affairs and the central government with national concerns.

In Drayton's confederacy, however, a citizen's sovereignty would not have been divided between the nation and the state. A people's ultimate allegiance, according to the chief justice, was to the preservation of their natural rights of life, liberty, and property. As he had done with the relationship between the king and his American subjects, Drayton applied the Lockean compact theory of government to the United States confederation. He considered the Articles a contract voluntarily agreed to by sovereign states for specific and limited purposes. Like all contractual obligations, the states were "at liberty to declare themselves absolved from all obedience to that government" if Congress persistently violated the arrangement (108). But this agreement worked both ways. The Carolinian also suggested that if a state violated any

of the Articles, Congress could bar it from its deliberations and even "proceed against such state" with the "utmost vigor of arms . . . until it shall have
paid due obedience" (109).

The contents of Drayton's speech dominated the General Assembly's discussion of the Articles. Eventually the legislature proposed twenty-one amendments, more than any other state. Of these, at least fifteen are attributed to
Drayton's recommendations. The fate of the Articles had the assemblymen's
highest attention on January 31, 1778, when they elected a new delegation to
the Continental Congress. Drayton, as South Carolina's foremost authority
on the national charter, was the legislature's indisputable first choice. Christopher Gadsden, Arthur Middleton, and Henry Laurens (who had already
been a delegate) were also selected. Gadsden and Middleton declined to
serve, however. Drayton was disappointed by their decision, as he was deprived of serving alongside two close friends. The General Assembly replaced
them with Thomas Heyward Jr., a thirty-one-year-old lawyer, planter, and
signer of the Declaration of Independence, and John Mathews, a thirty-four-
year-old lawyer and former assistant judge.[59]

Drayton waited nearly a month before leaving for his new post in York. Perhaps delaying his departure was the fire which swept through downtown
Charleston on January 15, consuming over 250 homes. There is no indication
of Drayton's losses, if any, but as a leading official he undoubtedly helped to
provide relief to those left destitute by the calamity. When Drayton did finally
set out for Pennsylvania in his four-wheeled chaise in late February 1778, he
brought along his ten-year-old son, John, so he could supervise the boy's education while in Pennsylvania.[60] Although Drayton must have been saddened
over leaving the rest of his family behind, he was eager to perform his new duties as a congressional delegate. His actions during the previous four years had
made an indelible impression on South Carolina's rebellion and garnered him
enormous recognition and respect among residents throughout the state. Now,
with his election to the Continental Congress, he had an opportunity to
broaden his reputation and leave an equally lasting mark on America's Revolution. Drayton failed to realize this dream, but not for lack of trying.

59. *JCC*, 11: 652–6; *SC&AGG*, 5 February 1778; Godbold and Woody, *Christopher Gadsden*,
169.

60. *SC&AGG*, 5 March 1778; John Lewis Gervais to Henry Laurens, 23 February 1778, John
Lewis Gervais Letters, 1772–1801, SCHS; John Drayton, *Carolinian Florist*, viii; Drayton, *Memoirs*, 1: xxvi.

CONGRESSIONAL DELEGATE

Drayton perhaps labored harder than any other congressional delegate in helping to realize American independence. During his seventeen months in the Continental Congress, the Carolinian served on more standing and ad hoc committees than anyone save young Gouverneur Morris of New York. Some of the more important duties Drayton performed on these boards involved rectifying abuses and problems within the army and reaffirming the authority of the central government over the states in matters of war and peace. When he was not busy with committee work, he participated in numerous debates on the floor, introduced resolutions, and wrote lengthy circular letters to friends and officials back home in South Carolina apprising them of national affairs. In his remaining spare time, Drayton continued researching for his history of the Revolution and thwarting British peace offerings that failed to recognize American independence.

Following a five-week journey up the Atlantic coast, Drayton and his young son rode into the little town of York, Pennsylvania, on the morning of March 30 "amidst much foul weather." Of course, York was not the original meeting place of the American Congress. The delegates had been forced to retreat from Philadelphia the previous September to escape General John Burgoyne's advancing army. The new location was a farming community of eighteen hundred located approximately ninety miles west of the capital; compared to Philadelphia, America's largest metropolis, York was inaccessible, dull, and cramped. North Carolina congressman Cornelius Harnett complained that it was "the most inhospitable scandalous place I was ever in."

Suitable lodgings were scarce and expensive. Many delegates also found the food unpalatable and the water sickening.[1]

Before the food and water at York could wreak havoc with Drayton, he entered the modest courthouse in the center of town where Congress met to present his appointment credentials. Afterwards, he sought out Henry Laurens, president of the body, who described the "true Situation" in America. Public affairs "looked extremely gloomy," Laurens somberly told his colleague, "everything was dark and dangerous." Congress's treasury was exhausted, its currency was falling precipitously in value, and the Articles of Confederation were still unratified. Perhaps the gravest problem facing Whig leaders, however, was the miserable condition of the American army stationed at nearby Valley Forge. Severe shortages of clothing, shoes, and food left nearly a third of the troops unfit for duty. The bitterly cold weather only added to the soldiers' miseries, compelling many to desert. Unless some "great and capital change suddenly takes place in that line," General George Washington warned Congress in December, "this Army must inevitably be reduced to one or another of these three things: Starve, dissolve or disperse." As a basis for discussion, Washington made numerous suggestions for increasing recruitment and reforming the clothing and commissary departments. Congress responded by dispatching a committee of its own members to Washington's headquarters to "promote a speedy reformation in the army." It remained there for three months conferring with the commanding general, studying conditions first hand, and investigating and reforming the staff departments.[2]

Just two days after taking his congressional seat, Drayton was deeply immersed in this "Herculean work," as Pennsylvania delegate Joseph Reed labeled it. On April 2 Congress added him to a committee to confer with the newly appointed commissary general, Jeremiah Wadsworth, in drawing up new regulations for the agency. According to Washington, the commissary department was in a "very deplorable situation." Much of the problem re-

1. Drayton to Laurens, 29 March 1778, *HLP*, 13: 54; Cornelius Harnett to William Wilkinson, 28 December 1777, *LDC*, 8: 490; Lynn Montross, *The Reluctant Rebels: The Story of the Continental Congress, 1774–1789* (New York: Barnes & Noble, 1950), 209–10, 222.

2. *JCC*, 10: 294; Laurens to John Lewis Gervais, 3 May 1778, *HLP*, 13: 239; Laurens to John Rutledge, 4 May 1778, *LDC*, 9: 598; George Washington to the President of Congress, 23 December 1777, and George Washington to the Committee of Congress with the Army, 29 January 1778, in John C. Fitzpatrick, ed., *The Writings of George Washington* (Washington, D.C.: United States Government Printing Office, 1931–1940), 10: 192–8, 365–94; *JCC*, 9: 1073.

volved around fraud and waste committed by inattentive, indolent, and corrupt deputies within the department.[3]

Drayton attacked the problem with his usual enthusiasm, according to Laurens, who noted that his colleague "has given earnest of his determination to set his face against fraud in every shape & to call upon those Men who detain unaccounted Millions." In their report submitted two weeks later, Drayton and the committee recommended that Congress endow the commissary general with full authority to appoint and remove any officer in his department and to require each commissary officer to immediately inform the legislature upon learning of any frauds and abuses in his bureau. To make positions in the department attractive to competent (and, they hoped, honest) men, the committee increased the commission earned by assistant purchasing commissaries on all money they disbursed, and that earned by the commissary general on all sums paid by him to his deputies. Finally, to encourage greater responsibility among the department's offices, it required purchasing commissaries to make monthly reports to the deputy commissaries in their districts, and ordered the commissary general to make periodic reports to Congress. The plan was adopted on April 14. Unfortunately, these reforms only temporarily solved the problems within the commissary department. By the end of the year the spiraling costs of the war and rapid depreciation of the country's currency made it increasingly difficult for the American government to adequately supply its troops.[4]

Drayton's enthusiasm in ferreting out fraud in the commissary department earned him a special assignment to Washington's headquarters at Valley Forge. Official records fail to mention this appointment, but evidence in Laurens's correspondence suggests that Congress sent Drayton to the headquarters in early May on a fact-finding mission. What information he was to gather, however, remains unclear. What is known is that Drayton met with Washington and his young aide-de-camp Colonel John Laurens (Henry Laurens's son); Major General Baron von Steuben, a former Prussian officer

---

3. Joseph Reed to Thomas Wharton, 1 February 1778, *LDC*, 9: 4; George Washington to the Committee of Congress with the Army, 29 January 1778, in Fitzpatrick, *Writings of George Washington*, 10: 392.

4. Laurens to William Livingstone, 19 April 1778, *LDC*, 9: 445–6; *JCC*, 10: 302, 327, 344–8; Erna Risch, *Supplying Washington's Army* (Washington, D.C.: United States Government Printing Office, 1981), 179–81; E. Wayne Carp, *To Starve the Army at Pleasure: Continental Army Administration and American Political Culture, 1775–1783* (Chapel Hill: University of North Carolina Press, 1984), 44–50, 176–7.

who served as the army's new drill instructor; Major General Marquis de Lafayette, a twenty-year-old French nobleman and protégé of the commanding
general; and Captain Pierre Charles L'Enfant, an engineer who later designed the basic plans for the nation's capital. During his stay at Valley Forge
Drayton also observed troop drills and was pleasantly surprised by the "rapid
advance" made by the soldiers under von Steuben's command.[5]

When Drayton returned to York on May 21, he presented Laurens with a
"sketch" of the encampment at Valley Forge. What his report said is unknown, unfortunately, because it was not recorded in either the journals
or the papers of the Continental Congress, nor is it found among Henry
Laurens's letters. But evidence of its content may be reflected in Drayton's
appointment to two committees in late May: one to increase recruiting and
the other to rectify abuses in the post office. Like his report to Laurens, however, these committee's recommendations, if any, are not included in the
congressional records.[6]

One "grand subject" thoroughly recorded in Congress's journals, though,
is the spirited debate over half-pay pensions for officers on a lifetime basis
after the war. General Washington, who believed that practically all human
actions were motivated by self-interest, considered this measure absolutely
necessary to stem the tide of experienced officers resigning from the army.
Congress began debating the general's suggestion just a few days before
Drayton's arrival in York. According to Laurens, his colleague quickly joined
the discussion, voicing opposition to the measure with "much energy & per-
spicuity." Like Washington, Drayton had a pessimistic view of human nature,
but unlike the Virginian, he did not think officers would resign without the
lure of half pay for life. If some of them refused to reenlist, so be it; Drayton
did not want such self-centered men holding high military positions anyway.
He was willing to risk his life and fortune to help achieve American independence—without pay. In fact, he had allegedly donated his previous year's income toward the Revolution in South Carolina. Drayton believed true patriots should make similar sacrifices for the American cause. Moreover, the
measure was unfair to enlisted soldiers, who faced an equal risk to their lives
as the officers. After nearly six weeks of heated argument, Congress finally

5. Henry Laurens to John Laurens, 5 May 1778, and Von Steuben to Laurens, 16 May 1778,
HLP, 13: 251–2, 307; Henry Laurens to Lafayette, 5 May 1778, Henry Laurens to Von Steuben,
5 May 1778, and Drayton to Von Steuben, 21 May 1778, *LDC*, 9: 603, 606, 726–7.
    6. Henry Laurens to von Steuben, 25 May 1778, *HLP*, 13: 340–1; *JCC*, 11: 532–50.

reached a compromise on May 15: half pay to officers for seven years after the war.[7]

Drayton's willingness to make personal sacrifices to advance the American cause is also reflected in his exhausting work schedule. Within seven weeks after arriving in Congress, he was serving on five of the eight standing committees: Appeals, Indian Affairs, Marine, Commerce, and Foreign Affairs. Only John Bayard Smith of Pennsylvania served on as many permanent boards.[8] Drayton's legal experience, dealings with Native Americans, and service as a ship's captain may explain his selection to the first three committees, while his eagerness to serve and varied talents probably account for his appointment to the latter two panels.

As demanding as service in five permanent committees might first appear, the duties required from most of them were apparently nominal. The Committee on Indian Affairs, for example, met only twice while Drayton was in Congress: to award a medal to the chief of the Delaware nation for his friendship toward the United States and to order the distribution of goods to western Indians in hopes of gaining their support. Likewise, Drayton's service on the Foreign Affairs Committee consisted of two meetings, both times to consider letters from American ambassadors in Europe. His duties on the Commerce Committee were even more limited, amounting to one gathering to instruct American agents to discharge debts contracted in obtaining crucial military supplies from France. On the other hand, Drayton was much more active as a member of the Marine Committee, which met on more than a dozen occasions for such purposes as urging navy commissioners in New England to outfit continental frigates to "annoy the enemy," determining what to do with prisoners taken at sea, and resolving sundry complaints and petitions from ships' captains and crews.[9]

Probably Drayton's most meaningful and demanding work with regard to these permanent panels was his service on the Committee on Appeals, an an-

---

7. Henry Laurens to John Lewis Gervais, 3 May 1778, *LDC*, 9: 576; *JCC*, 10: 373–4; Herbert J. Henderson, *Party Politics in the Continental Congress* (New York: McGraw-Hill, 1974), 121–4.

8. Calvin Jillson and Rick K. Wilson, *Congressional Dynamics: Structure, Coordination, and Choice in the First American Congress, 1774–1789* (Stanford, Calif.: Stanford University Press, 1994), 122. The other standing committees were Medical, War, and Treasury.

9. *JCC*, 11: 537, 590, 559, 622; 10: 356; 11: 537, 555, 620, 621, 625, 685, 724, 727, 749, 812, 814; 12: 909, 933, 971; 13: 103; Records of the Continental Congress, reel 55, item 42, vol. 5, pp. 98–101, National Archives and Records Administration.

tecedent of the United States Supreme Court. Congress created this five-member board in January 1777 to hear and adjudicate appeals from the sentences of state admiralty courts in cases of captures. One of the most consequential of such appeals Drayton heard while a member of this committee involved the celebrated case of the sloop *Active*. The record of the appeal reveals much not only about the evolution of national authority but also about Drayton's role in the case and his opinion on this important subject.

The case began in August 1778 when Connecticut sailor Gideon Olmsted (or Olmstead) and three other mariners were captured by the British on the open sea, taken to Jamaica, and placed on board the sloop *Active* to help sail it with arms and supplies to New York, which was occupied by the British. On the night of September 6, Olmsted and his companions were able to seize the vessel and steer northwest toward Egg Harbor, New Jersey. However, their good fortune changed two days later when Thomas Houston, captain of the Pennsylvania brig *Convention*, captured the *Active* against the New Englander's angry protests. Houston carried the *Active* into Philadelphia (reoccupied by the patriots by this time), where he claimed it as his prize. Olmsted also filed a claim to the British vessel and its contents. The case was tried before Judge George Ross and a jury, who awarded the daring Connecticut sailors only one-fourth of the prize. The remaining booty went to the captain and crew of the *Convention* and the state of Pennsylvania. Outraged by this decision, Olmsted promptly appealed his case to Congress, which duly referred the matter to the Committee on Appeals.[10]

On December 12 the committee heard arguments in the statehouse from lawyers representing both sides. Three days later it issued a report, written by Drayton, reversing the decision of the Pennsylvania court. This verdict, although arrived at jointly by all committee members, provides another telling example that Drayton supported a powerful central government, at least in certain matters. Concerning this affair, Drayton and his associates argued almost syllogistically that the federal government was the sole authority invested with the supreme power of war and peace, that the power of executing the law of nations was essential to the supreme power of war and peace, and therefore, the central government must determine the legality of all captures on the high seas; otherwise, juries would possess the ultimate power of exe-

10. Hampton L. Carson, "The Case of the Sloop *Active*," *Pennsylvania Magazine of History and Biography* 16, no. 4 (1892): 385–8; Kenneth W. Treacy, "The Olmstead Case, 1778–1809," *Western Political Quarterly* 10 (September 1957): 675–8.

cuting the law of nations in all cases of capture. Such a construction, the committee maintained, would involve "many inconveniences and absurdities" that would invariably destroy a vital part of the powers entrusted to Congress, thereby disabling it from giving satisfaction to foreign nations complaining of violations of neutralities, treaties, or "other branches" of the law of nations. Drayton and his colleagues understood that if the embryonic American government was to gain the respect of other countries, it must have a final voice on matters of war and peace.[11]

The Pennsylvania Court of Admiralty felt differently and refused to execute the committee's decree on the grounds that it violated a state law prohibiting appeal or reexamination of facts established by a jury. The Committee on Appeals was frustrated by Pennsylvania's challenge to its authority and submitted a report to Congress on January 18, 1779, including all the facts of the trial, the appeal, and the refusal of the state court to execute its decree. To compel the body to reaffirm its authority in this matter, the committee further informed the delegates that they would not proceed in this case or hear any others until their rulings were given full efficacy. Seven weeks later Congress established the central government's authority by issuing a strongly worded report declaring the Committee on Appeals's right to reexamine all questions of maritime capture, regardless of contrary state laws. Although the ruling did not end the power struggle between the national government and the state of Pennsylvania concerning this case, it did eventually confirm federal authority on matters of prize captures. In doing so, it marked a milestone in federal authority and, according to one authority, contributed to the establishment of the "priceless principle" that the "laws of the United States shall be recognized as the supreme law of the land."[12]

Of course, not all of Drayton's congressional duties were so momentous. Most of his work involved serving on ad hoc committees created to address the many mundane requests and inquiries sent to Congress. During his seventeen months as a delegate, the energetic Carolinian served on nearly ninety

11. *JCC*, 13: 134–7, 281–4; Hampton, "The Case of the Sloop *Active*," 391; Henry J. Bourguignon, *The First Federal Court: The Federal Appellate Prize Court of the American Revolution, 1775–1787*, vol. 122 of American Philosophical Society *Memoirs* (Philadelphia: American Philosophical Society, 1977), 101–9.

12. *JCC*, 13: 86–92, 134–7, 183, 252–3, 270–1; Hampton, "The Case of the Sloop *Active*," 398; Mary E. Cunningham, "The Case of the *Active*," *Pennsylvania History* 12 (October 1946): 229–47.

of these boards—no less than six times the number served by the average delegate for the same time period. Congressional leaders appointed him to these many panels because congressmen who were "talented and efficient enough to be elected to standing committees," explain two authorities on the Continental Congress, "were the most likely candidates for election to the constantly increasing number of ad hoc committees." If the number of committee assignments is truly a reflection of a delegate's talent level, Drayton must be regarded as one of the ablest men to have served in the Congress. President Laurens evidently thought so; in speaking of Drayton he explained that he wanted a man of the Carolinian's "abilities & diligence" to be "ever present" in Congress.[13]

The nature of business in the numerous ad hoc committees on which Drayton served varied enormously. Some of the most important included ruling on charges against Whig leaders accused of malfeasance in office, assisting southern states in crushing Indian resistance along their frontiers, and creating strategies for increasing recruitment in the Continental battalions, regulating the Continental mail, and eliminating price gouging by merchants. However, most issues Drayton confronted while serving on these temporary boards were much less important. At least three-fourths involved addressing such minor requests and complaints as petitions from sailors over the proper division of captured booty, demands from civilians for payment due them, appeals from officers seeking suspension or delays in executions of soldiers, requests from foreigners desiring to join the Continental army, and reports of violations against the American flag, among many other matters. Despite their relatively minor significance, these numerous inquiries consumed enormous amounts of Drayton's time and energy.

While not sitting on committees, Drayton was often participating in congressional debates. These deliberations were frequently noisy, disorderly, and sometimes acrimonious. Members carried on conversations with their neighbors and wandered about the room during debates. Many addressed the group without first being recognized by the chair, interrupted speakers who had the floor, and spoke "too long and too often." New Hampshire delegate Josiah Bartlett was "sorry to say" that "sometimes matters of very small importance waste a good deal of precious time by the long and repeated speeches and chicanery of gentlemen who will not wholly throw off the law-

13. Wilson and Jillson, *Congressional Dynamics*, 117, 121; Henry Laurens to Rawlins Lowndes, 17 May 1778, *LDC*, 9: 701–2.

yer even in Congress." Drayton, as a gifted orator with strong views, expressed his opinion on many issues. Unlike many of his colleagues, though, he was a "good speaker" who, according to Bartlett, was "not given to the chicane common to lawyers."[14]

The often loquacious and disorderly nature of argument on the floor prompted Drayton and fifteen other members to sign a pledge on April 12, 1778, to meet punctually at the beginning of the sessions, to speak no more than ten minutes on any topic, and to support order, decency, and politeness in debate. This oath motivated Congress the following month to adopt eighteen rules for "better conducting of business." Unfortunately, the leadership of Drayton and his fifteen cohorts in this matter failed to have a lasting impact on their colleagues. Just four months later South Carolina delegate John Mathews found the "thirst for Chatering so extremely prevalent that it absolutely disgusts me," he wrote Thomas Bee, and opined that it might deliver a "fatal stab" to the American cause.[15]

Somewhere between the committee work and the debates, Drayton managed to find time to pen lengthy circular letters to friends and officials in South Carolina informing them of northern political and war news. According to Laurens, Drayton devoted "all his leisure minutes" toward collecting and transmitting information. "He is a perfect Miser in gathering, but very liberal in diffusing," he wrote John Lewis Gervais, "and by his means Carolina will be fully informed, the great end will therefore be assured and I must avail myself of the advantages of so good a Colleague." Although few of Drayton's letters to South Carolina have survived, evidence from other sources reveal that he corresponded regularly with printer Peter Timothy, who sometimes published the information in his newspaper, and with John Rutledge, Rawlins Lowndes, and Christopher Gadsden. Gadsden returned the favor by apprising Drayton of affairs in South Carolina.[16]

Although no personal correspondence between Drayton and his wife have

14. Frech, "The Career of Henry Laurens," 154; Bartlett to William Whipple, 27 July 1778, and Bartlett to Whipple, 20 June 1778, *LDC*, 10: 360, 144.

15. Delegates' Pledge of Order, 12 April 1778, *LDC*, 9: 403; *JCC*, 11: 534–5; Mathews to Bee, 22 September 1778, *LDC*, 10: 683.

16. Henry Laurens to John Wells, 31 May 1778, Laurens to John Lewis Gervais, 15 July 1778, Laurens to Gervais, 23 June 1778, *LDC*, 9: 790; 10: 282, 180. Evidence of Drayton's correspondence with South Carolina leaders is found in: *SC&AGG*, 16 July 1778; *Gazette of the State of South Carolina*, 26 August 1778; *SCG*, 1 July 1778; *HLP*, 13: 466, 550; *LDC*, 10: 17–8, 80, 230, 286; 12: 327; Walsh, *Writings of Christopher Gadsden*, 122, 126–9, 131–4, 146–8, 150–4, 159–60.

survived, he undoubtedly informed her about his general duties in Congress and provided her with advice on managing their plantations. One of Dorothy Drayton's responsibilities was providing medical care for sick slaves, a duty she took quite seriously. On one occasion she even brought two slaves ill with rheumatic fever into the main house so that she could better give them "good nursing." Because of her careful medicinal treatments—or perhaps despite them—both bondsmen fully recovered from their illness. Yet Mrs. Drayton's duties as a plantation mistress did not consume all of her time and energy. Her numerous house slaves and plantation overseers allowed her time to visit with close friends such as Eliza Lucas Pinckney and Mrs. Pinckney's daughter Harriott Horry at their country estates. Dorothy Drayton also spent time in Charleston, attending concerts and plays and visiting with friends, who returned the social calls with visits to her plantation manor.[17]

Despite the onerous demands of his many official and unofficial duties, Drayton still continued to research material for his history of the Revolution. According to son John, Drayton spent much of his time copying congressional documents. He also conducted research in the Philadelphia library and received assistance from fellow delegates Joseph Reed and Charles Thomson, the longtime secretary to Congress who was collecting data for his own history of the Revolution.[18]

Drayton temporarily put aside his history project in late April 1778 to once again frustrate the efforts of British peace commissioners. On the twentieth of that month Congress received a disturbing packet from George Washington, which included what appeared to be a conciliatory proposal from Prime Minister North. In an accompanying letter, the commanding general informed Congress that the British in Philadelphia were distributing copies of the offer throughout America. This "insidious proceeding," he wrote, "is certainly founded on principles of the most wicked, diabolical baseness, meant to poison the minds of the people and detach the wavering, at least, from our cause." Fearing the "malignant influence" it would have on the un-

17. Dorothy Drayton to Elizabeth Trapier, 7 December 1778, enclosed in Eliza L. Pinckney to Harriott Horry, 7 December 1778, in Pinckney, "Letters of Eliza Lucas Pinckney," 152–5.

18. Drayton, *Memoirs*, 1: xxvi; Drayton to Joseph Reed, 22 April 1779, in Samuel Hazard, ed., *Pennsylvania Archives*, First Series (Philadelphia: Joseph Severns, 1853), 7: 329–30; T. Matlock to Drayton, 22 April 1779, ibid, 7: 330; Boyd S. Schlenther, *Charles Thomson: A Patriot's Pursuit* (Newark: University of Delaware Press, 1990), 204–5, 258–60.

decided, Washington urged Congress to "expose in the most striking manner, the injustice, delusion and fraud it contains."[19]

At first Congress believed the documents were merely a product of the Philadelphia Britons' conniving. But the proposal was indeed true. With the patriots' decisive victory at Saratoga in October 1777 and the Franco-American alliance signed in early February 1778, many Britishers lost hope of ever subjugating the Americans. Perhaps most discouraged was Prime Minister North, who on February 17 asked Parliament to pass a bill for the appointment of commissioners to offer peace to America on almost any terms they could secure—except independence. The men selected for this mission were not professional diplomats but simply active supporters of the North administration. Heading the delegation was Frederick Howard (fifth earl of Carlisle), a young, callow, and politically inexperienced nobleman known more for his wardrobe and gambling losses than any political leadership. The group's unofficial leader was William Eden, a close friend of Howard and an ambitious undersecretary of state and member of Parliament. George Johnstone, former governor of West Florida and partisan for America, completed the commission.

Preparatory to sending these commissioners, Lord North dispatched by express his conciliatory offer to America in hopes of forestalling another military campaign and the ratification of whatever alliance American diplomats may have concluded with France. In his proposal, the prime minister announced that Britain would no longer insist on the right to tax the North American colonies, and would repeal the Tea Act and the Massachusetts Government Act. As magnanimous as these terms may sound, they failed to give the patriots the one thing they absolutely demanded: recognition of their independence.[20]

President Laurens was insulted by this "spurious draught," as he labeled North's offer, and appointed a committee to draft a strong denunciation of

19. Washington to the President of Congress, 18 April 1778, in Fitzpatrick, *Writings of George Washington*, 11: 277–8.

20. Alan S. Brown, "The British Peace Offer of 1778: A Study in Ministerial Confusion," *Papers of the Michigan Academy of Science, Arts, and Letters* 40 (1955): 249–53; Weldon A. Brown, *Empire or Independence: A Study in the Failure of Reconciliation, 1774–1783* (Baton Rouge: Louisiana State University Press, 1941), 229–30, 244–5; Charles Ritcheson, *British Politics and the American Revolution* (Norman: University of Oklahoma Press, 1954), 262–9; Lewis Einstein, *Divided Loyalties: Americans in England during the War of Independence* (Boston: Houghton Mifflin, 1933), 77–80.

it. For this task he selected Drayton, Gouverneur Morris, and Francis Dana, men who he felt would return it "decently tarred & feathered." Drayton and his fellow committeemen did not disappoint the president. The report they submitted on April 22 declared that the Crown and Parliament were offering conciliation at this time because they finally realized the "impracticability of subjugating this country" and so were trying to "extricate themselves from the war upon any terms." Drayton and his fellow committee members strongly advised Congress against conferring with any British commissioners until their government either withdrew its fleets and armies or acknowledged America's independence. The Congress unanimously approved the committee's recommendations and ordered them, together with Lord North's speech to Parliament and the draft of his conciliatory offer, published in newspapers throughout America. Laurens assured Washington that such action would "blot out Pages of the British Instructions" to the commissioners.[21]

However, Drayton wanted to do more than "blot out" the commissioners' instructions; he aspired to use them as an instrument to compel France and Spain to sign a military alliance with the United States. On May 1 he introduced a resolution calling on Congress to inform the courts of France and Spain that Great Britain was intending to seek a reconciliation with the United States; that Congress believed Britain would consent to America's independence only upon the "most absolute compulsion"; and that the American states desired financial aid and an immediate declaration of war by France and Spain against Britain to "enable these United States to continue the war and with the blessing of God to establish their Independence." The delegates passionately debated Drayton's motion until that afternoon when they finally resolved to appoint a committee of three to draft such instructions to American diplomats in Paris and Madrid. The committee had little opportunity to perform this assignment, however, because the following day official texts of a Franco-American alliance arrived in York. A jubilant Congress quickly and unanimously ratified the treaties. To hearten others with this exciting news, Drayton, with President Laurens's encouragement, made a "very good abstract" of the treaties for publication in the *Pennsylvania Packet*.[22]

21. Henry Laurens to James Duane, 20 April 1778, *LDC*, 9: 457; *JCC*, 10: 367, 375–9; Laurens to Washington, 5 May 1775, *HLP*, 13: 256; Nathan R. Einhorn, "The Reception of the British Peace Offer of 1778," *Pennsylvania History* 16 (July 1949): 193–4.

22. Drayton's Proposed Resolution, 1 May 1778, *LDC*, 9: 551–2; *JCC*, 10: 374–80, 411, 413–4; Laurens to John Lewis Gervais, 3 May 1778, *HLP*, 13: 241; *Pennsylvania Packet*, 2 May 1778. The official treaties were signed between France and the United States in February 1777 but did not arrive in Congress until May 2.

News of America's alliance with France failed to discourage the British peace commissioners, who sent a message to Congress on June 13 expressing their desire for Americans to have the "irrevocable enjoyment of every privilege" that would lead to the "tranquility of this once happy empire"—short of a "total separation." The envoys followed this unwelcome remark with an even more offensive one by referring to America's new ally, France, as an "insidious" nation that could not be trusted. If the contents of this insulting letter were not damaging enough to their mission, George Johnstone's tactless attempt to bribe at least one congressman with high office and £10,000 sterling in exchange for helping restore Anglo-American unity certainly ruined any chance the diplomats had of success. An irritated Congress responded to the commissioner's offensive conduct on June 16 by establishing a committee (on which Drayton served) to draft a resolution for preventing any correspondence with the enemy. Later that afternoon the committee submitted its report, written in Drayton's hand, recommending that authorities in each state implement the most effective measures to stop "so dangerous and criminal a correspondence." Congress approved the committee's resolution the next day.[23]

Although Drayton coauthored this resolution, he evidently thought it did not go far enough toward thwarting the British envoy's nefarious machinations. The following day he made an "extraordinary Motion," according to Laurens, calling upon all congressmen to present before the house any letters they had received from the commissioners or individuals from Great Britain concerning Parliament's recent peace offering. Drayton understood that his motion would "cause uneasiness," but he told his colleagues that he "did not come into Congress to acquire friends, but determinately & boldly to discharge the duty of a Citizen." In defending his proposal, Drayton argued that congressmen should not associate privately with "individuals from abroad," especially those in public office, because it would ultimately destroy freedom of debate in Congress. The group rejected the Carolinian's motion, largely due to the determined efforts of Henry Laurens, who felt that it was a "dangerous attempt to stretch the powers of Congress" and would prevent him, as president, from communicating with the British diplomats.[24]

Drayton had little time to brood over this defeat because later that day the

23. Laurens to Horatio Gates, 13 June 1778, *LDC*, 10: 87; Carlisle Commission to Continental Congress, in Beatson, *Naval and Military Memoirs*, 6: 429–31; *Pennsylvania Packet*, 4 July 1778; *JCC*, 11: 608, 616.

24. Henry Laurens to Washington, 18 June 1778, and Drayton's Notes for a Speech in Congress, 17 June 1778, *LDC*, 10: 132, 114–5.

house assigned him to a committee of five to prepare an official reply to the commissioners' letter of June 13. In its brief report submitted and unanimously adopted four days later, the committee, reflecting the anger Congress held toward the peace envoys, said of those messengers, "Nothing but an earnest desire to spare the further effusion of human blood could have induced them to read a paper containing expressions so disrespectful to his most Christian majesty, the good and great ally of these states, or to consider propositions so derogatory to the honor of an independent nation." Only when King George III provided an "explicit acknowledgment" of America's independence or withdrew his fleets and armies from North America, the letter firmly concluded, would the Congress consider a treaty of peace and commerce with Great Britain.[25]

Since other pressing duties prevented the committee from addressing every point in the commissioners' "fallacious and incompetent" offer, Drayton took it upon himself to "add pretty severe strictures" to it in a more meticulous and reproachful reply. In his public letter written to the envoys on June 17, he first defended the French court against the envoy's charges that it offered an alliance with the United States to foil Britain's recent peace offerings to the United States. This assertion was blatantly untrue, Drayton countered, because it was "notorious" that France made its offer to the United States on December 16, 1777—a full month before Prime Minister North communicated any "plan of accommodation" to Parliament. The Carolinian respectfully refused to charge the commissioners with a "designed falsity" in their accusation, but he nevertheless told them such deceitful conduct on their part should at least warn the American people "to be upon their guard against you."

Having thus vindicated the honor of America's "good and great ally the King of France," Drayton next addressed the commissioners' proposals one by one. Their offer of representation in Parliament was worthless, he told them, because Americans are "too well acquainted with the *insignificancy* of the Scotch representatives" there to expect that Americans, if allowed to serve in the Commons, would "possess any importance" in that political body. Drayton regarded the envoys' proposal to discharge America's debts equally disingenuous since Britain could not even pay off its own deficit. Nor was their offer to "extend every freedom of trade" to America any more sincere, he added, because the colonists were all too familiar with Britain's "nat-

25. *JCC*, 11: 608, 615.

ural inclination" to monopolize commerce. If the commissioners were really serious about ending the war, then have King George withdraw his forces, Drayton declared, "and hostilities are instantly ended." Anyway, America would never reunite with Britain, he stressed, for "having tasted independence, she will ever be anxious to possess it again." Adding to the impossibility of a future reconciliation was the fact that any negotiations on the part of Congress with Great Britain would violate America's treaty with France, resulting in a loss of international respect and thus any hope of receiving additional foreign succor. Under these circumstances, Drayton announced, Britain *"will absolutely hold us at mercy."*

Believing Britain's offer, if adopted by Congress, would ultimately place America at that nation's mercy, Drayton next abusively charged King George III and Parliament with sending the commissioners to invite Americans to "surrender to the justice and mercy of our most unjust and vengeful enemies":

> Enemies who have starved to death our countrymen taken prisoners, loading them while alive and in their power with every insult. Enemies who gave stretch to their savage allies, to murder our old and unarmed farmers, and their helpless women and children; Enemies who have plundered our country, burned our towns, and armed son against father, servant against master, and brother against brother, in order to subject us; Enemies who have moved even Hell itself to accomplish their purpose of blood, ruin and tyranny; Enemies utterly abandoned to corruption, destitute of public virtue, deaf to the voice of justice, and dead to the feelings of humanity.

Such an enemy certainly cannot be trusted to honor their agreements, proclaimed Drayton. Anyway, the United States is independent *"de facto et de jure,"* he boldly concluded, and "will maintain her station at the expense of her last drop of blood."[26]

As if to symbolize this determination to maintain America's independence, the Congress resolved in late June to reassemble at its former meeting place in Philadelphia, which the British army had recently evacuated. But when the delegates arrived there, they were horrified to see the red brick State House (later renamed Independence Hall), which the British had used as a hospital, in a condition "disgraceful to the character of civility." The necessity of repairing the State House kept Congress from reassembling until July 7. How-

---

26. Drayton to the Carlisle Commissioners, 17 June 1778, is found in the *Pennsylvania Gazette*, 20 June 1778; the *Gazette of the State of South Carolina*, 27 July 1778; and *LDC*, 10: 116–21. See also Laurens to Washington, 18 June 1778, *LDC*, 10: 132.

ever, the building's "filthy and sordid" condition did not prevent the delegates from celebrating the second anniversary of American independence with a "grand festival" at the City Tavern on Second Street. After a "very elegant" dinner, President Laurens proposed the obligatory thirteen toasts, the last of which was: "May the Union of the American States be perpetual."[27]

But the Union's permanency was far from assured. By late June the legislatures of Maryland, New Jersey, and Delaware were still refusing to ratify the Articles of Confederation. Their unwillingness caused some delegates to fear that a confederation would never occur. John Mathews of South Carolina declared, "if we are to have no Confederation until the Legislatures of the Thirteen States agree to one, than we shall never have one, and if we have not one, we shall be literally a rope of sand, and I tremble for the consequences that will follow at the end of this War." In hopes of expediting matters, Congress on May 9 ordered the delegates to submit all amendments to the Articles suggested by their respective states. Drayton proudly presented South Carolina's twenty-one alterations, most of which stemmed from his January 20 speech on the national charter before the state legislature. His pride turned to disappointment six weeks later when Congress methodically rejected all proposed changes to the constitution.[28] All of Drayton's efforts in formulating his corrections, supporting them with elaborate arguments, and creating a new plan of government were for naught. However, his despondency was overshadowed by a larger concern over the possible deleterious effects Congress's action on this matter might have on the confederation. Drayton was convinced that his amendments were essential toward correcting what he believed were dangerous ambiguities and defects in the document. Congress's rejection of his alterations gave him some concern about the future of the American union.

Thus when Congress presented a form for ratification of the Articles to the delegates to sign on July 1, Drayton hesitated to affix his name because he did not think himself authorized to do so unless the delegates of the other twelve states would "agree to sign it likewise." To implement the Articles without the support of all thirteen states, as the document required was establishing a bad precedent, Drayton believed. However, two other members of

27. Henry Laurens to Rawlins Lowndes, 15 July 1778, *HLP*, 14: 31–2; Josiah Bartlett to John Langdon, 13 July 1778, *LDC*, 10: 268; *Pennsylvania Packet*, 6 July 1778.

28. John Mathews to Thomas Bee, 7 July 1778, *LDC*, 10: 235; *JCC*, 11: 485, 556, 625, 628, 631, 652–5.

the South Carolina delegation, Thomas Heyward and John Mathews, disagreed and felt themselves authorized to sign the Articles "notwithstanding One or even two States were to refuse." They maintained that realization of the confederation was more important than uncompromising obedience to principle in this case. Somehow Heyward and Mathews convinced their hesitant colleague of the importance of ratifying the compact. On July 9 Drayton reluctantly signed the Articles of Confederation.[29]

Two days later, Congress received word that the thirty-gun French frigate *La Chimère* carrying Conrad Alexander Gerard, France's newly appointed Minister Plenipotentiary to the United States, had recently landed off Chester, Pennsylvania, a small town on the Delaware River approximately fifteen miles south of Philadelphia. Congress quickly organized a committee, consisting of five of its most respected members, for the special purpose of receiving Monsieur Gerard "with proper honours." Those chosen for this assignment included Drayton, John Hancock, William Duer, Richard Henry Lee, and Daniel Roberdeau. The following day this welcoming committee departed for Chester with empty carriages and a military escort. Drayton brought along his eleven-year-old son John to witness the momentous event. The boy was not disappointed. When the American entourage arrived at their destination later that morning, elegantly dressed sailors aboard *La Chimère* saluted them with a discharge of the ship's guns and three loud cheers. After a brief, formal meeting aboard the frigate, Gerard and the Americans debarked under more salutes and set off for Philadelphia. When the dignitaries arrived in the capital in the afternoon, General Benedict Arnold, military commander of the city, provided them with a sumptuous dinner accompanied by "military music."[30]

However, Congress could not officially welcome Gerard for three more weeks because the State House was not yet restored to proper condition. In the meantime, Henry Laurens asked Drayton to write a speech for the singular event, which was adopted in modified form. On August 6 the carefully staged ceremony finally occurred. The president, surrounded by all the dele-

29. John Mathews to Thomas Bee, 7 July 1778, *LDC*, 10: 234–5; *JCC*, 11: 677; Paul Horne, "Forgotten Leaders: South Carolina's Delegation to the Continental Congress, 1774–1789" (Ph.D. diss., University of South Carolina, 1988), 225–6.

30. *JCC*, 11: 685; Records of the Continental Congress, reel 136, item 114, p. 6, National Archives and Records Administration. The preceding account is based on an extract from Drayton's manuscript book printed in Drayton, *Memoirs*, 1: xxii.

gates, sat on a platform in a mahogany armchair before a large table covered in green cloth. Two members of Congress presented Gerard to the assembly. The French minister bowed to the president and to the entire house, and they bowed in return. He then addressed the delegates in French, expressing the "sincere regard" King Louis XVI has for "everything which relates to the advantage of the United States," and his desire to help establish the young nation on an "honorable and solid foundation." When Gerard finished, Laurens nervously replied that the "virtuous citizens" of America can never forget the French king's "beneficent attention to their violated rights," which will bring Great Britain to a "sense of justice and moderation" and thus "secure peace and tranquility" to America "on the most firm and honorable foundation." The ceremony ended with more bowing. All present then went to the City Tavern for a lavish dinner followed by twenty-one toasts, each one accentuated by the firing of cannon.[31]

Gerard's arrival in Philadelphia provoked the Carlisle commission to renew its efforts at reconciling the Americans with their mother country. In an open letter to Congress on July 11, the envoys addressed the stated preconditions for negotiations: recognition of America's independence and withdrawal of all British forces. Concerning the first of these, the commissioners asserted that as far as independence meant the "entire privilege of the people of North America to dispose of their property and to govern themselves without any reference to Great Britain beyond what is necessary to preserve that union of force in which our mutual safety and advantage consists," they believed that their letter of June 10 already complied with Congress's demand for a recognition of independence. On the other hand, withdrawal of British forces was unacceptable, the diplomats remarked, because Britain needed them to protect American loyalists and to counter the intervention of their "ancient enemy," France.[32]

Congress refused to dignify the commission's offensive letter with a response. Drayton nevertheless replied with a scathing message published in the *Pennsylvania Packet*. He first attacked the emissaries' self-serving definition of independence. "By your construction" of the term, he began, the United States would be in an "*inexplicit dependence*" upon Britain. If you are

31. Drayton's Draft Address to Conrad Alexandre Gerard, 16–20 July 1778, *LDC*, 10: 289–90; *JCC*, 11: 754–7; Elias Boudinot to Hannah Boudinot, 8 August 1778, *LDC*, 10: 406; *Pennsylvania Packet*, 8 August 1778.

32. The Carlisle Commission's July 11 letter to Congress is found in the *Pennsylvania Packet*, 21 July 1778, and *HLP*, 14: 20–2.

really serious about your proposal, he told them, then "you must mean the independence we mean," an America independent of Great Britain. "We ask nothing more, we will accept nothing less."

Drayton also refused to accept the commissioners' denial that Great Britain adjusted its demands, refusals, and concessions to America according to its standing in the war. He reminded them that from 1774 to 1777, when America was "destitute of arms" and had "but a raw soldiery," the king and his ministers were "deaf to her supplications for redress of grievances" and "breathed nothing but unconditional submission on our part." However, now that British forces had suffered more than 35,000 casualties and the United States had recently signed an alliance with France, Lord North and his "coadjutors" have been "goaded by the situation of their affairs" to "ben[d] their knees" before America.

Because America's position in the conflict was better than ever, Drayton openly wondered why the commissioners felt Britain's most recent olive branch would find acceptance, especially since Congress had earlier rejected a similar proposal when the patriots' affairs were "in the most ruinous situation." Can you "gravely expect that your appeal will now be sustained," he asked,

> now that our affairs are not only *en bon train* but that we have every moral assurance of decisive victory and success! Are we not in pursuit of your forces? Has not your grand army retired to Islands for safety? Are you not at war with the House of Bourbon . . . ? Your inferior army is full reduced by draughts to the defense of your capital in Europe; a proof that you will receive no more land reinforcement. You are on the brink of perdition, and yet you pretend to hold dominion over us, and to reason us into an *independent dependence*—a jargon of words—a very chaos of ideas. Your Excellencies have been so long in the school of deception, and seem so fond of the art that . . . you are resolved to deceive yourselves.

To illustrate the envoys' deceptive nature, Drayton concluded his address with some extracts from George Johnstone's letter to congressman Francis Dana in which the messenger attempted to bribe the American in exchange for his assistance in promoting the "object of their commission."[33]

Drayton believed that Johnstone's subterfuge deserved more than public reproach, so on August 11 he presented a carefully prepared motion to Congress proposing that they censure the commissioner's conduct "in the strong-

---

33. Drayton to the Carlisle Commissioners, 18 July 1778, in the *Pennsylvania Gazette*, 21 July 1778; and *LDC*, 10: 295–302.

est terms." He urged his colleagues to expose Johnstone as an "object of universal detestation" and to discontinue all communication with a person who has "dared to seduce you." Drayton also pushed the legislative body to end all correspondence with the other commissioners, men whom he said came from the "same school of venality." Congress thought Drayton's last request too extreme, but did pass a resolution prohibiting communications with Johnstone.[34]

This resolution provoked a reply from the two other peace commissioners—Frederick Howard and William Eden—who claimed that they had no knowledge, "either directly or indirectly," of their colleague's private correspondence with Congressman Dana until they saw it published in the press. Although the two men believed Johnstone's integrity required no vindication from them, they nevertheless felt compelled to explain that the governor, in making his offer to Dana, was motivated by a desire to "promote and establish the liberties, peace, opulence, security and permanent happiness" of all Americans. After defending their colleague, Howard and Eden took the opportunity to repeat their attacks on the Franco-American alliance, again asserting that France proffered the treaties only upon learning of Britain's earlier "plan of accommodation" with America. When these particulars are "duly considered," they undiplomatically concluded, the "designs of France, the ungenerous motives of her policy, and the degree of faith due to her professions, will become too obvious to need any farther illustration."[35]

Congress refused to allow such a slanderous attack against itself and America's ally go unchallenged. It accordingly assigned Drayton, whose previous letters to the British envoys demonstrated his ability as a polemicist, to compose a "detailed refutation" of the commissioner's "sophisms." Assisting him in this assignment was the French minister Gerard, who provided information surrounding the Franco-American alliance in hopes that it would help "offset the work of the commissioners, whose object," he informed his superiors, "has only been to sow doubts and defiance among the people, and to arouse the Tories."[36]

34. Drayton's Notes for a Speech in Congress, 11 August 1778, *LDC*, 10: 424–5; *JCC*, 11: 770–3.

35. *Pennsylvania Packet*, 12 September 1778.

36. The congressional journals make no reference to this assignment. However, according to Gerard, Drayton was charged "under the secret auspices of Congress" to make this rebuttal "in his own name." Conrad Alexander Gerard to Comte de Vergennes, 12 September 1778, and 10 September 1778, in John J. Meng, ed., *Despatches and Instructions of Conrad Alexander Gerard, 1778–1780: Correspondence of the First French Minister to the United States with the Comte de Vergen-*

Drayton likewise had the ability to inflame the fury of others. After warning the British envoys that they would not find his observations upon their declarations to Congress "very agreeable," he launched into a defense of the Franco-American alliance. "Pardon me if I introduce a serious idea," Drayton sarcastically began. "I will be short; nay, I will use but a single word. INDEPENDENCE! This is proposed by the alliance with France," he explained; it "is not to be found in your offers." Drayton took exceptional offense to the commissioners' assertion that France had always been an "enemy to all civil and religious liberty," especially when he considered Britain's recent behavior toward America. "Witness your penal laws against Roman Catholics, and the rejected petitions of Dissenters. Witness the reigns of Charles the Second and his successor. Witness the present reign in Britain; the stamp act, the Quebec bill, the contemporary and subsequent outrages of laws and arms respecting America. Your excellencies ought to have looked at home, before you ventured to cast your eyes and censures abroad."

Nearly as offensive to Drayton was the commissioners' continuing claim that France had tendered an alliance with the United States for the purpose of frustrating Britain's plans to appease its former American colonies. Using the information provided by Gerard, Drayton went into painstaking detail to compare the chronology of events surrounding the Franco-American negotiations with those involving Parliament's passage of its conciliatory bills. Nearly three thousand words later, all he could conclude was that Lord North had presented his acts to Parliament two months after France made its offers to American diplomats in Paris. It was this development, Drayton explained, that caused a nervous Great Britain to change its proposals to Congress from "unconditional submission" to terms "only short of Independence."

Drayton next cleverly turned against the envoys their insistence that these new terms gratified all of America's "just claims." With this statement, he told his adversaries, you must also admit that "when you began the war, we had just claims . . . that notwithstanding our most humble petition in behalf of our just claims, you refused to grant those claims . . . that for three years you have by force of arms, and all the horrors of war, endeavoured to reduce us to unconditional submission, notwithstanding we had just claims." In light

---

nes (Baltimore: Johns Hopkins University Press, 1939), 281, 267. According to Drayton, the "measures of Congress" prevented it from making "any observations" upon the commission's declaration of August 26 (*Pennsylvania Packet*, 12 September 1778). Congress evidently did not want to become involved in a nasty and fruitless public debate with the envoys, so it unofficially asked Drayton to make an appropriate reply.

of these facts, Drayton argued, there is "no mistake or doubt" that Britain should have redressed America's "just claims" when it first made them. Instead, that country "enormously added" to its inhumanity by "letting loose . . . all the calamities of war" upon Americans to force them to abandon their honorable demands. "Your injustice has ruined thousands of our families," Drayton cried. "You have unjustly burned our towns and ravaged our country. Fathers, mothers, brothers, and friends, mourn the loss of their children, brothers and friends, by your injustice slain in the field of battle, scalped in their peaceable dwellings, murdered in your horrible prisons. America, by your injustice has lost thousands of her best citizens, and has been obliged to expend millions of her treasure." However, with the United States's alliance with France, Americans were now able to "receive satisfaction," the Carolinian said, "for all the damage which we, through your injustice, have received in supporting our just claims."

Finally, Drayton found hypocritical the commissioners' assertion that Louis XVI offered his support to the American cause out of self-interest. True, France would benefit if Great Britain, a bitter enemy, lost its lucrative American colonies. But can Britain claim that its own offers are based upon a desire to promote the "liberties, peace and permanent happiness" of Americans? Drayton asked rhetorically. "No!" he exclaimed:

> Her whole system of government since the year 1763, has operated—her laws have been enacted—her arms have been used for the very contrary purposes. Her ministers and Parliaments have long oppressed in order to plunder us. When we were unarmed, she ungenerously drew her sword upon us. She treated our most humble petitions for "peace, liberty and safety," with silent contempt. . . . Her veterans unjustly burned our towns, ravaged our country, and slaughtered our citizens. She let loose her Indian allies to massacre the unarmed, the aged, the sick, the infant, the matron, wife and virgin. Her generals and admirals in cold blood, in their prisons and prison ships, murdered our countrymen by suffocation, filth, hunger and nakedness.

These many British atrocities revealed to Drayton the true intentions behind the emissaries' self-professed generous offers to America. "Generous measures proceed from magnanimity," he concluded, "not cruelty—from choice, not necessity."[37]

37. Drayton to the Carlisle Commissioners, 4 September 1778, in *Pennsylvania Packet*, 12 September 1778, and *LDC*, 10: 559–70. Drayton later published this letter as *The Genuine Spirit of Tyranny, Exemplified in the Conduct of the Commissioners, Sent by the King of Great-Britain to bully, delude or bribe the Inhabitants of the American States Out of their freedom and property* (Poughkeepsie, N.Y.: John Holt, 1778).

Drayton's abusive public rejoinder probably played little part in the commissioners' decision to leave the country the following month. His aim in writing and publishing the letter was not to discourage the British envoys but to encourage vacillating Americans to join the colonial cause. Still, Drayton's public message perhaps motivated the British envoys, before departing, to publish a final "Manifesto and Proclamation" crafted to create a division between the people and the American legislature. The commissioners first charged the Congress with unlawful behavior by rejecting their "most honorable terms" and accepting the French treaties without first obtaining the consent of the state assemblies or their constituents. Therefore, all responsibility for the continuation of the war rests entirely with Congress, they said, and for "all the miseries with which it must be attended." To further undermine public confidence in the American legislature, the emissaries warned Americans of the "continued train of evils" they were "blindly and obstinately exposing themselves" to if they continued allowing Congress to behave so unlawfully and recklessly. In hopes of either encouraging or compelling the people to oppose the dictates of that body, they offered a general pardon until November 11 to all Americans who would accept reconciliation—and dire punishment to all who refused.[38]

The "insidious nature" of this offer, Drayton wrote a friend, inspired him to furnish the departing envoys with "some provision for their Sea store," which he hoped would "lie heavy upon their stomachs" during their voyage back to Britain. In an essay published in the *Pennsylvania Packet*, Drayton notified the commissioners that both their behavior and their published manifestos have been nothing but an entertaining diversion to Americans. He admired their persistence, but felt compelled to inform them that they were wasting their time because "the materials you are at work upon are rather of a firmer nature." Consequently, their attempts to "foment popular divisions and partial cabals" would never succeed. Their failure, as well as Britain's recent military and diplomatic troubles, Drayton asserted, were a direct result of that country's recent atrocities against America. These "horrid enormities" have "call[ed] down the vengeance of Heaven upon your nation," he declared. "That vengeance is now shaking your nation to the very centre: She feels the dreadful shock, and trembles in despair."

Drayton further explained that the Americans, by refusing Britain's offer, were simply following the magnanimous precedent established by Britishers

38. *Pennsylvania Packet*, 15 October 1778.

in 1692 when they refused a similar offer from James II following his de-
throning during the Glorious Revolution. The commission's grand promises,
like those of the last Stuart king, were merely the mark of weak minds who
had failed at all other means of compulsion or persuasion. Nor were their departing threats honorable "to your masters, to your nation, or to yourselves,"
he chided. "It is an outrage upon humanity. It is a proof of a narrow and base
mind." Drayton later may have wished to retract this last remark, considering
that he ended his letter with a threat of his own. "I warn you," he told the
envoys, "that as you burn our towns, so shall I urge to decimate your legions.
. . . God has raised us to independence, and we rest assured that Britain cannot deprive us of it. . . . Your arts have failed, your force has failed, and we
are not yet, and I trust never shall be so quite mad as to compliment Great
Britain with our obedience."[39]

Drayton's warning failed to intimidate the departing commissioners, but,
along with his earlier writings against the British envoys, this final letter
pleased many Whigs and their supporters both at home and abroad. George
Washington thought so highly of the Carolinian's "very good addresses" that
he ordered them distributed throughout occupied New York to instill hope
in the patriots residing there. Additionally, John Adams, who was serving as
a diplomat in Paris, remarked that Drayton's replies to the commissioners
were read in the French capital "with an Avidity that would surprise. . . . It is
not one of the least Misfortunes of Great Britain," Adams wrote his friend
James Warren, "that she has to contend with so much Eloquence, that there
are such painters to exhibit her atrocious Actions to the World and transmit
them to posterity, every publication of this kind seems to excite the Ardour
of the French nation and of their Fleets and Armies, as much as if they were
Americans." On the other hand, Drayton's essays undoubtedly produced passions of another kind within many Britishers when they read them in the
London press.[40]

In just his first six months as a delegate, Drayton had proven himself an invaluable member of the Congress. He had performed much more than his

39. Drayton to William Alexander, 29 October 1778, *LDC*, 11: 144; Drayton to the Carlisle
Commissioners, 24 October 1778, in *Pennsylvania Packet*, 29 October 1778; and *LDC*, 11: 104–9.
40. Washington to Charles Scott, 21 December 1778, in Fitzpatrick, *Writings of George
Washington*, 12: 475; John Adams to James Warren, 4 August 1778, in Robert J. Taylor, Gregg
L. Lint, and Celeste Walker, eds., *The Papers of John Adams* (Cambridge, Mass.: Belknap Press,
1983), 6: 347; *Remembrancer* (London), 1778, pp. 306–10, 1779, pp. 54–64.

share of committee work, participated in many debates, introduced important resolutions, and penned official and unofficial speeches and essays on behalf of the American legislature. His eagerness to serve, his abundant energy, his selfless dedication, and his many talents all garnered him admiration from peers both in and out of Congress. However, Drayton's contentious personality coupled with the emergence of several dangerously divisive issues would soon turn much of this praise into scorn—even from a fellow Carolinian.

CONGRESSIONAL DISHARMONY

William Henry Drayton enjoyed controversy; indeed, he seemed to thrive on it. However, the almost constant partisan strife that consumed Congress from mid-1778 to mid-1779 saturated even his passion for polemics. This political partisanship was rooted in the delegates' disparate interests, ideologies, and objectives concerning the Revolution. Over time, members grouped themselves into coherent factions as Congress confronted a number of military, diplomatic, and fiscal emergencies.[1] During Drayton's last year as a delegate, the factionalism reached its zenith over two of the most divisive issues to be addressed: the suitability of American diplomats in France and proposed peace terms. Drayton's contentious spirit and strong opinions naturally led him to take a prominent role in the discordant debates, and in the process he gained new political enemies and intensified disagreements with old ones. As if this discord was not enough, Drayton quarreled bitterly with General Charles Lee—a dispute that nearly resulted in bloodshed—and publicly ridiculed King George III. However, his most passionate feud—and in certain respects his most petty—occurred with Henry Laurens. Only Drayton's unexpected death ended their expanding estrangement.

Political and personal differences existed between Drayton and Laurens long before their service together in Congress. They first clashed in 1769

---

1. Jack N. Rakove, *The Beginnings of National Politics: An Interpretive History of the Continental Congress* (New York: Knopf, 1979), xv; Joseph L. Davis, *Sectionalism in American Politics, 1777–1787* (Madison: University of Wisconsin Press, 1977), 4–5; Henderson, *Party Politics*, 161–2.

over South Carolina's nonimportation agreement. Drayton's public opposition to certain elements of that boycott prompted Laurens to label the young
political neophyte a "Creature of Administration." The differences between
the two intensified six years later—after Drayton joined the American
cause—over control of South Carolina's rebellion. At least in action, Laurens
was a cautious and moderate Whig who often tried to obstruct more determined action proposed by Drayton and other extremists. His social views of
the Revolution, however, were anything but moderate. Unlike Drayton and
many other South Carolinians, Laurens did not mistrust or fear the tyranny
of "the people," an attitude reflected in his desire to reduce the economic gap
between the rich and the poor.[2]

Drayton, on the other hand, was a man of strong, determined, sometimes
even reckless action. Attempts by Laurens and other moderates to thwart his
aggressive proposals angered him. Fueling Drayton's hostility toward
Laurens was the latter's refusal in 1776 to satisfy his plea for a military command. And although Drayton tolerated some political participation by the
common people—primarily as a means of gaining their support for the American cause—he certainly did not support Laurens's more egalitarian social
objectives.

Despite their past quarrels and conflicting political and social ideologies,
Drayton and Laurens got along reasonably well during their first months together in Congress. Laurens, who also served as president of the Congress,
provided important guidance and information to his fellow Carolinian. Drayton, in turn, followed Laurens's leadership and voted similarly with him on
most issues. However, as Drayton became more familiar with national affairs
and with his new surroundings, he began taking a separate stand on many
questions. Accelerating the two men's estrangement were their separate congressional duties. As president, Laurens performed countless administrative
tasks, while Drayton, as a common member, served on numerous committees. His service in these boards, moreover, brought him new friendships
with such men as Gouverneur Morris of New York, William Paca of Maryland, and Elbridge Gerry of Massachusetts.

Even if Drayton and Laurens had spent more time together, their distinc-
tive personalities would have prevented a deep relationship from developing
anyway. Laurens possessed an erratic and irascible personality, which was
sometimes exacerbated by a severe case of gout. At times he could become

2. Laura P. Frech, "The Republicanism of Henry Laurens," *SCHM* 76 (April 1975): 73–4.

"irritatingly self-righteous," a trait manifested in his strict moral convictions, religious enthusiasm, and a puritanical lifestyle. On other occasions Laurens displayed a truculent streak, as when he threatened to kick the congressional secretary, Charles Thompson, from the president's platform upon which they were both standing or when he interrupted a speech by John Penn of North Carolina by singing from the president's chair, "Poor little Penny, Poor little Penny; Sing tan-tarra-ra-ra." Such antagonistic behavior earned Laurens the reputation as one of the most abrasive delegates who ever served in Congress.[3]

Laurens's irascible and self-righteous personality and abstemious habits clashed with Drayton's contentious and conceited temperament and profligate lifestyle. Drayton had strong convictions and enjoyed voicing them, often in deliberately provocative language. He also possessed a supercilious streak. With his patrician heritage, college education, and numerous accomplishments, Drayton considered himself equal—and perhaps superior—to the elder Carolinian, the son of a saddler who never attended college. On several occasions Laurens complained that Drayton failed to show him the respect he, as the senior delegate from South Carolina, expected from his junior colleague. And Drayton's self-indulgent lifestyle—although curtailed since his younger days—offended Laurens's ascetic sensibilities.

Given their past hostilities, political differences, and conflicting personalities, it was perhaps inevitable that Drayton and Laurens would quarrel in the politically charged Congress. It appears that their rupture began over a series of minor affairs. Only a month after he arrived in York, Drayton made Laurens "very angry" by "Excelencising the President." Unfortunately Laurens failed to explain or elaborate on his cryptic comment. Perhaps Drayton made a motion to bestow the presidency with some honor or title; if so, it was not recorded in the congressional journals. Nevertheless, several weeks later Drayton again offended Laurens by monopolizing the services of Moses Young, secretary to the president and the South Carolina delegation, with numerous and lengthy personal letters. Laurens was so indignant, in fact, that he refused Drayton the further use of Young's services. In retaliation, Drayton denied Laurens the "honor" of adding his signature to official messages he (Drayton) wrote to South Carolina on behalf of the state's delegation.

3. Frech, "The Career of Henry Laurens," 346; Schlenther, *Charles Thomson*, 160–1; David D. Wallace, *The Life of Henry Laurens* (New York: G. P. Putnam's Sons, 1915), 317; Rakove, *Beginnings of National Politics*, 260.

When Laurens confronted his colleague on this matter, Drayton "jocularly replied" that he "should not labour for A B and C." However, Laurens suspected that Drayton omitted his signature from these letters to promote himself rather than Laurens for the "benefit of posterity." His suspicions were raised later that summer when he inadvertently learned that Drayton had showed the other South Carolina delegates—and possibly others both in and out of Congress—a letter from Christopher Gadsden which contained derogatory remarks against the president. With this, Laurens could no longer suppress his hostility toward Drayton. In September 1778 he severely reproached his fellow Carolinian on some unknown matter in front of Samuel Adams. Drayton later confessed to Laurens that he was upset by the "manner & substance" of his expressions and requested that "when you differ in opinion with me & think my conduct deserving of your disapprobation, you will reserve the subject for a private hour."[4]

However, Drayton soon diverted his anger at Laurens to another foe, General Charles Lee. His enmity toward Lee began in July 1776 when the general, while organizing the defense of Charleston preparatory to the impending British naval assault, criticized Drayton's design of a bastion and ordered its dismemberment. Five months later Lee exposed himself to a counterattack when British forces captured him in Basking Ridge, New Jersey, after he had ignored Washington's numerous pleas to join the main army. The British took Lee to New York, where they kept him in close confinement until his exchange in April 1778. Drayton, eager to vindicate his reputation as a military engineer, went out of his way in his charge to the Charleston grand jury in October 1777 to accuse Lee of disobeying the commanding general's "repeated orders" and "*loitering*" when he should have *bounded* forward."[5]

Lee opened himself to further criticism only two months after his exchange when he made what Washington described as a "shameful retreat" during the battle of Monmouth. The Englishman replied with an imprudent and insulting letter demanding an apology from Washington and a court-

---

4. Henry Laurens to John Lewis Gervais, 3 May 1778, *HLP*, 13: 241; Laurens's Notes on the Conduct of William Henry Drayton, 12 April 1779, *LDC*, 12: 327 n. 3; Laurens to John Laurens, 6 July 1778, ibid., 10: 230–1; Gadsden to Drayton, 4 July 1778, in Walsh, *Writings of Christopher Gadsden*, 134–44; Godbold and Woody, *Christopher Gadsden*, 178–85; Drayton to Laurens, 16 September 1778, *LDC*, 10: 649–50.

5. Drayton, Charge to Charleston Grand Jury, in Niles, *Principles and Acts*, 93.

martial so that he could defend his conduct "to the world."[6] The Virginian refused the first request but readily granted Lee's wish for a court-martial, which found him guilty of disobeying orders, making an unnecessary and disorderly retreat, and acting disrespectfully toward the commanding general. Despite the seriousness of these offenses, Lee received only a one-year suspension from the army. Still, the verdict and punishment shocked the self-righteous Englishman, who urged friends in Congress to fight against ratification of the decision.

As with so many issues before Congress at this time, many delegates acted on personal and partisan considerations in debating the Washington-Lee quarrel. Perhaps the most biased of all was Drayton. He opposed Lee not only for having insulted his skills as a military engineer but also for acting disrespectfully toward Washington, whom Drayton considered a "freeman above all praise." In July 1778 he wrote the commanding general a "tribute of thanks" for the "important victory" at Monmouth, and assured him that he was "tenderly and anxiously interested in every thing respecting your safety and glory."[7] In other words, Drayton would do everything in his power to ensure that Lee lost in his dispute with Washington.

Accordingly, when Congress began discussing Lee's case in October 1778, Drayton fought vigorously for a vote approving or disapproving the verdict and sentence as a whole. Those friendly to Lee, on the other hand, demanded votes on each individual charge. This arrangement would have allowed members who were convinced of his guilt of the lesser charge—disrespect to Washington—but not the more serious ones—disobeying orders and making an unnecessary retreat—to express their opinion. But Drayton strongly opposed any opportunity to drop charges that would help cleanse Lee's tarnished reputation while at the same time damaging Washington's authority. Largely through the Carolinian's efforts, Lee's supporters lost their fight for separate votes. Congress was now forced to decide between either Washington or Lee—a judgment the Englishman was doomed to lose. On December 5 it approved the ruling of the military court.[8]

Although Lee was not surprised by Congress's decision, he nevertheless sought revenge against Drayton for his leading role in securing congressional

6. John Alden, *General Charles Lee: Traitor or Patriot?* (Baton Rouge: Louisiana State University Press, 1951), 230.

7. Drayton to Washington, 5 July 1778, *LDC,* 10: 223.

8. "Charles Lee Papers," NYHS *Collections,* 4: 152–3; *JCC,* 12: 1185, 1188, 1195; Alden, *Charles Lee,* 253.

confirmation of his sentence. In early February the general sent a message to Drayton, by way of South Carolina delegate Richard Hutson, censuring him for misrepresenting his conduct at Basking Ridge in his charge to the Charleston grand jury. In his reply, Drayton politely stood by his accusation, which he claimed was substantiated by information solicited from Major John Eustace, Lee's aide-de-camp. As a sign of his fairness, though, Drayton offered to retract his statement "in the most pointed terms" if Lee could prove to him that it was groundless.[9]

But the general refused to defend his conduct on the battlefield to the "tribunal" of William Henry Drayton—"a mere common member of Congress." Instead, he answered the chief justice in deliberately offensive language, probably with the intention of provoking him to issue a formal challenge. Lee first cleverly turned Drayton's accusation against his favorite American, George Washington. "You must suppose him either miserably deficient in understanding, or in integrity as a servant of the public," Lee chided, "when you suppose that he would suffer a man, for a single day, to act as his second in command, whom he knows to be guilty of such abominable military treason. This ingenious supposition, therefore, is, in my opinion, a greater affront to the General than to myself." Nevertheless, Lee still considered Drayton a scoundrel for "aggravat[ing] the calamities of an unhappy man" (himself), who had "sacrificed everything" for America's cause. Nor did the general expect an apology from a man who lacked "common humanity, common sense, or common decency."[10]

Lee's insults failed to provoke Drayton, who by this time only wanted to end the quarrel. Discarding the veil of politeness he had shown in his first letter, Drayton explained that he had neither the time nor the inclination to "enter into a competition" over who could "raise the most ingenious supposition, say the keenest thing, and pen the most finished period with parenthesis." Nor did he have the desire to continue corresponding with a man "legally disgraced for being guilty of abominable military treason against a community of the most liberal, just, generous and . . . merciful people on the face of the globe."[11]

If Drayton thought Lee would allow him to cast the last insult, he was wrong. In a scathing reply, the Englishman again tried to provoke the Carol-

9. Drayton to Lee, 3 February 1779, "Charles Lee Papers," NYHS *Collections*, 3: 305–6.

10. Lee to Drayton, 5 February 1778, ibid., 3: 307–8.

11. Drayton to Lee, 8 February 1778, ibid., 3: 308–9.

inian into issuing a challenge. "Until very lately I was taught to consider you only as a fantastick pompous dramatis Personae," he began, "a mere Malvolio never to be spoke or thought of but for the sake of laughter, and when the humour for laughter subsided, never to be spoke or thought of more—but I find I was mistaken." If this string of insults did not get the desired reaction, Lee added:

> I find that you are as malignant a Scoundrel as you are universally allow'd to be a ridiculous and disgusting Coxcomb. You are pleas'd to say that I am legally disgrac'd—all I shall say in reply is, that I am able confidently to pronounce that every man of every rank in the whole Army who was present at the tryal, every Man out of the Army, every man on the Continent who has read the proceedings of the Court Martial . . . is of opinion that the stigma is not on him on whom pass'd but on those who pass'd this absurd iniquitous and preposterous sentence—for to be just, I do not believe you quite blockhead enough to think the charges had a shadow of support. . . . As to the confirmation of the curious sentence, I do not conceive myself at liberty to make any comments on it, as it is an affair of Congress for which Body I ever had and ought to have a profound respect, I shall only lament that they are disgrac'd by so foul a member as Mr. William Henry Drayton. . . . If you think the terms I make use of harsh, or unmerited, my Friend Major [Evan] Edwards is commission'd to point out your remedy.[12]

However, Lee's scurrilous attack had no effect on Drayton, who promptly returned the dispatch unopened. Lee stubbornly sent another challenge through his aide-de-camp, Colonel Eleazor Oswald, who notified Drayton of the letter's contents. The Carolinian coolly shook off the challenge, explaining that although custom had sanctioned dueling with the military, it had not done so with the judiciary; and that such a conduct in a chief justice of South Carolina, as he was, would appear as a "public outrage on government, society, and common decency." He therefore refused to "sacrifice his public reputation" and "outrage his public character" merely to gratify General Lee "in the line of his profession." Still, for many days thereafter Drayton walked to and from Congress armed with a sword—one of the weapons Lee had designated—just in case he met the belligerent general, who also resided in Philadelphia.[13] By this time, however, Lee was busy quarreling with other ene-

12. Lee to Drayton, 15 March 1779, ibid., 3: 317–8. Malvolio, a character in Shakespeare's *Twelfth Night*, is a ridiculously conceited, self-righteous person who is made a laughingstock by other characters in the play.

13. Drayton, *Memoirs*, 1: xxiii–xxiv.

mies. He soon retired to Virginia, where he worked diligently—although unsuccessfully—to resurrect his fallen reputation.

Drayton had likewise turned his attention to another opponent, although a much more threatening one—King George III. The British monarch, in a November 26, 1778, speech to Parliament, charged France with secretly supplying arms and "other aid" to his "revolted subjects" in North America prior to signing an alliance with the United States, conduct he claimed violated treaties with Great Britain. To punish France—as well as to quash America's rebellion—George III pressed Parliament to make "the most active exertions . . . against all our enemies."[14]

As he had done with previous attacks against the Franco-American alliance, Drayton responded to King George's belligerent speech with detailed arguments and biting sarcasm. He first claimed that Louis XVI had a right to form an alliance with America because Britain's "dangerous war" against the United States posed a hazard to France's interests. Nor was there any treaty precluding the French from entering into "formal engagements" with an "independent nation." As to the charge that France had clandestinely supplied the patriots with arms and supplies while still at peace with Britain, "I have no reason to think that your Majesty has proof on this point," Drayton replied, "the Congress know of no such supply." He also found it "somewhat singular" that George III had the audacity to accuse France of committing "open hostilities and depredations" against England when, in fact, Britain had commenced hostilities with that nation in June 1778 by capturing two frigates belonging to the French court. If France had really offended "your Crown and honor," Drayton told the king, then you should have instantly declared war against your neighbor. George III's refusal to make such a proclamation at that time demonstrated to Drayton, at least, that Britain was too weak to fight France. It was therefore "absolutely necessary to your existence and future security," he warned His Majesty in bidding farewell, that you make the "painful operation" of "amputating America from Great Britain." If you "deliberate long upon it, you may be lost."[15]

While Drayton was castigating the British monarch, he was also participating in one of the most bitter and protracted conflicts in the history of the Con-

14. *The Parliamentary History of England from the Earliest Period to the Year 1803* (London: T. C. Hansard, 1806–1820), 19: 1276.

15. Drayton to the King of Great Britain, 13 February 1779, in *Pennsylvania Packet*, 18 February 1779, and *LDC*, 12: 61–8.

gress—the Lee-Deane imbroglio. This dispute centered around Silas Deane, a Connecticut merchant whom Congress sent to France in early 1776 to procure military stores and to encourage French support of the patriot cause. Two years later Deane, along with congressional ambassadors Arthur Lee and Benjamin Franklin, negotiated commercial and military treaties with the French government. Soon thereafter, Congress, responding to charges from the suspicious Arthur Lee that the Yankee merchant was using his official position to advance his mercantile business, recalled him home to explain the alleged financial irregularities. When Deane finally appeared before the body on August 15 to defend his conduct, debate arose over whether the report he was presenting should be oral or written. During the discussion, President Laurens was dismayed to discover that his fellow legislators had "absolutely taken sides as it can be supposed Gentlemen are capable of in a purely unbiased Assembly."[16] Around Arthur Lee rallied most New England delegates, led by Samuel Adams, and a few southern ones, including the Lee brothers of Virginia (Richard Henry and Francis Lightfoot Lee) and Henry Laurens. Opposing this "Adams-Lee junto," as it has been called, were the "Deaneites," a mixture of delegates from the middle and southern states.

This contest was in part an ideological struggle between the "imperatives of revolutionary purity" and the "dictates of pragmatism." Members of the Adams-Lee junto, most of whom favored an ascetic revolutionary morality and classical republicanism, considered themselves the "guardians of the integrity of the Revolution." They believed war profiteering by Deane and others posed a serious threat to the Revolution—no matter the outcome of the war. Much more menacing to the Adams-Lee faction, however, was Deane's support of France's war aims, which included regaining control of the Newfoundland fisheries—something New Englanders desperately wanted for themselves. France, in its humiliating defeat in the Seven Years' War, lost almost all of its North American possessions, including Canada, to the English. By assisting the Americans against Great Britain, France hoped to recover some of its lost territories—despite claims otherwise in the treaties of alliance with the United States. The Adams-Lee junto vigorously opposed France's subtle duplicity, which they considered a threat to American autonomy.[17]

On the other hand, partisans of Deane, especially southerners, were pressured to carefully nurture the French alliance with Britain's shift of the war

16. *JCC*, 11: 787; Henry Laurens to Rawlins Lowndes, 18 August 1778, *LDC*, 10: 474.
17. Henderson, *Party Politics*, 193.

to the South in 1778. They regarded the junto's attempts to control American foreign policy, exemplified by its ability to have Deane replaced by New Englander John Adams, as a danger to amicable relations between the United States and France. Moreover, many Deaneites either refused to believe the charges against the Yankee merchant or felt that some private involvement was inevitable in secretive commercial transactions.[18]

According to Laurens, Drayton appeared "strongly attached" to the Deaneites, which prompted the president to recommend the "fillet and scales of Justice" to his "worthy Colleague." Coming from a man with no legal education or training, this condescending lecture on the law must have incensed Drayton, who was, after all, chief justice of South Carolina. Nevertheless, it appears that Drayton's association with the Deaneites stemmed more from an opposition to Lee than support of Deane. In a letter to Laurens, Drayton revealed his antipathy for the Connecticut merchant and others who appeared to enrich themselves by mixing private cargoes with trade carried on in behalf of Congress. "I am entirely of opinion that there is not only much more villainy in the transaction of our public Affairs than we can fathom. This Spanish [mixed] Cargo discovers new wheels which have been running to private advantage under the guidance of public agents. What can be done!" he asked. From Drayton's perspective, perhaps little—at least against Silas Deane. The Carolinian was faced with the difficult decision of having to choose between two men both of whom he considered harmful to the nation's interest. In the end, he concluded that Arthur Lee posed a greater threat than Deane because of the former's poor standing with the French government. French minister Gerard, who wanted Lee recalled because of his close ties with the Adams-Lee junto, furtively informed selected delegates, including Drayton, that Lee was persona non grata in the French court. With Britain's redirection of the war to the lower South in fall 1778, Drayton believed South Carolina's future security depended on cooperating with Gerard and nurturing the nascent Franco-American alliance.[19]

For three months Congress periodically debated Deane's fate without allowing the Connecticut merchant to present his defense. His patience exhausted, Deane appealed his cause directly to the people with a lengthy dia-

18. Ibid., 193–7; Davis, *Sectionalism*, 16, 19; Neil Thomas Storch, "Congressional Politics and Diplomacy, 1775–1783" (Ph.D. diss., University of Wisconsin, 1969), 229–30.

19. Henry Laurens to Rawlins Lowndes, 18 August 1778, *LDC*, 10: 474; Drayton to Laurens, 30 November 1778, *HLP*, 14: 544 n. 1.

tribe in the December 5 issue of the *Pennsylvania Packet*, in which he charged Arthur Lee with opposing the French treaty and accused Congress of denying him justice by refusing to hear his defense. The New Englander's inflammatory broadside surprised and infuriated his antagonists, particularly President Laurens, who urged colleagues to punish Deane for his "highly derogatory" remarks against Congress. When the group refused, Laurens angrily resigned the presidency. John Jay of New York, an acknowledged Deane supporter, replaced him.[20]

Henry Laurens was not the only member of Congress disgusted with Deane's publication. Thomas Paine, secretary to the Committee on Foreign Affairs and a champion of Arthur Lee, published nine articles in the Philadelphia press under his famed pseudonym "Common Sense" lambasting Deane's public address and his conduct while in France. In supporting the assertions, however, Paine rashly released privileged information concerning treaty negotiations with France, which implied that Louis XVI had supplied materials to the rebellious colonies before recognizing them. This insinuation provoked the wrath of Conrad Gerard, who believed "Common Sense"was impugning the French Crown and threatening to provoke Britain into declaring war against France. The French minister therefore urged Congress on January 5, 1779, to "take measures suitable" to remedy Paine's "indiscreet assertions." Henry Laurens, a friend of Paine, led a small group of delegates imploring the delegates to hear the Englishman's defense before deciding his fate. However, Drayton believed Paine's disclosures not only violated Congress's trust in him, but, more importantly, jeopardized America's crucial alliance with France. Arguing that Congress must punish Paine for his flagrant misconduct, Drayton, along with Gouverneur Morris, James Duane, John Penn, and Richard Hutson, led a much larger group pushing for his dismissal as secretary of the Committee for Foreign Affairs. Laurens warned Paine that Congress would likely vote to dismiss him. The Englishman denied his enemies this pleasure by resigning his commission on January 8. His sudden resignation caused many delegates to suspect that someone had informed Paine of his fate. When a motion was adopted the next day requiring all members to admit whether they communicated the previous day's proceedings to the former secretary, Laurens declared that he had not only informed Paine that Congress would dismiss him but also encouraged him to examine the journals

20. *JCC*, 12: 1203–6.

to learn who had fought to deny him due process. Laurens, knowing the Englishman's fondness for quarreling, probably hoped the skilled polemicist would use the information to publicly disgrace Drayton and other anti-Paine members. The notes Drayton made on Laurens's behavior in this affair demonstrate that to Drayton, at least, that this was the former president's motive.[21]

Drayton's suspicions were confirmed two months later when Paine impugned him in the March 16 issue of the *Packet.* Whereas the Englishman had earlier praised Drayton for attacks against the British monarch, he now classified the Carolinian's February 13 message to King George III as a "dead match of *dulness.*" The letter's physical appearance also did not appeal to Paine, who remarked that it was "ornamented at the top, like an ale-house-keeper's sign, with the letters W. H. D." Escalating the pettiness of his critique, Paine next belittled Drayton's opening sentence to the king: "Your royal voice to your Parliament on the 27th of November last, has at length, reached the ears of freemen on the western shore of the Atlantic." Paine commented on the absurdity of referring to the passage of the king's voice across the Atlantic to America as a nine-week journey when it should have taken only nine hours, according to his estimate of the velocity of sound. However, he revealed his real reason for attacking Drayton with the concluding quip: "The Devil backs the King of England, and S. Deane backs W. H. D. because he has good 'ears,' and they are not 'shut.'" In other words, Drayton behaved in an inconsistent and partisan manner, according to the Englishman, by allegedly urging Congress to hear Deane's defense but denying him this same opportunity.

Paine, still not purged of his anger, attacked again four days later, this time criticizing Drayton's efforts in coauthoring a pamphlet entitled *Observations on the American Revolution.* In October 1778, Congress had appointed Drayton to a committee with Gouverneur Morris and Richard Henry Lee to publish an account of the British commissioners' peace overtures with "such notes and explanations" as "shall appear proper."[22] Four months later they had presented a 122-page white paper which not only documented the negotiations with the Carlisle commission but also catalogued, often in vivid

21. David F. Hawke, *Paine* (New York: Harper & Row, 1974), 86–91; John Keane, *Tom Paine: A Political Life* (Boston: Little, Brown, 1995), 175–80; Jack Fruchtman Jr., *Thomas Paine: Apostle of Freedom* (New York: Four Walls Eight Windows, 1994), 113–8; Frech, "The Career of Henry Laurens," 380–2; Thomas Burke and William Henry Drayton's Notes of Proceedings, 8 January 1779, *JCC*, 13; 37.

22. *JCC*, 12: 1063.

prose, British barbarities and excesses against America. According to Paine—
and modern historians—Morris performed the "chief share" in penning this
publication. Nevertheless, Drayton, who had already written several replies
to the commissioners and had gathered much material for his history of the
Revolution, certainly provided valuable assistance in producing the pamphlet.

On the other hand, Drayton may not have wanted credit as coauthor of
the report, given Paine's assessment of it. According to him, Morris and
Drayton had failed to give adequate treatment to America's early military efforts. "Why Mr. Morris and Mr. Drayton have, in utter silence, passed over
the affairs of Trenton and Princeton, and taken a flight from Staten Island to
Saratoga, I cannot conceive," Paine chided. "As historians they have reversed
the line of facts, and as writers they have not made most of their metaphors."
Perhaps Drayton and Morris were "so exceedingly industrious in supporting
Deane's impositions," Paine offered, "that they [did] not have time to attend
any other kind of duty." In concluding, he encouraged both men to reevalu-
ate their usefulness to Congress.[23]

Drayton did not reply to Paine's petty attacks. So many other people were
publicly castigating the Englishman at this time that he may have thought it
would be unfair—as well as a waste of his time and abilities—to add to the
censure. Instead, Drayton focused his attention on a much more serious
threat—one that could end his service in Congress. In early March he had
received a letter from Pierce Butler, adjutant general of South Carolina, informing him that the legislature had recently refused to reelect him as a delegate to Congress. Butler explained that the people "so sensibl[y] feel the want
of their chief justice at home, that they cannot consent to let him be absent
any longer. You must therefore . . . return to us as soon as you can," he
pleaded, because "we stand in much need of you at this critical juncture."
Worried over this news, Drayton presented the letter before the Congress
and asked whether he should continue serving. Not wanting to lose a valuable
member, the body quickly determined that a private letter "does not vacate
Mr. Drayton's seat." In the end, South Carolina evidently did not need its
chief justice as much as Butler implied, for the legislature soon reelected
Drayton to fill a vacancy left when Edward Rutledge declined to serve. Drayton's reelection perturbed some members of the Adams-Lee junto, particularly Arthur Lee, who remarked that it was "another melancholy omen for

23. *Pennsylvania Packet*, 20 March 1778; and *Virginia Gazette*, 16 April 1779.

the public . . . to permit W. H. D. to try for another year what mischief he can do."[24]

Indeed, Drayton's reelection allowed him to participate in another protracted and hotly contested congressional battle—the struggle over the Newfoundland fisheries. This five-month feud began innocently in mid-February 1779 when Conrad Gerard made two requests of Congress: to appoint a minister plenipotentiary to take part in the peace negotiations whenever they might occur and to make a list of "ultimata" it wanted to insist upon as conditions for ending the war. In making these requests, Gerard was reacting to recent news that Spain had decided to present the British with an ultimatum: either Britain must accept its offer as a mediator of peace, or Spain would enter the war on the side of France. Since Spain's ultimatum might lead to peace, Gerard wanted Congress to act quickly before the opening of the next military campaign. However, he strongly encouraged the members to seek peace on the basis of independence alone, explaining that "the pride of Great Britain was too high, and her abilities too great, to submit to extraordinary demands." In reality, though, it was Gerard and France that did not want Congress to insist on excessive claims, especially access to the Canadian fisheries. France wanted the fisheries for itself, not only for their economic value but also because it felt that a prosperous fishing industry was essential for building and training its naval fleet. Gerard also warned Congress to tone down its demands over navigation rights to the Mississippi because the king of Spain might refuse to help the United States if it insisted on this privilege, a privilege Charles III believed his country needed in order to adequately govern its American possessions.[25]

On February 17 Congress appointed a committee to consider Gerard's message. In a report submitted six days later, the committee ignored the French minister's surreptitious threats and recommended that Congress insist, as part of any peace treaty, on the United States's right to fish off the banks of Newfoundland and on free and open navigation of the Mississippi

24. *JCC*, 13: 300–1; ibid., 14: 891–2; Arthur Lee to John J. Pringle, 18 July 1779, Records of the Continental Congress, reel 128, item 102, vol. 3, p. 64, National Archives and Records Administration.

25. Gerard to John Jay, 9 February 1779, in Francis Wharton, ed., *The Revolutionary Diplomatic Correspondence of the United States* (Washington, D.C.: United States Government Printing Office, 1889), 3: 39–40; William Henry Drayton's Notes of Proceedings, 15 February 1779, *LDC*, 12: 72; Orville T. Murphy, *Comte De Vergennes: French Diplomacy in the Age of Revolution, 1719–1787* (Albany: State University of New York Press, 1982), 368–9.

River. Gerard vigorously objected to these territorial demands for two reasons: Britain would submit to them only by force of arms; and the king of France, who was willing to help the United States achieve independence, would not, however, "lengthen the war a day" to aid America's "excessive demands." To get Congress to withdraw these ultimata, Gerard solicited political support from delegates who believed that victory was impossible without French aid, and especially from southern members who were anxious for more French assistance and a Spanish alliance to help protect their region against further British attacks. One individual whom Gerard earnestly entreated was William Henry Drayton.[26]

When Congress began debating the fisheries and Mississippi River demands in mid-March, the house quickly split largely along sectional lines. New Englanders, of course, supported the fisheries, but had no interest in the navigation of the Mississippi. Southerners, on the other hand, viewed access to the Mississippi as indispensable to their region's economic development, but would gain nothing from the right to fish off Newfoundland. One notable exception to this sectional partisanship was Henry Laurens, who sided with the New England states owing to his merchant's awareness of the "importance of ships and sailors" and from principle of "valuing all commercial privileges."[27]

Drayton's position on this divisive topic was also exceptional, but for a different reason. Unlike most delegates, he opposed both ultimata. Drayton was concerned not with protecting the interests of either New England or the South but with ending the war before the enemy launched another campaign. The fact that the British military was poised over South Carolina at this time partially explains this unique stand in the controversy. Drayton also thought it was fruitless to make demands that the allies would not support and which America could not gain on its own.

During the debate over the fisheries question, Drayton repeatedly argued that the United States had lost its "pretended right" to fish off Canada when the colonies renounced their allegiance to Great Britain. Moreover, because the fisheries would only benefit three or four states, he believed it was not worth continuing the war merely to obtain this right. Unlike Laurens, Drayton was unwilling to sacrifice the lives and fortunes of thousands of South

26. *JCC*, 13: 194, 219–35; Storch, "Congressional Politics," 102.
27. Horne, "Forgotten Leaders," 287; Frech, "The Career of Henry Laurens," 422; Wallace, *Henry Laurens*, 340.

Carolinians just so New Englanders could harvest the rich bounty of the Newfoundland fisheries. Instead, he wanted Congress to inform Britain that the United States would agree to peace in exchange for a recognition of American independence—nothing more. Most delegates, however, strongly opposed his suggestion.[28]

Since Congress refused to remove either the fishery or the Mississippi ultimatum, Drayton next sought to place conditions on them pleasing to both France and Spain. On March 22 he introduced a motion urging the house to demand that Great Britain acknowledge the United States's right to fish off the Canadian coast. This proposal is quite odd considering that he opposed such an ultimatum. However, Drayton attached a clever qualification: that the United States's allies did not have to continue supporting the war in order for the Americans to obtain this acknowledgment. He knew that a majority of Congress would not support the New Englanders' demands for the fisheries if the allies would not assist the United States in its attempt to secure them. Drayton was right. Every New England state opposed his motion, while every other state—except New Jersey—supported it. His motion passed.[29]

Two days later Drayton, along with Thomas Burke of North Carolina, led a move to attach the same condition to the demand for free navigation of the Mississippi. This time, however, only North Carolina and Georgia—two states seriously threatened by the British—voted for the qualification. Although South Carolina was equally endangered by the enemy, Drayton and Laurens divided the state's vote with contrary ballots. In the end, though, Drayton and Burke's position won out, as Congress later withdrew the Mississippi ultimatum from the peace terms.[30]

Although some southern congressmen were perturbed with Drayton for his stance on the Mississippi ultimatum, their disagreement with him paled in comparison to the anger they felt toward Henry Laurens for his persistence in voting with the New Englanders on the question of fishing rights. Most upset with Laurens were the delegates from North Carolina—John Penn, Whitmell Hill, and Thomas Burke—who ineptly tried to pressure him back into the southern fold. A well-meaning Drayton joined in this political

28. Henry Laurens's Notes of Debates, 1 July 1779, and 8 May 1779, *LDC*, 11: 133–4; 12: 439; Frech, "The Career of Henry Laurens," 421.

29. *JCC*, 13: 350–1; Storch, "Congressional Politics," 104–5.

30. However, Congress did request that Spain grant the United States permission to navigate the Mississippi south of the thirty-first parallel. *JCC*, 13: 369–70.

power play, which infuriated Laurens and led to an irreparable breach between the two South Carolinians.

On April 2 Penn, Hill, and Burke sent an "official memorial" to the South
Carolina delegation expressing their surprise that Laurens supported the
continuation of hostilities so that New England could secure the right to fish
off the Canadian coast, an astonishing position considering that South Carolina was "so feeble in Internal strength and resources" that if attacked by the
British it would have to rely heavily on its neighbors for military assistance.
They bluntly notified Drayton and Laurens that North Carolina was "not in
a condition" to assist South Carolina if attacked by the enemy, nor did they
believe it would be inclined to offer any. Intensifying their pressure, the
North Carolinians enclosed a letter they threatened to send to their governor, Richard Caswell, urging him to recall the state's militia from South Carolina because Laurens's vote on the fisheries question indicated that their
southern neighbor had the strength and resources necessary for carrying on
the war without any outside assistance. Therefore, "any further exertions of
our State," they concluded, "may be very well dispensed with."[31]

Drayton was unduly disturbed by this message and took it upon himself to
mollify the indignant North Carolina delegation. Without consulting
Laurens on this delicate matter, he urgently replied that South Carolina "absolutely stands in need of the Sisterly aid of North Carolina" with Britain's
expanding military presence in Georgia. Regarding Laurens's voting record
on the fisheries, Drayton ventured that South Carolinians would "pointedly
oppose" his stance on this issue. He therefore begged them not to send their
letter to Governor Caswell, despite Laurens's conduct, because "it might
greatly distress a State entirely in unison with you in opinion on the point in
view, a State standing in need of your assistance & sensible of your efforts in
her favour."[32] The North Carolina delegation, perhaps influenced by Drayton's pleas, did not carry out their threat.

Even before Drayton wrote this reply, Laurens, ever suspicious of his colleague, accused him of having foreknowledge of the North Carolina delegates' letter to the South Carolinians. He therefore requested Drayton's "explicit and candid opinion" of it. In other words, were Penn, Hill, and Burke
serious about their threat? However, Laurens virtually guaranteed a nonre-

31. North Carolina Delegates to the South Carolina Delegates, 2 April 1779, and North
Carolina Delegation to Richard Caswell, 2 April 1779, *LDC*, 12: 277–8, 274–6.
32. Drayton to the North Carolina Delegates, 3 April 1779, *LDC*, 12: 282.

sponse by also charging Drayton with supporting the North Carolinians in the affair.[33]

Drayton brushed off Laurens's ungentlemanly accusations. Additionally, he refused to give his opinion on the "propriety of the measures" adopted by the North Carolina delegation, explaining ambivalently that "as the subject is new, of high importance, & you are well able to form a judgment, I beg leave to decline giving an opinion which there is no necessity I should hazard." On the other hand, Drayton felt obliged to inform Laurens of his recent letter to the North Carolinians.[34]

Drayton's preference for "illusion and ambiguity" was the last straw for Laurens. "[H]ere you have drawn a line between us," he declared in his April 4 reply to Drayton, "henceforward I will neither receive from you, nor trouble you with a Letter of controversy." Abandoning all possibility of ever reconciling with his fellow Carolinian, Laurens instead widened the rift between them by lambasting Drayton for his letter to the North Carolina delegation:

> Did the Measures adopted by the Gentlemen of North Carolina point, in your view, Sir, to no higher an object than aid to a sister State, which it is neither in their Power to direct or restrain? Were you less affected by an attempt of violence upon the suffrages of free Citizens as well as upon the honor of all these Independent States, than you were by the groundless apprehensions of temporary evils to your own? Do you think Sir, that *your* ardent requests can lull the resolutions of those Gentlemen or warp their inclinations from the pursuit of a duty which they hold indispensably necessary? Did not you feel a little for the breach of plighted faith and honor to keep secret deliberations upon a point, the disclosure of which may dash our infant Independence against the Stones? Or did you think me blind?

Instead of concluding his letter with the customary deferential veneration, "Your most obedient and humble servant," Laurens scrawled, "Comprehending all proper Ceremonies, Your faithful Colleague."[35]

Laurens's indifferent valedictory reflected a deeper resentment toward Drayton. Heretofore, the two Carolinians had, for the most part, kept their differences from becoming too personal. But Drayton's involvement in the dispute with the North Carolina delegation convinced Laurens that his colleague,

33. Laurens to Drayton, 3 April 1779, *LDC*, 12: 283–4.
34. Drayton to Laurens, 4 April 1779, *LDC*, 12: 285.
35. Laurens to Drayton, 4 April 1779, *LDC*, 12: 290–1.

whom he now referred to as "Black Coat" in his correspondence, was determined to ruin him politically. Laurens feared that he was "in danger of being betrayed & sacrificed by a man" who, he felt, "ought to love & support me." He therefore sought to protect his reputation and simultaneously blacken Drayton's by informing Whig leaders both in and out of Congress that he was blameless for the "late general and visible want of harmony" between himself and his fellow Carolinian. Laurens also started making detailed notes regarding Drayton's alleged misconduct in Congress—even recounting earlier arguments between them. In doing so, Laurens was possibly building a case to justify his own voting record in Congress if it ever became an issue in South Carolina. He already suspected Drayton of sending messages to their home state detailing his position on the fisheries debate. Laurens retaliated by seizing every opportunity to discredit his colleague by recording incidents showing that Drayton had either mistreated him or behaved foolishly as a delegate. In addition to earlier disputes with Drayton concerning the abuse of Moses Young's services, the omission of signatures from official dispatches, and the debates over the fisheries, Laurens wrote several "minutes" in late spring depicting their differences over how much in taxes South Carolina should pay in 1779. Laurens argued that the Palmetto State could not pay its allotted share—as several northern states already had—because it did not receive nearly as much money for its exports. Hereupon Drayton asked Laurens to prove the "disproportionate price" of commodities between their home state and those in the north. He also smartly pointed out the inconsistency of "combating against a high tax" while urging the continuation of hostilities to gain rights to the Canadian fisheries. "Now what can I call this," an irritated Laurens later wrote privately, "less than matchless effrontery?"[36]

Drayton, too, was waging his own public-relations campaign—one to portray Laurens as a traitor to the state and region. Congress in those days met behind closed doors, swore its members to secrecy, and kept private journals—all so the delegates could feel free to speak and vote as they wished.

36. Laurens to the North Carolina Delegates, 8 April 1779, and Henry Laurens to John Laurens, 8 April 1778, in *LDC*, 12: 310–1; Burnett, *Letters of Members*, 4: 423 n. ("Black Coat" reference); Richard Henry Lee to Henry Laurens, 5 September 1779, Henry Laurens Papers, Kendall Whaling Museum, Sharon, Mass.; Frech, "The Career of Henry Laurens," 441–2; Henry Laurens's Notes of Debates, 12 June 1779, and 19 May 1779, *LDC*, 13: 53–4 and 12: 493–4; Henry Laurens's "Minutes on the Motion for Taxing the States," and Henry Laurens's "Anecdote on Mr. Drayton's Manners on Question of Taxation, April 29–12 June 1779," Henry Laurens Papers, SCHS.

But Drayton wanted to remove this comfort from Laurens. On March 31 he proposed that Congress begin publishing its journals from the previous January so members' conduct "could be known to their constituents." For the future, Drayton suggested that every week Congress send copies of its journals to the state legislatures, which could then publish extracts from them in local newspapers. Those parts deemed top secret, of course, would be omitted. The house summarily adopted the proposal. Unfortunately for Drayton, Congress decided that debates on the peace ultimata were "private business" and not appropriate for publication or outside discussion. Despite this preclusion, information detailing Laurens's votes on the fisheries question somehow reached South Carolina. When Laurens learned of this, he accused Drayton of transmitting these secret details to their home state. Drayton immediately denied the charge, asserting that "If the intelligence has been transmitted to South Carolina, it was not by me." His denial did nothing to diminish Laurens's suspicions, however. Indeed, Laurens was so fed up with Drayton by this time, that he wished to leave Congress just so he would no longer have to endure the "insinuations & malicious intimations of a Man as wicked & as designing as human nature is capable of." Until then, Laurens continued writing letters back home defending himself against Drayton's alleged accusations that he was "too closely connected with the Eastern States."[37]

Drayton and Laurens temporarily put aside their differences in early spring 1779 to join forces in helping South Carolina defend itself against an impending British invasion. In 1778 Britain had decided to turn its North American war effort toward the lower South, where it believed the patriots were relatively weak and the loyalists both numerous and pugnacious. These loyalists, together with the southern Indians, would presumably support British forces in first gaining control of Georgia, the weakest of the thirteen American colonies, then pacifying South Carolina and extending British control northward. The plan began to unfold in late December 1778 when 3,500 British troops captured Savannah at little expense. Encouraged by this easy victory, General Augustine Prevost marched north from Savannah with nearly three thousand troops toward the British military's next main objective, Charleston.

37. *JCC,* 13: 394–5; Henry Laurens's Notes of Debates, 19 June 1779, *LDC,* 13: 83; Henry Laurens to John Laurens, 2 May 1779, and Henry Laurens to John Laurens, 21 September 1779, Henry Laurens Papers, Kendall Whaling Museum, Sharon, Mass.

South Carolina faced this invasion with a militia seriously weakened and depleted from a recent and unsuccessful expedition in East Florida. The gravity of the situation in South Carolina was driven home to Drayton and Laurens in January 1779 when Rawlins Lowndes informed them that the state's resources were "by no means adequate" against a British assault; therefore, military assistance was "apparent and indispensable." Congress responded by adding Drayton to a committee to consult with General Washington on the "most proper means" for defending the lower South. Drayton desperately urged the commanding general to send naval assistance to South Carolina, but the idea was "generally exploded," Laurens noted, because of Congress's "feeble funds" and the poor circumstances of the nation's naval forces. Washington could not spare any troops "to the Southward," either. In the end, Congress could do little except order Brigadier General Casimir Pulaski's legion of cavalry and light infantry to South Carolina and request the governments of North Carolina and Virginia to send all possible aid, including men, ammunition, and arms, to Charleston.[38]

Drayton and Laurens knew this paltry support would prove inadequate against Britain's growing military force in the South. Their fears were soon confirmed when fellow South Carolinian General Isaac Huger arrived in Congress, upon orders from President John Rutledge, to make a personal plea for increased military assistance. He informed the group that South Carolina could not raise enough militiamen to "do much mischief against the enemy" because so many men needed to remain home to prevent the slaves from rebelling or deserting to the British. Lieutenant Governor Thomas Bee, in a private letter to Drayton, added that the troops sent by North Carolina and Virginia were largely unarmed, and Pulaski's legion, if it arrived in time, would probably be too exhausted from its long march to fight effectively. Bee therefore implored Drayton to "exert all your influence with Congress to send forward some other and more durable relief."[39]

Accordingly, Drayton and Laurens made a radical proposal to Congress that they believed would solve South Carolina's manpower shortage: the cre-

38. Rawlins Lowndes to Henry Laurens, 15 January 1779, Laurens to Lowndes, 31 January 1779, and George Washington to Henry Laurens and Thomas Burke, 18 March 1779, in Henry Laurens Papers, SCHS; James Lovell to Richard Henry Lee, 17 August 1779, *LDC*, 13: 381; *JCC*, 13: 125, 132–3; Drayton to Benjamin Lincoln, 4 February 1779, *LDC*, 12: 9.

39. Farley, "The South Carolina Negro," 79–80; Thomas Bee to Drayton, 2 and 5 April 1779, Records of the Continental Congress, reel 86, item 72, pp. 485–90.

ation of an African American regiment. This recommendatic
not what Bee had in mind when he made his request. The idea,
from Lieutenant Colonel John Laurens, Henry Laurens's idea
four-year-old son, who was desperate to satisfy his desire for r
and eager to demonstrate his humanitarian sentiment by raisir.ͫ and commanding an elite regiment of black troops. The elder Laurens, who opposed
slavery on religious and humanitarian grounds—an attitude he developed
only after making his fortune in the slave trade—strongly supported his son's
proposal. On the other hand, Drayton, a large-scale slaveholder who accepted the "peculiar institution" with no moral qualms, held a different opinion of African Americans. Nevertheless, as with his stance on the lower class's
role in government, he was willing to grant blacks some additional rights and
opportunities if it helped defend his home state and secure American independence.[40]

Perhaps further encouraging Drayton and Laurens to make the radical
proposal was news of the looting and plundering by Prevost's troops in their
march toward Charleston. Among the plantation estates specifically targeted
by the British were those along the lower Ashley River. It is not known
whether the British ransacked Drayton's own estate. Certainly his reputation
and status in the Whig party would mark him and his property for British
vengeance. Dorothy Drayton recognized this fact and fled with their daughter Mary north to the hospitable protection of Daniel Horry's (Harriott Pinckney's husband) Hampton plantation on the Santee River. Evidently Dorothy did not feel entirely safe here either, as she and her young daughter later
fled westward into the Peedee region.[41]

Also escaping from Prevost's marauding troops were John Drayton and his
teen-aged wife Rebecca. However, the elderly patriarch did not fare as well
as his younger relatives in this general exodus. While crossing the west
branch of the Cooper River, John Drayton was taken with a seizure and died
in a tavern at Strawberry Ferry on the opposite side. Before expiring, however, he disinherited his eldest son in a final angry act for Drayton's having

40. Henry Laurens's Draft Committee Report, 25 March 1779, *LDC*, 246–7; Gregory D.
Massey, "A Hero's Life: John Laurens and the American Revolution" (Ph.D. diss., University of
South Carolina, 1992), 306–7; Gregory D. Massey, "The Limits of Antislavery Thought in the
Revolutionary Lower South: John Laurens and Henry Laurens," *JSH* 63 (August 1997): 509–13.

41. Eliza L. Pinckney to Tom Pinckney, 17 May 1779, Pinckney, "Letters of Eliza Lucas
Pinckney," 152–6.

refused his urgent requests to return to South Carolina to help the state in its desperate plight.[42]

What John Drayton did not know is that William Henry Drayton, along with Laurens, was assisting South Carolina in its time of need by working vigorously to secure passage of their extraordinary proposal to raise a regiment of black troops. They argued that a force composed of blacks not only offered military advantages but also prevented the British from inciting "revolts and desertions by detaching the most Enterprising and vigorous Men from amongst the Negroes." Their arguments, coupled with Huger's account of South Carolina's predicament, finally convinced Congress to adopt the plan on March 29. Specifically, it recommended that South Carolina and Georgia muster three thousand blacks and form them into separate corps commanded by white officers. Congress agreed to pay one thousand dollars to the slave owners for each enlisted slave and to give black soldiers their freedom at the conclusion of the war. However, the house recognized that this measure might involve "inconveniences peculiarly affecting" the two states. Therefore, it allowed authorities in South Carolina and Georgia to make the final decision over whether or not to implement the plan.[43]

As Congress had anticipated, white South Carolinians generally received this remarkable scheme "with horror" and "much disgust," considering it a "very dangerous and impolitic step" that was pregnant with "terrible consequences." With the "citizens at large" opposed to the measure, the South Carolina legislature overwhelmingly rejected it, despite the looming British threat.[44] This reluctance to fill the depleted ranks with black troops would come back to haunt South Carolinians in the spring of 1780 when British forces finally attacked Charleston and successfully occupied the state.

The tenuous truce between Drayton and Laurens was shattered in April over their opposing stands in a new controversy surrounding the composition of the foreign service, an issue entangled with the Lee-Deane dispute and the debate over peace terms. On March 24 Congress received a report from a committee that had been reviewing the foreign affairs of the United States. In

---

42. John Drayton, *Carolinian Florist*, xxv.

43. *JCC*, 13: 374, 385–8; Pete Maslowski, "National Policy toward the Use of Black Troops in the Revolution," *SCHM* 73 (January 1972): 10–1; Thomas Burke's Draft Committee Report and Henry Laurens's Draft Committee Report, [ante March 25, 1779], *LDC*, 12: 244.

44. Christopher Gadsden to Samuel Adams, 6 July 1779, in Walsh, *Writings of Christopher Gadsden*, 166; David Ramsay to William Henry Drayton, 1 September 1779, *DHAR*, 2: 121.

the course of its examination, the committee had discovered many complaints against the American commissioners in Europe that they believed were "highly prejudicial" to the "honor and interests" of America. It therefore urged Congress to replace Benjamin Franklin, Ralph Izard, Arthur Lee, and William Lee with new appointments. Rather than dismiss all the diplomats, however, Congress decided to judge each case individually. When the delegates began discussing the status of Arthur Lee, a "fiery debate" erupted between the Adams-Lee junto and the Deaneites, who wanted Lee recalled. Many Deane partisans were still enraged by the junto's treatment of the Yankee merchant the previous fall, and eagerly took advantage of this opportunity to attack his nemesis Arthur Lee. Fueling the Deaneites' assault was their conviction that Arthur Lee held anti-Gallican sympathies, a characterization carefully planted in Congress by Deane and especially Gerard, who was anxious to have the Virginian "flushed out" of the foreign service. For this reason, many southerners like Drayton who wanted to cultivate friendly relations with France also supported Lee's recall. The Adams-Lee junto, on the other hand, wanted someone who would protect America's claim to fishing rights off the Canadian coast and believed Lee was just the man they needed.[45]

The Adams-Lee faction fired the first shot in this dispute on April 15 when Samuel Adams declared that he had information from the "highest authority in America" that Arthur Lee "possessed the confidence of the Court of Versailles." Adams refused to name his source, but his phrase "highest authority in America" obviously referred to Gerard. Drayton and William Paca, a Maryland delegate and prominent Deane supporter, were astonished by this pronouncement, especially since they had been led to believe "upon good grounds" that the conduct of Lee was "disgustful" to the French court, "unconciliatory" to its citizens, and "prejudicial" to the "honor & interest" of France. To "precisely ascertain" the accuracy of Adams's declaration, Drayton and Paca applied to Gerard. The French diplomat happily presented the two southern delegates with a letter from the Comte de Vergennes, the minister of foreign affairs at Versailles, to Gerard which included the pregnant

45. *JCC*, 13: 363–7; Storch, "Congressional Politics," 129–45; H. James Henderson, "Congressional Factionalism and the Attempt to Recall Benjamin Franklin," *W&MQ*, 3d. ser., 27 (April 1970): 251; William C. Stinchcombe, *The American Revolution and the French Alliance* (Syracuse: Syracuse University Press, 1969), 66; Louis W. Potts, *Arthur Lee: A Virtuous Revolutionary* (Baton Rouge: Louisiana State University Press, 1981), 228; Rakove, *Beginnings of National Politics*, 256–7; Henderson, *Party Politics*, 200–1.

statement: "I confess to you, that I fear Mr. Lee and those about him." The French minister further informed Drayton and Paca that Arthur Lee's "imprudent conduct" had on several occasions "created the highest disgust" in both the French and Spanish courts, which he believed no longer had "that confidence in the said Commissioner which is necessary to give success to the negotiations of a foreign minister."[46]

Drayton and Paca laid this "decisive information" before Congress on April 30 and urged the body to recall Lee. Failure to do so, they argued, would "prove unconciliatory abroad, ruinous to the public finances at home, & an impediment" to securing American independence. Laurens, who was particularly irritated by Drayton's "illicit practices" with the French minister, made a vigorous but unsuccessful attempt to block discussion of Drayton and Paca's report with parliamentary privileges.[47]

Despite this damning intelligence, Congress voted by the narrowest of margins not to recall Lee. Still, members of the junto were outraged, but not surprised, by Drayton's conduct in this dispute. "I expected W. H. D. would take precisely the part he has," Arthur Lee wrote his brother Richard Henry, "his character is too much of the Catilianarian cast for him to remain long among honorable men. Turbidus, inquietus, atrox—he should be always dealt with as one, who, tho' your friend today, may betray you tomorrow." Richard Henry agreed. "Can anything fit more exactly than 'foul, restless, wicked'?" he replied. "No glove ever fitted his hand better than this character does the Man." Drayton and the anti-Lee forces were not so easily vanquished, however. In a cunning move, they provoked public outcry against Lee by publishing Drayton and Paca's incriminating memorandum in newspapers throughout the country, an action that helped pave the way for Lee's recall in late September 1779.[48]

The heated debate over Arthur Lee's fitness to serve in the foreign service rekindled the feud between Drayton and Laurens. Adding fuel to the burning

46. *JCC*, 14: 533–7. See also the Comte de Vergennes to Conrad Alexandre Gerard, 26 October 1778, in Meng, *Despatches and Instructions*, 538; Paca and Drayton to Congress, 30 April 1779, *LDC*, 12: 410–1; Storch, "Congressional Politics," 133–4.

47. Paca and Drayton to Congress, 30 April 1779, and Henry Laurens's Notes of Debates, 30 April 1779, in *LDC*, 12: 410–1, 408–9.

48. Arthur Lee to Richard Henry Lee, in Burnett, *Letters of Members*, 4: 423 n; Richard Henry Lee to Henry Laurens, 5 September 1779, Henry Laurens Papers, SCHS; Stinchcombe, *American Revolution*, 71–2; Potts, *Arthur Lee*, 236–7; Storch, "Congressional Politics," 136–7; James Lovell to Samuel Adams, 12 August 1779, *LDC*, 13: 363.

quarrel was the involvement of both men in the bitter conflict between General Benedict Arnold, military governor of Philadelphia, and local civil authorities, who were upset with the general for his close association with known loyalists, his questionable financial dealings, and his unwillingness to cooperate with them in the operation of the city. In early January 1779 the executive council of Pennsylvania filed eight charges against Arnold that collectively accused him of using his office for personal gain. The charges were eventually brought to the attention of Congress, which ruled that there was insufficient evidence to support six of the allegations. The Pennsylvania council was upset with this ruling, and imprudently published a protest to Congress's decision and audaciously asked the house for a joint conference between the two bodies to "remove . . . all grounds of discontent."[49]

As with so many previous issues, the congressional delegates divided into opposing factions on this controversy, particularly the question whether the house should meet with the Pennsylvania authorities. The Adams-Lee group, including Henry Laurens, supported such a meeting, while Drayton, Gouverneur Morris, Edward Langworthy, and John Penn opposed it because the council, by publishing its complaint, had "directly and positively appealed to the Public & stand as the accusers of Congress to their constituents"; therefore, the delegates could not "consistently and with the honor & dignity of Congress" confer with that body until it had "made reparation." Drayton supported this reasoning and further "talked of the duty of every man to know & to feel his own dignity." By making such an argument, Drayton and his cohorts had cleverly switched the focus of the debate from Arnold's conduct to Congress's honor and dignity. However, Henry Laurens suspected "Party spirit of the most dangerous tendency," not congressional honor, as a more likely explanation for the division in the house. It appeared to him that virtually all anti-Arnold delegates belonged to the eastern (or Adams-Lee) bloc while the pro-Arnold members were attached to the middle and southern (Deaneite) interest. The former president sensed hypocrisy in the behavior of the latter and acridly noted that the same men who in December had refused to support him in punishing Silas Deane for his "affrontive Publication" involving Congress were now attacking the Pennsylvania council for a similar offense.[50]

---

49. *JCC*, 13: 377.

50. Ibid., 374–8; Henry Laurens's Notes of Debates, 26 March 1779 and 29 March 1779, in *LDC*, 12: 249–50, 260.

Laurens's charge of hypocrisy may have applied to some in the pro-Arnold (or anti-Pennsylvania) faction, but the accusation does not appear to accurately reflect Drayton's role in this controversy. Instead, Drayton's backing of Arnold on this issue probably stemmed less from concurring with the general's case and more from a desire for vengeance against the Pennsylvania council. That local body had first angered Drayton several months earlier with its haughty refusal to comply with the decision made by the Committee of Appeals (of which Drayton was a member) regarding the *Active* case. The Pennsylvania group had further angered the Carolinian when it made several petty charges against his friend Gouverneur Morris. Drayton believed the accusations against Arnold were similarly minor, the product of a hypersensitive body. Drayton therefore may have viewed the Arnold controversy as an opportunity to seek revenge against the Pennsylvania authorities and, as in the *Active* case, affirm the supremacy of Congress's decisions in military matters.

In late March Drayton and John Penn again moved to exclude the Pennsylvania council from the proposed conference, repeating "almost verbatim" their previous arguments on the subject. Hereupon an irate Laurens "intimated" to them the "danger of refusing to confer" with the Pennsylvanians and suggested that the council had "causes to complain of some deficiencies, some delinquencies on the part of Congress." His warnings had the desired effect, as Congress—except Drayton and a few other stalwarts—agreed to meet with the Pennsylvania group. At the April gathering the two sides agreed that the Continental Congress and the military must give "proper regard" for the government of Pennsylvania. Drayton reluctantly swallowed this compromise, perhaps owing to its vague nature, but found unpalatable a proposal ordering General George Washington to convene a court martial to hear the charges against Arnold. Along with John Penn and Edmund Burke, Drayton made several unsuccessful motions to delay the decision indefinitely. Despite these parliamentary maneuverings, Congress resolved that Arnold should be tried by a military court, which found him guilty of violating the articles of war and using military forces for his private use.[51]

Although the Pennsylvanians received much of what they wanted in their meeting with Congress, some were still violently upset with Drayton and others for having taken the opposing stand in the Arnold controversy. In July 1779 two city officials, accompanied by eight Continental soldiers, attempted to break into the residence of Edward Langworthy, a delegate from Georgia

51. Henry Laurens's Notes of Debates, 29 March 1779, *LDC*, 12: 260–1.

and a vocal member of the anti-Pennsylvania faction. The ruffians failed to enter the house and kidnap Langworthy as the Georgian feared, but they did verbally insult the elderly housekeeper and "dangerously wound her in the head." Langworthy informed John Jay, president of the Congress, of the harrowing incident and added that he had learned from "knowledgeable sources" that the same men planned to seize Drayton, Morris, and Deane and "force them to appear before the [Pennsylvania] Committee." Perhaps as a result of Jay's intervention, the alleged kidnapping attempts never occurred. Nevertheless, the existence of such violent threats between local and national leaders reveals the dangerous divisions at the time regarding the federal relationship between Congress and the states, a small yet striking portent of things to come for the young nation.[52]

The feud between Drayton and Laurens did not always revolve around such significant issues. In early April, for example, Laurens became convinced that Drayton had tried to conceal the fact that John Jay, as president of the Continental Congress, had given him some letters from the governor of South Carolina, which Laurens felt the president should have instead delivered to himself as the "eldest & the first named" delegate. That Drayton kept these letters for several days only stoked Laurens's anger. When he confronted his colleague, Drayton answered evasively. Hereupon, Laurens departed "full of contempt for Men capable of so much meanness & mean quibbling."[53]

Laurens got even in early June when he learned that Drayton had "obliterated" several parts of a memorial from Dr. John Morgan after Congress had received it and referred it to a committee. Laurens eagerly brought this indiscretion to the entire group's attention. In his defense, Drayton explained that he had "expunged" some "severe epithets" in order to *"make it go down the better,"* but President Jay replied that the congressman had had no right to "alter a single Iota" from the memorial. When Drayton attempted to further "justify his practice," Laurens quickly cut him short by calling for the order of the day.[54]

The feud between Drayton and Laurens even carried over into the question of how Congress should celebrate the third anniversary of America's

52. Edward Langworthy to John Jay, 25 July 1779, Records of the Continental Congress, M247, reel 98, item 78, vol. 14, pp. 271–3, National Archives and Records Administration.

53. Henry Laurens's Notes on the Conduct of William Henry Drayton, [12 April 1779?], *LDC*, 12: 326.

54. Henry Laurens's Notes of Debates, 3 June 1779, *LDC*, 13: 19–20.

declaration of independence. On June 24 Drayton and Gouverneur Morris proposed that the house chaplain prepare sermons "suitable to the occasion." Congress readily passed this resolution. However, when another delegate moved that President Jay plan an entertainment and celebration for July 5 (July 4 fell on a Sunday), Laurens and thirteen other congressmen objected. Drayton, on the other hand, not only supported this measure, he further aggravated his puritanical associates by urging Congress to also exhibit "certain grand fireworks" on the "glorious anniversary" of American independence. He argued that all ancient and modern nations traditionally celebrated "particular days of festivity." The best example of this, Drayton underscored, was Greece's Olympic Games.

Laurens was astonished that his "Honorable Colleague" could be so joyous while his home state was "bleeding at every vein." The United States of Holland and the Cantons of Switzerland had never indulged in such "expensive feasts" during their fights for independence, he replied. As for the Olympic Games, these and "other fooleries" had "brought on the desolation of Greece." As a countersuggestion, Laurens thought it would be more appropriate for Congress to spend the day "fasting & mourning" instead of participating in "joy & mirth."

"I would have Gentlemen when they talk of history discover that they knew something about it," Drayton smartly answered. The Olympic Games were not created for the celebration of anniversaries, he said, nor did they bring on the ruin of Greece. Rather, they were "calculated for improving bodily strength—to make Men athletic & robust." Laurens was too infuriated with Drayton to think of an appropriate comeback until the next day when he entered in his journal the rhetorical query: "Is drinking Madeira Wine from 5 to 9 o'Clock then sallying out to gaze at fire works, & afterwards returning to Wine again, calculated to make Men athletic and robust?" In the end, Drayton's more popular proposal won out. On July 5 Congress—excluding Laurens and a few other abstemious members—joined local military and civil leaders at the City Tavern for a "very elegant dinner" followed by a "brilliant exhibition" of fireworks.[55]

Less than two weeks later the delegates were witnesses to a bombshell of another sort when Drayton and John Dickinson made one of the most incredible proposals ever introduced on the floor of the Congress: that the group immediately adjourn to Washington's camp to actively participate in

55. Ibid., 2 July 1779, *LDC*, 13: 135–6; *Pennsylvania Packet*, 6 July 1779, supplement.

"such important Operations as shall be judged most expedient for advancing the welfare of these States." This extraordinary motion was in response to a statement made by Gerard on July 12, in which he informed Congress that France wanted the United States to launch a "vigorous and successful campaign" to bring Great Britain to a "proper sense of all the disappointment which [it] shall meet with." Drayton and Dickinson, two men eager for military service and glory—as well as disgusted with the counterproductive political factionalism rampant in the lawmaking body—believed Congress could better promote the American cause by fighting rather than legislating. However, the other congressmen considered their proposal so preposterous that they refused to even address it. "[T]his shews more of valour in those Gentlemen than of the Wisdom & reflection of grave Senators," Laurens privately reflected, "but who can restrain the ardor of fighting Men when an opportunity offers?"[56]

If Drayton could not lead charges against the enemy, he at least wanted to legislate attacks on them. On July 19 he introduced a motion ordering the Continental navy to burn and destroy towns in Great Britain and the British West Indies in retaliation for the enemy's "ravages and devastations" against "defenseless towns" in Connecticut. This time the Congress not only addressed Drayton's proposal but also adopted it.[57]

This was Drayton's last important action in Congress—an appropriate ending to the career of one of America's most aggressive and contentious patriots. Shortly thereafter he came down with a "putrid nervous fever," probably typhus, from which he did not recover. A Philadelphia newspaper reported that Drayton's "sedentary life" and "incessant attention" to congressional business had "insensibly impaired" his health, making him susceptible to diseases. Drayton attended his last session of Congress on August 7. Ten days later he asked to be excused from his service on the Marine Committee. Thereafter, congressional physicians confined Drayton to bed and worked to drain an abscess that had developed on his torso.[58]

One individual not at his bedside at this time was Henry Laurens. Not

56. *JCC*, 14: 835–6, 830; Henry Laurens to John Laurens, 17 July 1779, "Correspondence between Hon. Henry Laurens and His Son John, 1777–1780," *SCHM* 6 (October 1905): 146. Dickinson would soon serve as a brigadier general in the Delaware militia.

57. *JCC*, 14: 851–2.

58. Jesse Root to Oliver Ellsworth, 8 September 1779, *LDC*, 13: 478; *Pennsylvania Packet*, 31 September 1779; Drayton, *Memoirs*, 1: xxvi; *JCC*, 14: 976–7.

until August 31, when he learned that Drayton was deathly ill, could Laurens put aside his resentment and ask to visit his sick colleague. Drayton, who knew he was dying, welcomed him. Laurens recorded the emotional death-bed reconciliation: "When I approached his Bed he clasped my hand & wept affectingly. After recovering his voice he signified his great satisfaction at seeing me & particularly requested I would write a state of his case to Mrs. Drayton—the Physicians think him dangerously Ill, say he may live one or two weeks longer."[59] Actually, just four days later, at one o'clock on the morning of September 4, William Henry Drayton died.

Congress ordered Henry Laurens, John Mathews, and Cornelius Harnett to superintend Drayton's funeral and administer his affairs. Unfortunately for historians, one of their acts included destroying "many valuable papers" Drayton had collected for his history of the Revolution because they alleg-edly contained "many secrets of State" which the administrators thought should not "fall into the hands of his family." One scholar has speculated that Laurens ordered the destruction of these papers because they may have in-cluded "anti-Laurens sentiments," but there is no evidence to substantiate this assertion. Fortunately for posterity, though, Drayton's papers relating to South Carolina's revolution escaped this "general ruin." These documents, later arranged, edited, and published by son John Drayton, remain one of the most valuable sources on the early rebellion in the Palmetto State.[60]

Because embalming was not commonly practiced in America during the eighteenth century, Congress ordered Drayton's remains quickly buried in the Christ Church (Episcopal) cemetery in Philadelphia. Accordingly, at 6:00 P.M. on the evening of September 4, the Congress, members of the Pennsyl-vania government, and a number of "strangers of distinction," gathered at the church to pay their final respects. Reverend William White, rector of Christ Church and one of the congressional chaplains, presided over the fu-neral. Unfortunately Reverend White's eulogy has not been preserved, but perhaps it resembled one published in a Charleston newspaper the following month, which reads:

> The death of the Hon. William Henry Drayton . . . at so early a period of
> life is very much regretted by all his countrymen, but exceedingly so, by those

59. Henry Laurens to Richard Henry Lee, 31 August 1779, *LDC*, 13: 434.

60. *JCC*, 15: 1020; William M. Dabney, "Drayton and Laurens in the Continental Con-gress," *SCHM* 60 (April 1959): 81–2; Drayton, *Memoirs*, 1: vii; Solomon Lutnick, "William Henry Drayton's *Memoirs*," in *The Colonial Legacy*, ed. Lawrence H. Leder (New York: Harper & Row, 1973): 207.

that knew him well. He had a head to contrive, a temper to persuade, and a hand to execute plans of the most extensive utility to his country; few men possessed an equal knowledge of the human heart, or a superior vigour of soul. His enterprizing great mind encouraged him to attempt, what, to the cold and phlegmatic, appeared impossible; and his attempts were generally crowned with success. By his death, the American States have lost one of their principal supporters, and posterity may regret, that his early fate prevented him from exerting his great Talents towards organizing this new world into a great, happy, and flourishing empire.[61]

Indeed, it is interesting to speculate on the impact Drayton might have played in erecting the nascent nation had he not died in the prime of life. His strong opinions on the Revolution's purpose, his many valuable talents, his enormous energy, and his dream of immortality all suggest that he would have had a considerable influence on the direction of the young republic.

61. *JCC*, 15: 1020; *Pennsylvania Packet*, 31 September 1779; *Gazette of the State of South Carolina*, 13 October 1779.

REQUIEM FOR A REVOLUTIONARY

William Henry Drayton's untimely death in September 1779 at the age of thirty-seven robbed him of not only the opportunity to help shape the young republic but also the joy of raising his two children and watching them become productive citizens. Sadly, Dorothy Drayton was also deprived of this pleasure less than a year later when she succumbed to an unknown illness in the summer of 1780. She was thirty-three. Her two orphaned children, twelve-year-old John and five-year-old Mary, lived the remainder of their childhood with various relatives and friends, including their maternal grandmother, Mary Golightly, and later with Arthur Middleton's family. Of the two children, less is known about Mary, whose recorded life, like those of most eighteenth-century women, can be summed up in a few sentences. She married Thomas Parker, scion of a respectable South Carolina family and a man of "great learning and respectability in the law." The couple had five children, one of whom they named William Henry.[1]

Much more is known of John Drayton, who continued the family's tradition of distinguished public service. He read law in the office of his father's schoolmate and friend Charles Cotesworth Pinckney. After six years of applying himself "closely to the study of Law," John Drayton was admitted to the Charleston bar and opened a legal practice in 1788. Steering him toward the legal profession was his desire to overturn his grandfather John's "iniquitous, confused and contradictory" last will and testament, which disinherited his

---

1. John Drayton, *Carolinian Florist*, xxxii.

father. It galled him that his uncle Charles, who "did not exert himself much in his behalf" following the death of his parents, had come to inherit Drayton Hall, which he considered to be his father's, and therefore his own, birthright. Perhaps fueling the younger Drayton's bitterness was his uncle's "constant trimming on both sides" during the Revolution, a cause for which his father had given his life. Charles Drayton had served in the army until the fall of Charleston in 1780, but following British occupation of the city he took the occupiers' protection and tried to remain neutral. Although relatives cursed Charles Drayton for "such politics & such principles" and believed that he "deserv[ed] to suffer," his neutrality did not appear to harm him either financially or politically. Following the Revolution the government did not amerce his estate, and voters elected him to several state offices, including assemblyman, senator, lieutenant governor, and delegate to the state convention that ratified the Constitution.[2]

However, John Drayton was not about to let his "fence-riding" uncle off so easily. In 1793 he attempted to overturn his grandfather's will and "claim his inheritance as heir at Law" by filing a suit against his uncles Charles, Glen, and Thomas, who served as executors of the patriarch's estate. Although John Drayton failed to break his grandfather's will and obtain Drayton Hall from Charles, the court did award him one-fourth of his grandfather's property and instructed the executors to pay their nephew "a fair and reasonable sum of money" for the use of this land from the time they obtained it as well as "a reasonable allowance" for the work performed by the slaves on those plantations. This legal decision proved financially disastrous for the three uncles, reducing them from gentlemen of "considerable substance" to gentlemen of "limited means."[3]

On the other hand, the money and property John Drayton received from the ruling provided him with the financial independence to become active in public service. His interest in civic affairs had been encouraged by his late father, who John claimed had brought "him forward by gradual advances for a knowledge of public affairs; fondly hoping, that one day, he might be useful

2. Ibid., xxix; Charles C. Pinckney to Arthur Middleton, 5 January 1782, in Barnwell, "Correspondence of Arthur Middleton," 61; Edward Rutledge to Arthur Middleton, 14 February 1782, ibid., 5; Edward Rutledge to Arthur Middleton, 26 February 1782, ibid., 8; Edward Rutledge to Arthur Middleton, 14 April 1782, ibid., 12.

3. Henry William DeSaussure, *Reports of Cases Argued and Determined in the Court of Chancery of the State of South Carolina* 4 vols (Columbia, S.C.: Cline & Hines, 1817), 1: 250; Griffin, "Eighteenth Century Draytons," 349.

to his country."[4] John's political achievements equaled and perhaps surpassed those of his father, who certainly would have been proud of his son's many accomplishments. While still in his twenties and early thirties, John Drayton served as warden of Charleston in 1789, as a member of the South Carolina House of Representatives from 1792 to 1798, and as lieutenant governor from 1798 to 1800. Upon the death of Governor Edward Rutledge on January 23, 1800, thirty-three-year-old John Drayton became governor of South Carolina on an interim basis until his election to a full two-year term in December 1800. As governor, he actively promoted the establishment of South Carolina College (later the University of South Carolina) in Columbia to advance public learning and to further unify the different sections of the state. Following his term as governor, he served as a warden of Charleston and one of its representatives in the state senate until 1808, when he again won election as governor. In 1812 President James Madison appointed him federal judge of the U.S. District Court in South Carolina, a post he held until his death in 1822.

Although John Drayton had a long and illustrious career as a politician and jurist, he is perhaps most remembered for his achievements as a writer and botanist. In 1794 he published his *Letters Written during a Tour through the Northern and Eastern States of America*, which critically compared South Carolina's educational system with that in Massachusetts and found many shortcomings in the former. John Drayton used his findings as evidence of the need for an institution of higher learning in the state. Even more influential was his 1802 publication *A View of South Carolina, as Respecting Her Natural and Civil Concerns*, a work modeled after Thomas Jefferson's *Notes on Virginia*. In it, John Drayton demonstrated his extensive knowledge of botany and skill as an artist with his inclusion of many watercolor drawings. The work was translated into several languages and was favorably reviewed throughout Europe. The recognition received from this work earned him membership into the Royal Society of Sciences in Germany in 1804. In the last years of his life Drayton devoted himself to compiling and editing his father's papers, which he published in 1821 in two volumes under the title *Memoirs of the American Revolution, from Its Commencement to the Year 1776, Inclusive; as Relating to the State of South Carolina and Occasionally Referring to the States of North Carolina and Georgia*. This compilation, which contains a lengthy biographical sketch of William Henry Drayton, is as much a history of the Revolution in South Carolina as it is a lasting tribute to his father's many contributions to the epochal event.

4. John Drayton, *Carolinian Florist*, xxviii.

*   *   *

Without exception, no other individual had as great an impact on South Carolina's rebellion as did William Henry Drayton. No other South Carolinian pushed harder for independence or labored more to preserve it. No other local patriot held as much power or wielded it with as much vigor. No other South Carolinian, finally, served the American cause in as many official and unofficial roles. As the leading Whig polemicist in the lower South, Drayton led the forces for independence in the region with rousingly revolutionary speeches and publications that instilled disgust within the people for the king, Parliament, and placemen while inspiring confidence within the public for the American cause. Particularly important were his judicial charges and letter to the Continental Congress, which forcefully argued for Americans' inherent rights and denied parliamentary authority over the colonies. The patriotic emblems and mottos he designed for both the provincial currency and the state seal helped to reinforce these ideas within the populace.

But Drayton sought to do more than merely open the people's eyes to the efficacy of independence; he also desperately wanted to silence the opposition and sway the indecisive. To that end, Drayton exercised his broad powers and enormous energy, intellect, and guile to successfully suppress loyalism both in Charleston and the backcountry. In the same manner, Drayton often outmaneuvered his conservative colleagues to push them toward more warlike action. Drayton certainly did more than his share to prepare the province for a clash with the mother country in his recruitment of soldiers from North Carolina and Virginia, his arming and manning of warships in the fledgling provincial navy, his designing of the plan for Charleston's defense, and his acquisition of valuable arms and ammunition. As if this was not enough, Drayton also helped to bolster the American cause in Georgia. As a result of Drayton's numerous accomplishments, South Carolinians were much better prepared than they would have been otherwise for the painful break with the mother country and the subsequent armed conflict.

Drayton's influence extended beyond simply pushing his fellow South Carolinians toward independence and preparing them for war. He also helped shape the purpose of the local rebellion by exercising the significant influence he held in all three branches of the state government. Unlike the often radical means he used in achieving and preserving independence, however, Drayton's objectives for the Revolution were quite conservative—an attitude shared by most of the South Carolina elite. In joining the American cause, Drayton did not seek to destroy artificial privilege, to promote social

mobility, or to make way for the "natural aristocracy." In addition to perceived unconstitutional and despotic British measures against America, another motivating factor compelling him to switch allegiances was a desire to
perpetuate the status quo by protecting the local gentry's domination of political and social affairs from perceived threats by both the placemen and the
people. This objective is evident in Drayton's proposal to the Continental
Congress in 1774 for the creation of a permanent governing council in each
province comprised of local men of wealth. Although that body did not adopt
the Carolinian's suggestion, local Whig leaders managed to achieve a similar
objective by placing enormously high property qualifications for officeholding in the 1778 state constitution, of which Drayton was allegedly both
"father and mother." Likewise, when the Continental Congress proposed a
federal charter circumscribing much of the state's political, military, and economic power, Drayton felt compelled to create an alternate plan of union
that preserved much of the local government's (i.e., the elite's) authority.

However, Drayton's desire to maintain the social and political status quo
was superceded by an even stronger desire to ensure American victory against
Britain. He was therefore willing to allow the lower orders a limited number
of additional rights and opportunities in exchange for their support of the
Revolution. With this ulterior motive in mind, he selected artisans to serve
on Revolutionary committees and urged increased political representation
for the backcountry, religious equality for followers of the dissenting faiths,
and freedom to slaves willing to fight for the American cause. Although
Drayton feared that giving the people additional liberties might encourage
them to demand an equal share in government, he felt that such potentially
threatening measures were necessary in order to avoid even greater evils
under British rule.

Despite the passage of these democratic measures, the Revolution in
South Carolina remained a "remarkably conservative" movement with only
minor institutional changes. Indeed, David Ramsay, a participant in the rebellion, argued that the transition from the status of colony to that of sovereign state was "marked by a conscious attempt to avoid change."[5] This allowed the elite unfettered dominance over all aspects of South Carolina life
through the remainder of the century. It is somewhat ironic—and perhaps
sad—that Drayton, who worked so hard to realize this goal, did not live to
fully enjoy the product of his labor. Yet for at least the last five years of his
life Drayton basked in more power and prestige than he ever dreamed of
achieving before the Revolution. Thus, in the final analysis, the Revolution

5. Weir, *Colonial South Carolina*, 332–3; Ramsay, *History of South Carolina*, 1: 152.

perhaps had a greater impact on Drayton's life than he had on it. Among many other things, Drayton's involvement in the Revolution can therefore further illuminate the self-aggrandizing agenda of our founding fathers.

It is partly this fact that has influenced some historians to label Drayton an "ambitious and unscrupulous politician . . . completely lacking in ideological, even moral principles," a Whig with "no commitment to the cause of Independence beyond the hope that it would further his own career."[6] True, Drayton sought to protect the elites' status and influence in politics and society, but such an acerbic assault on his motivations, convictions, and goals is both unfair and inaccurate. Drayton's 1774 constitutional arguments for a reorganization of the British Empire and his later arguments for independence were not propaganda designed to hide narrow self-interest, as some scholars have suggested. They were meant, in part, to explain why control of the reins of local government by local leaders was essential for the protection of Americans' liberty and for effective management of the colonies. Like many of his class, Drayton believed that an independent, educated, and propertied native elite with a major economic stake in the welfare of the province were best able to govern. Although arguably a self-serving rationalization, patrician dominance of politics and society and the protection of property and liberty were inseparable in the eyes of most lowcountry elite. Thus when the home government threatened the elites' political control, undermining effective administration of the province by appointing inept, sycophantic placemen to the most desirable provincial offices and imperiling Americans' inherited rights by enacting seemingly unconstitutional measures against the colonies, Drayton felt compelled to offer a settlement that would remove the placemen from power, repeal the despotic Intolerable Acts, and correct the constitutional and institutional differences between the colonies and the mother country. When Britain refused to support the provincial elites and rejected America's calls for a redress of grievances, he felt no alternative available but to abjure the Crown. In the final analysis, then, a desire for effective local government and protection of Americans' inherited rights, coupled with pure self-interest, explains Drayton's motivation in first opposing parliamentary supremacy and later supporting the quest for independence. His mixed motives in the American cause therefore help explain the mixed consequences of South Carolina's rebellion.

6. S. R. Matchett, " 'Unanimity, Order, and Regularity': The Political Culture of South Carolina in the Era of the Revolution" (Ph.D. diss., University of Sydney [Australia], 1980), 406; Dabney and Dargan, *William Henry Drayton*, xii.

BIBLIOGRAPHY

PRIMARY SOURCES

Manuscripts

Charleston County Library, Charleston, S.C.
    Miscellaneous Records of Charleston County
Clements Library, University of Michigan, Ann Arbor
    Henry Clinton Papers
    Thomas Gage Papers
    Miscellaneous Manuscripts
    Nathaniel Greene Papers
    Shelburne Papers
Drayton Hall, Charleston
    Charles Drayton Papers
Earl of Dalhousie, Brechin Castle, Brechin, Angus
    Dalhousie Muniments: Papers Relating to the Drayton Family
Historical Society of Pennsylvania, Philadelphia
    William Henry Drayton, "History of the Confederation."
    Gratz Collection, Old Congress
Kendall Whaling Museum, Sharon, Mass.
    Henry Laurens Papers
Library of Congress
    James Grant Papers
National Archives and Records Administration
    Records of the Continental Congress

National Library of Scotland, Edinburgh
  Erskine Murray Correspondence
New York Public Library
  American Loyalist Transcripts
  John Bowie Papers
Shrubland Hall, Coddenham, Suffolk, Ipswich, U.K.
  Middleton Papers
South Carolina Department of Archives and History, Columbia
  British Public Records Office Relating to South Carolina
  Charleston County Deeds
  Charleston County Inventories
  Charleston County Memorials
  Charleston County Wills
  Colonial Memorials
  Colonial Plats
  Council Journals
  Court of Common Pleas
  Charles Garth Letterbook
  Robert Gibbes Collection
  Journals of the Commons House of Assembly
  William Lowndes Papers
  Marriage Settlements
  Miscellaneous Records of South Carolina
  Renunciation of Dower
  Revolutionary Manuscripts
  Royal Land Grants
South Carolina Historical Society, Charleston
  Drayton Family Papers
  John Drayton, "History of the Drayton Family."
  Thomas Elfe Account Book
  John Lewis Gervais Letters
  Henry Laurens Papers
  Manigault Family Papers
  Peter Manigault Letterbook
  Pinckney Family Papers
South Caroliniana Library, University of South Carolina, Columbia
  William Henry Drayton Papers
  Christopher Gadsden Diary
  Christopher Gadsden Miscellany
  Oliver Hart Papers
  James Glen Papers

Joseph Kershaw Papers
Henry Laurens Papers
Manigault Family Papers
Charles Pinckney Papers
Simms-Laurens Collection
South Carolina Provincial Congress Papers
William Tennent Papers
Southern Historical Collection, University of North Carolina, Chapel Hill
William Lowndes Papers
University of South Carolina, Columbia
British Public Records Office, Colonial Office, Series 5

Printed Government Records

Beatson, Robert, ed. *Naval and Military Memoirs of Great Britain.* London: J. Strachan, 1790.

Clark, William B., William J. Morgan, and Michael J. Crawford, eds. *Naval Documents of the American Revolution.* 10 vols. to date. Washington, D.C.: United States Government Printing Office, 1964–present.

Cooper, Thomas, and David J. McCord, eds. *Statutes at Large of South Carolina.* 10 vols. Columbia: A.S. Johnston, 1836–1841.

Davies, K. G., ed. *Documents of the American Revolution, 1770–1783.* 20 vols. Dublin: Irish University Press, 1972–1979.

DeSaussure, Henry William. *Reports of Cases Argued and Determined in the Court of Chancery of South Carolina.* 2 vols. Philadelphia: R. H. Small, 1854.

Edwards, Edele, ed., *Journals of the Privy Council, 1783–1789.* Columbia: University of South Carolina Press, 1971.

Ford, Worthington C., ed. *Journals of the Continental Congress, 1774–1789.* 34 vols. Washington, D.C.: Government Printing Office, 1904–1937.

Gregorie, Anne K., ed. *Records of the Court of Chancery of South Carolina, 1671–1779.* Washington, D.C.: American Historical Association, 1950.

Hazard, Samuel, ed. *Pennsylvania Archives.* First Series. Philadelphia: Joseph Severns, 1853.

Hemphill, W. Edwin, and Wylma Wates, eds. *Extracts from the Journals of the Provincial Congresses of South Carolina, 1775–1776.* Columbia: University of South Carolina Press, 1960.

Hemphill, W. Edwin, Wylma Wates, and R. Nicholas Olsberg, eds. *Journals of the General Assembly and House of Representatives, 1776–1780.* Columbia, University of South Carolina Press, 1970.

Journal of the Commissioners for Trade and Plantations, 1768–1775. 14 vols. London: Her Majesty's Stationery Office, 1920–1938.

"Journal of the Council of Safety for the Province of South Carolina, 1775." South
Carolina Historical Society *Collections*, vol. 2. Charleston: South Carolina Historical Society, 1858.

"Journal of the Second Council of Safety." South Carolina Historical Society *Collections*. Vol. 3. Charleston: South Carolina Historical Society, 1859.

Journals of the House of Commons, 1547–1874.

Journals of the House of Lords, 1509–1829.

"Minutes of the Executive Council, May 7–October 14, 1777." *Georgia Historical
Quarterly* 34 (March 1950): 19–35.

"Miscellaneous Papers of the General Committee, Secret Committee and Provincial
Congress, 1775." *South Carolina Historical and Genealogical Magazine* 8 (July 1907):
132–50; (October 1907): 189–94.

"Papers of the First Council of Safety of the Revolutionary Party in South Carolina,
June–November 1775." *South Carolina Historical and Genealogical Magazine* 1 (January 1900): 41–75; (April 1900): 119–35; (July 1900): 183–205; (October 1900):
279–310.

The Parliamentary History of England from the Earliest Period to the Year 1803. 36 vols.
London: T. C. Hansard, 1806–1820.

Saunders, William L., and Walter Clark, eds. *The Colonial and State Records of North
Carolina, 1662–1790.* 26 vols. Raleigh, N.C.: P. M. Hale, 1886–1907.

Simpson, William. *The Practical Justice of the Peace and the Parish-Officer, of His Majesty's Province of South Carolina.* Charles Town: Robert Wells, 1761. Reprint. New
York: Arno Press, 1972.

Thorpe, Francis N., ed. *The Federal and State Constitutions.* 7 vols. Washington: Government Printing Office, 1909.

Letters, Memoirs, Pamphlets, Travel Accounts, Collections

A Backsettler. *Some Fugitive Thoughts on a Letter Signed Freeman, Addressed to the High
Court of Congress in Philadelphia.* Charlestown: 1774.

Bargar, B. D., ed. "Charles Town Loyalism in 1775: The Secret Reports of Alexander
Innes." *South Carolina Historical Magazine* 63 (July 1962): 125–36.

Barnwell, Joseph, ed. "Correspondence of Charles Garth." *South Carolina Historical
Magazine* 31 (April 1930): 124–53.

Barnwell, Joseph, ed. "Correspondence of the Honourable Arthur Middleton." *South
Carolina Historical Magazine* 27 (January 1926): 1–29; (April 1926): 51–80.

Bennett, John, contributor. "Charleston in 1774 as Described by an English Trav-
eler." *South Carolina Historical Magazine* 47 (July 1946): 179–80.

Burnett, Edmund C., ed. *Letters of Members of the Continental Congress.* 8 vols. Washington, D.C.: Carnegie Institute, 1921–1936.

Conway, Moncure, ed. *The Writings of Thomas Paine.* New York: G. P. Putnam's Sons,
1984.

"Correspondence between Hon. Henry Laurens and His Son John, 1777–1780." *South Carolina Historical and Genealogical Magazine* 6 (October 1905): 138–60.

Dalrymple, Sir John. *The Address of the People of Great Britain to the Inhabitants of America.* London: T. Cadell, 1775.

Historical Manuscripts Commission. *The Manuscripts of the Earl of Dartmouth.* 3 vols. London: Her Majesty's Stationery Office, 1895.

Davis, Robert S., ed. "A Georgia Loyalist's Perspective on the American Revolution: The Letters of Dr. Thomas Taylor." *Georgia Historical Quarterly* 81 (spring 1997): 118–38.

Drayton, John. *The Carolinian Florist of Governor John Drayton of South Carolina.* Charleston, 1798. Reprint. South Caroliniana Library of the University of South Carolina, 1943.

———. *Memoirs of the American Revolution as Relating to the State of South Carolina.* 2 vols. Charleston: A. E. Miller, 1821. Reprint. New York: New York Times & Arno Press, 1969.

Drayton, William Henry. *A Charge on the Rise of the American Empire, Delivered by the Hon. William Henry Drayton, Esq., Chief Justice of South Carolina to the Grand Jury for the District of Charleston.* Charleston: David Bruce, 1776.

———. *The Genuine Spirit of Tyranny, Exemplified in the Conduct of the Commissioners Sent by the King of Great Britain, to Bully, Delude or Bribe, the Inhabitants of the American States Out of their Freedom and Property.* Poughkeepsie, N.Y.: John Holt, 1778.

———. *The Letters of Freeman & c.,* London: 1771.

———. *A Letter from Freeman of South Carolina to the Deputies of North America Assembled in the High Court of Congress at Philadelphia.* Charleston: Peter Timothy, 1774.

———. *Speech to the Assembly, 20 January 1778.* Charleston: David Bruce, 1778.

———. *To His Honor John Adams Treutlan, Esquire, Governor and Commander in Chief of the State of Georgia. . . .* Charleston: David Bruce, 1777.

———. *To Their Excellencies Richard Viscount Howe, Admiral; and William Howe, Esq., General; of His Britannick Majesty's Forces in America, 1776.* Charleston: David Bruce, 1776.

Fenhagen, Mary Pringle, ed. "Letters and Will of Robert Pringle (1702–1776)." *South Carolina Historical Magazine* 50 (July 1949): 144–55.

Fitzpatrick, John C., ed. *The Writings of George Washington.* 37 vols. Washington, D.C.: United States Government Printing Office, 1931–1940.

Force, Peter, ed. *American Archives: Consisting of a Collection of Authentick Records . . . 1774–1776.* 4th ser., 6 vols; 5th ser., 3 vols. Washington, D.C.: M. St. Clair Clarke and Peter Force, 1837–1853.

Fortesque, Sir John, ed. *The Correspondence of King George III.* 6 vols. London: Mac-Millan, 1927–1928.

Garden, Alexander. *Anecdotes of the Revolutionary War, with Sketches of Character of Distinguished Persons.* Charleston: A. E. Miller, 1822.

Gibbes, Robert Wilson, ed. *Documentary History of the American Revolution: Consisting of Letters and Papers Relating to the Contest for Liberty, Chiefly in South Carolina.* 3 vols. New York: D. Appleton, 1853–1857. Reprint. Spartanburg, S.C.: The Reprint Co., 1972.

Greene, Jack P., ed. *The Nature of Colony Constitution: Two Pamphlets on the Wilkes Fund Controversy in South Carolina by Sir Egerton Leigh and Arthur Lee.* Columbia: University of South Carolina Press, 1970.

Hamer, Philip M., George C. Rogers, and David Chesnutt, eds. *The Papers of Henry Laurens.* 16 vols. Columbia: University of South Carolina Press, 1961–2000.

Hawes, Lilla M. "The Papers of Lachlan McIntosh, 1774–1779." Georgia Historical Society *Collections.* Vol. 12. Savannah: Georgia Historical Society, 1957.

Hotten, John C., ed. *The Original Lists of Persons of Quality . . . Who Went from Great Britain to the American Plantations, 1660–1700.* New York: Empire State Books, 1874.

Hutchinson, Orlando, ed. *Diary and Letters of His Excellency Thomas Hutchinson.* 2 vols. London: Sampson et al., 1883.

Johnson, Joseph. *Traditions and Reminiscences of the American Revolution in the South.* Charleston: Walker and James, 1851. Reprint. Spartanburg, S.C.: The Reprint Co., 1972.

Jones, E. A., ed. *The Journal of Alexander Chesney, A South Carolina Loyalist in the Revolution and After.* Ohio State University *Bulletin* 30 (October 1921). Reprint. Greenville, S.C.: A Press, 1981.

Jones, Newton B. "Writings of the Reverend William Tennent, 1740–1777." *South Carolina Historical Magazine* 61 (October 1960): 189–209.

Kepner, Frances R., ed. "A British View of the Siege of Charleston, 1776." *Journal of Southern History* 11 (February 1945): 93–103.

Klingberg, Frank J., ed. *Carolina Chronicle: The Papers of Commissary Gideon Johnston, 1707–1716.* Berkeley: University of California Press, 1946.

"Charles Lee Papers." New York Historical Society *Collections.* Vol. 4. New York: New York Historical Society, 1873.

"Letters from Henry Laurens to His Son John Laurens, 1773–1776." *South Carolina Historical and Genealogical Magazine* 5 (April 1904): 69–81.

"Letters of the Honorable Richard Hutson." *Charleston City Year Book* (1895): 313–25.

"Letters of Joseph Clay, Merchant of Savannah, 1776–1793." Georgia Historical Society *Collections.* Savannah: Morning News, 1913.

"Letters of Thomas Newe from South Carolina, 1682." *American Historical Review* 12 (January 1907): 322–7.

Malmesbury, Third Earl., ed. *Diaries and Correspondence of James Harris, First Earl of Malmesbury.* 4 vols. London: Richard Bentley, 1844.

Mathews, Maurice. "A Contemporary View of Carolina in 1680." *South Carolina Historical Magazine* 55 (July 1954): 153–9.

Meng, John J., ed. *Despatches and Instructions of Conrad Alexander Gerard, 1778–1780: Correspondence of the First French Minister to the United States with the Comte de Vergennes*. Baltimore: Johns Hopkins University Press, 1939.

Merrens, H. Roy., ed. *The South Carolina Scene: Contemporary Views, 1697–1774*. Columbia: University of South Carolina Press, 1977.

Merrens, H. Roy, ed. "A View of Coastal South Carolina in 1778: The Journal of Ebenezer Hazard." *South Carolina Historical Magazine* 73 (October 1972): 177–93.

Morison, Samuel E. *Sources and Documents Illustrating the American Revolution, 1764–1788, and the Formation of the Federal Constitution*. 2d. ed. Oxford, U.K.: Clarendon Press, 1929.

Moore, Frank, ed. *American Eloquence: A Collection of Speeches and Addresses, By the Most Eminent Orators of America with Biographical Sketches and Illustrative Notes*. 2 vols. New York: D. Appleton, 1857.

Moultrie, William. *Memoirs of the American Revolution, So Far as It Related to the States of North and South Carolina, and Georgia*. 2 vols. New York: David Longworthy, 1802. Reprint. New York: Arno Press, 1968.

Niles, Hezekiah, comp. *Principles and Acts of the Revolution in America*. Baltimore: William Niles, 1822. Reprint. New York: Burth Franklin, 1971.

O'Donnell, James H. III, ed. "A Loyalist View of the Drayton-Tennent-Hart Mission to the Upcountry." *South Carolina Historical Magazine* 67 (January 1966): 15–28.

Pinckney, Elise, ed. *The Letterbook of Eliza Lucas Pinckney, 1739–1762*. Chapel Hill: University of North Carolina Press, 1972.

———. "Letters of Eliza Lucas Pinckney, 1768–1782." *South Carolina Historical Magazine* 76 (July 1975): 143–70.

Ramsay, David. *History of the American Revolution*. 2 vols. Philadelphia: R. Aitken, 1789. Reprint. Indianapolis: Liberty Classics, 1990.

———. *History of the Revolution of South Carolina from a British Province to an Independent State*. 2 vols. Trenton: N.J.: Isaac Collins, 1785.

———. *History of South Carolina, from Its First Settlement in 1670 to the Year 1808*. 2 vols. Charleston: D. Langworth, 1809.

Salley, Alexander S., Jr., ed. *Documents Relating to the History of South Carolina during the Revolutionary War*. Columbia: State Co., 1908.

———, ed. *Narratives of Early Carolina 1650–1708*. New York: Charles Scribner's Sons, 1911.

Salley, Alexander S., Jr., and D. Huger Smith, eds. *Register of St. Andrews Parish, South Carolina 1754–1810*. Charleston: Colonial Dames of America, 1927. Reprint. Columbia: University of South Carolina Press, 1971.

Smith, Paul H., ed. *Letters of Delegates to Congress 1774–1789*. 24 vols. to date. Washington, D.C.: Library of Congress, 1976–.

"South Carolina Gleanings in England." *South Carolina Historical and Genealogical Magazine* 8 (October 1907): 211–9.

Taylor, Robert J., Gregg L. Lint, and Celeste Walker, eds. *The Papers of John Adams.* Cambridge, Mass.: Belknap Press, 1983.

Walsh, Richard., ed. *The Writings of Christopher Gadsden.* Columbia: University of South Carolina Press, 1966.

"Warren-Adams Letters." 2 vols. Massachusetts Historical Society *Collections* 72 and 73. Boston: Massachusetts Historical Society, 1917–1925.

Webber, Mabel L., ed. "Abstracts from the Records of the Court of Ordinary, 1764–1771." *South Carolina Historical and Genealogical Magazine* 35 (January 1934): 25–8.

————, ed. "Peter Manigault's Letters." *South Carolina Historical and Genealogical Magazine* 33 (January 1932): 55–62.

————, ed. "Register of St. Andrews Parish, Berkeley County, South Carolina 1719–1774." *South Carolina Historical and Genealogical Magazine* 14 (January 1913): 20–35.

————, ed. "The Thomas Elfe Account Book, 1765–1775." *South Carolina Historical and Genealogical Magazine* 35 (April 1934): 58–73; 39 (April 1938): 83–90; (July 1938): 134–42; 40 (July 1939): 81–6.

Weir, Robert M., ed. *The Letters of Freeman, Etc.: Essays on the Nonimportation Movement in South Carolina.* Collected by William Henry Drayton. Columbia: University of South Carolina Press, 1977.

Wharton, Francis B., ed. *The Revolutionary Diplomatic Correspondence of the United States.* 6 vols. Washington, D.C.: Government Printing Office, 1889.

Newspapers

Gazette of the State of South Carolina
Gentleman's Magazine (London)
Lloyd's Evening Post and British Chronicle
Pennsylvania Evening Post
Pennsylvania Gazette
Pennsylvania Packet
Publick Advertiser (London)
Remembrancer (London)
South Carolina and American Gazette
South Carolina and American General Gazette
South Carolina Gazette
South Carolina Gazette and Country Journal
Virginia Gazette

SECONDARY SOURCES

Books

Ackerman, Robert K. *South Carolina Colonial Land Policies.* Columbia: University of South Carolina Press, 1977.

Alden, John R. *General Charles Lee: Traitor or Patriot?* Baton Rouge: Louisiana State University Press, 1951.

————. *John Stuart and the Southern Colonial Frontier: A Study of Indian Relations, War, Trade, and the Land Problems in the Southern Wilderness, 1754–1775.* Ann Arbor: University of Michigan Press, 1944.

Ammerman, David. *In the Common Cause: American Response to the Coercive Acts of 1774.* Charlottesville: University Press of Virginia, 1974.

Bailyn, Bernard. *The Ideological Origins of the American Revolution.* Cambridge, Mass.: Harvard University Press, 1967.

Barker, G. F., and Alan H. Stenning, comps. *The Record of Old Westminster: A Biographical List of All Who Are Known to Have Been Educated at Westminster School.* 2 vols. London: Chiswick, 1928.

Bloch, Ruth H. *Visionary Republic: Millennial Themes in American Thought, 1765–1800.* Cambridge: Cambridge University Press, 1985.

Bourguignon, Henry J. *The First Federal Court: The Federal Appellate Prize Court of the American Revolution, 1775–1787.* American Philosophical Society *Memoirs.* Vol. 122. Philadelphia: American Philosophical Society, 1977.

Bowes, Frederick P. *The Culture of Early Charleston.* Chapel Hill: University of North Carolina Press, 1942.

Bradford, Melvin E. *A Better Guide Than Reason: Studies in the American Revolution.* La Salle, Ill.: Sherwood, Sugden, 1979.

Bridenbaugh, Carl. *Myths and Realities.* Baton Rouge: Louisiana State University Press, 1952.

Brown, Jane D. *The Catawba Indians.* Columbia: University of South Carolina Press, 1966.

Brown, John P. *Old Frontiers: The Story of the Cherokee Indians from the Earliest Times to the Date of their Removal to the West, 1838.* Kingsport, Tenn.: Southern Publishing, 1938.

Brown, Wallace. *The Good Americans: The Loyalists in the American Revolution.* New York: William Morrow, 1969.

————. *The King's Friends: The Composition and Motives of the Loyalist Claimants.* Providence, R.I.: Brown University Press, 1965.

Brown, Weldon A. *Empire or Independence: A Study in the Failure of Reconciliation, 1774–1783.* Baton Rouge: Louisiana State University Press, 1941.

Bull, Kinloch, Jr. *The Oligarchs in Colonial and Revolutionary Charleston: Lt. Governor William Bull II and His Family.* Columbia: University of South Carolina Press, 1991.

Burnett, Edmund C. *The Continental Congress.* New York: Macmillan, 1941.

Butter, Ruth L. *Doctor Franklin: Postmaster General.* New York: Doubleday, Doran, 1928.

Campbell, Peter F. *Some Early Barbadian History.* St. Michael, Barbados: Caribbean Graphics & Letchworth, 1993.

—————. *Chapters in Barbados History*. Bridgetown: Barbados Museum and Historical Society, 1986.

Carleton, John D. *Westminster School: A History*. London: Rupert Hart-Davis, 1965.

Carp, E. Wayne. *To Starve the Army at Pleasure: Continental Army Administration and American Political Culture, 1775–1783*. Chapel Hill: University of North Carolina Press, 1984.

Cashin, Edward J. *The King's Ranger: Thomas Brown and the American Revolution on the Southern Frontier*. Athens: University of Georgia Press, 1989.

Chancellor, Beresford. *The XVIIIth Century in London*. London: B. T. Batsford, 1920.

Clarkson, L. A. *The Pre-Industrial Economy in England, 1500–1750*. London: B. T. Batsford, 1971.

Clemens, Samuel L. *Mark Twain's Autobiography*. 2 vols. New York: Harper & Bros., 1924.

Clowse, Converse D. *Economic Beginnings in Colonial South Carolina, 1670–1730*. Columbia: University of South Carolina Press, 1971.

Cohen, Lester H. *The Revolutionary Histories: Contemporary Narratives of the American Revolution*. Ithaca, N.Y.: Cornell University Press, 1980.

Coleman, D. C. *The Economy of England, 1450–1750*. London: Oxford University Press, 1977.

Crouse, Maurice. *The Public Treasury of Colonial South Carolina*. Columbia: University of South Carolina Press, 1977.

Crowe, Jeffrey, and Larry E. Tise, eds. *The Southern Experience in the American Revolution*. Chapel Hill: University of North Carolina Press, 1978.

Dabney, William M., and Marion Dargan. *William Henry Drayton and the American Revolution*. Albuquerque: University of New Mexico Press, 1962.

Davis, Joseph L. *Sectionalism in American Politics, 1777–1787*. Madison: University of Wisconsin Press, 1977.

Davis, Nora. *Fort Charlotte on the Savannah River and Its Significance in the American Revolution*. Greenwood, S.C.: Daughters of the American Revolution, Star Fort Chapter, 1949.

Edgar, Walter B., and N. Louise Bailey, eds. *Biographical Directory of the South Carolina House of Representatives*. Vol. 2. Columbia: University of South Carolina Press, 1977.

Einstein, Lewis. *Divided Loyalties: Americans in England during the War of Independence*. Boston: Houghton Mifflin, 1933.

Foster, Joseph. *Alumni Oxonienses: The Members of the University of Oxford, 1715–1886*. 4 vols. Nendeln, Liechtenstein: Krause Reprint, 1968.

Frakes, George E. *Laboratory for Liberty: The South Carolina Legislative Committee System, 1719–1776*. Lexington: University of Kentucky Press, 1970.

Fraser, Walter J. *Patriots, Pistols, and Petticoats: "Poor Sinful Charlestown" during the American Revolution*. Columbia: University of South Carolina Press, 1976.

Fruchtman, Jack, Jr. *Thomas Paine: Apostle of Freedom.* New York: Four Walls Eight Windows, 1994.

Godbold, E. Stanley, Jr., and Robert H. Woody. *Christopher Gadsden and the American Revolution.* Knoxville: University of Tennessee Press, 1982.

Green, V. H. H. *A History of Oxford University.* London: B. T. Batsford, 1974.

Greene, Jack P. *The Quest for Power: The Lower Houses of Assembly in the Southern Royal Colonies, 1689–1776.* Chapel Hill: University of North Carolina Press, 1963.

Gregg, Alexander. *History of the Cheraws, 1730–1810.* New York: Richardson, 1867.

Greven, Philip J. *The Protestant Temperament: Patterns of Child-Rearing, the Religious Experience, and the Self in Early America.* New York: Knopf, 1977.

Gruber, Ira. *The Howe Brothers and the American Revolution.* New York: Atheneum Press, 1972.

Hatley, Tom. *The Dividing Paths: Cherokees and South Carolinians through Era of Revolution.* New York: Oxford University Press, 1993.

Haw, James. *John and Edward Rutledge of South Carolina.* Athens: University of Georgia Press, 1997.

Hawke, David F. *Paine.* New York: Harper & Row, 1974.

Heisser, David C. R. *The State Seal of South Carolina: A Short History.* Columbia: South Carolina Department of Archives and History, 1992.

Henderson, Herbert James. *Party Politics in the Continental Congress.* New York: McGraw-Hill, 1974.

Higginbotham, Don. *The War of American Independence: Military Attitudes, Policies and Practices, 1763–1789.* New York: Macmillan, 1971.

Howe, George. *History of the Presbyterian Church in South Carolina.* 2 vols. Columbia, S.C.: Duffie & Chapman, 1870.

Hudson, Charles M. *The Catawba Nation.* Athens: University of Georgia Press, 1970.

Irving, John B. *The South Carolina Jockey Club.* Charleston, S.C.: Russell & Jones, 1857. Reprint. Spartanburg, S.C.: The Reprint Co., 1975.

James, Coy Hilton. *Silas Deane—Patriot or Traitor?* East Lansing: Michigan State University Press, 1975.

Jillson, Calvin, and Rick K. Wilson. *Congressional Dynamics: Structure, Coordination, and Choice in the First American Congress, 1774–1789.* Stanford, Calif.: Stanford University Press, 1994.

Jones, John. *Balliol College: A History, 1263–1939.* Oxford, U.K.: Oxford University Press, 1988.

Jones, Lewis P. *The South Carolina Civil War of 1775.* Lexington, S.C.: Sandlapper Store, 1975.

Joyner, Judith R. *Beginnings: Education in Colonial South Carolina.* Columbia, S.C.: Wentworth, 1985.

Keane, John. *Tom Paine: A Political Life.* Boston: Little, Brown, 1995.

Klein, Rachel N. *Unification of a Slave State: The Rise of the Planter Class in the South*

Carolina Backcountry, 1760–1808. Chapel Hill: University of North Carolina Press, 1990.

Labaree, Leonard W. *Conservatism in Early American History*. Ithaca, N.Y.: Cornell University Press, 1948.

Lambert, Robert S. *South Carolina Loyalists in the American Revolution*. Columbia: University of South Carolina Press, 1987.

Lewis, Lynne. *Drayton Hall: Preliminary Archaeological Investigation at a Low Country Plantation*. Charlottesville: University Press of Virginia, 1978.

Lipscomb, Terry W. *The Carolina Lowcountry: April 1775–June 1776*. Columbia: South Carolina Department of Archives and History, 1994.

McCrady, Edward. *The History of South Carolina in the Revolution, 1775–1780*. New York: Macmillan, 1901.

———. *The History of South Carolina Under the Royal Government, 1719–1776*. New York: Macmillan, 1899.

Madden, Richard C. *Catholics in South Carolina: A Record*. New York: University Press of America, 1985.

Maier, Pauline. *From Resistance to Revolution: Colonial Radicals and the Development of American Opposition to Britain, 1765–1776*. New York: Knopf, 1972.

Mallet, Charles E. *A History of the University of Oxford*. 2 vols. New York: Longmans, Green, 1924.

Meroney, Geraldine M. *Inseparable Loyalty: A Biography of William Bull*. Norcross, Ga.: Harrison, 1991.

Merrill, James H. *The Indians' New World: Catawbas and Their Neighbors from European Contact through the Era of Removal*. Chapel Hill: University of North Carolina Press, 1989.

Milling, J. Chapman. *Red Carolinians*. Chapel Hill: University of North Carolina Press, 1940.

Mingay, G. E. *Georgian London*. London: B. T. Batsford, 1975.

Montross, Lynn. *The Reluctant Rebels: The Story of the Continental Congress, 1774–1789*. New York: Barnes & Noble, 1950.

Mooney, James. *Historical Sketches of the Cherokee*. Chicago: Aldine, 1975.

Morris, Jan., ed. *The Oxford Book of Oxford*. Oxford, U.K.: Oxford University Press, 1978.

Murphy, Orville T. *Comte De Vergennes: French Diplomacy in the Age of Revolution, 1719–1787*. Albany: State University of New York Press, 1982.

Norton, Mary Beth. *Liberty's Daughters: The Revolutionary Experience of American Women, 1750–1800*. Boston: Little, Brown, 1980.

O'Donnell, James H. *Southern Indians in the American Frontier*. Knoxville: University of Tennessee Press, 1973.

Olwell, Robert. *Masters, Slaves, and Subjects: The Culture of Power in the South Carolina Lowcountry, 1740–1790*. Ithaca, N.Y.: Cornell University Press, 1998.

Owens, Loulie L. *Oliver Hart, 1723–1795: A Biography*. Greenville, S.C.: Baptist Historical Society, 1966.

———. *Saints of Clay: The Shaping of South Carolina Baptists*. Columbia, S.C.: R. L. Bryan, 1971.

Pancake, John S. *This Destructive War: The British Campaign in the Carolinas, 1780–1782*. Birmingham: University of Alabama Press, 1985.

Potts, Lois W. *Arthur Lee: A Virtuous Revolutionary*. Baton Rouge: Louisiana State University Press, 1981.

Rakove, Jack N. *The Beginnings of National Politics: An Interpretive History of the Continental Congress*. Baltimore: Johns Hopkins University Press, 1979.

Ravenel, Harriott H. *Charleston, the Place and the People*. New York: Macmillan, 1906.

———. *Eliza Lucas Pinckney*. New York: Charles Scribner's Sons, 1898.

Risch, Erna. *Supplying Washington's Army*. Washington, D.C.: United States Government Printing Office, 1981.

Ritcheson, Charles. *British Politics and the American Revolution*. Norman: University of Oklahoma Press, 1954.

Robbins, Caroline. *The Eighteenth-Century Commonwealthmen: Studies in the Transmission, Development and Circumstance of English Liberal Thought from the Restoration of Charles II Until the War with the Thirteen Colonies*. Cambridge, Mass.: Harvard University Press, 1959.

Robinson, W. Stitt. *James Glen: From Scottish Provost to Royal Governor of South Carolina*. Westport, Conn.: Greenwood Press, 1996.

Salley, Alexander S., Jr. *The History of Orangeburg County, South Carolina: From Its First Settlement to the Close of the Revolutionary War*. Orangeburg, S.C.: R. Lewis Berry, 1898.

———. *The Seal of the State of South Carolina*. Columbia, S.C.: The State Co., 1912.

———, ed. *Delegates to the Continental Congress from South Carolina 1774–1789, with Sketches of the Four Who Signed the Declaration of Independence*. Columbia, S.C.: The State Company, 1927.

Saye, James H., ed. *Memoirs of Major Joseph McJunkin: Revolutionary Patriot*. Richmond, Va.: *Watchman and Observer*, 1847. Reprint. Greenwood, S.C.: *Index-Journal*, 1925.

Schimizzi, Ernest and Gregory Schimizzi. *The Staten Island Peace Conference: September 11, 1776*. Albany: New York State American Bicentennial Commission, 1976.

Schlenther, Boyd S. *Charles Thompson: A Patriot's Pursuit*. Newark: University of Delaware Press, 1990.

Schwartz, Richard B. *Daily Life in Johnson's London*. Madison: University of Wisconsin Press, 1983.

Siebert, Wilbur H. *Loyalists in East Florida 1774–1785*. Deland, Fla.: Florida State Historical Society, 1929.

Singer, Charles G. *South Carolina in the Confederation*. Philadelphia: University of Pennsylvania Press, 1941.

Sirmans, M. Eugene. *Colonial South Carolina: A Political History, 1663–1763.* Chapel Hill: University of North Carolina Press, 1966.

Smith, Daniel Blake. *Inside the Great House: Planter Family Life in Eighteenth-Century Chesapeake Society.* Ithaca, N.Y.: Cornell University Press, 1980.

Snapp, J. Russell. *John Stuart and the Struggle for Empire on the Southern Frontier.* Baton Rouge: Louisiana State University Press, 1996.

Spruill, Julia Cherry. *Women's Life and Work in the Southern Colonies.* Chapel Hill: University of North Carolina Press, 1938. Reprint. New York: W. W. Norton, 1972.

Starr, Rebecca. *A School for Politics: Commercial Lobbying and Political Culture in Early South Carolina.* Baltimore: Johns Hopkins University Press, 1998.

Stinchcombe, William C. *The American Revolution and the French Alliance.* Syracuse, N.Y.: Syracuse University Press, 1969.

Sutherland, Dame Lucy. *The University of Oxford in the Eighteenth Century: A Reconsideration.* Oxford, U.K.: Oxford University Press, 1972.

Sutherland, L. S., and L. G. Mitchell, eds. *The History of the University of Oxford: The Eighteenth Century.* Oxford, U.K.: Clarendon Press, 1986.

Townshend, Leah. *South Carolina Baptists, 1670–1805.* Florence, S.C.: Florence Printing, 1935.

Vipperman, Carl J. *The Rise of Rawlins Lowndes, 1721–1800.* Columbia: University of South Carolina Press, 1978.

Wallace, David D. *South Carolina: A Short History.* Chapel Hill: University of North Carolina Press, 1951.

———. *The Life of Henry Laurens, with a Sketch of the Life of Lieutenant-Colonel John Laurens.* New York: G. P. Putnam's Sons, 1915.

Walsh, Richard. *Charleston's Sons of Liberty: A Study of the Artisans, 1763–1789.* Columbia: University of South Carolina Press, 1959.

Weiner, Marli F. *Mistresses and Slaves: Plantation Women in South Carolina, 1830–1880.* Urbana: University of Illinois Press, 1998.

Weir, Robert M. *"A Most Important Epocha": The Coming of the Revolution in South Carolina.* Columbia: University of South Carolina Press, 1970.

———. *Colonial South Carolina: A History.* Millwood, N.Y.: KTO Press, 1983.

Wertenbaker, Thomas J. *The Golden Age of Colonial Culture.* New York: New York University Press, 1942.

Whitney, E. L. *Government of the Colony of South Carolina.* Baltimore: Johns Hopkins University Press, 1895.

Wood, Peter. *Black Majority: Negroes in Colonial South Carolina from 1760 through the Stono Rebellion.* New York: Knopf, 1974.

Wood, Gordon S. *The Creation of the American Republic, 1776–1787.* Chapel Hill: University of North Carolina Press, 1969. Reprint. New York: W. W. Norton, 1972.

———. *The Radicalism of the American Revolution.* New York: Knopf, 1992.

Woodward, Grace. *The Cherokees.* Norman, Ok.: University of Oklahoma Press, 1963.

Wyatt-Brown, Bertram. *Honor and Violence in the Old South.* New York: Oxford University Press, 1986.

Young, Alfred F., ed. *The American Revolution: Explorations in the History of American Radicalism.* De Kalb: Northern Illinois University Press, 1976.

Zahniser, Marvin R. *Charles Cotesworth Pinckney: Founding Father.* Chapel Hill: University of North Carolina Press, 1967.

Articles

Adair, Douglass. "Fame and the Founding Fathers." *Fame and the Founding Fathers: Essays by Douglass Adair,* ed. H. Trevor Colbourn. New York: W. W. Norton, 1974.

Alden, John R. "John Stuart Accuses William Bull." *William and Mary Quarterly,* 3d ser., 2 (July 1945): 315–20.

Aldridge, Alfred O. "Thomas Paine and Comus." *Pennsylvania Magazine of History and Biography* 85 (1961): 70–5.

Anzilotti, Cara. "Autonomy and the Female Planter in Colonial South Carolina." *Journal of Southern History* 63 (May 1997): 239–68.

Baskett, Sam S. "Eliza Lucas Pinckney: Portrait of an Eighteenth Century American." *South Carolina Historical Magazine* 72 (October 1971): 207–19.

Bennett, John. "Historical Notes." *South Carolina Historical and Genealogical Magazine* 18 (January 1917): 96–9.

Bogna, Lorence W. "Parents and Children in Eighteenth Century Europe." *History of Childhood Quarterly* 2 (summer 1974): 1–31.

Boyer, Larry. "The Justice of the Peace in England and America from 1506–1776: A Bibliographic History." *Quarterly Journal of the Library of Congress* 34 (October 1977): 315–26.

Breen, Timothy H. "Horses and Gentlemen: The Cultural Significance of Gambling among the Gentry of Virginia." *William and Mary Quarterly,* 3d ser., 34 (April 1977): 239–57.

Brown, Alan S. "The British Peace Offer of 1778: A Study in Ministerial Confusion." *Papers of the Michigan Academy of Science, Arts, and Letters* 40 (1955): 249–60.

"Bull Family of South Carolina." *South Carolina Historical and Genealogical Magazine* 1 (January 1900): 76–89.

Burrows, Edwin G., and Michael Wallace. "The American Revolution: The Ideology and Psychology of National Liberation." *Perspectives in American History* 6 (1972): 167–308.

Calhoon, Robert M., and Robert M. Weir. "The Scandalous History of Sir Egerton Leigh." *William and Mary Quarterly,* 3d ser., 26 (January 1969): 47–74.

Cann, Marvin L. "Prelude to War: The First Battle of Ninety Six, November 19–21." *South Carolina Historical Magazine* 76 (October 1975): 197–214.

Carson, Hampton L. "The Case of the Sloop *Active*." *Pennsylvania Magazine of History and Biography* 16, no. 4 (1892): 385–98.

Cashin, Edward J. "'The Famous Colonel Wells': Factionalism in Revolutionary Georgia." *Georgia Historical Quarterly* (supplement 1974): 137–56.

Chandler, Alfred D. "The Expansion of Barbados." In *Chapters in Barbados History*, ed. Peter F. Campbell. St. Ann's Garrison, Barbados: Barbados Museum and Historical Society, 1986.

Chesnutt, David R. "'Greedy Party Work': The South Carolina Election of 1768." In *Party and Political Opposition in Revolutionary America*, ed. Patricia Bonomi. New York: Sleepy Hollow Press, 1980.

Clayton, J. Glenwood, and Loulie L. Owens, eds. "Oliver Hart's Diary of the Journey to the Backcountry." *Journal of the South Carolina Baptist Historical Society* 1 (November 1975): 18–30.

Clifton, James. "The Rice Industry in Colonial America." *Agricultural History* 55 (July 1981): 266–83.

Coclanis, Peter A. "Death in Early Charleston: An Estimate of the Crude Death Rate for the White Population of Charleston, 1722–1732." *South Carolina Historical Magazine* 85 (October 1984): 280–91.

————. "The Rise and Fall of the South Carolina Low Country: An Essay in Economic Interpretation." *Southern Studies* 24 (summer 1985): 143–66.

Cohen, Sheldon S. "The *Philippa* Affair." *Georgia Historical Quarterly* 69 (fall 1985): 338–54.

Coon, David L. "Eliza Lucas Pinckney and the Reintroduction of Indigo Culture in South Carolina." *Journal of Southern History* 42 (February 1976): 61–76.

Cowan, Thomas. "William Hill and the Aera Iron Works." *Journal of Early Southern Decorative Arts* 13 (November 1987): 1–31.

Crouse, Maurice A. "Cautious Rebellion: South Carolina's Opposition to the Stamp Act Congress." *South Carolina Historical Magazine* 73 (April 1972): 59–71.

Cunningham, Mary E. "The Case of the *Active*." *Pennsylvania History* 12 (October 1946): 229–190.

Dabney, William. "Drayton and Laurens in the Continental Congress." *South Carolina Historical Magazine* 60 (April 1959): 74–82.

Davis, Harold E. "The Scissors Thesis, or Frustrated Expectations as a Cause of the Revolution in Georgia." *Georgia Historical Quarterly* 61 (fall 1977): 246–57.

Dethloff, Henry C. "The Colonial Rice Trade." *Agricultural History* 56 (January 1982): 231–43.

Doolittle, I. G. "College Administration." In *The History of the University of Oxford: The Eighteenth Century*, ed. Lucy S. Sutherland and L. G. Mitchell. Oxford, U.K.: Oxford University Press, 1986.

Duffy, John. "Eighteenth-Century Carolina Health Conditions." *Journal of Southern History* 18 (August 1952): 289–302.

Einhorn, Nathan R. "The Reception of the British Peace Offer of 1778." *Pennsylvania History* 16 (July 1949): 191–214.

Farley, M. Foster. "The South Carolina Negro in the American Revolution, 1775–1783." *South Carolina Historical Magazine* 79 (April 1978): 75–86.

Ford, Paul L. "Lord Howe's Commission to Pacify the Colonies." *Atlantic Monthly* 77 (June 1896): 758–62.

Frech, Laura P. "The Republicanism of Henry Laurens." *South Carolina Historical Magazine* 76 (April 1975): 68–79.

Freeman, Joanne B. "Dueling as Politics: Reinterpreting the Burr-Hamilton Duel." *William and Mary Quarterly*, 3d ser., 53 (April 1996): 289–318.

Geiger, Florence G. "St. Bartholomew's Parish as Seen by Its Rectors." *South Carolina Historical and Genealogical Magazine* 50 (October 1949): 173–203.

Gillette, Jane B. "American Classic." *Historic Preservation* 43 (March–April 1991): 23–7, 71–2.

Gould, Christopher. "South Carolina and the Continental Associations: Prelude to Revolution." *South Carolina Historical Magazine* 87 (January 1986): 30–48.

Green, V. H. H. "The University and Social Life." In *The History of the University of Oxford: The Eighteenth Century*, ed. Lucy S. Sutherland and L. G. Mitchell. Oxford, U.K.: Clarendon Press, 1986.

Greene, Jack P. "Bridge to Revolution: The Wilkes Fund Controversy in South Carolina, 1769–1775." *Journal of Southern History* 29 (February 1963): 19–52.

———. "The Gadsden Election Controversy and the Revolutionary Movement in South Carolina." *Mississippi Valley Historical Review* 56 (December 1959): 469–92.

———. "The Role of the Lower Houses of Assembly in Eighteenth-Century Politics." *Journal of Southern History* 27 (November 1961): 451–74.

———. "Slavery or Independence: Some Reflections on the Relationship among Liberty, Black Bondage, and Equality in Revolutionary South Carolina." *South Carolina Historical Magazine* 80 (July 1979): 193–214.

Hamer, Philip M. "John Stuart's Indian Policy during the Early Months of the American Revolution." *Mississippi Valley Historical Review* 17 (December 1930): 351–66.

Harmon, George D. "The Proposed Amendments to the Articles of Confederation." *The South Atlantic Quarterly* 24 (July 1925): 298–315.

Harrold, Frances. "Colonial Siblings: Georgia's Relationship with South Carolina during the Pre-Revolutionary Period." *Georgia Historical Quarterly* 73 (winter 1989): 7–44.

Hatch, Nathan O. "The Origins of Civil Millennialism in America: New England Clergy, War with France, and the Revolution." *William and Mary Quarterly*, 3d ser., 31 (July 1974): 407–30.

Haywood, Robert C. "Mercantilism and South Carolina Agriculture, 1700–1763." *South Carolina Historical Magazine* 60 (January 1959): 15–27.

Henderson, H. James. "Congressional Factionalism and the Attempt to Recall Benjamin Franklin." *William and Mary Quarterly*, 3d ser., 27 (April 1970): 246–67.

Hoffman, Ronald. "The 'Disaffected' in the Revolutionary South." In *The American Revolution: Explorations in the History of American Radicalism*, ed. Alfred F. Young. De Kalb: Northern Illinois University Press, 1976.

Horne, Paul A., Jr. "The Evolution of a Constitution: South Carolina's 1778 Document." South Carolina Historical Society *Proceedings* (1988): 7–15.

———. "William Henry Drayton and the Articles of Confederation." South Carolina Historical Society *Proceedings* (1990): 23–9.

Huford, Jon R. "Enough Gunpowder to Start a Revolution." *Southern Studies* 23 (fall 1984): 315–8.

Jensen, Merrill. "The American People and the Revolution." *Journal of American History* 57 (June 1970): 5–35.

Jordan, Winthrop. "Familial Politics: Thomas Paine and the Killing of the King, 1776." *Journal of American History* 60 (September 1973): 294–308.

Kramnick, Isaac. "Reflections on Revolution: Definition and Explanation in Recent Scholarship." *History and Theory* 11 (1972): 26–63.

Lefler, Hugh T. "Promotional Literature of the Southern Colonies." *Journal of Southern History* 33 (February 1967): 3–25.

Lemisch, Jesse. "The American Revolution Seen from the Bottom Up." In *Towards a New Past: Dissenting Essays in American History*, ed. Barton J. Bernstein. New York: Pantheon, 1968.

Lutnick, Solomon. "William Henry Drayton's Memoirs." In *The Colonial Legacy: Early Nationalist Historians*, ed. Lawrence E. Leder. New York: Harper & Row, 1973.

McMurry, Allan J. "The North Government and the Outbreak of the American Revolution." *Huntington Library Quarterly* (1971): 141–58.

Maclear, J. F. "The Republic and the Millennium." In *The Religion of the Republic*, ed. Elwyn A. Smith. Philadelphia: Fortress Press, 1971.

Madden, Richard C. "Catholics in Colonial South Carolina." *Records of the American Catholic Historical Society of Philadelphia* (March 1962): 11–42.

Maier, Pauline. "The Charleston Mob and the Evolution of Popular Politics in Revolutionary South Carolina, 1765–1784." *Perspectives in American History* 4 (1970): 173–96.

———. "Early Revolutionary Leaders in the South and Problem of Southern Distinctiveness." In *Southern Experience in the American Revolution*, ed. Jeffrey J. Crow and Larry E. Tise. Chapel Hill: University of North Carolina Press, 1978.

———. "John Wilkes and American Disillusionment with Britain." *William and Mary Quarterly*, 3d ser., 20 (July 1963): 373–95.

Manigault, E., and Gabriel Manigault. "The Manigault Family of South Carolina from 1685–1886." *Transactions of the Huguenot Society* 4 (1897): 48–84.

Martin, J. M. "The Rise in Population in Eighteenth-Century Warwickshire." *Dugdale Society Occasional Papers* 23 (1976): 3–50.

Maslowski, Pete. "National Policy toward the Use of Black Troops in the Revolution." *South Carolina Historical Magazine* 73 (January 1972): 1–17.

Massey, Gregory D. "The Limits of Antislavery Thought in the Revolutionary South: John Laurens and Henry Laurens." *Journal of Southern History* 63 (August 1997): 495–530.

Mazlish, Bruce. "Leadership in the American Revolution: The Psychological Dimension." In *Library of Congress Symposia on the American Revolution*. Washington, D.C.: Library of Congress, 1974.

Meroney, Geraldine. "William Bull's First Exile from South Carolina, 1778–1781." *South Carolina Historical Magazine* 80 (April 1979): 91–104.

Morgan, Philip D. "Work and Culture: the Task System and the World of Lowcountry Blacks, 1700–1880." *William and Mary Quarterly*, 3d ser., 39 (October 1982): 563–98.

Morgan, Thurmond T. "The Fate of the Ship *Prosper.*" *South Carolina Historical Magazine* 93 (July 1993): 202–4.

Mouzon, Harold A. "*Defense:* A Vessel of the Navy of South Carolina." *American Neptune* 13 (January 1953): 29–50.

——. "The Ship *Prosper,* 1775–1776." *South Carolina Historical Magazine* 69 (January 1958): 1–10.

Olson, Gary D. "Loyalists and the American Revolution: Thomas Brown and the South Carolina Backcountry, 1775–1776." *South Carolina Historical Magazine* 68 and 69 (October 1967 and January 1968): 201–19, 44–56.

Olwell, Robert A. "'Domestic Enemies': Slavery and Political Independence in South Carolina, May 1775–March 1776." *Journal of Southern History* 55 (February 1989): 21–48.

Olsberg, R. Nicholas. "Ship Registers in the South Carolina Archives." *South Carolina Historical Magazine* 74 (October 1973): 189–279.

Owens, Loulie L. "A Nail in Time." *Sandlapper* 9 (January 1976): 16–22.

——. "Oliver Hart and the American Revolution." *Journal of the South Carolina Baptist Historical Society* 1 (November 1975): 2–17.

——. "South Carolina Baptists and the American Revolution." *Journal of the South Carolina Baptist Historical Society* 1 (November 1975): 31–45.

Phillips, Ulrich B. "The Course of the South to Secession." *Georgia Historical Quarterly* 21 (March 1937): 1–49.

Robson, Eric. "The Expedition to the Southern Colonies, 1775–1776." *English Historical Review* 66 (October 1951): 535–60.

Rogers, George C., Jr. "The Charleston Tea Party: The Significance of December 3, 1773." *South Carolina Historical Magazine* 75 (July 1974): 153–68.

Rowlands, Marie. "Society and Industry in the West Midlands at the End of the Seventeenth Century." *Midland History* 4 (spring 1977): 48–60.

Salmon, Marylynn. "Women and Property in South Carolina: The Evidence from

Marriage Settlements, 1730–1830." *William and Mary Quarterly*, 3d ser., 39 (October 1982): 655–85.

Schlesinger, Arthur M. "Political Mobs and the American Revolution, 1765–1776." *Proceedings of the American Philosophical Society* 99 (August 1955): 244–50.

Sharrar, G. Terry. "Indigo in Carolina, 1671–1796." *South Carolina Historical Magazine* 72 (April 1971): 94–103.

Sirmans, M. Eugene. "Charleston Two Hundred Years Ago." *Emory University Quarterly* 19 (fall 1963): 129–35.

———. "The Legal Status of the Slave in South Carolina, 1670–1740." *Journal of Southern History* 28 (November 1962): 462–73.

———. "The South Carolina Royal Council, 1720–1763." *William and Mary Quarterly*, 3d ser., 18 (July 1961): 373–91.

———. "Politicians and Planters: The Bull Family of Colonial South Carolina." *South Carolina Historical Association Proceedings* (1962): 32–41.

Smith, D. E. Huger. "An Account of the Tattnal and Fenwicke Families in South Carolina." *South Carolina Historical and Genealogical Magazine* 14 (January 1913): 3–19.

Smith, Glenn Curtis. "An Era of Non-Importation Associations, 1768–1773." *William and Mary Quarterly*, 2d ser., 20 (January 1940): 84–98.

Smith, Henry A. M. "The Ashley River: Its Seats and Settlements." *South Carolina Historical and Genealogical Magazine* 20 (April 1919): 75–122.

———. "The Upper Ashley and the Mutations of Families." *South Carolina Historical and Genealogical Magazine* 20 (July 1919): 151–98.

Snapp, J. Russell. "William Henry Drayton: The Making of a Conservative Revolutionary." *Journal of Southern History* 57 (November 1991): 637–58.

Sparks, Randy J. "Gentleman's Sport: Horse Racing in Antebellum Charleston." *South Carolina Historical Magazine* 93 (January 1992): 15–30.

Stein, Stephen J. "An Apocalyptic Rationale for the American Revolution." *Early American Literature* 9 (winter 1975): 211–25.

Stephenson, Orlando W. "The Supply of Gunpowder in 1776." *American Historical Review* 30 (January 1930): 271–81.

Stokes, Durwood T. "The Baptist and Methodist Clergy in South Carolina and the American Revolution." *South Carolina Historical Magazine* 73 (April 1972): 87–96.

Stourzh, Gerald. "William Blackstone: Teacher of Revolution." *Jahrbuch fur Amerikastudien* 15 (1970): 184–200.

Sutherland, Lucy S. "The Curriculum." In *The History of the University of Oxford: The Eighteenth Century*, ed. Lucy S. Sutherland and L. G. Mitchell. Oxford, U.K.: Oxford University Press, 1986.

Thomas, P. D. G. "Charles Townshend and American Taxation in 1767." *English Historical Review* 83 (January 1968): 33–51.

Treacy, Kenneth W. "The Olmstead Case, 1778–1809." *Western Political Quarterly* 10 (September 1957): 675–91.

Villers, David H. "The Smythe Horses Affair and the Association." *South Carolina Historical Magazine* 70 (July 1969): 137–48.

Wallace, David D. "Gage's Threat—Or Warning?" *South Carolina Historical Magazine* 47 (July 1946): 190–3.

Walsh, Richard. "Christopher Gadsden: Radical or Conservative Revolutionary?" *South Carolina Historical Magazine* 63 (July 1962): 125–36.

——. "The Charleston Mechanics: A Brief Study, 1760–1776." *South Carolina Historical Magazine* 60 (July 1959): 123–44.

Waterhouse, Richard. "Economic Growth and Changing Patterns of Wealth Distribution in Colonial Lowcountry South Carolina." *South Carolina Historical Magazine* (October 1988): 203–17.

——. "England, the Caribbean, and the Settlement of Carolina." *Journal of American Studies* 9 (December 1975): 259–81.

Watson, Alan D. "The Beaufort Removal and the Revolutionary Impulse in South Carolina." *South Carolina Historical Magazine* 84 (July 1983): 121–35.

——. "Placemen in South Carolina: The Receiver Generals of the Quitrents." *South Carolina Historical Magazine* 74 (January 1973): 18–30.

Weir, Robert M. "Beaufort: The Almost Capital." *Sandlapper* 9 (September 1976): 43–4.

——. "'The Harmony We Were Famous For': An Interpretation of Pre-Revolutionary South Carolina Politics." *William and Mary Quarterly*, 3d ser., 26 (July 1969): 473–501.

——. "Rebelliousness: Personality Development and the American Revolution." In *The Southern Experience in the American Revolution*, ed. Jeffrey Crow and Larry E. Tise. Chapel Hill: University of North Carolina Press, 1978.

——. "The South Carolina as Extremist." *South Atlantic Quarterly* 74 (winter 1975): 86–103.

——. "The 'Violent Spirit': The Reestablishment of Order, and the Continuity of Leadership in Post-Revolutionary South Carolina." In *An Uncivil War: The Southern Backcountry in the Revolution*, ed. Ronald Hoffman and Thad W. Tate. Charlottesville: University Press of Virginia, 1985.

——. "Who Shall Rule at Home: The American Revolution as a Crisis of Legitimacy for the Colonial Elite." *Journal of Interdisciplinary History* 6 (spring 1976): 679–700.

Whitmire, Beverly T. "Richard Pearis, Bold Pioneer." *Proceedings and Papers of the Greenville County Historical Society* (1962–1964): 75–85.

Wood, Gordon S. "A Note on Mobs in the American Revolution." *William and Mary Quarterly*, 3d ser., 23 (October 1966): 635–42.

——. "Rhetoric and Reality in the American Revolution." *William and Mary Quarterly*, 3d ser., 23 (January 1966): 3–32.

Wyatt-Brown, Bertram. "Honour and American Republicanism: A Neglected Corollary." In *Ideology and the Historians,* ed. Ciaran Brady. *Historical Studies* 17. Dublin: Lilliput Press, 1991.

Zuckerman, Michael. "Penmanship Exercises for Saucy Sons: Some Thoughts on the Colonial Southern Family." *South Carolina Historical Magazine* 84 (July 1983): 152–66.

Dissertations, Theses, and Unpublished Papers

Arneman, Dana P. "The Medical History of Colonial South Carolina." Ph.D. diss., University of South Carolina, 1996.

Barnwell, Robert W., Jr. "Causes of Backcountry Disputes Prior to Revolution." Master's thesis, University of South Carolina, 1928.

———. "Loyalism in South Carolina, 1765–1785." Ph.D. diss., Duke University, 1941.

Boles, Rayford B. "The South Carolina Judiciary, 1669–1769." Ph.D. diss., University of Georgia, 1978.

Carter, Mary F. "James Glen, Governor of South Carolina: A Study in British Administrative Policies." Ph.D. diss., University of California at Los Angeles, 1951.

Clow, Richard B. "Edward Rutledge of South Carolina, 1749–1800: Unproclaimed Statesman." Ph.D. diss., University of Georgia, 1976.

Coon, David L. "The Development of Market Agriculture in South Carolina, 1670–1785." Ph.D. diss., University of Illinois, 1972.

Cunningham, Carol R. "The Southern Royal Governors and the Coming of the American Revolution, 1763–1776." Ph.D. diss., State University of New York–Buffalo, 1984.

Ferrari, Mary C. "Artisans of the South: A Comparative Study of Norfolk, Charleston and Alexandria, 1763–1800." Ph.D. diss., College of William and Mary, 1992.

Frech, Laura Page. "The Career of Henry Laurens in the Continental Congress, 1777–1779." Ph.D. diss., University of North Carolina, 1972.

Griffin, Dorothy Gail. "The Eighteenth Century Draytons of Drayton Hall." Ph.D. diss., Emory University, 1985.

Griffiths, John III. "'To Receive Them Properly': Charlestown Prepares for War." Master's thesis, University of South Carolina, 1992.

Horne, Paul. "Forgotten Leaders: South Carolina's Delegation to the Continental Congress, 1774–1789." Ph.D. diss., University of South Carolina, 1988.

Knepper, David M. "The Political Structure of Colonial South Carolina, 1743–1776." Ph.D. diss., University of Virginia, 1971.

Lane, George W., Jr. "The Middletons of Eighteenth Century South Carolina: A Colonial Dynasty, 1678–1787." Ph.D. diss., Emory University, 1990.

Lilly, Samuel A. "The Culture of Revolutionary Charleston." Ph.D. diss., Miami University (Ohio), 1971.

Massey, Gregory D. "A Hero's Life: John Laurens and the American Revolution." Ph.D. diss., University of South Carolina, 1992.

Matchett, S. R. "'Unanimity, Order and Regularity': The Political Culture of South Carolina in the Era of the Revolution." Ph.D. diss., University of Sydney (Australia), 1980.

Poythress, Eva B. "Revolution by Committee: An Administrative History of the Extralegal Committees in South Carolina, 1774–1776." Ph.D. diss., University of North Carolina, 1975.

Shatzman, Aaron M. "Servants into Planters, The Origin of American Image: Land Acquisition and Status Mobility in Seventeenth Century South Carolina." Ph.D. diss., Stanford University, 1981.

St. Georges, Laurent M. "Population Control and Guerilla Warfare as Decisive Factors in the American Revolution." Master's thesis, University of South Carolina, 1988.

Starr, Raymond G. "The Conservative Revolution: South Carolina Public Affairs, 1775–1790." Ph.D. diss., University of Texas, 1964.

Stokes, Durwood T. "The Clergy of the Carolinas and the American Revolution." Ph.D. diss., University of North Carolina, 1968.

Stone, Richard G., Jr., "The Privy Council of South Carolina, 1776–1790: A Study in Shared Executive Power." Ph.D. diss., University of Tennessee, 1973.

Storch, Neil Thomas, "Congressional Politics and Diplomacy, 1775–1783." Ph.D. diss., University of Wisconsin, 1969.

Stuckey, Heyward. "The South Carolina Navy and the American Revolution." Master's thesis, University of South Carolina, 1972.

Taylor, Rayford B. "The South Carolina Judiciary, 1669–1769." Ph.D. diss., University of Georgia, 1978.

Waterhouse, Richard. "South Carolina's Colonial Elite: A Study in the Social Structure and Political Culture of a Southern Colony, 1670–1760." Ph.D. diss., Johns Hopkins University, 1964.

Weir, Robert M. "The Stamp Act Crisis in South Carolina." Ph.D. diss., Case Western Reserve, 1966.

Weir, Robert M. "William Tennent III." (1969). Unpublished manuscript in the William Tennent Papers. South Caroliniana Library, Columbia, South Carolina.

INDEX